Local Economies in Transition

Local Economies in Transition

Policy Realities and Development Potentials

Edward M. Bergman, editor

Duke Press Policy Studies

Duke University Press   Durham 1986

© 1986 Duke University Press
All rights reserved
Printed in the United States of America
on acid-free paper ∞
Library of Congress Cataloging-in-Publication Data
Main entry under title:
Local economies in transition.
(Duke Press policy studies)
Bibliography: p.
Includes index.
1. Urban economics—Addresses, essays, lectures.
2. Urban policy—United States—
Addresses, essays, lectures. 3. Economic development
—Addresses, essays, lectures.
I. Bergman, Edward M. II. Series.
HT 321.L63 1986 330.9173′2 85-25413
ISBN 0-8223-0549-6
ISBN 0-8223-0693-x (pbk.)

Contents

Tables and Figures

Tables

Figures

Preface

This book derives much of its inspiration from my efforts to teach urban economic development planning during the turbulent 1970s and 1980s. Graduate students are among the first to detect weaknesses in the available literature, particularly where evidence has worn thin and guides to action appear unreliable. Moreover, my collaborative encounters with our alumni and policy officials reinforced the sense that events were rapidly eroding the stock of principles available to the development professions.

Colleagues at Chapel Hill and elsewhere were reaching similar conclusions based on their teaching and research. I therefore took the opportunity to sort through the large volume of scholarly work appearing simultaneously in several disciplines that has focused attention on local economies. Discussions with Mike Luger, Rob Mier, Bob Beauregard, John Hekman, Emil Malizia, Jean-Louis Sarbib, Norman Glickman, Thierry Noyelle, Wilbur Thompson, and, most particularly, Harvey Goldstein, contributed directly to the shape of this book. The influential works of Wilbur Thompson, Bennett Harrison, Norman Glickman, and John Friedmann also figure prominently in the book's ambition to address the intersection of evidence and action that I consider vital to development planning.

Editorial assistance from Scott Verner, Bob Mirandon, and Reynolds Smith considerably tightened the selection and writing of various chapters. Becky Crane typed seemingly endless drafts of my chapters with care and dispatch, as was true of Ellen McLamb who typed the full bibliography, which Marla Engel and Brad Torgan helped assemble. Didi Dunphey drew the figures thoughtfully from the barest of sketches. Stacey Ponticello created a thoroughly organized index from notations supplied by chapter authors. And at every stage of this undertaking valuable support was always available from the Department of City and Regional Planning and the Center for Urban and Regional Studies of the University of North Carolina at Chapel Hill.

At this point the editor and publisher would like to thank the following for permission to reproduce copyrighted material: *American Planning Association Journal* for "Dynamics and Structural Change in Metropolitan Economies" by E. Bergman and H. Goldstein; "The Growth and Restructuring of Metropolitan Economies" by R. Phillips and A. Vidal; "Advanced Services and the System of Cities" by T. Noyelle; "Business Activities of Not-for-Profit Organizations" by W. Wiewel and R. Mier; "City Venture Corporations: Initiatives in U.S. Cities" by C. Bradford and M. Temali; "The Role of Labor Mobility in a National Urban Policy" by F. James and J. Blair; "High Technology and Local Economic Development" by E. Malecki; and Sage Publications, *Urban Affairs Quarterly,* for "Transforming Cities and Employment Policies for Displaced Workers" by J. Kasarda.

Final acknowledgments are due to each of my coauthors. My tasks as editor were lessened considerably and made uncommonly rewarding by their timely, cooperative efforts. And while each must bear responsibility for individually authored chapters, overall responsibility for this volume is mine alone.

E. M. B.

Introduction: Policy Realities and Development Potentials in Local Economies

It is now widely accepted that economic development has taken its place among the principal policy activities carried out at state and urban levels.[1] Acceptance came so rapidly and completely that many local officials overlook the fact that few of them would have posed it as one of their important responsibilities a decade or two ago. While progressive local governments have always been concerned with individual economic problems of their communities, these problems had typically been seen as the separate concerns of existing programs or agencies. Dealing with them as parts of a general policy for local economic development was not a common practice.

It also was often said of national economic policy then (as now) that a rising tide lifts all boats. Evidence was offered that city economies remained seaworthy and remarkably healthy throughout the 1960s and early 1970s despite a few remaining problems. While the distributive fairness of the rewards that a local economy offered its participants remained an unresolved matter, local officials seldom needed to concern themselves with trying to treat the fundamental economic health of their communities. How one understood the mechanics of urban economies or planned for their development were only occasionally worthwhile endeavors.[2] There seemed very little need for urban economic development policy and even less need to assess its potential importance in coming decades.

The 1970s entirely changed local policymakers' view of economic development. The national economic tide on which all boats floated began to ebb and flow with disturbing regularity. And, in the face of business downturns, inflationary pressures, international competition, and record high interest rates, national economic policies seemed ineffectual—possibly culpable. Domestic urban policy instruments available to local planners varied widely in their development effectiveness from place to place (Burns and Van Ness 1981) and, it appeared, might be capable of only partially relieving the problems urban areas were facing—higher unemployment, permanent loss of public and social services, worn-out public facilities, and depleted public treasuries. The economic tide had receded unevenly. Many boats had gone adrift, while others, often those in the Sunbelt region, rose on a flood of mobile capital and reinvestment.

By decade's end, nearly everyone acknowledged that national and local economies performed much differently than before. At the national level the urban policy statements of two successive administrations documented the extent of local distress but in essence argued trends in the movement of capital were either immutable or were necessary for the national economy to regain its former equilibrium.[3] Local officials were advised by these policy statements to accommodate deindustrialization trends, even to the point of adopting local policies that promoted further rounds of painful adjustment. The implied dismantling of communities set off a firestorm of controversy that still continues, several years after the initial release of the contested documents.[4]

As a corrective to the primacy conventionally accorded national purposes in the setting of local policy, Hanson (1983) has presented an alternative view of urban policy. His alternative would be based upon balanced considerations of local economies (their strengths, prospects, etc.) and the national interest: in other words, a national urban policy for the sound development of local economies. Consistent with Hanson's view of local economies is Jane Jacobs's (1984) stress on cities as the true wealth generators of nations. She contradicts

> the old mercantilist tautology that nations are the salient entities for understanding economic life. . . . Nations are political and military entities, and so are blocs of nations. But it doesn't necessarily follow from this that they are also the basic, salient entities of economic life or that they are particularly useful for probing the mysteries of economic structure, the reasons for rise and decline of wealth. (p. 31) [Rather, she contends,] economic life develops by grace of innovating; it expands by grace of import-replacing. These two master economic processes are closely related, both being functions of city economies. (p. 39)

These views are beginning to take root among development professions and in city administrations. One example can be drawn from the National League of Cities, which in 1983 urged its members to redefine their relationship to national policy initiatives by declaring:

> economic policy making should go beyond "national" totals to a concern with the *viability of local economies* [by adopting] . . . a perspective that views *the city as an economic unit* and that focuses on quality of life, jobs, cultural diversity, entrepreneurship, and productive activity. . . . *Local officials must take the lead in fashioning a conscious and aggressive economic role of city government.* This role must include the development of a much more precise understanding of the local economy together with policy development, planning, and decision-making processes in which the economic dimension of all city government actions are concerned. . . . City governments should have *the primary public sector role* in shaping local economic development. (p. 3; emphasis added)

In cities and regions throughout the nation, the idea is gaining acceptance that local government should meet community goals and deal effectively with the problems of exceptional growth (or decline) by mobilizing resources and capacities within its grasp and within an explicit economic development framework. Public officials are adopting a view that goes much beyond passive acceptance of economic development as merely a spatial manifestation of national urban, economic policies, or of private sector investment practices. The simple relabeling of previous policies or their administering agencies with "economic development" adjectives is less frequently the first and only step. The National League of Cities' resolution as excerpted above also argues the need to understand local economies and their changes to conduct policies more effectively. In so doing it echoes to a remarkable degree an earlier prophecy:

> We could well come to see our national economic and social well-being as highly dependent on greater analytical sophistication and more sensitive perception of time and change among local officials, their policy advisers and academics. If . . . the state of the national economy . . . reflects in turn the efficiency of the constituent local economies, then associations of local officials such as the National League of Cities, U.S. Conference

of Mayors, and the National Association of Regional Councils might ask in their own self-interest what they "can do for their country." One answer is: do not allow yourself to be so surprised, so often, by change. (Thompson 1980, 38)

Public officials do recognize that the changed reality of local economies and development prospects require a more thoroughgoing approach. We need serious dialogue on this newest area of public development policy, a dialogue in which we seek to understand the reality of what truly is happening to local economies before old policies are summarily relabeled or marginally different approaches are refabricated from the remnants of depleted assumptions.

Policy Realities

The best way to begin rethinking the range of local policy options is by examining the new realities that either limit or expand local options. The debate over urban policy during the late 1970s and well into the 1980s has been joined by another parallel set of debates about industrial policy.[5] All forms of urban policy appear unsuited to correct difficulties that beset the U.S. and local economies, particularly as the international division of labor places an ever larger number of domestic industries and local economies in direct competition with their foreign counterparts. Neither industrial producers or local officials are confident of how to conduct their affairs as the insular protection of a huge U.S. domestic market continues to dissolve under strong assaults of low cost or high quality imports.

International competition may be new to U.S. officials, but it is a commonplace situation for nearly all European cities and countries. To get our bearings in this changed division of labor, Glickman and Wilson have surveyed the practices of OECD countries and provide in chapter 1 a comparative appraisal of national urban-industrial policy frameworks that are used to guide urban economic development. Their chapter—"National Contexts for Urban Economic Policy" —synthesizes national and urban economic development strategies and concludes what future role state and local governments must play as national governments withdraw programmatic and policy support for domestic development.

As the national or federal partnership with cities that was established first in the 1930s (Gelfand 1975) continues to dissolve during the Reagan years, a parallel set of new discussions that dates from the mid-1970s has resuscitated the traditional but nearly dormant notion of local public-private sector arrangements.[6] Those who have studied local economies are aware that throughout the twentieth century, chambers of commerce, private development corporations, and other private sector groups usually work in close association with local government on urban development, where the private sector most often functions as the "senior" partner. This arrangement was not widely appreciated during the rapid federal-local partnership growth of the postwar period since private sector groups are usually content to operate in the background and assume no great importance in generally prosperous times. However, as citizen and worker constituencies pressure elected officials during economic downturns and as local public bodies cannot afford unilaterally the costs of urban development, public-private partnerships have once again become visible instruments of policymaking. Although all the uncertainties surrounding this shift in public-private sector responsibilities cannot be reviewed here (on which, see Bergman, forthcoming), they have resulted in one new view of the local policymaking process that is rapidly gaining prominence—if not yet widespread or enthusiastic endorsement—*corporatism*. As detailed in its burgeoning European-American literature and summarized by Clarke in chapter 2, corporatism departs from pluralism as a basis for policymaking that in corporatist guise is conducted by a few major controllers of resources, usually government, business, labor, or other principal resource-holding organizations. Clarke examines the corporatist potential embodied in a large number of Urban Development Action Grants from the federal government to cities that adopted one of four distinct types of public and private sector agreements.

The changes in U.S. and local economies that stimulated both national and corporatist alterations in local policymaking must be understood. The decade from 1967 to 1977 perhaps best typifies the transition from an era of general local prosperity to the beginnings of the current uneven, unstable state of local economies. Although this transitional period stimulated changes still under way in our policymaking apparatus, it also changed local economies. For this reason, we must pay close attention to the alterations in our nation's system of urban economic centers, alterations whose importance is not yet agreed upon and to which national and local economic development policy is still being addressed. Chapter 3 by Phillips and Vidal provides a two-period analysis of the nation's fifty largest metropolitan economies and a sample of fifty smaller metropolitan economies for this critical decade during which principal industrial sectors were restructured. Growth differentials and transitions offer a baseline comparison of sectoral alterations in these metropolitan economies grouped by major census region and disaggregated by their central city-suburban components. While industrial restructuring during the earlier 1967–72 period consisted mainly of the well-chronicled sectoral shifts away from manufacturing toward services and government (see chapter 7), the deleterious effects of these earlier shifts were generally confined to residents of central cities in the largest, most established metropolitan centers. The resultant mismatch was responsible for what was widely called the "urban crisis," but others saw it leading toward a concern for urban economic development (Harrison 1974). Overall, however, metropolitan (and even nonmetropolitan) economies continued to do well in aggregate terms. The latter period of transition (1972–77) finds the restructuring of the nation's industrial sectors accelerating as it also hosts some equally significant changes. As Bergman and Goldstein explain at length in chapter 4, far more basic changes took place from 1972 to 1977 as the U.S. macroeconomy and its metropolitan components experienced serious reversals from stagflation, internationalization, capital flight, energy cost escalations, record interest rates, and post–World War II highs in unemployment. This short list could be amplified as a narrative description of all difficulties faced during the mid-1970s; the authors instead placed emphasis on providing an empirical analysis of business cycle behavior and the underlying structural shifts that now complicate local policymaking but that also serve to propel each of 202 metropolitan economies along some unique, perhaps unrecognized economic development path.

Development Potentials

That policymaking frameworks or local economies have suddenly changed is not a fact lost on local officials who understand at an intuitive level that local economies no longer perform or respond to policy quite the way they once did. Moreover, an endlessly expanding series of bewildering development instruments, tools, programs, and action measures promoted for policy consideration appear suspiciously similar to repackaged versions from a previous era. While many such measures may indeed be coincidentally applicable to the new policy realities, there is so much contradictory guidance on their uses from the professional communities' topical literature that a local official would be justifiably apprehensive in selecting any particular development approach. Some of this difficulty is due to development theories that are in need of refurbishing or reformulation (Burns 1982). Prior theoretical understanding of the development consequences of, for example, various agglomeration economies, product cycles, enterprise "incubation," or systems of city economies are qualitatively altered by the changed conditions that Pred (1977), Bluestone and Harrison (1982), or Storper and Walker (1983) have identified. Further, there is a lingering predisposition to overlook even sound, theoretically based approaches in the hasty applications of the latest federal program initiative (e.g., enterprise zones) or in newly fashionable public-private projects that offer the appearance of immediate, direct impact. Needham's (1982) proper caution about the need to select complementary policy instruments with powerful but long-term indirect effects is instructive here as is Jacobs's (1984, ch. 7) compelling argument that successful urban economic development is built gradually, not suddenly "transplanted."

These precautions assume even greater significance for local economies caught in rapid transition. The development potential of these economies seldom hinges on a single, decisive policy initiative. Far more likely to be effective is an ensemble of selected measures strategically directed at modern factors of urban production through which long-term development forces are mobilized. These include (a) key industrial *sectors* that embody and further propagate production technologies, (b) *enterprises* that initiate and accumulate capital in communities, and (c) *labor* talents and availabilities. An understanding of these mobilizing factors is essential to local officials who wish to design sound policies for the development of local economies in transition.

Industrial sectors seem conventionally to be thought of as "winners" or "losers," depending on their stage in the product cycle and their technological resistance to international competition. Matters of industrial mix, diversification, or balance have similarly influenced previous development policies for reducing the local effects of national business cycles or for transferring dependence from declining to advancing industries.

These approaches consider industrial sectors as replaceable or adjustable elements of a local economy in the way that products and markets are viewed by corporate strategists. Policies are designed to "fine-tune" a blend of output sectors, each of which offers one or more desirable performance qualities (Thompson 1965; Conroy 1975): capital (or labor) intensity, wage levels and distribution, employment stability, secondary worker job opportunities, environmental and workplace risks, and so on. These individual qualities are indeed important considerations to local policymakers, but an emphasis on sectoral mix draws attention solely to simple portfolio strategies for aggregating singular attributes found in individual industries. Sometimes overlooked in a simple mix strategy are the intersectoral effects exerted on other components of local economies by a few key industries that are responsible for disproportionate changes in a local economy due to their area-wide influence. Drawing on Schumpeter and others, Scherer (1984) distinguishes among the effects with a conceptual matrix of technology-originating and technology-adopting industries. Norton (1979) has elsewhere demonstrated the technology-propagating qualities characteristic of the machine tool and electronics industries—what might be termed technology "carrier industries"—and argued their importance in local economic development. In chapter 5 Howland examines the components of change—net migration, net expansion, startups, and closures—in Norton's two industries and in the motor vehicle industry through three business cycle phases of the 1973 to 1982 decade. Her policy findings take explicit account of differential cyclical performance in these key sectors for city and suburban components of metropolitan economies. Malecki's chapter 6 then explores the overall significance of high-technology industries for local economic development. His synthesis of the pertinent literature presents guidance on policy issues of global mobility, corporate location, and economic growth to local officials considering a technology-based development strategy. As Harris demonstrates later in chapter 8, the technology and skilled workers inherent in high-tech carrier industries are often responsible for the propagation of new enterprises. In chapter 7 Noyelle brings another key sector to the reader's attention: advanced producer services. He demonstrates how the rapid emergence of advanced business or producer services has helped reshape the national system of cities. While advanced services are related to sectoral advances in production technology and telecommunication control of the sort treated in chapters 5 and 6, Noyelle argues that concentrations of advanced services in some local economies contribute to their emerging function as the command and control centers of corporate headquarters in the larger system of cities. Together, these three chapters argue forcefully the proposition that key industries are the *vehicles* of technology that help convey a local economy in its transition. Key industrial sectors therefore embody area-wide development potential rather than serving merely as replaceable elements in an industrial mix strategy.

The continuing debate over industry policies—particularly high-technology industry—tends to preoccupy local officials with industrial sectors, only one facet of modern urban production. Yet through the efforts to retain failing or relocating industries by plant closing notification laws and publicly supported worker buyouts, local policies have in fact already shifted attention away from industrial sectors per se (and their technologies, products, markets, etc.). The object of policy concern is thereby redirected to the *enterprise*, that is, to the kind of business organization through which capital and productive investments are mobilized, technologies are selected, production is organized and earnings are distributed. The discovery that policies toward industry and enterprise present distinctly different options came quickly in the wake of plant shutdowns, corporate divestiture, and capital mobility measures that Bluestone and Harrison (1982) describe. Until these consequences were experienced in nearly all urban economies and were chronicled in the press, public officials remained content to recruit branch plant production units of large corporations, particularly those enjoying product market oligopolies (Thompson 1965). Indifference to the local economy's composition of enterprise types was consistent with local public officials' traditional reliance on chambers of commerce or merchants' associations to encourage retail and service establishments. More decisive, however, was the implicit delegation of enterprise policy to industrial developers whose business it is to recruit corporate buyers of industrially zoned, developed, and serviced real estate for branch plant or office operations (Conway 1980; Feagin 1983). That private industrial developers are oriented primarily to a commissionable or speculative flow of corporate property transactions and are less inclined toward fostering a stable group of permanent enterprises became apparent to public officials when industrial developers proved unable to retain (or replace) their mobile corporate clients in local economies.

Enterprise policies have since come under more direct public scrutiny, and local policy now goes well beyond plant retention and buyout measures, as interest in the small business policy revolution clearly reveals (Friedman and Schweke 1981). The rediscovery of small business—or, more precisely, new enterprise—as a vital force in advanced capitalism emerged first in the 1970s as the beginning of an unsettled debate regarding its job-creating potential, and debate continues along neo-Schumpterian lines of argument that place emphasis on its innovative function. Local policy officials are increasingly attracted by the prospect of stimulating vital new enterprises and a small business culture that continues to spin off relatively permanent, employment-generating investments in the local economy. While public officials often entertain the entrepreneur's classic hope that at least one or two might enjoy spectacularly successful growth, they face the risks of new enterprise buyouts posed by distant, out-of-town corporations.

Whether viewed as major job generators or the origin of innovative practices, new business development is regarded as a key enterprise policy for local economies in transition. One approach to promoting new enterprises tries to adopt policies that enhance the demonstrated correlates of new enterprise startups. Building on research conducted by the Brookings Institution Economic Studies Program, Harris analyzes Dun and Bradstreet data on new enterprise startups in both branch operations and independent firms between 1976 and 1980 across a sample of thirty-five cities with substantial proportions of high-technology industries. Her analysis in chapter 8 of the factors that contribute to new high-technology startups in these cities demonstrates the primary importance of high-skill labor supplies and urban agglomerations of high-technology industry. Another approach stresses the universal needs of all new enterprises for a protected "incubator" environment, backed up with effective management and financial support. A major effort along these lines was initiated by City Ventures Corporation, a spinoff from Control Data

Corporation's President William Norris. Bradford and Temali examine the results of twenty-one City Ventures Corporation (CVC) contracts with partner cities that through 1982 commingled public funds, corporate equity positions, and Control Data Corporation's PLATO system to help incubate new enterprise ventures in CVC Business and Technology Centers. In chapter 9 they conclude their review of the mixed results obtained through City Venture Corporation contracts, and they supply caveats for local officials concerned about the extent of public sector benefits and private sector policy involvement. Rather than focus on factors or incubators supportive of high-tech startups, chapter 10 starts from the premise of community needs for goods or services and the survival of urban not-for-profit organizations. In chapter 10 Wiewel and Mier chronicle community efforts to establish new business enterprises in Chicago with the assistance of the Center for Urban Economic Development. Their observations about the criteria and measures of success are intended for the benefit of community organizations and local officials who consider technical assistance to fledgling establishments an important policy element.

Policies for industrial sectors and enterprises make important contributions, but labor may be the most underrated element in many areas' potential for successful economic development. Policies directed toward labor must keep two objectives in balance: workers' ability to supply critical production skills and to provide consumer markets for those locally supplied goods and services that together are essential for local economies' development. Adequacy and stability of earned incomes required by working households to provide family needs and tax-supported community services is the second objective. Earlier chapters placed central emphasis on the widely acknowledged importance of labor skills. Malecki (chapter 6) and Harris (chapter 8) reviewed the use of high-skill labor as a condition (and proxy) for high-technology industry, Harris placed primary importance on skilled labor supply as a determinant of entrepreneurship in high-technology enterprise startups, and Wiewel and Mier (chapter 10) mentioned the importance of community workers in establishing community-based enterprises.

The overlap between labor, industry sectors, and enterprises is sometimes so entangled in development initiatives such as worker-owned firms, producer cooperatives, and proposed labor-management-government accords (Reich 1983; Bowles, Gordon, and Weisskopf 1983) that labor policy per se is often difficult to isolate.[7] But this complexity demonstrates vividly how important the establishment of local policy toward labor can be to an area's development potential. One example of mixed labor and enterprise policy is examined by Van Horn, Beauregard, and Ford in chapter 11. They report the results of a demonstration program operated by fourteen communities between 1980 and 1983 to develop their economies by simultaneously assisting small, minority business enterprises and by helping disadvantaged workers find jobs. Their evaluation of the Targeted Jobs Demonstration Program shows how effectively both objectives were pursued and illustrates the obstacles local officials might encounter in pursuing similar policies.

Improved policy measures of this sort, i.e., policies intended to ensure the viability of a local economy for the benefit of community residents, fall under what Clark (1983) calls the "Rawls Option." Named after a widely read book by John Rawls (1971) on the significance and meaning of social justice, Clark includes within this group of options all those intended to secure enduring, viable local economies and the overall well-being of communities. Chapters 5 through 11 discuss the development potential of local economies from this general frame of reference.

But Clark also groups another set of policies under the "Coase Option," a neoclassical efficiency argument that stresses national economic productivity and the hotly contested need for maximum adjustment potential in local economies and labor mobility by community workers. The primacy accorded aggregate efficiency and productivity objectives in all recent discussions of national urban or industrial policies (Clark 1982; Glickman and Van Wagner forthcoming) and the implications for the well-being of workers and their communities call for more attention to "Coase Option" policies of labor mobility. Since national job markets and career mobility are everyday realities to managerial, professional, and some technical workers, mobility policies are directed principally at skilled trades, operative or unemployed workers who hold roots in their communities.

If the "Coase Option" is to make sense and provide mobility incentives to workers who are tied most tightly to their communities, then they should gain some advantage by moving to other labor markets. Relying on longitudinal data through the mid-1970s for individual workers in fifty-three U.S. cities, Salinas tests three hypotheses in chapter 12 concerning labor mobility, subemployment, and declining vs. growing cities. Working from findings that show limited or no beneficial worker effects expected from mobility, Salinas offers a review of several alternative policy approaches and their relation to labor mobility.

James and Blair provide a review of recent literature and evidence that demonstrate the potential improvements in economic position available to workers who are willing to relocate. They conclude in chapter 13 that mobility policies alone are insufficient to balance economic outcomes among workers in different local economies but argue that needless barriers to mobility should be removed through selective reformulation of tax, housing, and social welfare policies. In chapter 14 Kasarda goes beyond James and Blair in proposing active policy measures to remove incentives that now "anchor" workers in cities that once offered "springboard" opportunities but whose economic function has drastically changed. His proposals hold with greatest force in the nation's largest, most established cities where, Kasarda shows with recent evidence, the discrepancy between resident labor skills and "knowledge-intensive" industries is the greatest.

The importance of themes sketched by chapters in each section of the book will be measured ultimately by their ability to stimulate useful debate about the economic future of local areas as the United States enters the next century. Analysts and researchers are likely to remain interested parties to these debates by virtue of their contributions to policy findings and scholarship. More important, the multiple and complex changes outlined here must be understood by those engaged in public policymaking: to do less invites irreversibly permanent development born of poor policy choice reached hastily or unreflectively. The potential for improved, deliberate policymaking stands a good chance of being realized as the themes presented in these chapters receive the attention of local officials who implement public policies as well as those analogously situated professionals in industry and other private sector groups whose development decisions affect the overall structure and performance of local economies.

Local economies and policies for their development are considerably different from a decade ago. We must now ask ourselves how improved economic development strategies can be devised and suited to the times and to the nature of different places. Of course, even improved economic development policies too quickly become the new, unquestioned conventional wisdom that continues to guide practitioners long beyond its useful life. Therefore, the best legacy for this book would be an ongoing dialogue among policymakers, analysts, and planners on the continued adequacy of our concepts and policies, eventually to become the basis for informed public dialogue in forums where the development of our local economies should ultimately be determined.

E.M. Bergman
July 1985

1   National Contexts for Urban Economic Policy

Norman J. Glickman and Robert H. Wilson

Introduction

In this essay we will discuss the economic environment in which urban policy in OECD countries is made.[1] We will look first at both long-term (structural) and cyclical factors operating at the national and international levels that affect urban economies. We also will outline national monetary and fiscal policies that are pursued primarily to cure national economic problems but which may have significant urban effects as well. It is useful to understand clearly the context of both economic events and policy when considering urban policies formulated at both national and local levels since economic and urban programs may conflict. Should this occur, policymaking can be difficult and inefficient.[2] In such cases the goal of economic efficiency will run counter to efforts to increase spatial equity or to revitalize declining areas. Government agencies whose main goals are to increase aggregate economic growth will be working at cross-purposes with those having urban missions, particularly redistributive ones. In such circumstances policy will not only fail to achieve goals, but political conflict will result as well.

Urban policy—we refer specifically here to efforts to promote the economic development[3] of cities and neighborhoods—has been a concern of national and subnational governments for some time. For several decades governments have implemented policies for declining or distressed areas to attain balanced urban growth (Allen 1978). Even in some growing cities, neighborhood development efforts have been pursued. These policies, which for the the most part sought to attract enterprises, have been designed on the assumption that the major determinants for firms to locate were area wages, existing industries, agglomeration economies and diseconomies, transportation access, natural resource endowment, special tax breaks, and other strictly local variables.

However, structural change in national and international economies is creating a new context for urban economic development policy. With the greater internationalization and integration of the world's economies, variables reflecting these phenomena should be given more consideration. Thus, local economic development can be seen increasingly as more dependent on the fate of an area's ability to attract employment in a worldwide market environment. In this view a locality's economic performance will be intimately tied to the success of the nation's economy and to the ways in which national employment is distributed among regions.

Our approach is summarized in figure 1.1. We see structural economic change (box 1) implying both shifts in industries and occupations (box 2) and urban and regional economies (box 3). Problems of

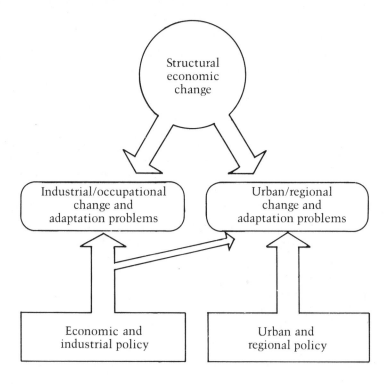

Figure 1.1. The context for urban policymaking

adaptation to structural forces result, including those that involve industrial restructuring, occupational change, and spatial movements of capital and labor. Two broad types of policy are used to respond to these problems. First, there are economic and industrial programs aimed at correcting economic imbalances and encouraging growth (box 4); second, there are urban and regional policies directed primarily at spatial problems (box 5). However, the economic (and other nonurban) policies also have unintended impacts in urban and regional economies that affect development efforts (see dashed arrow between box 4 and box 3). Therefore, the context of urban policymaking consists of the sets of economic and spatial phenomena (boxes 1–3) and the urban effects of nonurban programs.

The purposes of this chapter are to outline (1) the nature and significance of structural change (with particular emphasis on its spatial implications); (2) the impacts of policies focused on economic growth at the national level and on urban development and policy; (3) the nature and context of urban economic development efforts; and (4) the interconnection among policies undertaken at different governmental levels. We conclude with a series of questions about the future of urban development policy in its larger economic context.

Structural Change

Economic Aspects of Structural Change

In the past two decades many economic factors have become less readily controlled by central governments. For example, Keynesian demand management has become less successful, and more thoroughly internationalized economies have made national economic policy more difficult to implement. Moreover, structural change has played an important role in policymaking at all governmental levels. In the context of the 1970s and 1980s structural change has meant shifts in the composition of demand, production, and employment; more capital-intensive production; new technology; slower economic growth rates in most OECD countries; demographic transformations; changes in the international division of labor; and changing urban patterns (OECD 1979).

For our purposes it is important to highlight three critical aspects of structural change. First, on a national and international scale we have been witnessing the transition to what may be the third industrial revolution, one based on information processing, electronics, and bioengineering. Previous industrial transformations — one founded on coal and steam power in the nineteenth century and another (earlier in this century) built upon petroleum, chemicals, and automobiles—encouraged urbanization (Gordon 1976; Renaud 1982). The tendency in many industrial sectors toward economies of scale at high levels of production, rigid input-output relations among firms in industrial complexes, and economies due to urbanization itself (better infrastructure, highly skilled work force, and larger local markets) led to the spatial concentration of industry that in turn was a primary force in the development of cities during those periods. The present industrial revolution, along with cheaper auto-based transportation, has implications for increasing dispersion of population from large cities. There is clearly less need for large-scale production and face-to-face contact in commerce. Smaller, more decentralized units of production are becoming more common in this age as agglomeration economies decline in importance. As a result, new patterns of urban growth are emerging, with important ramifications for the future of urban policy.

Second, there has been a sharp slowdown of economic growth and a commensurate economic restructuring of industry. During the 1970s the rate of economic growth slowed dramatically, and unemployment and inflation rates rose.[4] "Stagflation" was the dominant economic situation as we entered the 1980s. In addition, there was a change in the distribution of employment. There has been a decline in the importance of manufacturing and a rise in the importance of services, both private and governmental. In 1969 nearly 28 percent of OECD workers were employed in manufacturing; by 1980 that percentage had fallen to 24 percent. Over the same period, service employment grew from 48 to 56 percent of the labor force. Government employment also increased, albeit at a decreasing rate in the 1970s.[5] These phenomena have had significant effects on those cities dependent on traditional manufacturing and service provision.

Moreover, world trade mushroomed, growing at about 20 percent annually from 1965 to 1979 (much faster than GNP), and the composition of trade changed; there was greater importation of assembled goods (much previously produced in OECD countries) from selected developing countries. The terms of trade for most OECD countries deteriorated sharply in the late 1970s, reflecting, in part, the rise of OPEC. Direct foreign investment increases were rapid, and the composition was changing as well (OECD 1981). Rather than exporting goods from the home countries, many firms invested abroad. Much direct foreign investment went to a few LDCs and to the southern rim of Europe, especially for assembly operations.

Two related aspects of the economic environment should be noted: capital mobility and the changing nature of the product cycle. With increased capital mobility—the greater ability to redeploy productive and financial resources in different parts of the world—corporations have closed plants in some regions and opened them in others (Bluestone and Harrison 1982). Sometimes these new sites are elsewhere in the firm's home country (e.g., a relocation from Paris to Lyons), while, increasingly, the new plant may be in another continent as transnational firms look for low-wage labor or new markets.

Significantly, the distribution of plant openings and closings has been uneven—some areas have gained, while others have lost from plant relocations. For instance, the relocation of assembly operations to low-wage areas in developing countries and Mediterranean Europe from Northern Europe has increased in recent years. Textile production that used to take place in Manchester, England, now may be located in Oporto, Portugal, or in a developing country. Central to capital mobility have been improved communications and transportation technology, lighter products, and the organization of business through conglomerate and transnational corporations.[6] Similarly, the guest worker (*Gastarbeiter*) phenomenon has involved distant migrations in the past two decades from North Africa and Southern Europe to the factories of Northern Europe; similarly, migration has occurred from the Caribbean and Latin America to North America. International migration (as with capital shifts) has allowed firms access to larger pools of low-wage labor. The major differences of the past twenty years compared to previous periods have been the *speed* and *distance* of capital mobility and, to a lesser extent, labor migration.

Changes in the product cycle also have contributed to increased capital mobility.[7] While research and development (R&D) and the earlier manufacturing phase tend to concentrate in areas with highly skilled workers—scientists, engineers, technicians, and skilled labor —during the later phases of the cycle a deconcentration of production takes place, particularly in areas of relatively low labor costs. Thus, economic activity will tend to locate outside areas that pioneered processes and products.

The current product cycle is being shortened because the length of time between the introduction of a new product and the saturation of that product's market is diminishing. The spatial implications of the shortened product cycle are twofold. First, even greater importance is being placed on R&D, suggesting that areas containing an environment conducive to nurturing new products will be stable; second, standardized manufacturing activities will be relocating to areas of low labor costs more quickly than in the past. This last feature contributes to rapid changes in capital's location.

A third part of structural change concerns a demographic evolution that has altered OECD cities in fundamental ways. Most important has been the virtual end of rural-to-urban migration that was so central to past urban growth. There are several reasons why this has happened, but the most important is simply that there are fewer potential migrants left in the countryside.[8] By 1980 about three-quarters of the population of OECD countries were living in cities, although the level of urbanization varied greatly among member countries.[9] Thus, migration has become a zero-sum game among cities—the population gain of one town is the loss of another. Potential job availability is an important attractive force for migrants.

Spatial Aspects of Structural Change

The economic restructuring of OECD economies has played itself out spatially as well as industrially. That is, areas have been affected differentially by structural change and other macroeconomic factors.[10] For example, there has been a relative (and sometimes absolute) loss of population in larger metropolitan areas. This is related directly to the slower job growth in big cities (in part, due to higher operating costs for firms) and to the greater importance attached to "quality of life" factors associated with less urbanized settings. Suburban development has continued in many countries. Jobs have been taken away from large cities[11] and decentralized to smaller cities. As a result, OECD cities with populations between 50,000 and 100,000 grew by 30 percent, three times the growth rate during the 1970s of cities of

500,000 or more (Renaud 1982). In some cases entire metropolitan areas (the center cities and their suburbs) have lost population. That is, there has been some "deurbanization" (OECD 1983c).

Two major trends have been at work. On one level the decline of these larger cities has been directly connected to the concentration of heavy, traditional industry in those cities;[12] in addition, there has been a noticeable decline in the importance of agglomeration economies, as noted above. At the same time there are examples of rapid growth in other regions,[13] especially those tied to resources development, high-technology industry, and recreation. Also, increases in service employment have occurred in a few large cities because of the location of international corporate headquarters (for instance, in London, New York, Paris, Tokyo, and, most recently, Houston) and employment in corporate-related services (accounting, law, finance, etc.); also, the location of these corporate management functions in certain large cities has increased corporate control over decentralized production activities located in smaller towns (Cameron 1983). Many of these large cities are also governmental centers, another factor that compensates for the loss of manufacturing jobs. Overall, however, the first trend has dominated, and employment decline has been felt in the larger metropolitan areas of the OECD.

There also has been a rise in the importance of small- and medium-sized cities, due mainly to the decentralization of jobs in manufacturing and services from larger cities. Services have grown in these cities as thresholds of economies of scale have been reached. Finally, many smaller cities have grown on the basis of good environmental and living conditions.

Because of these trends there have been severe problems for some neighborhoods and downtown areas, particularly in declining metropolitan areas. Some central business districts have lost firms to their suburbs, and many neighborhoods have suffered from bad housing and public services; often these neighborhoods are populated by ethnic minorities.[14] In response to these developments there have been many public programs aimed at structural adjustment both in the economic and spatial spheres.

Responses to Economic Change

The Spatial Impacts of Economic Policy

Attempts to increase economic growth and to achieve positive adaptation have included tax and spending programs, macroeconomic policy, industrial strategies, research and development subsidies, job training, infrastructure provision, and foreign trade programs (OECD 1982b). Even though these policies focus on industries and occupations with little attention paid to location, they have not been spatially neutral. Direct spending by central governments, for example, can affect local growth via the multiplier effects that come with exogenous expenditures.[15] Thus, expenditures on roads, schools, infrastructure, and social transfers have direct effects on areas receiving funds. Through the multiplier effect, additional indirect gains occur to the extent that leakages to other regions are small.

Thus, in looking at the effect of national policy on regions and cities, one would want to know the distribution of spending and taxes. There are regional gainers and losers from this process.[16]

National macroeconomic policy—particularly countercyclical policy—affects cities and regions differentially. Cyclical behavior depends on local factors such as industry mix, unemployment rates, labor supply characteristics, age of capital, wage levels, and resource endowment. Thus, regions specializing in durable goods industries are likely to have more volatile cyclical patterns than regions concentrated in services and agriculture (Victor and Vernez 1981). Using the same reasoning, regions will have different cyclical timing. Therefore, when a national government attempts to reduce cyclical inflation by raising interest rates, the results will have different effects in those areas having firms with large amounts of capital debt. Similarly, low-interest rate regimes would aid areas that are growing and where companies are in need of cheap credit. The main point is that no matter what local economic projects are being attempted by cities, they will be influenced (positively or negatively) by national countercyclical policy.

There are other, probably more important, ways in which national economic and social policies affect regions. Many tax and spending programs create incentives for private firms to channel investment to particular areas. Tax and other microeconomic policies provide important illustrations of this phenomenon, although, we must emphasize, the phenomenon is general. To increase economic growth and international competitiveness, governments often provide (microeconomic) tax subsidies in the form of (untargeted) depreciation allowances and tax credits.[17] By lowering the effective tax rate (and real cost) of capital, it is hoped that firms will increase capital formation and employment.

In the United States, for example, the 1981 Economic Recovery Tax Act (ERTA) produced effective tax rates on new investment between 16 and 21 percent, well below previous effective rates and the statutory rate of 46 percent (Gravelle 1982). Whatever the effect on investment levels of the tax treatment of capital, classes of capital will be affected differentially. In the case of ERTA, new equipment was given more advantageous tax status relative to structures, and short-lived equipment was favored over long-lived assets. Also there were important differences in tax rates among types of assets and industries, and new buildings were favored over old ones. For instance, there was an effective tax rate of −49 percent on computers (assuming a 6 percent inflation rate) compared to +11 percent on railroad equipment (Gravelle 1982). The uneven treatment of assets and industries is common in the tax codes of OECD countries.

How do tax laws such as ERTA affect local economic development? First, by allowing a quicker depreciation of assets the economic life of capital is reduced; thus, a machine that previously would be depreciated over ten years might now be written off in three years. This means that the asset would have no accounting life after the third year, and the firm would have a financial incentive to scrap and abandon that otherwise productive asset. The implications of this phenomenon are important: it will be more likely that older plants (often in large, older cities) will be closed and new investment will take place in newer, growing regions. Second, structures in older regions would be at a disadvantage to those in newer ones because tax laws often encourage construction of new facilities over the rehabilitation of older ones. Other facets of tax policies often have spatial consequences.[18]

We have given the example of tax laws' implications for urban development and policy. It also could be shown that for other national economic policies—industrial policies, research and development, procurement, and infrastructure, among others—different kinds of incentives are generated for the location of private activity. Such "urban impact analyses" can show how the set of policies aimed primarily at economic growth affect urban and regional development, indirectly or inadvertently (Glickman et al. 1982). No comprehensive understanding of the "real" urban policy—that is, the explicit spatial strategies of countries and the implicit ones that result from nonurban programs—can be gained without urban impact analysis (Glickman 1980; OECD 1983b).

There are likely to be significant incentives for private capital formation in economic programs that run counter to the goals of urban policies. Our tax example provides a case in point. Although the intent of accelerated depreciation allowances is to increase investment and productivity, significant spatial consequences will occur as unintended by-products. With companies able to write off equipment faster, they will likely take older plant and equipment out of service sooner than previously. The fact that this older equipment is often in older manufacturing cities will mean disinvestment there. However, it is in precisely those cities that the concern for urban development policy is the strongest.

In addition to public programs attempting to increase national economic growth there have been a range of policies aimed explicitly at the spatial dislocations caused by structural change. While some policies have been directed specifically to the social consequences of economic distress, we are particularly interested in those policies designed to deal with the economic dimensions of spatial dislocation. National policies targeted to distressed urban areas include revitalization and redevelopment schemes, infrastructure provision, training programs, and capital subsidies. The economic justification for these programs is that the market-clearing solution leaves substantial underused resources. Spatially targeted national policies have attempted to reduce market failures, to control negative externalities, and to lower the costs of transacting business. When successful, these policies probably lead to increases in Gross National Product that would not occur otherwise, since, in the absence of these policies, resources in these areas would be underemployed. These spatially targeted national policies are usually of greater concern to distressed or declining cities. The economic policies, however, aimed at positive adaptation to structural change often have their strongest effects in growing cities. Therefore, a critical conflict exists in attempts to stimulate national investment and in efforts to rejuvenate declining manufacturing centers. The important policy questions are: can national economic growth and urban revitalization be made more compatible, and can economic and industrial policy become more "region sensitive"?

Economic Change and Political Conflict

It appears that a new context for urban policy has emerged, one in which national and international phenomena and policies may limit the effectiveness of local actions. We have seen this in the case of attempts to adjust to structural change. In addition, there are important conflicts between policies aimed at growth and those designed to increase spatial equity and urban development.

Increasingly, nation-states find themselves caught in a set of external and internal conflicts. At the external level, ways must be found to increase economic growth in an ever-uncertain internationalized economy and negotiate with trading partners (Glickman and Alford 1982).[19] But, simultaneously, the modern nation-state also must deal with a set of consequences that are internal to the nation. In the case of the international sector, nations find themselves trying not only to relate to external forces but to the social and spatial consequences of a changing world. For example, the United States negotiates with Japan over automobile imports but must also deal with the consequences of import penetration and the investment policies of U.S. auto firms on autoworkers and the Midwestern region. Similarly, the struggles over EEC agricultural policy have both external and internal consequences among members of the Community; witness recent "wine" and "pasta" wars. These battles are not only about industries but involve regional (e.g., Detroit) and occupational (e.g., farmers, autoworkers) dimensions.

While issues such as "free trade versus protectionism" rage at the national level, decisions about trade policy have significant local impacts (U.S. Congressional Budget Office 1979). Semiconductor firms and textile companies have quite divergent views about the benefits of free trade, and the cities in which such firms are clustered will be affected in important ways by decisions about trade barriers. Coalitions of citizens—groupings based on regional, industrial, class, and other backgrounds—have pressured the state (at both the national and local levels) to preserve jobs lost to foreign competition, to aid trade-distressed communities, and to formulate industrial strategies to improve international competitiveness. Often, the goals of these disparate groups are contradictory, and governments are forced into political quagmires. At the local level, for example, pressures placed on governments to cushion the effects of dislocation often lead to fiscal crisis.

In addition, industrial capitalist nations face problems resulting from faster capital mobility. Transnational corporations argue for tax privileges, with the threat to relocate to another country as a bargaining chip. Countries increasingly find themselves in bidding wars over factory locations (e.g., Austria and Spain over a General Motors plant). Capital mobility—seen by many as the key to capital accumulation and prosperity—also can bring with it significant locally felt social costs. Plant relocations mean loss of employment and often increases in health problems, family violence, and other social pathologies (Bluestone and Harrison 1982). The loss of factories means a declining local tax base and, simultaneously, increased municipal costs for unemployment compensation and other welfare-related expenditures. As communities face a downward spiral of jobs and public revenues, fiscal problems result. Under such circumstances, even the most aggressive local growth policies will have trouble succeeding in the face of so many closed factories and shops.

Yet it is the movement of capital—both in space and among industrial sectors—that is central to the workings of the economic systems of OECD countries. Moreover, as noted earlier, mobility is encouraged by tax laws. Therefore, urban economic development policy may conflict with national goals of economic efficiency as epitomized by the dictates of capital mobility.

Urban Economic Development Strategies

Structural change and the policies that try to promote adaptation provide the context for urban economic development efforts. Both the phenomena—shifts in industries, new technology, changes in location patterns, greater private capital mobility—and the national programs tied to adjustment make the environment for promoting growth in a certain area much more complicated.

Economic Rationale for Urban Development Policy

The essence of the problem faced by urban economic development decisionmakers, both in the design of targeted national policies and local government policies, is to induce existing enterprises to expand, to attract new enterprises, and to prevent firms from closing. While the means available to address this problem are circumscribed by the prevailing economic and political system (and vary among nations and among levels of government), the objective is the same: to increase investment and employment in a city or neighborhood. This can be done with a variety of tools, including labor training programs, capital subsidies, land policies, facilities and infrastructure provision, tax incentives, and attempts to enhance the relative attractiveness of the city (or neighborhood) to firms.

Two general rationales serve as the basis for designing policies. First, investments may not occur in a city even though it is a desirable location because the benefits of the locale to enterprises are unknown or they are incorrectly perceived. In this case the appropriate policy is simply one of promoting the relative attractiveness of the area.[20] The second, and more common, situation is that the city does not represent the most desirable location, perhaps due to market failures, and policy must be designed to improve the cost or revenue structure that an enterprise faces there.

Firms incur operating costs for labor, capital, raw materials or intermediate goods, utilities (power, water, sewage), land and facilities, transportation, storage, and taxes. Many of these costs, as well as revenues resulting from sales, will vary. The location decision for a firm will theoretically involve choosing the most profitable location. Urban policies will be effective only if they can significantly affect the cost or revenue structure faced by a firm, relative to other cities. Most strategies are designed to reduce the costs of companies, although some attempt to affect the demand for the enterprises' product.

Traditional Urban Economic Development Strategies

While the specific form of cost-reduction development strategies varies substantially among countries and among various levels of governments in the same country, measures generally can be classified by the type of input being affected.

Labor costs. A variety of targeted national policies and local government initiatives are designed to reduce the cost of labor. Government programs in training, retraining, and education attempt to improve the skill level of the work force (found in such OECD countries as the Netherlands, Denmark, the United States, and Great Britain, OECD 1983a). Labor subsidies through tax credits can be used to reduce labor costs (used in the United States, Canada, Great Britain, and Sweden). These policies also are often directed to a certain segment of the labor force, e.g., the unemployed. Subsidized housing programs for workers may make an area more attractive to prospective firms (Johnson and Cochrane 1981).

Capital costs. Government programs can attempt to affect the cost of capital in particular areas through a wide variety of instruments such as capital grants (in Great Britain, the Netherlands, Austria, and the United States), direct loans or loan guarantees that effectively reduce interest rates, and investment tax credits (in the United States, OECD 1983a). These strategies tend to be in the purview of national governments (which may target the incentives to depressed areas) since local governments usually are incapable of generating the necessary revenue or they lack requisite taxing authority. However, given the shortage of capital, new financing mechanisms and institutions are emerging in the United States, such as venture capital and economic development corporations, that mobilize capital for development (NCUED 1978; U.S. Conference of Mayors 1980; Litvak and Daniels 1979).

Land and facilities. Reduction in the cost of land or facilities for enterprises that locate in an area represents perhaps the most common strategy available to local governments. (It is used in West Germany, Austria, Great Britain, Sweden, and the United States, Johnson and Cochrane 1981; U.S. Conference of Mayors 1980; OECD 1983a.) Land assembly and below-market land prices provided by the public sector are often critical for the redevelopment of distressed areas of large cities as well as in countries with relatively limited amounts of developable land.

Infrastructure provision and utility charges. Policies dealing with the provision of water, sewage disposal, transportation facilities, and energy can be designed to lower the operating costs of firms, thus giving a city a comparative advantage (OECD 1983a; Johnson and Cochrane 1981; U.S. Conference of Mayors 1980). The expansion of road networks to underdeveloped areas has been used specifically as a development tool (in Great Britain, Canada, and the United States). The provision of infrastructure is frequently the joint responsibility of various levels of government and often involves public or quasi-public enterprises. Inadequate investment in maintenance leads to infrastructure that operates poorly and can adversely affect the operating costs of firms, thus making the area relatively less attractive to firms (for the United States, see Choate and Walter 1981).

Taxes. Another set of strategies attempts to lower taxes to a firm through preferential rates on land, production, or income (as in Japan, the Netherlands, and the United States, Johnson and Cochrane 1981; OECD 1983a; National Council for Urban Economic Development (NCUED) 1978).

Government regulation. Attempts can be made to reduce the costs imposed on firms through government regulation (Aronson and Shapiro 1981). This strategy can assume a variety of forms such as expediting procedures for acquiring permits, relaxing land use or environmental regulations, relaxing minimum wage laws, etc. (OECD 1983a; U.S. Conference of Mayors 1981).

Technical assistance. As a variation of promotional activities, local governments also may provide technical assistance to prospective firms. Assistance in evaluating the costs and revenues of a particular area can be very beneficial to prospective firms, particularly for smaller firms (OECD 1983a; Johnson and Cochrane 1981; U.S. Conference of Mayors 1980).

In addition to approaches that attempt to affect a firm's cost structure, a small number of policies are designed to affect a firm's revenue by creating demand for its products. This creates an incentive for it to locate in the area. One procedure is for a government to adopt a procurement policy whereby a preference is given to goods and services produced by local enterprises. One could even include various types of franchises awarded by government in this category as well as policies that facilitate the export of goods and services. While one could imagine, at least for large metropolitan areas, a Keynesian approach to development through the management of demand, local governments are not likely to be invested with the necessary powers. These demand-oriented policies are of less importance than the cost-oriented efforts but are mentioned for completeness.

Government programs for economic development often consist of a mix of several policy instruments. Urban renewal programs, for example, have combined land assembly, infrastructure provision, tax abatement, and other tools.[21] The purpose of using several instruments in combination is twofold. First, if the prevailing cost structure in an area is very poor, then several means to reduce costs will more likely be needed. Second, by using several strategies, the program can be "tailored" to the locational needs of a particular industry or city.

Most of the strategies described here result in costs to government. There are direct costs in the construction of facilities, and indirect costs such as tax expenditures (revenue foregone) on tax credits. A government that must make numerous concessions to attract firms does so with the hope that the enterprise will have a large multiplier effect and that the higher levels of economic activity will more than compensate for the public expenditures. Whether or not the cost/benefit ratio is acceptable, the earlier discussion suggests that many traditional tools, particularly related to cost reduction for business, may already be less effective.

Recent Approaches to Urban Economic Policy

With significant pressure on governments, increased attention has been placed on developing new strategies for economic development. While the traditional strategies are still used, governmental authorities are experimenting with new tools, three of which will be discussed here: the public/private partnership, research and development support, and community-based economic development.

There have been suggestions for greater cooperation between the public and private sectors, particularly in the United States (OECD 1983a). The form of these public-private partnerships can vary substantially. In some cases there is simply increased dialogue between public policymakers and representatives of business; at other times, there are joint ventures involving private and public capital (NCUED 1978). One of the most common examples of close cooperation between the public and private sectors occurs in central city revitalization where land assembly and infrastructure improvements by local governments are essential for large-scale redevelopment. The increase in the number of public-private partnerships, at least in the United States, represents a greater direct involvement by the public sector in development ventures and suggests that local governments are assuming an entrepreneurial role.

Another increasingly common response is governmental support for research and development. While support for R&D activities—an integral part of industrial policy—is largely the concern of national governments due to competition in the international arena, some subnational governments attempt to attract and nurture R&D in the hope that they will spin off other activities, particularly manufacturing. Research and development is attractive for several reasons. First, firms tend to employ high-income, well-trained individuals. Second, unlike manufacturing, there is little chance that R&D facilities will locate "off shore" given their strategic importance. And, finally, the very nature of R&D—creation and innovation—makes it an exceptional resource for long-term economic stability; while a single product will pass through the various phases of the product cycle, the pressure for the development of new products will continue to exist.

Public sector efforts to attract R&D face several constraints. These activities require a certain level of intellectual and technical resources in the environment, most often found in the research facilities of large universities.[22] The second constraint is that any nation will have relatively few R&D centers, creating intense competition among possible locales. Consequently, successful economic development induced by R&D will be found in very few places.

The severe economic distress suffered by some areas has resulted in experimentation with strategies not heretofore common in market economies. These include community-based economic development, neighborhood cooperatives, and worker buy-outs of existing enterprise, among others. Some of these efforts do not necessarily require supportive public sector involvement, but they are increasingly being adopted by locales faced with significant economic problems (Aronson and Shapiro 1981). These efforts involve attempts to increase social control of capital, and since they are tied geographically to a working population, they could reduce the mobility of capital.[23] Even though such activities affect only a small part of most OECD economies, they are important to note as one creative response to the increased mobility of capital and the resulting disinvestment in some areas.

Urban Policy Issues

The new structural context affects urban economic policymaking in many important ways. We will now discuss the implications of the larger economic context on urban policy in five policy areas: tax concessions and tax burdens, growth policy for smaller cities, policy to attract manufacturing employment, development strategies for service sector employment, and employment generation.

Just as economic slowdown places intense pressure on national governments to adopt policies conducive to growth, localities (even those in structurally favorable positions) suffer from the same pressure. Many policies designed specifically to lower business costs often shift tax burdens from business to consumers and lead to a reduction in the level of nonbusiness services. Research from the United States has shown that tax abatement schemes for attracting enterprises to cities have, at best, a marginal effect on location decisions. Yet these concessions result in lower tax revenue for the locality (Harrison and Kanter 1978; Bahl 1980). While the cost-benefit ratio may not be attractive for tax concessions, governments are faced with a "prisoner's dilemma" in that no single locality will risk the possible consequences of not offering these concessions. Cities, like many national governments and labor unions, find themselves in a relatively weak bargaining position during this period of slow growth and increased capital mobility.

One of the effects of slow economic growth and economic restructuring has been that small and medium-sized cities are relatively favored, at least with respect to the location and expansion of manufacturing. The potential for success of the cost-reduction development strategies in these cities is relatively high, at least as compared to traditional manufacturing cities. Even here, though, one must be cautious. While these cities as a group may be able to offer lower costs than traditional manufacturing centers to many types of firms, the relatively large number of medium- and small-sized cities in a country (not to mention those in other countries) means intense competition among cities in this group; that is, localities may be in direct competition for the same kinds of companies (Johnson and Cochrane 1981). Historical studies have shown that the entrepreneurial efforts of businessmen and public officials, not structural imperatives, have often been the cause for the success of cities (Perry and Watkins 1977). This research suggests that relatively few smaller cities will significantly improve their relative positions in spite of favorable conditions.

Further caution must be applied to any city, particularly smaller cities, that focuses development efforts on attracting manufacturing enterprise. Increasing the number of manufacturing jobs has often been the principal goal of both urban and regional economic development programs. High employment multipliers and the importance of proximity to interindustry linkages justified this goal. In today's environment, however, branch plant locations of large corporations (both nationally and internationally), technological change, and the shortening of the product cycle suggest that the basis for pursuing manufacturing employment as the major goal has been somewhat eroded. The relative attractiveness of LDCs for manufacturing in some traditional sectors, such as textiles, and in some new sectors, such as the assembly operations in microelectronics, may mean that the benefits of growth of manufacturing employment, at least in some industries, may be short-lived.

Another important effect of structural change on urban policy concerns changes in the sectoral composition of employment. Manufacturing employment has represented a steadily decreasing share of employment for some time, while the share of service sector employment has risen. This creates yet another dilemma for urban policy that attempts to capitalize on this growth by expanding service sector employment. Increases in some types of service employment, such as retail trade and government, are rather rigidly tied to increases in urban population and local consumption and, consequently, these sectors cannot serve as principal mechanisms for development strategies.[24] On the other hand, several service sectors, such as finance, insurance, and other producer services, are export-oriented, and the spatial distribution of these activities and the administrative and management components of corporations are likely to be important in the evolution of urban networks in advanced industrial economies (Stanback et al. 1981). While the locational needs of services should be the subject of extensive research and incorporated into the design of urban economic development policy, employment in service activities is largely bifurcated, requiring some highly trained workers as well as a large number of unskilled or low-skilled workers (Stanback et al. 1981). Economic development via service sector employment, therefore, must be qualified in two ways. The implications for income distribution are probably less than desirable, and the multiplier effects of service sector employment on the local economy will probably be less significant than those traditionally found in manufacturing.

Urban economic development strategies must incorporate a better understanding of the contemporary job generation process. While policies have generally tried to attract new enterprises (often large employers), employment levels are more dependent on the differences between jobs created by new firms and closures of others and on the contraction and expansion of existing firms. Also, employment in small firms is relatively more important than that of large firms (Birch 1979). These findings strongly suggest that greater attention must be focused on the creation of small firms and on the economic viability of existing firms (Aronson and Shapiro 1981).

Our discussion suggests that some traditional urban strategies may be less effective in the new environment created by structural change and that the design of new strategies is certainly problematic. In the following section, we will raise a number of critical issues concerning the new context of urban economic development.

Concluding Remarks

Our argument, sketched in figure 1.1, has been that during this period of structural economic change and increased competition in the world economy, national governments are faced with serious dilemmas in formulating economic and urban policy. Among other things, structural change involves differential growth rates among industrial sectors; thus, policies that place priorities on high-growth sectors will reinforce the impact of structural change. As a result, traditional manufacturing regions will likely suffer further decline, while other areas may grow rapidly. To counter this dispersion of growth rates, national policies for promoting growth must be made consistent with, or be complemented by, programs for urban revitalization and stabilization. In other words, national policies must be devised that reconcile the possible conflict between national economic growth and urban revitalization (Hanson 1983). At present this is generally not the case.

At the local level decisionmakers (especially those in traditional manufacturing areas) are faced with disinvestment and intense competition for new employment. The evolving economic context suggests that some traditional economic tools may have become less effective and that a posture of adaptation, flexibility, and experimentation in policymaking are needed in this period. There are at least three problems facing local governments. First, local governments may not be legally empowered to pursue some innovative efforts in local economic development, such as mobilization of capital or public-private partnerships. Second, many localities do not have the fiscal capability to meet the infrastructure requirements essential for economic development. With this in mind, new approaches to policy should be considered. And, finally, even in areas where governments have traditionally had competency, such as in education and training, major new efforts will be required to meet the employment and skills requirements of the emerging economy.

The political conflict inherent in this period of change, with its winners and losers, also complicates local economic decisionmaking. Pressures on the local public sector for enhancing the local business environment and widespread opposition to new taxes could well lead to declines in the provision of local social services. In addition, the standard tools of local development planners have limited effectiveness in this period of high capital mobility.

The implications of structural change on a particular local economy are fairly clear and can be derived through an analysis of the economy and its comparative advantages. Thus, we can look at Manchester or Osaka, for instance, examine their industrial mixes and fiscal bases, and forecast their potential for development, at least in broad terms. Moreover, the economies of various city types (e.g., manufacturing-based, service-dominated) may be analyzed within the context of structural change. On the other hand, it is difficult to be precise about implications of the national economic and urban policies for local economic development efforts. Since these policies are the result of highly variable political outcomes, subject always to negotiating and bargaining among many actors, national policies and their local effects will vary from country to country and will change over time.

In considering the economic and political environment in the United States, however, there are reasons for predicting that urban economic development planning will fall increasingly to state and local governments, and these governments will assume new functions and responsibilities. This is coming about because of the withdrawal of the federal government from a variety of urban aid programs under the Reagan administration's New Federalism schemes. If the level of urban services is not to fall, states and localities must become greater providers of services.

In the United States, national economic policy has placed the burden of economic adjustment largely on the industries and firms themselves, and current tax policy that provides incentives for new investment encourages relocation. Some protectionist trade policies (which protect market shares for U.S. firms) try to provide a few industries with a transition period to make internal adjustments required for competition in the international market. As with industries, cities and regions are left responsible for adjustments to the spatial dimensions of structural change, at least under current U.S. urban policy. The federal government is assuming less of a role in infrastructure provision, and various economic development grant programs are still in place but at low levels of funding. By default, public sector action for promoting economic development must be assumed by state and local governments if it is to occur.

The constraints placed on local development activities, due to structural change, are rendering traditional roles of state and local governments and the tools used by these governments less effective. A combination of circumstances, including stiff international competition and national policies, may force local economic actors, both private and public, to create new institutions and policies designed to strengthen local economies and prepare for the future.

Author's Note: An earlier version of this chapter was prepared for the OECD Project Group on Urban Economic Development. This research was supported in part by the Mike Hogg Research Support Fund of the University of Texas at Austin. The views expressed here do not necessarily represent those of the OECD or the University of Texas.

2 Urban America, Inc.: Corporatist Convergence of Power in American Cities?

Susan E. Clarke

Introduction

In recent years many Americans have found the Japanese model of cooperative relations between business and government interests to be an intriguing answer to the malaise of the American economy. The search for ways to better coordinate these interdependent interests, in a manner appropriate to the American context, continues to be elusive at the national level. At the local level, however, the compelling need to accommodate the demands of economic interests and electoral constituencies has prompted local officials to devise new policy structures and procedures bringing together public and private development interests. These local approaches range from project-specific partnerships to institutionalization of these relations in quasi-governmental organizations with policymaking authority. Such arrangements contrast sharply with the pluralist "street-fighting politics" and distributional coalitions dominating local politics over the last two decades. They also differ from the historically close but less formal relationship between American business and local governments and suggest important changes in interest group organization and decisionmaking processes in American cities. In particular, to the extent that these local arrangements bring organized interests into local policymaking structures, they indicate a nonpluralist convergence of power in American cities—the emergence of Urban America, Inc.

This essay examines evidence of this newest convergence of power in terms of the concept of interest representation. Using this concept to frame the issue moves one away from a narrow concern with the mechanisms of public-private partnerships to a consideration of how different modes of interest representation are adopted in response to a pervasive local governance problem: the need to make binding long-term policy decisions about local development in the face of short-term, often conflicting, needs of functional and territorial interests.

The concept of interest representation encompasses two analytic dimensions: differences in the demand pattern, or how interests are organized, and differences in the decisional structures, the ways in which interests are represented in the policymaking process.[1] The heart of the scholarly debate centers on whether observed variations in these dimensions can be accommodated by the pluralist paradigm or whether they reflect patterns more accurately described by corporatist models.[2] To date, analyses of changing interest representation patterns have focused on national politics in advanced industrial economies, primarily in Europe and Japan, where there is substantial variation in the forms of interest organization and in the means by which organized interests participate in policy formation processes. The possibility of corporatism in the United States is rejected.[3] But this lack of evidence of corporatist patterns in the United States may be a result of looking for the wrong thing—peak associations of interest groups—in the wrong place—the national political arena. This essay argues that the properties of new decisional structures and policymaking procedures in local economic development policymaking suggest patterns of interest representation in local American politics that are not adequately explained by interest group pluralism models.

The Concept of Interest Representation

The renewed scholarly attention to analysis of interest representation stems from a sense that existing models are inadequate in explaining contemporary political phenomena.[4] This began with efforts to apply American-derived models of interest group pluralism to postwar European politics. These early comparative studies increased scholarly appreciation of the different forms of interest group organization and the various ways in which organized interests participate in policymaking processes, particularly in nonelectoral arenas. By the mid-seventies the apparent declining capacity of political parties and interest groups to facilitate collective action and the rise of new types of links between groups and government led many scholars to move away from the structural-functionalist framework and pluralist assumptions guiding previous empirical studies of interest group activity (Almond 1983, 248). A good number now work with some version of the broader concept of "interest intermediation"—the processes by which groups mediate between society and the state. This concept draws attention to a range of relationships, pluralist and nonpluralist, between groups and government. As Berger (1981) points out, it contrasts with structural-functionalist views of interests and interest group functions in several important ways: interest group formation and organization is viewed as problematic and not determined by socioeconomic structures alone; interest groups may play a wide range of roles and, consequently, have a variety of different relationships with governing authorities rather than perform a singular interest articulation and aggregation function; and the relationship between patterns of interest representation, political stability, and economic growth is viewed as a central empirical issue (Berger 1981, 1–11). Each of these distinctions rests on a key element in the interest representation approach: some modes of representation involve an active state role in influencing interest formation and in bringing interests into policymaking processes.[5]

The primary empirical referents for the concept of interest representation are pluralist and nonpluralist, or "corporatist," patterns of representation. A major distinction is their interpretation of the extent to which demands made on the local state are seen as unstructured and emanating from the felt needs of groups, as in the pluralist view, or structured to some extent by the state itself. In pluralist views, public authority acts as a constant, neutral broker among policy interests; state power, authority, and activity are explained by group activity (see Truman 1951; Wilson 1973). State responsiveness to the demands of interest groups is portrayed as a function of the level and intensity of those demands; the state is not seen as having autonomous interests of its own or as an active policy advocate. Thus, the interest group pluralism model interprets policy formulation as a response to, and limited by, groups organized around felt needs and able to make policy demands; the process is characterized by bargaining and negotiating among interests and between interests and government. This diversity of interests and bargaining was initially associated with greater political stability. But, as specialized interests increase and policy demands grow more numerous, some now view the overload of demands and the inability of the political system to cope with and arbitrate among competing demands as contributing to political instability.[6]

But the pluralist model lacks any theoretical criteria for distinguishing among state responses to these demands when they include efforts, such as co-optation, cooperation, or incorporation, to shape group relations with government. This results in an inability to predict the circumstances under which such responses occur in nonelectoral policy arenas (see Nedelmann and Meir 1979). As a consequence, interest group pluralism models are inclined toward labeling of state–interest group linkages rather than explaining or predicting the circumstances or consequences of such linkages. For example, pervasive and persistent linkages of groups to decision structures may be interpreted as "preferred access" relations, "iron triangles" of reciprocal influence, or the most acceptable "minimal winning coalition" solution to articulating demands, channeling conflicts, and reaching compromises on further policy agreements. Furthermore, this ahistorical approach cannot account for historical trends toward greater penetration of state and civil associations; this includes contemporary trends toward giving interest groups policymaking status and incorporating them into quasi-public decision structures. This inability to account for changing state roles is a critical limitation to the utility of pluralist models in explaining contemporary local policymaking.

In contrast, corporatist theorists accept the state as, under some circumstances, an active agent in interest mobilization and policy formation processes. Although policy decisions in the corporatist model also are ultimately depicted as the product of group activity, policymaking is seen as rooted in objective interests, with the state actively promoting interests rather than merely brokering exogenous pressures. In this view of public authority the state is not only an arena for interest group activity but capable of interests and initiatives separate from the sum of group pressures. Corporatist views are not wedded to instrumentalist views of the state, however; that is, state interventions are not necessarily or permanently identifiable with any one set of interests, particularly in the short term (see Nordlinger 1981).

Yet in focusing on these trends toward more structured linkages between state decisional structures and economic interest groups, particularly tripartite business-government-labor arrangements, some corporatist models appear to restrict the use of the term "corporatist" to static institutional arrangements. The key analytic element, however, is not an ideal-type configuration but the extent to which policymakers "define and channel the relationships of groups to the policy process" (Anderson 1979). In "corporatist" processes, therefore, mobilization and policy participation are intentionally created and structured through public policy.

Neither pluralist nor corporatist views are wholly adequate in explaining contemporary political processes. Sole reliance on pluralist perspectives for the study of local politics leads to three analytic dead ends: a static focus on the distribution of influence among currently existing and active groups rather than consideration of evolving patterns of activity and representation of affected interests; an atheoretical view of the changing role and activities of public authority, both in shaping interest group activity and structuring group links to policymaking processes; and an inability to explain changing urban policy agendas, particularly shifts from social consumption, or distributional policies, to economic policy issues. Applying corporatist perspectives to the analysis of local policy processes addresses two of these issues: local policy agenda changes and interest group formation can be linked to the influence of capital accumulation needs on public activities; and, over time, it is anticipated that these needs cause the local state to become increasingly active in shaping interest group activity in economic policy arenas.[7]

But, unfortunately, most corporatist analyses of interest representation processes continue to confound the demand structure and decisional structure dimensions when these are more usefully viewed as distinct. In this analysis the intent is to consider whether interest representation in local decision structures and policy processes in the local economic development arena can be more adequately explained by pluralist or corporatist models; for the sake of clarity, these relations between groups and government will be described as pluralist and nonpluralist, or "corporatist-like," policy processes.

The Local Context of Interest Representation

What puts the Inc. in Urban America, Inc. is an observable trend toward greater inclusion of private interests in public policymaking forums. This "attribution of public status to interest groups" (Offe 1981) in local policy processes challenges structural-functionalist assumptions about interest group roles and activities; it also contradicts the pluralist policy model in which groups pressure government but remain external to the decision process. This blurring of public authority and private interests contributes to a dissonance between analytic models and local political reality similar to that stirring a reconsideration of the relations of state and society in comparative studies of national politics. European scholars have responded with analyses that reconsider the adequacy of existing paradigms and introduce new theoretical approaches to the study of local politics.[8] In contrast, American scholars have mapped the local impacts of larger economic changes but have given less attention to the adequacy of current paradigms in illustrating or explaining the new political phenomenon.[9]

Yet there are grounds for anticipating that these local political changes, particularly in the economic development policy arena, are more likely to resemble nonpluralist patterns of interest representation and to be more adequately explained by models drawn from corporatist theories. To begin with, local officials face a territorial imperative to devise effective means of accommodating conflicts between functional and territorial interests in local policymaking processes; to fail to do so risks the loss of electoral support and private investment. Local governments, therefore, need ways to reach consensus on development issues.

Given the interjurisdictional competition fostered by the fragmented federal system in the United States, business interests are assured of receptive local audiences in most communities. Business demands for local government support are constant, therefore, backed by the implicit threat of relocation to another, more "responsive" jurisdiction. In the face of economic crises, however, there is evidence that many businesses are "upping the stakes" and seeking greater political certainty. For some this involves demands that local governments not only share business costs through conventional subsidies but that they also share business risks through investments of public capital in private enterprises. Many firms also have a strong interest in arriving at agreements on the "rules of the game" that can survive electoral changes and reduce the potential for disruption of their economic activities. This often leads to efforts by business interests and local officials to remove economic development policymaking from pluralist policy bargaining processes and to lodge this authority in special agencies or organizations.

Until recently, the ability of citizen groups to influence development decisions hinged on their ability to mobilize against the project itself, frequently through protest tactics (Lipsky 1968; Mollenkopf 1981). The history of federal development programs and local development initiatives is fraught with these veto activities. Now, however, there is increasing evidence that community groups are becoming actively involved in development projects, often as "partners" with developers and local government on specific projects or in citywide policy forums. (For examples, see Fosler and Berger 1982; National Commission on Neighborhoods 1979; Friedman and Schweke 1981; National Economic Development and Law Center 1983; Berger et al., 1982). In addition to this new focus of community organizational activities, local officials may become actively involved in organizing certain diffuse constituencies into new organizations and viable partners. Local government's incentives for influencing the formation of new community-based groups include concerns that these interests are significant but unorganized market components, such as small businesses or, as in the case of neighborhood groups, that they may potentially mobilize around issues of market failure and hamper redevelopment efforts.

Although there may be alternative means of political access and influence available to each of these interests, the substantive policy issues—the transformation of land uses and the allocation of public investment funds—and the imperative to reach coherent decisions on these questions provide business, government, and local citizen groups with the incentive to reach mutually agreeable decisions. Each controls resources needed by the others, although the level of awareness may vary by city and over time. It is anticipated that this territorial imperative to work out consensual procedures for local economic development policymaking encourages a trend toward nonpluralist, corporatist-like relations between groups and government in American local policymaking, even though relations between business, labor, and government in national politics continue to be characterized by pluralistic bargaining.[10]

Analysis of Local Interest Representation

Using the criteria identified in figure 1.1, this section assesses the extent to which linkages of interests and public authority in two types of local economic development decision structures resemble pluralist or nonpluralist interest representation patterns.[11] Linkages are nonpluralist, or more corporatist-like, for example, to the extent that interests are designated by the local state for inclusion in authoritative decision structures, that designated interests act as "trustees" for the larger interests they represent rather than their specific groups or areas, that these representatives are incorporated into policy formation and implementation processes, that behaviors of both interest group members and government change as a result of these joint decisions, and, although difficult to determine, that these structured linkages are more important in determining economic development policy than electoral or bureaucratic modes of representing interests. Not all these conditions are likely to be met, but they signify relations between groups and government that cannot be explained by pluralist paradigms.

While there is a plausible theoretical argument for anticipating more structured modes of interest representation in local economic development policy arenas, there are fewer bases for anticipating variations in interest representation patterns in terms of local characteristics. This study is a first effort at empirical analysis of local interest representation patterns in economic development policymaking.[12] It uses project-level information to determine the extent to which local governments expand Urban Development Action Grant (UDAG) partnerships to include other interests, such as minority business groups or neighborhood associations, as formal partners in the development project. Governments that expand these parnerships beyond the federally required business-government partnership can be said to be actively structuring interests by bringing these groups into the project and making them formal participants in its implementation. The advantage of using this program-specific information to examine the broader question of interest representation is that it provides concrete information on the actual involvement of different interests, their responsibilities, and their anticipated benefits—the "partnership" label acquires substantive meaning. Also, it is possible to match this information on partnership arrangements with contextual information on the cities involved; this allows some interpretation of the conditions under which different relations between groups and local government occur. The drawbacks, of course, also stem from the nature of the data. These UDAG partnerships are not broad systems of interest representation characterizing a policy arena in a city but are specific to certain projects. It is not possible, therefore, to generalize about local interest representation patterns on the basis of project-specific data, even for the city involved. But the analysis does allow for systematic consideration of whether, and under what conditions, cities bring groups into policy processes about development decisions. To the extent that UDAG projects only involve the federally required partnership of business and government, they suggest "business as usual"; to the extent that local governments choose to bring in other groups, they suggest an active effort to alter pluralist policy formation processes.

Information on city-wide economic development policymaking processes also is presented to overcome some of the limitations of the project-specific data. This information complements the UDAG data but is not based on a random sample of cities; it reflects institutional development in sixty cities with experience in more than one federal development program and was gathered in intensive interviews with local economic development officials in those cities. The information distinguishes among types of policy structures and is not intended to be statistically representative of the population; rather, it is suggestive of the characteristics of interest representation patterns in local economic development policymaking.

Types of Partnerships

From recent research on project-specific public-private relationships in the Urban Development Action Grant program, four types of partnerships can be identified.[13]

The simple partnership of business and government, mandated by the UDAG program, is the dominant mode found (49 percent) but involves no active structuring of interests by the local government. The other partnership types involve some active structuring of inter-

Table 2.1 Partnership types over time (in percentages)

	1978	1979	1980	1981
City/private	53	52	47	48
City/private/nonprofit	28	30	23	23
City/private/other public	18	11	18	18
City/private/nonprofit/other public	2	7	13	12

est representation by the local government, generally either inclusion of other local nonprofit and neighborhood interests (23 percent), other governmental units (17 percent), or a partnership involving both horizontal and vertical coordination of local groups and other governmental units (19 percent).

Over time there is more structuring of interests in local partnerships. In the initial years of the UDAG program the Carter administration sought to fund a "reasonable balance" of residential, industrial, and commercial projects. (See Gatons and Brintnall [1985] for discussion of program changes.) During this period the inclusion of neighborhood groups (or neighborhood-based projects) could give a city's application an advantage in the funding competition, but there was no formal requirement that nonbusiness groups be included.[14] The composition of UDAG partnerships is therefore a local choice; the evidence suggests that more complex interest representation patterns begin to emerge as cities become more experienced with the UDAG program and, perhaps, as groups become more familiar with the potential benefits from inclusion in development projects.

The Local Economic Context

This analysis indicates that economic stress contributes to differences in interest representation. The simpler partnership forms, representing only business and government interests, are more frequently found in less distressed cities; these cities are not actively structuring interests at the project level, although the least distressed cities are more likely to have partnerships with nonprofit-neighborhood involvement than more distressed cities. With more economic stress there is greater structuring of interests in project-level partnerships: in the economically distressed cities one is most likely to find partnerships with the most complex range of interest representation

—involving nonprofit groups and other public agencies as well as the investor-producer and government interests.

These findings support evidence from case studies that local economic stress is the most common factor underlying the formation of public-private partnerships (Fosler and Berger 1982; Committee for Economic Development 1982). Generally, the interpretation of this relationship centers on the assumption that such market changes increase economic uncertainty and raise the need to share economic risks, particularly in cities with declining economic growth. Yet existing pluralist accounts provide little specification as to why the rate or direction of economic change would influence the ways in which interests are involved in policy processes. Friedland's research (1980), in fact, suggests that the resurgence of reinvestment interests in local sites, rather than the decline of interest, is the precursor of more cooperative ventures.

As noted above, in the corporatist perspective crises in capital development processes and changing capital accumulation needs contribute to an increase in nonpluralist linkages between groups and decision structures. But the relationship between levels of crisis or distress and the form of these more structured links, as well as variations in types of interest representation, remain unspecified. Neither perspective adequately accounts for the generation and problematic transformation of the needs created by local economic stress into demands for different forms of interest representation.

In addition, it appears that economic diversification is related to more conventional, less structured interest representation. Cities with greater economic diversity—measured here as having a high proportion of nonheadquarters relative to firm headquarters—are more likely to have simple partnerships between business and government. Cities with high proportions of headquarters in their

Table 2.2   Partnership types by economic distress[a] (in percentages)

	High	Medium	Moderate	Low
City/private	43	50	59	57
City/private/nonprofit	21	28	27	36
City/private/other public	22	13	10	7
City/private/nonprofit/other public	13	9	5	0

a Distress as measured by the UDAG criteria for funding eligibility.

Table 2.3 Partnership types by ratio of subsidiaries to headquarter firms[a]
(in percentages)

	High Ratio of Subsidiaries	Low Ratio of Subsidiaries
City/private	52	47
City/private/nonprofit	24	26
City/private/other public	15	18
City/private/nonprofit/other public	9	9

a Calculated by author from data reported in Ward's *Corporate Directory,* 1980.

economic base are more likely to have more active structuring
of interests. It may be, as Jones and Bachelor (1984) claim, that local
economies with significant numbers of large, multiplant industries
are more vulnerable to threats of relocation than communities with
more locally based, small capital firms. Local officials, labor, and
citizen groups would have greater incentives to seek more structured
interest representation as a means of increasing certainty and
information.[15]

The Local Political Context

While economic change may create the need for more structured
linkages, this is not an automatic response nor is it likely to be an
unvariegated one. The findings on UDAG partnerships indicate that
local political features are important determinants of variations in
interest representation patterns. Several alternative outcomes could
plausibly be anticipated. Business interests, for example, could find
more formal links to be useful when other means of interest
articulation, such as parties and neighborhood organizations, are
vital and operative; under such circumstances the need to mobilize a
countervailing effort on the behalf of economic interests would
encourage business involvement in more formal ties. Accordingly,
where party ties and social organization are weak, less business
involvement in politics may be anticipated because it is less necessary
—business interests can rely on their systemic power and local revenue dependency rather than resort to direct efforts to influence policy processes (Stone 1980). On the other hand, in weakly articulated
local systems, economic interests may see opportunities to easily

overcome their numerical disadvantage by dominating the local political system (Martin 1973). These data do not allow testing of these
alternative hypotheses, but the evidence indicates that more structured interest representation is associated with certain political
features. For example, cities with mayor-council and nonpartisan
governments have more structured interest representation.

Cities with mayor-council governments are more likely to actively
structure interest representation to include neighborhood and
nonprofit groups as well as to create complex partnerships that include
other governmental units. Cities with nonpartisan voting systems
also are more likely to have greater neighborhood and nonprofit representation than cities with partisan structures; the latter are more
likely to feature vertical integration of other governmental units.
The form of executive administration, therefore, appears to be a key
feature that influences whether cities actively seek to include neighborhood and nonprofit groups. Other studies of the significance of
formal political structures for local policymaking processes (Lineberry
and Fowler 1967; Liebert 1974) suggest that unreformed political
structures—those with ward organizations and mayor-council forms
—may encourage interest representation and accommodation among
interests through electoral politics and bargaining processes. In

Table 2.4a Partnership type by local government organization
(in percentages)

	Ward/at-large		Mayor-council/city manager	
City/private	52	52	47	53
City/private/nonprofit	24	24	25	21
City/private/other public	18	10	16	17
City/private/nonprofit/ other public	6	15	11	9

Table 2.4b Partnership type by partisan structure (in percentages)

	Partisan	Nonpartisan
City/private	52	52
City/private/nonprofit	20	27
City/private/other public	18	13
City/private/nonprofit/other public	10	9

Table 2.5 Partnership type by development bureaucracy expertise[a]
(in percentages)

	High	Moderate	Low
City/private	47	49	63
City/private/nonprofit	25	24	25
City/private/other public	16	18	6
City/private/nonprofit/other public	12	8	6

a Measured by prior involvement in federal development programs, starting with
urban renewal through UDAG.

reformed structures, however—those with at-large elections and city
manager or commission forms—the limited political access and lack
of political cues that hinder the formation of electoral coalitions
may prompt the development of more structured links between interest groups and the state to assure the representation of producer-
investor interests and to remove policy decisions from direct political accountability.

Cities with greater bureaucratic expertise have more structured
interest representation in general; cities with more prior bureaucratic development experience tend to form partnerships with a
broader representation of interests. The most distinctive pattern is
the relationship between cities with little prior involvement in federal community development programs and simple partnerships: this
could reflect a lack of bureaucratic experience in coordinating groups
or spreading development benefits to a range of groups. Although
other federal development programs have required representation of
specific interests, these representatives generally serve in consultative roles with primarily advisory powers. (See Advisory Commission on Intergovernmental Relations 1979.) Representatives of specific
affected interests did gain policymaking authority in some local Community Action Programs in the late 1960s and early 1970s, but this
is an aberration from the basic pluralist pattern (see Greenstone and
Peterson 1973). The UDAG requirements for contractual agreements
between business and government before submission of a funding
application are a departure from the business-government relations
in the Model Cities and Urban Renewal programs as well as from the
more broad-based citizen participation initiatives of the Community Action Program. The relationship between prior bureaucratic

experience with federal development programs and more complex interest representation, therefore, is more likely to be a reflection of the degree to which constituencies are organized around local development issues than experience with different interest representation modes.

In situations where the formation of, rather than the composition of, structural relations among interests is in question, these new linkages may appear threatening to local administrative domains; it is plausible that partnerships may be more likely to occur in cities where there is no entrenched development bureaucracy to resist such changes. But, even where such bureaucracies are in place, demands on elected and administrative officials may create overload symptoms that prompt the creation of more formal coordinating arrangements (see Diamant 1982).

A more indirect political influence is associated with regional location. The data reveal that more complex partnerships with broader interest representation are found in the cities of the Northeast and Midwest. While these are the regions with the greatest levels of economic distress, they also are characterized by dense networks of distributional coalitions demanding discrete benefits from local policymakers (Olson 1982). The simple, limited forms of interest representation are found most frequently in the South and the West, noted for the relative absence of these coalitions.

Also, it appears that moderated forms of interest representation are associated with some types of projects more than others. Residential and mixed-use UDAG projects are more likely to include nonprofit and neighborhood groups. Such projects are more likely to be found in residential areas where dissent by local residents is often a barrier to redevelopment (see Mollenkopf 1981); the inclusion of nonprofit and neighborhood groups, therefore, may be a means of managing potential conflict. These projects also are more amenable

Table 2.6 Partnership type by region (in percentages)

	Northeast	Midwest	South	West
City/private	40	44	62	62
City/private/nonprofit	18	32	24	23
City/private/other public	25	14	12	10
City/private/nonprofit/other public	17	10	2	5

Table 2.7 Partnership type by project type (in percentages)

	Commercial	Industrial	Residential	Mixed
City/private	50	53	50	37
City/private/nonprofit	25	7	39	30
City/private/other public	16	27	7	18
City/private/nonprofit/ other public	9	12	4	15

Table 2.8 Partnership type by policy benefits (in percentages)

	Leverage Ratios[a]		Distributional benefits[b]	
	Low	High	No	Yes
City/private	45	57	52	44
City/private/nonprofit	29	11	20	32
City/private/other public	15	23	20	11
City/private/nonprofit/ other public	11	9	8	13

a More private dollars generated by each public dollar invested than in the average leverage ratio.
b Grant agreements set aside housing, construction jobs, investment funds, etc., for specific groups or areas.

to the inclusion of these groups since they involve activities—housing and commercial enterprises—that such groups often have experience in and regard as direct, short-term gains. Industrial projects, on the other hand, are less likely to be situated in residential areas, and nonbusiness groups will have fewer skills or resources to contribute, but they are of sufficient scale to require packaging of different forms of assistance and tend to result in the most complex partnerships. These findings suggest that the nature and characteristics of the enterprise or policy issue will influence the likelihood of more complex interest representation; more formal relations may appear less necessary, and less beneficial, under certain conditions.

Finally, it appears that more structured partnerships are associated with different policy choices, in particular with distributional benefits. In table 2.8 projects with above-average leverage ratios —greater private dollars over public dollars—are more likely to have simple partnerships or to bring in other federal units than projects with less profitable ratios. Projects with larger public capital investments and less private equity are more likely to have a broader range of interests represented. The more efficient enterprises in terms of leverage ratios, therefore, are the least likely to spread benefits among local interests. On the other hand, greater representation of interests is associated with UDAG partnership agreements that specify the benefits, such as jobs for minorities and low-income housing, to be received by particular groups or areas. At the discretion of local officials, UDAG loan agreement terms stipulate the reuse of program income from repaid loans, the "partners" (including neighborhood, minority, and nonprofit groups) to be "cut in" on the deal, parcels of publicly owned land to be utilized, housing set-asides for low-income households, job set-asides for minority contractors and workers, and other fiscal and nonfiscal benefits from UDAG-supported development. If the UDAG project involves equity investments by the local government and the other partners, successful developments include sharing the net cash flow from the project. Analysis of UDAG project agreements indicates that these nonmarket conditions—fiscal and social—are most likely in unreformed cities where community groups have greater political access (Clarke and Rich 1982b). Those in the partnership, or represented by the formal partners, gain discrete benefits, while those outside the partnership do not, even though they may be influential in electoral or bureaucratic linkage modes.

In sum, project-specific partnerships are a means of representing those interests affected by development in the project formulation and implementation process. This analysis suggests that over time cities become more active in structuring interest representation at the project level; this increased complexity involves both greater vertical coordination of other governmental units and horizontal integration of local interests into a common decisionmaking forum. As the level of economic distress increases, so does the active structuring of interest representation on UDAG projects. But active structuring occurs less often in cities with more diverse economic bases than in cities dominated by headquarters. Cities with mayor-council governments, with nonpartisan voting systems, with greater bureaucratic development experience, and those in the Midwest and Northeast are more likely to be actively structuring local interests into project-level partnerships. This also is more often the case for projects involving residential and mixed use development. This suggests an increase in active channeling of interests to project-level joint decision structures congruent with the criteria established for identifying nonpluralist linkages; the type of structuring that occurs, however, appears more influenced by noneconomic factors than the corporatist arguments would suggest.

City-Wide Interest Representation Patterns

It appears that there is more widespread designation of interests in specific development projects than in city-wide policy formulation processes. While there is some evidence of intentional structuring of interests in local economic development policymaking processes, the majority of local officials interviewed in sixty cities reported pluralist patterns of interest representation. Local economic development activities are relatively new local policy concerns, and the question of who can and should make these policy decisions is still an unresolved political issue in many communities.

Most officials (71 percent) for example, reported that local economic development efforts began in the early 1970s. In most instances (52 percent), they began in response to regional and local economic decline—specific plant closings, slumps in downtown sales, and so on are referred to as the "reason" for the city's economic development interest. In a few cases, often in western cities, officials referred to the supply of federal funds as fueling their interest in economic development activities (18 percent); one official explicitly ascribed his city's interest to "getting some of what the Eastern cities are getting."

Furthermore, most cities formulate economic development policy in units with some electoral accountability. Task Forces in the mayor's office, for example, and other units reporting directly to the executive branch (39 percent) and identified as the "lead agency" for economic development policy formation are the most direct means of electoral accountability over economic development policy. More indirectly accountable are bureaucratic units, such as departments of economic development, reported as the "lead agency" in formulating economic development policy (57 percent).

These interviews suggested that, over time, many cities previously relying on bureaucratic and quasi-independent organizations for economic development policy formation are reverting to more direct mayoral controls. In some cities, community development policy formulation has been the province of specialized bureaucracies, special authorities, and quasipublic organizations removed from direct political accountability. Now, however, many local officials view the economic development arena as a means of regaining executive control over these policy decisions. Several officials explicitly described recent reorganizations of their community development policy structures as meeting just this end. In part this may be due to the withdrawal of many federal programs supporting these local bureaucracies and quasi-independent organizations; it also may indicate, however, the nonprogrammatic nature of current economic development practices that center on tax incentives, deregulation, and "civic leadership." While these shifts bring economic development policies back into the political arena, it is not clear yet that they increase the options for popular control of economic development decisions.

It is clear that few cities currently share economic policy formation decisionmaking authority with small business, labor, or neighborhood interests. Although the majority of cities report that these local interests have some advisory capacity (68 percent) in economic development policymaking forums, the sharing of decisionmaking authority with small business (15 percent), labor (10 percent), or neighborhood interests (7 percent) is less frequent. There is evidence of more structured, nonpluralist arrangements — the intentional channeling of interests to decision structures — in some (32 percent) local economic development policymaking.

This analysis indicates that the actual sharing of public authority with affected interests appears more common in specific public-private development projects rather than in city-wide policy formulation processes. Whether this shared authority is symbolic or material, whether risks to the groups from inclusion outweigh the gains, or whether the greater representation of interests leads to greater public control over specific public investments remain to be seen. In the UDAG program there is evidence that public-private partnerships do make a difference — greater interest representation is associated with wider distributional benefits. This corroborates arguments that more structured, nonpluralist modes are a means of overcoming the inequities of pluralist interest representation and result in more equitable distribution of policy benefits (see Black and Burke 1983; Schmitter 1981; Safran 1983).

Local Representation Modes and Effective Representation

There are drawbacks, however, to these nonpluralist modes of interest representation. The creation of structured linkages of interest groups and the state involves public authority in "political architecture" (Anderson 1979); that is, it entails visible identification of normative criteria for inclusion in policymaking, the establishment of priorities, goals, and objectives, and the likely exclusion of other interests. Thus, the legitimacy of arrangements sharing policymaking authority among public and private interests is always vulnerable. Their objective basis for legitimacy is weak, given that their formation and authority are designated by public officials on the basis of the "contribution" of "affected" interests or particular groups. As a consequence, local officials engender further conflict and instability in policymaking processes in the very process of establishing more structured modes intended to manage local development conflicts. This inherent instability is suggestive of a cyclical process. Ruin (1974) points out that demands for greater individual participation are often met with further group incorporation into policymaking processes (also see Schmitter 1983). That is, the response to dissatisfaction with existing linkages is to extend representation to new interests. The "solutions," however, do not lead to quiescence but to further demands for access and representation since the base of representation and inclusion is open to continual challenges. The conflict generated by this "political architecture" may eventually lead to further layers of structured linkages.

It is clear, for example, that to define groups "out" of the policy community or to define their demands as inappropriate will risk fomenting challenges to the political structure itself. Not only is this an issue of *who* is to be considered an "affected" interest and, therefore, a potential partner in development policymaking processes, it also is a question of *what* is to be represented—big or small capital, organized or unorganized labor, community associations or development corporations.

Furthermore, to the extent that development policy formation procedures provide for substantive representation of interests, their efficiency is likely to be hampered. This loss of relative efficiency may be less likely if policy representation becomes a professional role within interest associations. This professionalization, however, creates a passive relationship between the membership and the policy system; members are distant from their policy representatives, and these representatives may come to more clearly identify with other representatives on some issues than with the membership or constituencies they represent (see Lehmbruch 1982; Schmitter 1983). Interest associations, particularly territorially based organizations, face the tensions of multiple demands from diverse constituencies: representatives must serve their organizational interests while negotiating and compromising on joint development policy decisions. These dual responsibilities, sometimes conflicting, make it difficult to retain the membership's belief that its interests are being aggressively served by its leadership. Tensions between the type of decision mode appropriate to economic decisions and the type of interest representation necessary for effective policymaking threaten the stability of both structured and unstructured linkages.

Neither pluralist nor nonpluralist, "corporatist-like," interest representation modes offer significant promise of more representative, equitable local development policies. Pluralist modes leave out the less organized, and bargaining modes of policy formulation cannot address the long-term distributional effects of local development decisions. Yet shifting policy responsibilities to more structured modes of representing interests may ultimately reduce public voice and participation in development politics. To date, challenges to economic development policies are fragmented and sporadic; they center on the costs of specific projects, such as Poletown in Detroit, rather than on the need to create new representative mechanisms for formulating such policies. Yet, as public intervention in local economic development processes increases, these institutional issues become more pressing. Actual popular control of local economic development decisions would entail greater public control of productive assets than is likely in the current American political economy, but there is a need for analysts and planners to consider approaches to policy representation that lead to desired ends. This discussion must center on the normative issues of who should be represented and toward what ends as well as on the analysis of advantages and disadvantages of different ways of representing interests. For example, greater voice in either pluralist or nonpluralist arrangements will not lead to greater popular control if groups are unclear about the demands to be made. Thus, there is a need for systematic development of the criteria to be used when "investing in the public interest" if it is to lead to greater public benefits from publicly supported private investment. This presumes that efficiency and equity are not incompatible local development concerns and that the current definitions of efficient investments are too narrowly drawn. The UDAG experience offers direct evidence that greater public representation and greater distributional benefits than would be provided through market processes are possible and viable in local projects. Developing alternative public investment criteria appears a necessary precondition if either pluralist or more structured interest representation mechanisms are to lead to more equitable local economic development policies.

Author's Note: Valerie Bunce first suggested that the corporatist literature might be useful in my research on urban economic development policymaking processes; in subsequent discussions, Bryan Jones, Margit Mayer and Ed Bergman have been quite helpful in sorting out the advantages and limitations of this approach. Michael J. Rich, Edward Goetz, and Angela Hendricks had major responsibilities for interviewing local economic development officials in sixty cities; these interviews were conducted with the partial support of a Northwestern University Faculty Grant and the Center for Urban Affairs and Policy Research at Northwestern University. This analysis is part of an ongoing research project on the Urban Development Action Program with Michael J. Rich. I am responsible for the interpretations presented here but gratefully acknowledge the help I received from these colleagues. Mary French, June Ince, and Debbie Bataghva, at the University of Colorado at Boulder, prepared the manuscript for publication.

Restructuring and Growth Transitions
of Metropolitan Economies: The Context
for Economic Development Policy
Robyn S. Phillips and Avis C. Vidal

During recent decades population and employment have decentralized dramatically from older central cities to nearby suburban
communites, from metropolitan to nonmetropolitan areas, and from
the older, densely settled regions of the Northeast and Midwest to
the newer, rapidly growing regions of the South and West. At the
same time major changes have taken place in the U.S. economy and
the national labor force. These changes have greatly altered the structure of metropolitan economies and the types of employment opportunities available to urban residents. They provide the context for
local and national policies directed at urban economic development.

The broad patterns of intrametropolitan employment dispersion
have been widely recognized. They include the shift of manufacturing toward low-density locations on the urban fringe during most of
this century; the decline of manufacturing employment in older
central cities beginning soon after the close of World War II; the
gradual weakening of retailing and wholesaling in an increasing number of central cities as their suburbs have expanded; the relative
vitality of the service sector in central cities, especially in the years
after 1960; and the widespread, vigorous growth of suburban economics (sec, for example, Kain 1975; Hamer 1973; Sternlieb and Hughes
1977; Struyk and James 1975).

Regional shifts in economic activity and the relative vitality of
newer cities are long-lived phenomena and have been well-
documented historically (e.g., Perloff 1960). More recently, an article
by Sternlieb and Hughes (1977) described this regional dynamic
as "sweeping employment and population growth away from older
metropolitan centers of the Northeast and North Central states to
the newer growth poles of the South and West." Drawing on data

from the 1960–1975 period, the authors grimly observed that the Sunbelt regions are growing at twice the national rate, "leaving the older northern sections of the country at best approaching a steady state condition." Working in combination with the long-term suburbanization of population and employment (Harrison 1974; Kain 1975), and the more recent resurgence of nonmetropolitan areas (Fuguitt and Voss 1979; McCarthy and Morrison 1979), these movements have eroded the economic vitality of many older central cities.

Unfortunately, systematic information on the details of this process has been rare, with the result that policy debates about urban economic development problems and their solutions have sometimes been inadequately informed. For example, while the decline of central city manufacturing and the concomitant growth of service and government employment have long been recognized, the relative magnitude of these changes has not been clear. Some analysts have contended that metropolitan job losses in manufacturing have been offset by sizable gains in services, finance, insurance, real estate, and government (Black 1980). Others have argued that this was the exception rather than the rule (Solomon 1980). As a result, the relatively simple question of whether the number of jobs in central cities has been growing or declining has remained clouded (see also Ganz and O'Brien 1973; and James 1974). Similarly, local efforts to bolster sagging urban economies and to provide jobs for displaced workers often have focused heavily on attracting new businesses by means of public relations programs extolling the favorable business climate of the community and by offering various incentives such as land write-downs, tax abatements, or favorable financing through industrial revenue bonds. These strategies for local economic development overlook other important components of employment change: the retention and expansion of existing firms; the start-up of new, locally based business enterprises; and the substantial contribution of small firms to business vitality, particularly in contracting industries and in slow-growth localities (Birch 1981; Armington and Odle 1982; Meyer, Schmenner, and Meyer 1980).

At the same time that economic activity has been decentralizing out of older cities and regions, the national economy has been undergoing a fundamental restructuring, away from such long-established manufacturing sectors as primary metals, electrical machinery, and transportation equipment toward high technology and the growing service sector. This shift has meant significant growth in employment opportunities for workers in professional and technical occupations, for clerical workers, and for many service occupations, at the expense of skilled and unskilled blue-collar workers (Leon 1982; Bylinsky 1981; Treadwell and Redburn 1983).

The magnitude and implications of these long-term shifts became starkly apparent during the economic recession of 1982 that left thousands of workers in older regions and in declining industries jobless; many have little prospect of returning to their previous positions, even as the economy improves. Blue-collar workers have been particularly hard hit by these changes in the national economy. Recent figures from the Bureau of Labor Statistics indicate that there are 2 million fewer manufacturing jobs in the nation's industrial heartland today than a decade ago, a decline of 26 percent (Green 1983). As a result, unemployment rates are running near 15 percent in Michigan and Pennsylvania, and even higher in particularly hard-hit cities, such as Detroit and Youngstown. While these figures will certainly improve with national economic recovery, the number of jobs in traditional industrial sectors is expected to continue to decline as U.S. firms automate production to remain competitive with foreign producers, relocate production facilities to Mexico, Taiwan, or other areas with lower labor costs, or accept smaller world market shares due to foreign competition (Treadwell and Redburn 1983).

Successful efforts to attract growing industries to replace declining sectors of a local economy may help diversify local employment opportunities and strengthen the municipality's sagging tax base. They may not, however, provide jobs for displaced workers whose skills do not match the needs of new industries. This possibility is well-illustrated by the experience of Huntsville, Alabama. During the past decade Huntsville has made the transition from a weakening industrial base centered on cotton textiles to a burgeoning center for high technology. However, the city's high-technology firms largely employ either scientists and highly skilled technicians or low-skilled, low-wage assemblers; they have few openings for traditional blue-collar industrial workers. As a result, Huntsville's unemployment remains above 10 percent at the same time that local firms recruit computer scientists on the national market (Treadwell and Redburn 1983).

Informed policy choices concerning economic development at the local and national level require an understanding of the broad economic restructuring that is transforming the national economy and an appreciation for how these locational and structural shifts are affecting different types of metropolitan areas. This essay draws on a data base that describes the magnitude of these shifts, examines their impact on metropolitan economies and job opportunities for urban workers, and addresses the implications of these trends for policies directed at urban economic development.

Methodological Difficulties in Studying Urban Economies

Studies of economic trends in the nation's cities have been constrained by the difficulty of monitoring economic activity in urban areas. A central problem is that no single data source provides a complete enumeration of all employment at the local level. While the *Economic Censuses* represents the most detailed enumeration of local economic activity available nationally, it excludes employment in government, transportation, communication, public utilities, construction, finance, insurance, and real estate (FIRE). Moreover, only selected services are reported for individual cities. These omissions are critical, since a great deal of the recent growth in urban economies has been in sectors not covered by the *Economic Censuses* —particularly government, FIRE, and excluded services in health and education. These sectors are included in the *Census of Government* and *County Business Patterns*, but the reporting on government employment is incomplete and *County Business Patterns* data are reported for counties only, making it cumbersome to aggregate SMSA (Standard Metropolitan Statistical Area) totals and impossible to identify central city employment in many cases.

A second methodological issue encountered by efforts to monitor urban economic trends over time is the need to adjust data for changing central city and SMSA boundaries. Past experience has shown that failure to make such adjustments can obscure even major trends. For example, a recent study comparing data using 1950 city and SMSA boundaries with current figures based on 1972 boundaries finds almost no change in the central city's share of manufacturing employment between 1963 and 1972, despite sustained manufacturing job losses in central cities and consistent manufacturing gains in suburban areas during the nine-year period (Solomon 1980). Although time-consuming, failure to make boundary adjustments will tend to overstate actual economic growth (or to understate decline), since many SMSAS and some central cities have expanded their boundaries.[1]

A third measurement issue of increasing concern is the ability of the standard industrial classification (SIC) system to adequately represent the character of metropolitan jobs. The system has received minor modifications over the years, but its broad outlines have remained fixed. This greatly facilitates analysis of changes through time but makes important and rapidly evolving parts of urban economies difficult to monitor. For example, while it would be desirable to analyze recent trends in high-technology employment, these jobs are scattered among a variety of two- and three-digit SIC categories and are not readily identifiable.

Based on a data base that overcomes many of the methodological problems affecting previous studies of employment in urban areas, this chapter describes the long-run trends that are gradually altering the economies of the nation's cities. By combining information from several government sources, adjusting for SMSA boundary changes, and adding previously excluded sectors, the integrated data base reports employment trends in nine major nonagricultural sectors for one hundred metropolitan areas. These include the fifty largest SMSAS and a proportional, stratified sample of fifty small and mid-sized SMSAS. The data were compiled from the most current information that permits separate examination of central cities and their suburban rings. Thus, the data permit detailed analysis of long-term trends in urban economies through comparison of information from roughly similar points in the national business cycle (1967 and 1977) (see Vidal, Phillips, and Brown 1982).

Employment Trends in Large Metropolitan Areas

Employment in the fifty largest metropolitan areas grew at a rate virtually identical to the national average between 1967 and 1977, but the pattern of employment change differed from that found in the country as a whole. Large urban areas incurred absolute losses in manufacturing employment and grew comparatively slowly in most other sectors. As shown in table 3.1, economic gains in the nation's fifty largest metropolitan areas were concentrated in three principal sectors — services, government, and retail. The service sector

Table 3.1 Employment trends in 50 largest SMSAS, 1967–77

Sector	1967	1977	Change 1967–77 Number	Change 1967–77 Percent	Percentage change, U.S. employment 1967–77
Employment by Sector (ooo)					
Manufacturing	9,986	9,331	−655	−6.6	1.3
Retail	4,808	6,389	1,581	32.9	39.0
Services	5,006	8,279	3,273	65.4	59.3
Wholesale	2,172	2,493	321	14.8	25.0
Trans/Com	2,120	2,323	203	9.6	14.5
FIRE	2,039	2,859	820	40.2	43.0
Construction	1,508	2,139	631	41.8	24.4
Mining[1]	88	118	30	34.7	40.9
Government	3,314	4,974	1,660	50.1	27.2
Total	31,040	38,905	7,862	25.3	25.2

Source: Data for manufacturing, retail, services, wholesale, construction, and mining are from the *Economic Census* for 1967 and for 1977. Data for Trans/Com (transportation, communication, and public utilities) and FIRE (finance, insurance and real estate) are from *County Business Patterns*. Government employment data are from the *Census of Government*.
1 Mining figures exclude Salt Lake City in both years since data were not available in 1977.

expanded dramatically, accounting for more than 40 percent of total employment growth and two-thirds of net new business establishments during the 1967–77 decade. The retail and financial (FIRE) sectors also have provided expanding employment and business opportunities in large metropolitan areas. However, a substantial share of job gains in recent years has been in the public sector, with local and federal government jobs accounting for more than one in every five net new jobs added in large metropolitan areas over the 1967–77 decade, a rise of 50 percent.[2]

The diversity of experience among individual metropolitan areas has been very great, with strong regional dimensions. Thirteen SMSAS —all in the South or West—expanded their employment bases by more than one-half; two of these more than doubled during the decade (Fort Lauderdale – Hollywood and Anaheim – Santa Ana –Garden Grove). Five of these metropolitan areas registered job gains in all of the nine major industrial sectors. More commonly, modest job losses in manufacturing or mining employment were far outweighed by increases in other parts of the economy. At the other extreme, two entire metropolitan areas, New York and Baltimore, suffered a net loss of jobs. Between these extremes are found cities of highly varied circumstances. Declines in manufacturing employment were widespread and sometimes sharp; fourteen SMSAs saw manufacturing jobs fall off by more than 10 percent. Industrial job losses were typically offset by growth in services, government, retailing, finance, construction, and wholesaling.

Employment Trends in Central City and
Suburban Areas of Large SMSAs

A disproportionate share of recent economic growth in large metropolitan areas has taken place in suburban areas, while net job losses in older industrial sectors have been concentrated in central cities. High rates of employment growth in suburban areas reflect changes both in the locational factors of firms favoring lower density, outlying locations and in employment generated in suburban areas by population dispersal.

Total employment in central cities of the fifty largest metropolitan areas increased only 7 percent in aggregate from 1967 to 1977 (see table 3.2), well below the national growth rate of 25 percent. During this time these central cities lost more than 1 million net manufacturing jobs—one job out of every five—in addition to absolute declines in wholesaling and transportation. Losses in these sectors were offset by rapid and substantial employment gains in services, government, and FIRE. Together, these three sectors were responsible for more than 95 percent of net central city job growth in large SMSAs.

In contrast, suburban economies of the fifty largest SMSAs grew in all sectors, with total suburban employment increasing almost 60 percent between 1967 and 1977. In sectors that contracted in the central cities, the suburbs experienced employment growth. For example, suburban areas of the fifty largest SMSAs gained better than one manufacturing job for every three lost in central cities. Economic sectors that grew strongly in central cities grew even more rapidly in suburban areas. Service employment increased 35 percent

Table 3.2 Employment trends in central-city and suburban areas of
50 largest SMSAS, 1967–77[1]

		Central-city[2]		
			Change 1967–1977	
	1967	1977	Number	Percentages
Employment by sector (000)				
Manufacturing	5,091	4,081	−1,009	−19.8
Retail	2,583	2,661	78	3.0
Services	3,400	4,577	1,177	34.6
Wholesale	1,487	1,250	−237	−15.9
Trans/Com	1,805	1,639	−166	−9.2
FIRE	1,794	2,216	422	23.5
Construction	1,149	1,155	6	0.5
Mining	65	88	22	34.0
Government	2,487	3,594	1,107	44.5
Total	19,861	21,262	1,401	7.0

Source: See source citations for table 3.1.

1 Figures exclude the Nassau-Suffolk SMSA, which has no central city. Salt Lake City is also excluded from the minerals sector but included elsewhere.

2 Figures for the following sectors are for central county rather than central city: Trans/Com, FIRE, construction, mining, and government. As discussed in the appendix, this tends to overstate the level of central-city economic activity in either year and the estimated job

in central cities but 134 percent in suburban areas; FIRE employment grew 24 percent in central cities but 173 percent in suburban areas.

More significant than the relative rate of growth, which reflects the smaller initial base in outlying areas, is the absolute growth in number of jobs. In the late 1960s central cities of large metropolitan areas provided almost twice as many jobs as their surrounding suburbs. During the following decade suburbs gained more than four net new jobs for each net new job added in large central cities. Suburban areas captured virtually 95 percent of the gain in retail employment in large metropolitan areas in the 1970s, 63 percent of the growth in services, 47 percent in FIRE, and 99 percent of new construction jobs. Only for government employment did central cities maintain their dominant share.

City-by-city comparisons of employment change in the central city and suburban ring confirm the consistently strong performance

| Suburban areas | | | | Central-city share of employment gains 1967–77 (percentages) |
| | | Change 1967–77 | | |
1967	1977	Number	Percentages	
4,730	5,094	364	7.7	—
2,101	3,571	1,470	70.0	5.0
1,511	3,539	2,028	134.2	36.7
648	1,186	538	83.1	—
288	648	360	124.9	—
217	592	375	172.5	52.9
328	951	623	189.8	1.0
22	30	9	39.4	71.0
757	1,266	509	67.3	68.5
10,602	16,879	6,276	59.2	18.3

gain between 1967 and 1977 for these sectors. Excluding the nine SMSAs for which central county is the least good proxy—that is, those contained in a single county—lowers estimated central-city job gains over the period 1967–77: the estimated gain in FIRE employment drops from 24 to 15 percent, construction turns negative (−9.5 percent), and the loss in Trans/Com jobs increases from 9 to 15 percent.

of suburbs and the mixed economic experience of central cities. Except in manufacturing, suburban areas uniformly gained jobs during the 1970s, both in sectors that grew slowly nationally and in those that grew rapidly nationwide. The pattern is more mixed in central cities. Typically, central cities fared well in those sectors that expanded most sharply in the national economy; nearly all large central cities gained jobs in services, and most added employment in FIRE and government. However, despite rapid national growth in retailing, nearly half of all large central cities lost retail jobs during the decade. Central cities performed markedly less well for slow-growth sectors: nineteen lost employment in transportation and communication, twenty-five lost construction jobs, and twenty-eight lost wholesale employment. Manufacturing had the most widespread declines, with thirty-three of the fifty largest SMSAs losing manufacturing jobs in the central cities and fourteen in suburban areas.

Table 3.3 Central-city share of total employment for 50 largest SMSAS, 1967 and 1977[1]

Sector	Percentage of total employment	
	1967	1977
Manufacturing	51.8	44.5
Retail	55.1	42.7
Services	69.2	56.4
Wholesale	69.7	51.3
Trans/Com	83.9	66.3
FIRE	87.5	75.0
Construction	73.7	54.8
Mining	68.7	71.0
Government	72.3	68.7
Total	63.6	53.4

Source: See source citations for table 3.1.

1 Figures for manufacturing, retail, services, and wholesale excluded Nassau-Suffolk, which has no central city. Figures for the remaining sectors also exclude SMSAS contained in a single county, since all employment and establishments are allocated to the central county. These are Los Angeles, Anaheim–Santa Ana–Garden Grove, San Diego, Miami, Seattle, Riverside–San Bernadino, Phoenix, San Jose, and Fort Lauderdale. Actual sample sizes are therefore 49 and 40, respectively. The total central-city share is calculated from a combination for the first four sectors and the 40 SMSA sample for the last five sectors.

As a result of differential growth rates over the decade, the share of total metropolitan employment located in central cities has continued to decline. By the late 1970s nearly half the employment of large metropolitan areas was located outside the central cities, down from 64 percent a decade earlier (table 3.3). While all economic sectors suburbanized during the 1970s, employment dispersal was most pronounced for construction, wholesaling, and in transportation and communication. By the late 1970s retailing had replaced manufacturing as the most highly suburbanized sector, with nearly 60 percent of total metropolitan retail employment located outside central cities. Despite continuing job dispersal, employment in services, FIRE, government, transportation, and communication remain relatively centralized.[3]

Hence, the broad structural shifts taking place in the national economy have left their mark on the economic base of large metropolitan areas. Manufacturing declined sharply in importance in both central cities and surburban areas—in one instance the result of absolute losses and in the other instance the result of slow relative growth (table 3.4). Services and FIRE gained importance in suburban economies as well as in central cities, although three-quarters of the jobs in finance, insurance, and real estate remain in central counties. Wholesaling, transportation, and construction increased their share of total employment in suburban areas but lost ground in large cities. As private economic activity has decentralized, the public sector has come to account for a larger proportion of the employment base in large central cities. By the late 1970s, 17 percent of city workers were employed by local or federal government.[4]

Changing Job Opportunities in Large Urban Areas

The net impact of these sectoral patterns of growth and decline was to shift the economic base of large metropolitan areas away from

Table 3.4 Employment Base for Central-City and Suburban Areas of 50 Largest SMSAS, 1967 and 1977 (in percentages)[1]

Sector	Central city[2]		Suburban	
	1967	1977	1967	1977
Manufacturing	25.6	19.2	44.6	30.3
Retail	13.0	12.5	19.8	21.1
Services	17.1	21.5	14.2	21.0
Wholesale	7.5	5.9	6.1	7.0
Trans/Com	9.1	7.7	2.7	3.9
FIRE	9.0	10.4	2.1	3.5
Construction	5.8	5.4	3.1	5.6
Mining	0.3	0.4	0.2	0.2
Government	12.5	16.9	7.1	7.4
Total	100.0	100.0	100.0	100.0
Total employment (000's)	19,863	21,069	10,602	16,762

Source: See source citations for table 3.1.
1 Figures exclude the Nassau-Suffolk SMSA, which has no central city. Salt Lake City is also excluded from the mineral sector but included elsewhere.
2 Figures for the following sectors are for central county rather than central city: Trans/Com, FIRE, construction, mining, and government.

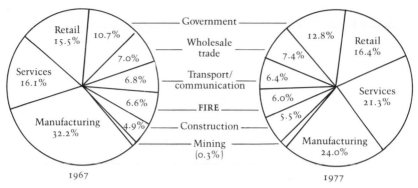

Figure 3.1. Employment base of 50 largest metropolitan areas, 1967 and 1977

manufacturing toward other sectors. Manufacturing accounted for nearly one-third of total metropolitan employment in the 1960s, but by the late 1970s fewer than a quarter of workers in large urban areas were employed in manufacturing (figure 3.1). During this period, services came to approach manufacturing in size, while retailing, FIRE, construction, and government all became relatively more important components of the economic base in large SMSAS.

Changes in the number and location of employment opportunities have directly affected the ability of urban residents to find suitable jobs, since industries vary greatly in the types of skills they require.[5] For example, over 90 percent of all jobs in the highly centralized financial sector are white-collar positions, more than half of which are held by clerical workers.[6] White-collar employment accounts for 60 percent of the jobs in the rapidly expanding service sector, and over one-third of all employees are professional and technical workers. Another 29 percent of jobs in the service sector are held by persons in service occupations.[7] In contrast, almost two-thirds of the manufacturing work force are craftsmen or operatives; only 12 percent are clerical workers, and even fewer are professional or technical workers.

Dynamic growth of the service sector, retailing, and government has increased the number of service jobs by almost one-half; these jobs constituted approximately 20 percent of all metropolitan jobs gained during the decade. Growth of the service sector also was responsible for the nearly 40 percent rise in the number of professional and technical workers. However, the largest absolute increase in metropolitan employment over the decade came among clerical workers, who increased in number by almost 2 million. Taken together, new white-collar jobs (i.e., those in clerical, service, sales, and professional/technical occupations) accounted for almost two-thirds of net metropolitan employment growth over the 1970s.

Employment in blue-collar occupations expanded slowly, growing by only 10 percent in ten years. Among craftsmen, large losses in manufacturing were more than counterbalanced by gains in other industries; other blue-collar workers fared less well. Lost positions for manufacturing operatives were barely offset by new openings in other sectors, leaving the number of available jobs about the same in 1977 as it had been a decade earlier; net new jobs for transportation operatives and for laborers were modest in number. Overall, the blue-collar jobs that constituted 39 percent of the metropolitan job base in 1967 captured only 16 percent of the increased employment in large SMSAs during the 1970s.

This changing mix of job opportunities carries important ramifications for the economic welfare of urban residents. Highly educated members of the work force face an expanding set of choices in the professions in a variety of technical posts and, to a lesser extent, in management and administration. These jobs typically pay well and carry the possibility of advancement. Rapid expansion of clerical work also will furnish opportunities for many. However, these positions frequently provide salaries that will not support a family at the median level of income. In addition, many types of clerical jobs have traditionally been held by women and are not actively considered by male job-seekers. Jobs for service workers, although relatively plentiful in number, often pay poorly; in many cases they do not provide enough income to maintain a family of four above the poverty line. Skilled blue-collar work, once a mainstay of many, is barely holding its own in metropolitan economies.

Regional Dimensions of Metropolitan Employment Growth

Regional[8] disparities in the rate of economic growth in recent years have been sharp, and considerable attention has been focused on the contrast between aggregate employment declines in many older Frostbelt central cities and vigorous economic expansion in the urban areas of the Sunbelt (e.g., Treadwell 1976; Sternlieb and Hughes 1977).

Table 3.5 Employment trends in 50 largest SMSAs by region, 1967–77 (employment in thousands)

Sector	Northeast[1] (N = 10)				North Central (N = 12)			
	1967	1977	Change	Percentage change	1967	1977	Change	Percentage change
Manufacturing	3,120	2,497	−623	−20.0	3,349	3,081	−268	−8.0
Retail	1,308	1,427	120	9.1	1,325	1,700	376	28.4
Services	1,614	2,280	666	41.3	1,249	2,008	759	60.8
Wholesale	687	637	−50	−7.3	597	660	63	10.6
Trans/Com	681	622	−59	−8.7	524	551	26	5.0
FIRE	740	866	125	16.9	495	679	184	37.3
Construction	356	401	45	12.6	377	487	110	29.1
Mining	15	16	1	8.2	11	7	−4	−33.3
Government	852	1,180	328	38.5	721	1,078	357	49.5
Total	9,373	9,926	552	5.9	8,648	10,252	1,604	18.6

Sector	South (N = 16)				West (N = 12)			
	1967	1977	Change	Percentage change	1967	1977	Change	Percentage change
Manufacturing	1,508	1,583	76	5.0	1,844	2,013	170	9.2
Retail	1,013	1,557	544	53.7	1,039	1,548	509	49.0
Services	974	1,921	947	97.2	1,074	1,907	832	77.5
Wholesale	426	588	161	37.8	424	552	127	30.0
Trans/Com	446	583	137	30.6	442	532	90	20.5
FIRE	390	623	233	59.9	387	641	254	65.7
Construction	439	699	260	59.3	305	520	215	70.3
Mining[2]	42	69	27	64.6	22	26	6	31.8
Government	865	1,449	585	67.6	805	1,153	347	43.1
Total	6,102	9,073	2,971	48.7	6,342	8,890	2,551	40.2

Source: Data for manufacturing, retail, selected services, wholesale, construction, and mining are from the *Economic Census* for 1967 and for 1977. Data for Trans/Com (transportation, communication, and public utilities), FIRE (finance, insurance, and real estate), and excluded services are from *County Business Patterns*. Government data include local and federal government employment figures from the *Census of Government; Annual Report of Federal Civilian Employment in the U.S.,* 1967; and *Annual Report of Employment by Geographic Area,* 1977.
1 Figures exclude Nassau-Suffolk.
2 Mining figures exclude Salt Lake City.

These differences in performance have been pervasive, extending across all types of economic activity. As a result, the common underlying trends of suburbanization and industrial restructuring appear in very different contexts. Perhaps because the contrast between overall regional growth rates has been so strong, the modest signs of weakening in Sunbelt cities and the relative vitality of Frostbelt suburbs has gone largely unnoticed.

Although the South and West together accounted for just over 40 percent of total U.S. employment in large metropolitan areas in the late 1960s, these regions captured nearly three-fourths of the total job gain in large SMSAS during subsequent years. Total employment in large metropolitan areas expanded 40 percent in the West and nearly 50 percent in the South between 1967 and 1977, in contrast to 19 percent growth in the North Central region and a 6 percent gain in the Northeast (table 3.5).

Notably, employment gains in large metropolitan areas located in the slow-growth regions have been limited largely to the nation's fastest growing economic sectors: services, FIRE, retail, and government. During the decade studied, large SMSAS in the Northeast and North Central regions added nearly 2 million government jobs, 1.5 million positions in the service sector, and nearly another million in retail and FIRE. However, employment in all sectors increased more slowly than the national average and far below the rate of growing regions. Moreover, gains in these sectors have been offset by sharp losses elsewhere. Indeed, large metropolitan areas in the Northeast lost 20 percent of their total manufacturing base during the 1970s in addition to absolute declines in wholesaling and transportation-related employment. Large SMSAS in the North Central region as a group also have suffered absolute declines in manufacturing and mining employment while managing to hold onto wholesaling and transportation activity.

The slow rate of economic growth in the large Northeastern and North Central SMSAS reflects substantial employment losses in central cities. Total employment declined 5 percent in central cities of large SMSAS located in the North Central region and fell by 12 percent in the Northeast from 1967 to 1977 (table 3.6). The largest job losses were in manufacturing, which dropped 30 percent in the industrial belt in the ten-year period. Sharp declines also were experienced in wholesaling, transportation and communications, and retail

Table 3.6 Employment trends in central cities and suburbs of 50 largest SMSAS by region, 1967–77[1] (employment change in thousands)

	Central city							
	Northeast[2] (N = 10)		North Central (N = 12)		South (N = 16)		West (N = 12)	
Sector	Change	Percentage change	Change	Percentage change	Change	Percentage change	Change	Percentage change
Manufacturing	−538	−32.6	−485	−27.4	−28	−3.2	42	5.2
Retail	−117	−16.5	−69	−10.1	130	20.2	135	24.6
Services	171	14.7	182	20.9	477	69.9	347	50.6
Wholesale	−138	−28.7	−96	−23.8	−25	−7.4	22	8.3
Trans/Com	−217	−39.4	−46	−10.1	46	11.7	52	12.8
FIRE	−16	−2.4	90	20.5	257	46.2	192	52.1
Construction	−87	−36.0	−39	−13.4	41	11.9	91	33.5
Mining[3]	0	−1.7	−3	−35.7	22	67.4	3	18.6
Government	210	36.5	215	37.4	395	63.3	288	40.3
Total	−723	−12.2	−253	−4.6	1,214	28.6	1,172	28.7

	Suburban							
	Northeast[2] (N = 10)		North Central (N = 12)		South (N = 16)		West (N = 12)	
Sector	Change	Percentage change	Change	Percentage change	Change	Percentage change	Change	Percentage change
Manufacturing	−85	−5.8	217	13.8	104	16.2	128	12.3
Retail	237	39.8	444	69.0	415	111.6	374	76.2
Services	496	109.9	578	151.9	470	161.0	485	125.0
Wholesale	88	42.8	159	82.8	186	197.9	105	67.3
Trans/Com	157	121.0	73	110.2	91	165.5	39	103.3
FIRE	141	152.9	95	167.4	76	152.0	62	338.8
Construction	131	113.2	149	176.2	220	229.2	123	387.9
Mining[3]	1	14.8	−1	−25.9	5	50.0	3	385.7
Government	118	42.7	142	96.1	190	78.8	60	65.0
Total	1,285	38.4	1,857	58.9	1,756	94.9	1,378	61.1

Source: See source citations for table 3.5. 1 Figures are for central county rather than central city for the following sectors: Trans/Com, FIRE, Construction, Mining, and Government. As noted in the appendix, using central county as a proxy for central city tends to overstate central-city job gains and to understate economic growth. The bias is largest for the West, where six of the twelve SMSAS are contained within a single county. 2 Figures exclude Nassau-Suffolk. 3 Mining figures exclude Salt Lake City.

employment. Aside from government, central city job gains were largely restricted to services, although finance, insurance, and real estate also grew modestly in the North Central region.

While central cities in these regions experienced sharp employment losses across most sectors, suburban economies prospered (table 3.6). Indeed, as a group, suburban portions of large SMSAS located in the Northeast and North Central regions grew much more rapidly than central cities in the South and West. Suburban employment more than doubled during the 1970s in services, transportation, FIRE, and construction in these relatively slow-growing regions. Together with substantial gains in retailing, wholesaling, and public sector employment, this growth expanded total suburban job opportunities by 38 percent in the Northeast and nearly 60 percent in the large metropolitan areas of the North Central states. Even manufacturing losses were small in suburban areas of the Northeast, while suburban manufacturing employment increased 14 percent in the North Central region.

While metropolitan employment gains in the northern regions have been heavily concentrated in suburban areas and in a few fast-growing sectors in central cities, large metropolitan areas in the South and West have enjoyed broad-based economic expansion. As elsewhere, the largest employment gains in southern and western SMSAS have been in services, with this one sector alone adding nearly 1.8 million net new jobs between 1967–77. Rapid growth in retail employment, finance, insurance, real estate, and construction industries contributed another 2 million new jobs. Gains also extended to sectors showing slow growth nationally, with even manufacturing registering employment increases. The public sector has been an important component of employment growth in the Sunbelt, with federal and local government providing one of every six net new jobs in large southern SMSAS and one of every seven in western cities.

Central city-suburban disparities are generally less distinct in the South and West, where central cities continue to grow across most economic sectors. Notably, central cities have captured over 40 percent of new economic activity in large SMSAS in recent years, expanding the employment base by nearly one-third. The strong performance of city economies in the South and West contrasted to substantial employment losses in their northern counterparts reflects

Table 3.7 Employment trends in 50 small and midsize SMSAS, 1967–77 (employment change in thousands)

Sector	SMSA Change	SMSA Percentage Change	Central city Change	Central city Percentage Change	Suburban area Change	Suburban area Percentage Change
Manufacturing	56	5.4	−6	−1.3	44	10.0
Retail	273	49.7	138	38.0	130	76.7
Services	367	79.3	146	63.5	201	99.0
Wholesale	59	30.7	17	13.0	37	72.7
Trans/Com[1]	41	22.1	11	14.0	6	62.3
FIRE[1]	71	47.1	17	25.0	11	123.5
Construction[1]	39	20.0	12	14.8	2	8.2
Mining[1]	8	23.7	1	19.4	1	37.5
Government[1]	107	23.8	28	18.3	14	28.6
Total	1,021	31.5	367	23.7	446	46.6

Source: See source citations for table 3.1.

1 Data for these sectors refer to central county rather than central city. Metropolitan areas for which the central county is coterminous with the SMSA boundaries are excluded from the central-city and suburban columns of these rows. Hence, central-city–suburban data are based on 24 of the 50 small and midsized SMSAS.

the relative vitality of the urban core as well as more expansive city boundaries.

These data highlight both the sharp regional disparities in metropolitan growth during the past decade and the relative strength of suburban economies throughout the country. In both central cities and their suburban rings, employment opportunities have grown much faster in the Sunbelt than in the Frostbelt, with two-and-one-half net new jobs added in the South and West for each new job in the Northeast and Midwest. While large central cities of the northern regions suffered a net *loss* of nearly 1 million jobs, those in the growing regions *added* nearly 2.5 million new jobs. Manufacturing has continued to grow in urban areas of the South and West while declining sharply in other metropolitan places. Even for sectors that gained employment in the Northeast and North Central regions, the gains have been small compared to those in southern and western cities. At the same time the suburban growth rate throughout the country was well above the national average. Economic activity has decentralized in metropolitan areas in all parts of the country, although Sunbelt central cities such as Houston have been more successful in capturing peripheral growth through their greater ability to expand boundaries through annexation.

Employment Trends in Smaller Metropolitan Areas

Small and mid-sized metropolitan areas have shown markedly stronger economic growth during recent years than large SMSAS, particularly for central cities. Trends from a sample of fifty smaller SMSAS indicate that growth was widely shared, with only two of the fifty SMSAS sampled registering employment declines (Jersey City and Utica-Rome). Small and mid-sized SMSAS shared in the important sectoral and locational shifts resulting from the erosion of older industrial sectors and suburbanization of economic activity. However, these shifts were less sharp than for larger cities, as were regional disparities.

Economic growth in small and mid-sized SMSAS more than kept pace with national trends and with large city gains. As shown in table 3.7, total employment rose more than 30 percent between 1967 and 1977, compared to a national growth rate of 25 percent over the same period. Growth rates in most sectors outpaced those in large metropolitan areas, although the pattern of growth mirrored activity in the nation as a whole. Services, retail, and FIRE grew most rapidly, jointly contributing seven of every ten net new jobs added to small metropolitan economies during the decade. Virtually all of the fifty smaller SMSAS surveyed gained jobs in these sectors, with most enjoying substantial growth.

Sectors that grew slowly on a comparative national basis fared markedly better in smaller SMSAS. Wholesaling employment rose 30 percent in the 1970s—twice the rate for large SMSAS—while transportation and communication employment increased 22 percent, compared to a 14 percent gain nationwide. Even manufacturing employment increased 5 percent, contrasted to a 7 percent loss in large SMSAS. Although nine of the fifty small SMSAS sampled lost manufacturing employment, rates of job loss were typically smaller than those experienced by larger metropolitan areas. Sixteen small and mid-sized SMSAS registered substantial manufacturing gains. The most dramatic of these increases came in the smaller urban areas of Florida and

Texas; for example, manufacturing employment more than doubled in the SMSAS of Fort Myers, Midland, and Lubbock.

Restructuring of the economic base was less dramatic in small urban centers than for larger cities. As elsewhere, the proportion of jobs provided by manufacturing fell markedly due to rapid growth in other sectors. However, despite rapid expansion in services and FIRE, these high-growth sectors continued to provide a smaller fraction of total employment in small urban centers than in large metropolitan areas. Still, they have been gaining importance and by the late 1970s were equal in size to manufacturing. Moreover, due to vigorous growth in the private sector, government employment actually diminished its share of total jobs during the decade, in contrast to large SMSAS where an increasing share of the work force was on the public payroll.

Central city economies fared better in small and mid-sized metropolitan areas than their counterparts in large SMSAS, although they still did not quite keep pace with the national economy. As shown in table 3.7, total central city employment grew 24 percent in the smaller metropolitan areas examined, contrasted to a 7 percent growth rate in the central cities of large SMSAS. Even manufacturing employment nearly held steady during the 1970s, and all other sectors experienced substantial job gains in central cities of small and mid-sized SMSAS. The largest and most rapid job gains came in services and retailing, which together accounted for nearly 80 percent of central city job growth in small SMSAS. Service employment rose more than 60 percent compared to a 35 percent gain in large central cities. Retail employment increased almost 40 percent in these cities—a sharp contrast to the very sluggish growth of retail activity in larger cities. In the public sector, the reverse situation prevailed, with local government employment playing a far less important role in job growth in small cities. Indeed, federal and local government employment accounted for fewer than one in every ten new central city jobs compared to four in every ten for large central cities.

Suburban areas have experienced a more rapid rate of employment growth than central cities for most sectors, although the absolute gains generally remained smaller than in central cities. Overall, suburban employment rose 47 percent between 1967 and 1977. Despite this strong performance, suburbs of small SMSAS did not grow as rapidly as suburbs in large metropolitan areas where total employment increased 59 percent. This fact, coupled with the comparative strength of central cities in smaller urban areas, makes central city–suburban disparities less sharp in small and mid-sized SMSAS. In contrast to larger places, central cities captured over 40 percent of total metropolitan job growth, one-half of all job gains in retail, 40 percent of service gains, and 30 percent of new wholesaling jobs. The central city share of new activity also was high for the financial sector, transportation and communication, and government, although it is not possible to say exactly how large since data for these sectors are reported for central county rather than for central city.

Economic activity in small and mid-sized metropolitan areas remains relatively centralized, roughly similar to the pattern found in large urban areas twenty years ago (Kain 1975). There was little discernible suburbanization of employment in smaller SMSAS in the 1970s, with the fraction of total employment located in the central city declining only slightly between 1967 and 1977. Aside from services, all other sectors remained markedly more concentrated than for large SMSAS, with the majority of nonmanufacturing jobs located in the central city. Manufacturing was the most dispersed sector, with the majority of manufacturing activity taking place outside the central city by the late 1970s.

Regional disparities also are apparent for small and mid-sized metropolitan areas, with those located in the South and West capturing a disproportionate share of economic growth. However, regional differences are less sharp than for larger urban areas, with most places gaining jobs in most sectors, regardless of region.

Implications for Economic Development Policy

Shifts in the location and characteristics of employment have affected the nation's cities in very different ways. Some urban areas have enjoyed fast-paced and diversified economic growth. Large urban areas such as Houston, Phoenix, and Denver have become well-known examples, but many smaller cities, such as Grand Rapids, Michigan, Fort Myers, Florida, and Stockton, California, have experienced broad-based economic gains as well. These metropolitan regions typically provide their residents with varied and expanding economic opportunities.

At the same time numerous central cities have experienced sluggish employment growth or registered moderate job losses. Chicago,

Boston, Pittsburgh, and Minneapolis–St. Paul are among the many cities in this position. A lesser number of cities have suffered severe employment declines: New York, Detroit, St. Louis, Baltimore, Newark, Atlanta, Philadelphia, and Dayton each lost more than 10 percent of its job base during the 1967–77 period. The effects of sluggish growth and even major job losses have been mitigated for some city residents, either because selected economic sectors have grown despite net overall decline or because nearby suburban employment has expanded. In Dayton, for example, the losses of over 35 percent of the manufacturing jobs, almost one-third of retailing positions, and more than one in every five jobs in wholesaling were to some extent offset by expansion of the employment in the services and financial sectors (up by 35 percent and 50 percent, respectively). The city of Atlanta lost more than one out of every ten jobs during the decade; however, vigorous suburban growth increased the employment base of the metropolitan area by more than 50 percent. In these cities, the adverse effects of the changing location and composition of employment are felt most sharply by those who lack the skills or mobility to take advantage of emerging opportunities. In a few cases—including New York, Jersey City, and Baltimore —entire metropolitan areas lost employment as the erosion of the traditional job base that has been under way in the central cities for some time spread to older suburban areas.

The diversity of cities' economic experiences and circumstances reinforces the unchallenged but sometimes forgotten fact that localities have different comparative advantages as producers of goods and services. Many communities would like to attract high-technology firms, but only a limited number can realistically expect to become centers for such industries. Efforts to reestablish a city's traditional industrial dominance are even more likely to be misplaced, however great their rhetorical and political appeal. Local development policies are most likely to succeed if they rest on a hard-nosed appraisal of local strengths *and* local weaknesses, and if they focus on economic sectors for which the city has at least a potential comparative advantage.

Recent experience shows that for most cities, losses in some sectors have been at least partly offset by gains in other sectors that may indicate opportunities for future growth. For example, a number of large cities with serious employment losses have a continuing specialization in finance and insurance. Even within manufacturing, growth opportunities may be found, e.g., Cleveland's relative success in the expanding rubber and miscellaneous plastics products business (Gurwitz and Kingsley 1982). Given this, the effectiveness of efforts to lure businesses to a distressed urban area—as would occur in proposed enterprise zones or other job development plans—will likely depend on the "fit" between the incentives offered, the specific locations within the city targeted for development, and the requirements and alternatives of firms in industries where the city has a continuing or emerging comparative advantage.

Despite the diversity of urban economic conditions, this analysis suggests the need for policies directed at local economic development to recognize that the difficulties facing individual communities are seldom unique or the result of purely local circumstances. Rather, they are part of a larger restructuring of the national economy as it responds to changing production and transportation technologies, shifting factor price differentials, population redistribution, and important changes in the international economy. Federal policies designed to alter these underlying causal phenomena, e.g., by promoting improved productivity or inducing change in the pattern of investment and disinvestment, will affect the nation's cities —albeit in varied ways. Concomitantly, successful state or local economic development policies will require acknowledgment of nationwide industrial and locational adjustments and of the locality's role in the national or regional economy.

A consistent theme in the assessment of employment trends in cities is the relatively strong economic performance of lower-density locations. Smaller metropolitan areas have been growing more rapidly than larger ones, and the job base of suburban cities and towns in all regions of the country has expanded vigorously. In contrast, large central cities of the Northeast and North Central regions have generally grown sluggishly or have experienced serious employment declines, and signs of weakening have begun to appear in the economies of central cities in the South and West. This pattern is a clear —and very durable—extension of trends that have been ongoing for most of the century and is a continuing reflection of both the changing economic advantages of different locations and the enduring preference of households for lower-density living.

The persistence of job-dispersal trends is of concern for at least two reasons. First, weak central city economies represent diminished revenue-raising capacity for local governments with no corresponding reduction in demands for service. Indeed, many large older cities face growing burdens—e.g., service provision to populations increasingly composed of poor and disadvantaged persons, the replacement or rehabilitation of aging infrastructure. The long-term character of employment shifts out of such central cities suggests the importance of developing funding sources that are not purely local, such as grant-in-aid programs, independent authorities with state- or federally backed bonding authority, or metropolitan-wide tax-base sharing, even if services are *delivered* locally.

Second, the process of adjustment to changing job location can be both difficult and costly. Minorities and the poor are among the last to follow jobs to the suburbs, and they are less likely than others in the population to successfully migrate to growing places. They are increasingly concentrated in older central cities with declining or only slowly expanding economies. Furthermore, disadvantaged persons in cities with declining economies, including minorities and female heads of households, are generally less well-off than disadvantaged persons in cities experiencing vigorous economic growth (*President's National Urban Policy Report* 1980). Given the desirability of integrating poor and disadvantaged workers into the economy, policies to facilitate the mobility of these workers to localities with greater opportunities would seem in order. However, unemployment rates in low-skilled occupations and among minorities are high relative to the rates for skilled workers and nonminorities, even in economically strong cities. This raises the possibility that migration of sizable numbers of disadvantaged workers from shrinking to growing metropolitan areas might have the result of displacing some of the disadvantaged workers already in growing cities. With or without mobility assistance, however, the need to upgrade the skills of many of these workers is clear.

Extensive shifts in the occupational structure of urban labor markets are indicative of the large and increasing role of job retraining in adapting to national economic change. The individual costs of economic restructuring are considerable for workers whose jobs are disappearing and whose skills are no longer in demand. Many of these workers will independently undertake the task of acquiring new skills; others will be encouraged to do so by their employers, often within the workplace. Some, however, are likely to require public assistance of some kind. Appropriate forms of assistance will vary, from cash support (e.g., extended unemployment benefits for workers displaced by foreign competition) to more comprehensive program packages including training, placement services, and mobility assistance.

The success of relocation strategies depends in part on the match between displaced workers and the employment opportunities available in growing metropolitan areas. Proposals to help relocate unemployed autoworkers from Detroit to Houston or San Jose, for example, presume that those displaced workers have skills appropriate to the available job opportunities in growing cities. Relocation strategies for displaced or disadvantaged workers also depend on the ability and willingness of such workers to move to new places and to accept the jobs that are available—even though these jobs may entail reductions in salary and seniority, at least initially.

Authors' Note: The authors would like to thank Professor H. James Brown, John F. Kennedy School of Government, Harvard University, for his assistance in conceptualizing and executing this research and for comments on earlier drafts of this essay. Funding for this research was provided by the U.S. Department of Housing and Urban Development; opinions are those of the authors and do not represent the position of the Department.

4 Dynamics, Structural Change, and Economic Development Paths

Edward M. Bergman and Harvey A. Goldstein

Through the mid-1980s local economics in all regions of the United States are undergoing the greatest distress since the Great Depression. During this period unemployment rates and business failures have reached post-1930s highs, while shrinking tax revenues and reduced capacities to finance needed capital improvements to dangerously worn-out infrastructure have virtually stripped local governments of the few means available to them to alleviate the distress.

The post–World War II incidence of local economic distress is of three general types. National recessions until the early 1970s raised unemployment rates in many local economies, but these recessions were of relatively short duration. More important, they were squeezed within an otherwise sustained, twenty-five-year period of economic expansion. Many local economies did not even experience an economic downturn because their high secular growth rates totally offset the effects of the recession.

Some local economies did suffer chronic distress as a result of structural changes in important local industries (e.g., New England textiles) and the concomitant disinvestment and movement of capital to other regions. Yet as painful as these dislocations were to the areas experiencing them, they were isolated exceptions to the general rule of economic growth and prosperity. Under these circumstances short-term relief from the federal government was politically feasible, and the long-term policy of encouraging population migration to growing areas, of the type now advocated by the President's Commission for a National Agenda for the Eighties (Hicks 1982), could be viewed as rational.

A second type of local economic distress is associated with the so-called urban crisis of the 1960s, which was actually a central city crisis. The loss of central city jobs and tax bases to the surrounding suburban jurisdictions meant severe economic distress within *parts* of local economies that was neither of short-term duration nor isolated to just a few metropolitan areas. Yet there was more optimism than pessimism that the central city distress could be alleviated through metropolitan equalization, through central city economic development initiatives, and in the long run by the rising tide of national economic growth (see Bergsman 1971, and Ganz and O'Brien 1973, for optimistic assessments at the time).

The third type of economic distress that almost all areas have felt at some point since 1970 (Syron 1978) differs from previous post–World War II periods of distress because it results from a series of strong cyclical downturns and from structural changes in the national economy. Since 1970 the national economy has been through four wrenching recessions and three recoveries. Occurring at the same time were shifts in the sectoral and spatial pattern of capital investment and employment across the U.S. system of local economies (Bluestone and Harrison 1982) and strong fluctuations in the prices of commodities that reflected the long-term transformations under way in the international economic system and the United States' position in it (Block 1977; Muller 1980; U.S. Department of Housing and Urban Development 1979). It is indeed difficult to disagree with language used in a bill to amend the Public Work and Economic Development Act of 1965 (U.S. House of Representatives 1983, pp. 2, 4): "Congress also recognizes that economic conditions and political relationships change and that legislation must address those changes . . . *there is continued need to assist in adjustment of change, which is the only permanent feature of our national, regional and local economies*" (emphasis added).

The prospects for continued simultaneity of strong cyclical behavior and structural change in the national economy—which then become transmitted to local economies—present local economic analysts and planners with situations in which their forecasts of local economic performance and assessments of the area's development prospects are increasingly unreliable. The fashioning of viable development strategies is dependent, in part, upon an accurate assessment of the area's development prospects. This assessment, however, hinges upon the local economic planner's ability to sort out observable changes and trends in local economic activity: one must be able to recognize those due to structural changes in the local economy and those due to its unique cyclical behavior.

This chapter offers recent evidence of cyclical performance of metropolitan economies in the United States and of changes in the economic structure of these areas. The evidence will be presented as important sources of insight into the dynamics of local economies and as an analytic aid in the design and planning of strategic economic development policies.[1]

Exogenous Influences on Local Economies in the U.S.

According to traditional regional economic development theory, the most important exogenous influences on local economies are changes in regional and national product markets of locally produced export goods. Either price changes due to increases or decreases in aggregate product demand or changes in the market share of local producers due to changes in competitive advantage can exert tremendous influence on the functioning of local economies. These changes can result from short-term market adjustments (seasonal or cyclical) or from the longer-term transformations in the structure of markets and institutions that guide markets.

In recent years a number of writers have noted a pair of changes in the macroeconomy that have not been well-incorporated into regional economic theory or into the emerging economic development planning literature. First, changes in the international division of labor have led to long-term changes in the structure of export product markets of locally produced goods and services as well as to changes in the cyclical behavior of local economies. Second, changes in the pattern of ownership and control of enterprises have led to changes in decisions on plant location, investment and disinvestment of capital, and spatially distributed job gains and losses that would not be predicted by traditional regional economic theory or by the analytic tools that regional economists have provided to planners over the years.

Changes in the International Division of Labor

The international economic system has undergone dramatic shifts in the last fifteen years. There have been the worldwide decentralization of traditional manufacturing industries, the increasing competitiveness of major U.S. trading partners, the fluctuations of the dollar, the rise of OPEC and resulting transformations in energy-producing industries, plus turmoil and realignment of international monetary markets (Block 1977; Barnet 1980; Glickman 1981). U.S. foreign and domestic economic policies experienced similar coping adjustments throughout the 1970s as Keynesian demand policies shifted to new concerns for national industry and supply-side policies. These various structural changes (and attendant policies) have had many important impacts on U.S. local economies through the foreign trade sector and through shifts in the magnitude and direction of international capital flows.

Foreign trade has become a larger component of the national economy and thus, on average, a larger component of U.S. local economies (both exports and imports as a percentage of Gross National Product have grown dramatically in the last thirty years, but particularly so in the 1970s). Exports of U.S. manufactured goods in general have decreased. The most important export mainstays are now agricultural products, agricultural machinery, selected high-technology equipment, and business services. These changes in the foreign trade pattern yield differential impacts on U.S. local economies because of industrial specialization in local economies. Local economies based upon industries that have undergone worldwide decentralization, or in which there has been substantial import penetration, are witnessing large-scale layoffs, plant shutdowns, and tax base erosion, as well as social, psychological, and medical distress. The economic distress in these local economies goes beyond distress that is cyclically induced; these economies are undergoing long-term structural change and readjustment. On the other hand, local economies with specializations in industries that have been able to enhance their international competitiveness and export product markets have performed relatively well. The adjustments they have made to the new order have been much less painful (Bergman and Goldstein forthcoming).

The changes in the international division of labor have led to shifts in the direction in U.S.-based direct foreign investment (DFI) and in the amount of foreign investment in the United States.[2] The increasing proportion of U.S. DFI in less-developed countries from the mid-1970s represents two risks to local economies: increased import competition for domestically produced goods and the opportunity cost of capital investment in U.S. manufacturing industries, although the differential regional impacts of the latter are unclear. It is plausible to argue that some of the overseas investment would have occurred in lower-wage regions in the United States, including the Southeast and Southwest. On the other hand, the increase in the U.S. DFI has led to increases in banking, finance, and related corporate services activity. Yet this increase has been concentrated in only a few large metropolitan areas such as New York, Chicago, San Francisco, and Los Angeles. Indeed, the increase in importance of U.S. DFI and international trade has been a major contributing factor to the emergence of corporate centers in which the principal export is now services rather than manufactured goods (see Noyelle 1983a).

Ownership and Control of Enterprises

The second major exogenous influence affecting the structure of U.S. local economies in recent years stems from changes in the pattern of ownership and control of enterprises. This has both international and domestic dimensions. The role of multinational corporations (MNCs) in organizing and controlling such a large proportion of international trade and their ability to shift capital rapidly anywhere in the world has been paralleled by the process of increasing conglomeration in the U.S. economy, by MNCs as well as by national corporations. By 1980 more than 70 percent of all private economic activity was controlled and operated by eight hundred conglomerate firms, while the remaining 30 percent was shared by 14 million firms (Muller 1980). This trend has been under way for a long time, but it started accelerating substantially in the late 1960s and again in the late 1970s. The importance of this change in enterprise ownership and control structure for plant location decisions and behavior has been addressed by Hamilton (1974), Collins and Walker (1975), Pred (1977) Bluestone and Harrison (1982), and Schmenner (1982).

Locational decisions of either branch plants within a firm or units within a conglomerate are seldom made on the basis of optimal criteria from the point of view of the particular establishment. Rather, locational choices are increasingly based on optimal criteria from the point of view of the parent corporation and thus reflect its hierarchical and geographic structure as a whole. In other words, classical location theory assumes the rational behavior of entrepreneurs selecting the maximal profit (or minimum cost) location for the single enterprise in which alternative locations are judged on the basis of their comparative advantages. This behavior can no longer be assumed for large corporations holding many branch plants or conglomerates with many types of enterprises under their corporate umbrellas. The principal implications of this change for local economies and their development prospects are twofold. First, an area's comparative advantage for different types of industries or operations may be outweighed by internal corporate criteria. Thus, local development planning strategies that emphasize either the enhancing of area advantages or the lessening of area disadvantages for attracting industries may not necessarily be effective strategies to pursue. Second, urban agglomeration economies are not likely to remain an important locational criterion for firms. Backward linkages within the local economy will be weaker as branch plants purchase a larger share of their inputs from other parts of the parent corporation that are located outside the local economy. The possible decline in importance of urban agglomeration economies would lead eventually to the weakening of the "glue" holding urban agglomerations together. This can mean a loss of an important function of many local economies that have depended upon their diversity, specialization and scale of support services, labor force, and intermediate product markets to attract and nurture the growth of young firms (i.e., the incubator function). The strengthening of corporate ties and the weakening of urban agglomeration economies together account for a good portion of the net shift of manufacturing from metropolitan to nonmetropolitan locations during the past two decades. Many of the newer local economies in the South and West have not been adversely affected by this trend since these areas were never based strongly on urban agglomeration economies in the first place.

The changes in the international economic order, combined with the conglomeration and the accelerating concentration of corporate ownership, control, and power in the U.S. economy, have led to visible changes in economic cyclical behavior that are still in flux (Glickman 1981, p. 6).

There has been a greater synchronization of our business cycle with those of our trading partners during the 1970s, although some of the coincident cyclical patterns can be attributed to worldwide oil and food price shocks. Should this trend continue, domestic business cycles could become more severe in the future. In previous decades the U.S. cycle was "out of phase" with many European countries; as a result, domestic cyclicality was dampered through interaction with other economies.

As shifts in the international economic order continue, they produce effects that ripple through national and subnational economies such that changes in the cyclical behavior of the U.S. economy occur simultaneously with changes in the cyclical behavior of constituent local economies (Bergman and Goldstein forthcoming). Current changes and prospects for future changes in local cyclical behavior are not well understood in large part because it is difficult to separate empirically cyclical performance and structural change in the short-term *and* because they are often interactive. The section below describes the results of an analysis of local cyclical behavior in relation to an area's longer-term growth and development trends. Understanding this relationship is one step in the task of improving the available set of tools for analyzing the interaction between cyclical performance and structural change of local economies.

The Cyclical Behavior of U.S. Local Economies

The cyclical behavior of local economies has recently been of interest to regional economists and local economic policymakers for at least two reasons. First, it has been recognized as necessary to accurately estimate the timing, amplitude, and duration of local economic downturns in order to design a *locally effective* set of countercyclical programs (Vernez et al. 1977). Second, knowledge of the cyclical behavior of local economies provides diagnostic information for the design of longer-term local economic stabilization policies (e.g., regional industrial diversification) to help minimize the costs associated with cyclical fluctuations (Thompson 1965; Conroy 1975).

The marked cyclical instability of local economies during the 1970s is primarily a reflection of the depth and frequency of national business cycles during this period. The 1960s was a period in which there was uninterrupted national economic growth for 117 consecutive months. The changes in the international economic order mentioned above, as well as national policies designed to deal with a stagflation economy, gave rise to the series of four national recessions and recoveries starting in 1970. How can the cyclical performance of U.S. local economies during this period best be described? How much variation in cyclical performance has there been among local economies? What is the relationship, if any, between a local economy's cyclical performance and its long-term economic growth and development performance? Finally, what is the policy utility of this type of evidence?

Early studies of local or regional cyclical behavior (Vining 1946; Neff and Weifenbach 1949; Borts 1960) attempted to identify those characteristics of local or regional economies that either are correlated with or predict their cyclical behavior. The results were often difficult to interpret because of limitations in the design of the studies, including problems of data availability.

King et al. (1972) later focused on understanding the relationship between local cyclical behavior and the secular growth rate of local economies. Performing a factor analysis of bimonthly total nonagricultural employment data over the 1957–69 period, the researchers found that almost all areas that had experienced rapid employment growth over the period were also cyclically stable and either led or were coincident with national cycles. These areas also were concentrated in the South, Southwest, and West. Areas that had experienced slow growth tended to exhibit cyclical instability and to lag behind the national cycles. These were concentrated in the Northeast and had high proportions of manufacturing employment.

In an analysis of the cyclical behavior of states and labor market areas, Vernez et al. (1977) found disappointingly little regularity in the timing, duration, and severity of cycles for a given area over time. This implies that the ability to predict the future cyclical behavior of an area's economy based upon its historical behavior is somewhat low. As a result, the researchers suggested that area cyclical behavior needed to be analyzed as a long-term (average) relationship between area and national employment growth rates because of both the idiosyncratic nature of discrete business cycles and the inadequate number of cases (cycles) for inferential purposes. Using regression analysis, the authors compared the area monthly employment growth rate to the national monthly employment growth rate for about 150 metropolitan areas for the period 1960–74. The results of this analysis led

Vernez et al. to three principal conclusions: (1) there is considerable variation among areas in the relationship between area and U.S. employment growth rates; (2) there is a distinct regional pattern among the Northeast, the South, and the West; and (3) large areas behave differently from small and medium-sized areas. Large areas exhibit very high conformity and very high responsiveness. The tendency to behave similarly to the United States as a whole was interpreted as a result of the relative diversity of industry mix in large metropolitan areas.

Local Cyclical Behavior, 1970–80

An extension of the regression model used by Vernez et al. (1977) was developed to analyze the cyclical behavior of 202 U.S. metropolitan economies over the period from January 1970 to December 1980. This period includes the duration of three complete national recessions and recoveries and the beginning of the fourth and deepest recession since the 1930s. The model is a particularly useful one because not only does it provide information about the relationship between cyclical behavior and secular growth trends, but it also differentiates the sensitivity to national economic expansions from sensitivity to national economic contractions.

The mathematical form of the regression model is described in the note below.[3] The model provides estimates of six characteristics of the cyclical behavior (and growth behavior) of each local economy during the 1970–80 period. A graphic description of the indicators of local cyclical and growth behavior should help to communicate their meaning and some of their relationships to one another (figure 4.1). The estimates of these indicators for each of the 202 U.S. metropolitan areas are given in appendix table 4A.1.

The degree of conformity or similarity of the cyclical behavior of the given local economy to that of the national economy is provided by the coefficient of determination (R^2) of the model. The degree of conformity tells the analyst the extent to which fluctuations in local employment are due to upturns and downturns in the national economy. Areas with $R^2 \geq .50$ are considered relatively high conformance areas. The estimates of the other characteristics of cyclical behavior (except for average monthly employment growth rate)

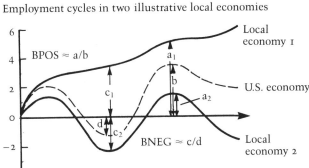

Employment cycles in two illustrative local economies

Cyclical characteristics of local economies

	Conformance of local to U.S. economy R_2	Local sensitivity to U.S. recession BNEG	Local sensitivity to U.S. recovery BPOS	Autonomous local growth ALPHA
Local economy 1	Low conformance: $R^2 \ll 0.5$	Inversely sensitive: BNEG < 0.0*	Mildly sensitive: BPOS > 0.0*	High: ALPHA $\gg 0$
U.S. economy				
Local economy 2	High conformance: $R^2 \gg 0.5$	Highly sensitive: BNEG ≥ 1.0	Moderately sensitive: BPOS > 0.5	Near zero ALPHA ≈ 0

*Often statistically insignificant

Figure 4.1.   Employment cycle for two hypothetical local economies

obtained from the regression model are not considered for areas of low conformance $(R^2 < .50)$.

The average monthly employment growth rate describes the *observed growth trend* for each area during the period. This is the mean value of the dependent variable $(\bar{Y}_t)$ in the regression model and thus can be calculated directly from the data.

The *sensitivity* of a given local economy to national employment expansions measures the percentage change in the level of local employment for each 1 percent increase in the level of national employment. Thus, for example, an area with a sensitivity coefficient of 1.5 will, on average, grow in response to the national economy at an annual rate of 3 percent when the national economy is expanding at the annual rate of 2 percent. Coefficients above 1.0 indicate that the area is disproportionately sensitive to the U.S. economy during expansionary periods of the latter. Values between 0.0 and 0.99 indicate an area is relatively insensitive to national economic expansion. A negative value indicates countercyclical tendencies: national economic expansions occur at the same time local employment levels contract. The estimate of the sensitivity from the regression model is the regression coefficient BPOS.

The sensitivity of a given local economy to national employment contractions (recessions) measures the percentage change in the level of local employment for each 1 percent decrease in the level of national employment. It is analogous to the local sensitivity to national economic expansions and is estimated in the model as the regression coefficient BNEG.

A useful indicator of local economic performance is the expected rate of economic growth when the national economy neither expands nor contracts. That is, in the absence of net growth or decline in the national economy, what is the *autonomous* linear growth rate of the local economy? The regression model provides an estimate of the local autonomous growth rate as the constant term, ALPHA. For example, an area with a positive ALPHA equal to 1.8 would grow at the annual rate of 1.8 percent in the absence of national employment expansion or contraction. About one-half of the 202 areas had positive autonomous growth rates.

The last indicator of local cyclical performance is *timing*; it is the average lead or lag ("*m*," or months) between local cycles and national cycles. Leads are positive numbers (1, 2, 3, or 6) and indicate that, on average, a local economy enters a recession and then enters a recovery some number of months before the national economy as a whole. A lag is represented by a negative number (−1, −2, −3, −6) and indicates that recession and recovery in the national economy, on average, have preceded the onset of a recession and subsequent recovery in a particular local economy. A value of 0 indicates coincidence of national and local cycles. The timing dimension of local cyclical behavior is not discussed below as it is a volatile short-term characteristic, although it, too, is included here and in appendix table 4A.1 for the sake of completeness.

The results contain several important findings. First, the degree of variation in local cyclical behavior among local economies has increased during the late 1970s when compared to the results obtained by Vernez et al. for an earlier period. Second, many metropolitan economies are not closely conformant with the U.S. economy. The growth rates of areas with low conformance to national economic fluctuations ($R^2 < .50$) are doubtless accounted for by other influences. Sometimes other cycles relatively independent of the national business cycle exert large influences on the local economy: investment cycles, export cycles, interest rate cycles, product cycles. Price fluctuations of the major export products, for example, often can overpower the influence of national business cycles. The results of this analysis do not attempt to account for the source of other influences on local economies exhibiting low conformance, but they do identify the need to investigate these influences if they are not already understood by local economic planners and policymakers. Third, the results show that many conformant local economies exhibit a high degree of asymmetry with respect to their sensitivity to upturns and downturns in the national economy.

The Cyclical Ratchet

The possibility that asymmetric cyclical behavior could lead to long-term decline and erosion of the base of central city economies has been posed by several researchers including Kain (1975) and James (1976). That is, if an area's employment base is strongly affected by cyclical downturns but is only weakly affected by cyclical upturns, the result is a one-way, net loss of jobs over the entire cycle, which may repeat itself in subsequent cycles. This phenomenon has been referred to as a ratchet effect. This use of the cyclical ratchet metaphor differs from the urban-scale ratchet originally hypothesized by Thompson (1965). The existence of a cyclical ratchet among conformant SMSAs during the 1970s is indicated by the distribution of areas in table 4.1. Areas in cells along the principal diagonal (upper left to lower right) display relative symmetric cyclical behavior; their sensitivity to upturns and downturns is of the same approximate order of magnitude. Areas in the cells above and to the right of the

Table 4.1 Positive versus negative sensitivity, 1970–80, areas of high conformance ($R^2 \geqslant .50$)

	BNEG < 0.80	0.80 ⩽ BNEG < 1.20	BNEG ⩾ 1.20
BPOS < 0.80	New Orleans New York San Antonio San Diego Trenton	Albuquerque Greensboro Jackson, MS Los Angeles Lynchburg Macon Nashville/Davidson Richmond San Francisco	Atlanta Chicago Jackson, MI Kansas City Memphis South Bend Springfield, MA

0.80 ⩽ BPOS < 1.20	Anaheim/Santa Ana
	Dallas/Fort Worth
	Oxnard/Simi Valley
	Riverside/San
	  Bernadino
	Tacoma
		Albany/Schenec-
		  tady/Troy, NY
		Baltimore
		Boston
		Cleveland
		Dayton
		Denver/Boulder
		Harrisburg
		Knoxville
		Lancaster
		Little Rock
		Louisville
		Mobile
		Philadelphia
		Poughkeepsie
		Reading
		Roanoke
		Wilmington
			Appleton/Oshkosh,
			  WI
			Elmira
			Fall River
			Grand Rapids
			Green Bay
			Indianapolis
			Madison
			Milwaukee
			New Bedford
			Paterson/Clifton
			Portland, OR
			Providence
			Rochester
			Rockford
			St. Louis
			Santa Rosa
			Scranton
			Springfield, MO
			Worcester
			York

BPOS ⩾ 1.20	Hartford Pittsburgh Racine Santa Barbara Stamford	Binghamton Bridgeport Canton Cincinnati Columbus, OH Minneapolis/St. Paul Nassau/Suffolk New Brunswick Omaha Toledo Wilkes-Barre	Billings Brockton Buffalo Eugene/Springfield Fargo/Moorehead Lowell Salinas/Seaside Sioux Falls Spokane Syracuse Utica/Rome

principal diagonal display cyclical ratchets in a positive direction. They are relatively insensitive to the national business cycle during downturns and are relatively sensitive during upturns. Areas in the cells below and to the left of the main diagonal display cyclical ratchets in a negative direction. High autonomous growth rates (ALPHA) explain those areas with ratchets in the negative direction but that have high average growth rates. Conversely those areas with positive ratchets but that are very slowly growing or declining secularly have very low autonomous growth rate components (see appendix table 4A.1).

The average employment growth rate of an area can be accounted for by three additive components: the autonomous growth rate, ALPHA (can be positive or negative); the growth rate due to the degree of sensitivity of the local economy to national economic expansions (positive if BPOS > 0.0); and the growth rate due to the degree of sensitivity of the local economy to national economic contractions (negative if BNEG > 0.0). Different combinations of values of the three components will lead to different average growth rates. On the other hand, it is possible to achieve a given average growth rate by several different combinations of values of the three components. For example, one area can achieve a high growth rate from a large positive ALPHA with BPOS and BNEG being close to zero, while another area can achieve the same high growth rate from a large BPOS, a BNEG close to zero or negative, and a negative ALPHA. A discrete set of local economic policies could be designed to decrease an area's sensitivity to national economic contractions, while a different set of policies might be designed to increase the area's autonomous growth rate.

Since the logical set of policies to increase (or decrease) any one of the three components may be contradictory to policies designed to achieve the others, one must often choose among the several strategies available. This discussion is meant only to suggest that the results of the analysis of local cyclical behavior and its relationship to longer-term growth performance can provide local policymakers with a useful framework for deciding which set of policies are coherent and most appropriate for a given economy. If the national economy performs as it did in the 1970s with very strong cyclical components, area economies undergoing low growth perhaps should focus on increasing the autonomous growth rate rather than trying only to make themselves immune to cyclical downturns.

The cyclical ratchet, as the metaphor implies, leads to unidirectional secular changes in the net employment growth rate of metropolitan economies. While these changes may be purely of a scalar nature—i.e., over the course of several business cycles there is a net increase or decrease in the total employment base due solely to asymmetric sensitivity to national business cycles—it is unlikely that all sectors of the metropolitan economy are affected proportionately. This is due to industry differences in product market orientation, area-specific competition advantages, and stages in the product cycle. It is the uneven effects of business cycles among sectors that can lead to long-term structural changes in metropolitan economies. Thus, long-term and repeated cycles can lead to what might be called a structural ratchet effect. This possibility is not new. Yet up until the 1970s it has not been one deserving much attention merely because the national economy and thus most metropolitan economies were not displaying pronounced and repeated cyclical fluctuations.

Structural Changes in Local Economies

Economic development planners and researchers have long relied upon a number of approaches for measuring and analyzing local economies. The most widely known and applied approaches examine the internal composition of a local economy in terms of standard classifications (e.g., SIC) for which data are readily available and its comparative composition with respect to some larger reference economy (e.g., U.S. economy). Such approaches work well so long as the composition of the local economy maintains a stable relationship to larger reference economies or if marginal changes in composition can be assumed to follow some well-understood continuum.

However, the record of the 1970s does not inspire confidence in the stability of relations to the national economy or in conventional assumptions concerning most of its subnational components. Accordingly, local economic development planners may be quite unaware of the basic, underlying structural changes that all metropolitan economies are to some degree experiencing, and they need to know how to assess the degree and direction of structural changes under way in their local economies.

Measures of Structure in Local Economies

Traditional ways of characterizing the metropolitan mix and share of particular industries provide a range of convenient indices: location quotients of industrial specialization or concentration, cumulative variances or deviations from U.S. industry mix profiles, and local effects inferred from shift-share residuals. Most are descriptive devices that provide useful measures, but one can seldom establish reliably the meaning of a single measurement in the absence of some conceptual or interpretive framework.

To examine matters of structure, i.e., patterns of basic interrelationships among sectors, analysts have come to adopt the conceptual apparatus of agglomeration economies. Agglomeration economies (or diseconomies) are thought to account for the identifiable, predictable complexes of industrial activity that contribute to the economic structure of particular metropolitan areas. Industrial clusters or complexes adhere together and shape the structure of metropolitan economies in strikingly distinctive variations. Reviews of several empirical tests of industrial complexes demonstrate a consensus about the configurations of such complexes and their importance to economic development planners and researchers (Czamanski and de Q. Ablas 1978; Cherniack 1980). However, agglomeration theory of industrial complexes hinges rather decisively on assumptions that postulate the continued need of independent firms in open markets for access to economies that urban and industrial concentration offer. Since corporate control of previously independent firms is known to have expanded rapidly in the past twenty years, the proportion of total producers relying on *corporate* scale economies has necessarily increased and the agglomeration ties that bind industrial complexes have weakened. This weakness is reflected in part by the rapid growth of nonmetropolitan industry throughout the 1970s, and it probably accounts for some of the early shifts in composition of metropolitan industrial complexes during the late 1960s (Cherniack 1980).

Other empirical investigations of metropolitan economies evade the weaknesses of defining structure purely in industrial terms by including many additional dimensions that are thought to characterize important aspects of economic structure. The application of statistical techniques that reduce many variables to a manageable handful of significant components allows a more exploratory approach to questions of economic structure. Early efforts by proponents of factorial ecology demonstrated both the promise and risks of including a much broader set of structural variables (Moser and Wolf 1961; Wood 1969; Alford 1972; Berry 1972; Ray and Murdie 1972; Keeler and Rogers 1973). For example, the risks of including demographic or social features of the population (racial, age, or family characteristics) as reflections of economic structure must be balanced against the gains such measures provide in the interpretation of structural factors. If the lags or leads between economic and demographic structure are short or if central relationships between them (e.g., labor force participation rates) remain fairly stable, one can introduce a rich mixture of potential measures and establish important structural connections. However, in the face of evidence that important structural and cyclical changes are in progress, particular care is required in the choice and analysis of contemporaneous structural measures.[4]

Measures of Structural Change in Local Economies

The importance of *changes* in structure of local economies has been recognized in recent years, although changes measured for individual industries or sectors remain a staple of regional analysis. Basic techniques such as shift-share analysis have traditionally focused more on the identification or presence of local industries' aggregate effect rather than on the structural meaning associated with a *pattern* of such effects. Early work by Thompson and Mattila (1959) to devise econometric models for postwar industrial development happened to include a study addendum of correlations of the *changes* in employment among two-digit SIC manufacturing industries for all forty-eight states during the late 1940s and mid-1950s. They noted which industry's growth or decline was correlated with that of others: the patterns of employment change in many durable and nondurable industries changed together as distinct groups. Their work clearly established the merits of investigating and interpreting patterns of particular industry changes in mix and share composition. With this information, an economic development planner would focus on developing compatible pairings of industries or avoiding pairings that were inversely correlated. Despite their call for further refinements and interpretations, little additional work along these lines has been

devoted to understanding how such changes affect the overall structure of metropolitan economies.

Cherniack's research has demonstrated ways in which *change* in
industrial complexes or clusters can be estimated. Adopting techniques similar to many of the studies of industrial clustering reviewed
by Czamanski and de Q. Ablas (1978), Cherniack derived industrial
clusters for all U.S. metropolitan economies in 1965 and again for
1970 by use of factor analysis. He then systematically compared the
estimated industrial clusters of both years by use of the RELATE algo-
rithm to determine the degree of shift in the composition and proportion of industries that comprise each period's industrial cluster.
(Cherniack also conducted a similar comparison of industrial clusters
estimated separately for the central cities and the suburbs of metropolitan areas.) His findings revealed that, overall, industrial complexes in metropolitan economies were similar for the two observations (p. 110), yet some three-digit industry components of the
clusters had indeed changed during the period. It should be noted
that this 1965–70 period coincided with the last five years of the
longest expansion phase in the postwar period and immediately preceded the series of recessions and recoveries characterizing all of the
1970s. An updating of this important research might well reveal
even more marked change in the composition of observed industrial
clusters as some industries continue to decline secularly, come under
increasing corporate control and influence, or relocate for numerous
reasons to the other metropolitan or nonmetropolitan areas or to
foreign countries.

Changes in economic structure also can be estimated by applying
factor analysis to measured *changes* in important dimensions of
metropolitan economies. Unlike Cherniack's ex post comparison of
change between individually estimated industrial complexes, this
approach instead builds on the earlier work of Thompson and Mattila
by directly employing change variables. It also extends work of the
present authors and others cited above by factor analyzing multiple
dimensions of economic structure that change between points in
time rather than analyzing such dimensions for a single period.

A desirable feature of this analytic method is the relevance to
economic development planners of the information output for each
metropolitan economy: factor scores that provide a clear index of
whether an area is above or below the U.S. average *change* are avail-

able for each metropolitan economy. By controlling for changes in all other metropolitan economies, these scores afford economic development planners a clear view of whether a local economy is close to, or far from, the average structural change for each of the key structural change factors. In general, factor scores with absolute values greater than one standard deviation from the mean offer convincing evidence that a local area is strongly influenced by the structural change effects of the factor in question. However, lower scores also provide valuable information concerning tendencies for change.[5] Two or more such tendencies may together suggest the potential and direction of substantial future changes.

Structural Change in Local Economies during the Mid-1970s

The economic instability and sluggishness of industrialized countries is by now also a commonplace fact in the United States. It has been characterized by stagflation beginning in the mid-1970s, record high interest rates as the United States entered its fourth recessionary contraction in less than a decade, and accelerated rates of capital mobility and industrial relocation across regions, states, and metropolitan areas.

To provide local planners with a good handle on the meaning of these important but broadly defined structural alterations of the U.S. economy, a more precisely measured set of significant changes in the country's constituent metropolitan economies was developed. Sixteen important measures[6] of economic change were compiled for each metropolitan area:

1. six changes in location quotient of important industrial sectors (manufacturing, distributive services, retail services, consumer services, producer services, and corporate complex functions);
2. five changes in average productivity and production costs (nonsupervisory wages, value added per worker, capital expenditures per worker, utility costs, and shipments per worker);
3. three changes in economic performance (per capita income, unemployment, and per capita savings); and
4. two measures of change in local fiscal burden (local property tax per capita and public debt per capita).

Table 4.2 shows how the application of factor analysis recombined these sixteen measures into six factors, each of which describe distinct properties of change in metropolitan economic structure. Together, the six factors account for 60 percent of all the variance in the original set of sixteen change measures for 202 metropolitan economies. The meaning of each factor is straightforward and is independent of the meaning associated with any of the other factors, i.e., they are orthogonal factors defined by varimax rotation procedures. (Scores for metropolitan economies are listed in appendix table 4A.1.)

Factor I is based on very high loadings (or correlations) with changes in location quotients for producer services and overall corporate functions. Thus, this factor represents a dimension of change in economic structure involving the growth or decline of *corporate complexes*—that is, the increased or decreased importance of this set of functions to metropolitan economies. The significance of corporate control was mentioned earlier in this article, and the importance of corporate complexes to economic development planners is laid out by Noyelle (1983).

Factor II is defined by a logical set of measures related to productivity: consistent changes in payrolls, value added, and capital expenditures per worker all load very heavily on the factor. Care must be taken in the interpretation of this factor for particular areas since it could capture traditionally defined productivity relationships in basic industry or it could also mirror the inflated value of products in resource-based industries during the mid-1970s (chiefly petroleum) and the localized boom in refining capacity and payrolls that were fueled by that boom. For these reasons, this factor will be considered to represent structural features of *price-productivity* changes in metropolitan economies. An economic development planner would be advised to investigate the local economy carefully and establish if the local area scores heavily on this factor due to genuine productivity effects of production technology, labor skills, or basic efficiency of area infrastructure. At the same time a planner also should examine the possibility that the ability of area industries to administer prices and meet labor wage bargains as described by Thompson (1965) may underlie this factor. Since the trend in price-productivity will affect an area's ability to retain production facilities and offer substantial labor incomes to its work force, economic development planners will find this a valuable indicator.

Factor III is formed by an inverse pattern of loadings: per capita income and per capita property taxes are moving together con-

Table 4.2 Economic structure change factors*

Changes** in measures of economic structure (1972–77)	Corporate headquarter Factor I	Price-productivity Factor II	Economic distress Factor III	Market center Factor IV	Manufacturing multiplier Factor V	Residentiary function Factor VI
Producer services (ΔL.Q.)†	.879					
Headquarter functions (ΔL.Q.)†	.888					
Nonsupervisory payrolls (ΔP.W.)		.751				
Value added (ΔP.W.)		.647				
Capital expenditures (ΔP.W.)		.665				
Income (ΔP.C.)			−.830			
Property tax (ΔP.C.)			.895			
Distributive services (ΔL.Q.)†				.784		
Value of shipments (ΔP.W.)				.656		
Manufacturing (ΔL.Q.)				−.445	.404	
Savings (ΔP.C.)					.607	
Unemployment (Δrate)					−.410	
Local public debt (ΔP.C.)					−.560	
Utility costs (Δrate)					.500	
Retail (ΔL.Q.)†						.606
Consumer services (ΔL.Q.)†						.747

Table 4.2 (continued)

---

* Factor loadings ≤ .40 were omitted from this summary for visual ease of relating variables to factors.

** Changes measured as follows:

ΔL.Q. = Changes between periods in value of location quotient.

ΔP.W. = Changes between periods measured per worker.

ΔP.C. = Changes between periods measured per capita.

Δrate = Changes between periods in conventionally measured rates.

† Indicates change measured between 1970 and 1977.

sistently but in opposite directions. The most straightforward interpretation suggests that areas which experienced increases in property taxes per capita also experienced losses in per capita income. While this could be thought of as an index of general distress for metropolitan economies, it also is possible that this factor concisely measures the *economic distress* usually associated with mobility of capital from some areas to others. That is, areas that lost wage- and tax-paying industries will have factor scores that show higher taxes per capita and lower income per capita, and those that gained wage- and tax-paying industries will have factor scores of opposite sign. In either case, economic development planners would need to ascertain whether higher-than-average scores on this trend for their areas are likely to continue. Policies that are directed at fiscal and income relief in capital loss areas should be reviewed in light of foreseeable demographic adjustments and development initiatives, particularly community economic development efforts. On the other hand, capital gain areas should plan early to devote reasonable proportions of early growth in per capita income and tax receipts to public investments that allow development of a vigorous, sustainable local economy.[7]

Factor IV consists of high factor loads that result from changes in the location quotient of distributive services and in the value of shipments per worker. This factor indicates that some metropolitan areas experienced noticeable shifts in the degree to which goods were shipped from local producers, transported by local carriers, warehoused by local companies, and distributed by local wholesalers. One interpretation of this factor suggests that it may measure increases in export production. However, the factor also includes a negative shift in the location quotient for manufacturing, i.e., a reduction of manufacturing concentration during this same period, which gives some pause. The factor is perhaps best seen as evidence of a local economy that is in transition, gaining (or losing) the principal features of a national or regional *market center*. Planners will want to carefully consider the implications of trends for their areas. Local areas that are in fact becoming market centers (i.e., not merely increasing relative market center functions due to losses of manufacturing) require well-designed improvements in transportation systems and wholesaling district development, accommodation of expected increases in support firms and industries, and projected export behavior of local manufacturers. Conversely, planners in areas that show trend reductions in market center concentration will want to be satisfied that such reductions are not merely temporary due to recent gains in manufacturing that may later be matched by expanded marketing and distribution of manufactured goods.

Factor V consists of several measures, all of which can be seen to revolve around relative changes in the concentration of manufacturing employment. Since the location quotients of manufacturing would increase most rapidly in places with lower levels of manufacturing activity, and since manufacturing grew only very slightly during the mid-1970s, this factor is probably measuring the induced changes in economic structure of areas that experience the multiplier effect of manufacturing change. Reductions in debt burden per capita reflect existing levels of public infrastructure debt that is spread over the growing work force and population of areas experiencing growth of manufacturing. Similarly, unemployment levels in those areas shift downward with added manufacturing and induced service employment while per capita savings rise as manufacturing payrolls ripple through household budgets to consumer markets. Utility rates also tend to increase as new manufacturing demand for energy expands. Opposite scores on this factor capture the structural changes that metropolitan areas experience when they lose manufacturing employment. Although similar in some respects to the economic distress factor, this factor is nevertheless distinct because it groups all impacts specifically associated with changes in the *manufacturing multiplier*.

Factor VI includes high loads from two closely related industry sectors associated with changes in residential demand: increased concentration of both retail services and consumer services. Changes in location quotient of these measures can result when consumer demand in an area that had previously expanded rapidly in the production of export goods and services (thereby temporarily depressing the location quotient of retail and consumer services) eventually induces permanent retail and service expansion. Stable or even slightly declining levels of local consumer demand in places that suddenly lose large shares of other industrial employment also show an increase in the measured concentration of retail and other consumer services. Although readily associated with conventional assumptions about economic base theory, this factor is probably best thought of as measuring more general shifts in the *residentiary functions* of economic structure within metropolitan areas.

Scores from each of the six factors show the degree to which any particular metropolitan economy is changing more than the average change of all 202 metropolitan economies, and the sign indicates direction of change. Since each factor measures change in proportion or rate of key economic indicators, a substantial factor score (i.e., greater than one positive or negative standard deviation from a standardized mean score of zero) identifies a place where important structural changes were under way through the late 1970s. The changes may continue or they may have already precipitated a consequent series of adjustments in policy and performance of which local economic development planners are doubtless aware. However, these major changes are basic evidence of forces that tend to propel a local economy along some long-term development path or trajectory. Therefore, this analysis should be used to form the initial basis for further inquiry and systematic conjecture about policy for future developments.[8]

Factor scores of less than one standard deviation clearly indicate less change relative to all other U.S. economies, but even small scores in the 0.4 to 0.9 range may indicate that a local economy has either just completed or is about to begin a period of substantial structural change. In such instances, local economic development planners would want to look for patterns of two or three modest factor scores to determine whether together they indicate a tendency for structural change. (Factors with modest scores also help analysts interpret the meaning of the significant changes in an area economy that are indicated by larger factor scores.) As one might expect, some of the largest metropolitan economies or those with industrial mixes most similar to the U.S. economy tend to show patterns of modest factor scores; conversely, small or relatively unique metropolitan economies frequently display substantial scores on one or more factors.

Policy Turbulence and Development Paths

The extraordinary economic turbulence of the 1970s and early 1980s brings with it a need for improved analytic perspectives toward policies for local economies. Economic development planners must become accustomed to the notion of planning during periods of simultaneous cyclical and structural change and to adopt improved approaches that account for these dynamics.[9] Of equal importance is the recognition that cyclical dynamics and structural changes constitute important evidence of how local economies are moving along some development path.

The evidence presented on cyclical behavior offers at least two new findings that planners must address. First, national business cycles can be eliminated as the principal causes of instability in nonconformant metropolitan economies. Knowing this allows local analysts to direct their attention toward other exogenous influences on their local economic cycles. Second, over half of all metropolitan economies are sufficiently conformant $[R^2 > .50]$ with the national business cycle that local countercyclical policies must be considered (Vernez et al. 1977). The high proportion of conformant metropolitan economies that experienced asymmetric contractions and expansions of their business cycles indicates the need for carefully tailored countercyclical or stabilization policies. The asymmetry of cyclical behavior also indicates direction and strength of forces that help push a local economy along its development path and through a consequent series of structural changes.

More important in the long run, however, are the asymmetric contractions and recoveries that may affect *different* industrial sectors or basic economic conditions in a given metropolitan area during each successive phase, thereby exaggerating structural changes already under way or perhaps inducing such changes. For example, the Chicago metropolitan economy is sufficiently large and similar to the U.S. economy that little structural change is apparent from an examination of its scores (see appendix table 4A.1). While some modest loss of headquarter function is indicated, clearer indications of dynamics in the Chicago SMSA economy are captured in its cyclical behavior: table 4.1 indicates the metropolitan economy is affected by a strong negative ratchet. Therefore, economic development planners would want to examine which specific sectors are affected adversely during these cycles and whether, for instance, such cycles are related to modest shifts in headquarter function.

Turning to questions posed by evidence of structural shifts in local economies, development planners can use this evidence to better understand the direction and comparative magnitude of specific structural changes that may frustrate or accelerate contemplated development strategies. Such evidence is particularly valuable for understanding metropolitan economies whose cycles do not conform closely to the U.S. business cycle because of unique local circumstances.[10] The Baton Rouge SMSA is a good example. Its cyclical behavior is quite unlike other cities and its cycle conforms poorly with the U.S. cycle ($R^2 = 0.21$), yet it exhibits two substantial change factors (scores greater than 1.00) and three additional modest change factors (scores greater than 0.40, but less than 1.00). From these factor scores alone one might infer that Baton Rouge has experienced substantial increases in price or productivity advantage, has lost some of its relative concentration in corporate complex activities, has increased its manufacturing distribution and market center (port) functions, and is reducing its level of fiscal and personal income distress. In this instance, local economic development planners in Baton Rouge can use such evidence to piece together a combination of substantial structural changes or tendencies for structural change to estimate whether it is headed along a recognizable and desirable development path. The momentum behind these structural changes is often sufficient to completely overpower the effect of some superficial policies or to disproportionately exaggerate effects of other policies. This potential has to be taken into account by local officials and planners if the economy seems to be headed along an undesirable path.

Finally, some local economies experience cyclical behavior *and* structural changes that are sufficiently strong to mark indelibly their development paths. One such example is the Stamford, Connecticut, SMSA. It is affected by a powerful positive ratchet whose growth effects through successive business cycles totally overwhelm its autonomous rate of decline. Moreover, it is quite apparent that these cyclical effects are closely related to Stamford's becoming a major corporate white-collar complex (Factor II) and to its acquiring markedly greater concentrations of retail, residentiary service functions (Factor VI).

These simple illustrations demonstrate the potential value of carefully examining the five cyclical characteristics and six structural change factors estimated for each metropolitan economy. Together, they afford economic development planners a coherent perspective of the dynamics under way in local economics.[11] The ability of economic development planners to devise sound policies and strategies and to guide their local economies through turbulent periods of continuous change may very will hinge on such perspectives.

Author's Note: Edward M. Bergman and Harvey A. Goldstein are professor and associate professor of city and regional planning at the University of North Carolina, Chapel Hill. They teach and conduct research in the areas of urban economic development, local economic and industrial policy, and planning theory. They are members of Planners Network. This research was supported by funds provided by the Office of Research and Development, Employment and Training Administration, U.S. Department of Labor, Contract #21-36-80-32. The authors gratefully acknowledge the valuable contributions of Nancy A. Paulson, Albert Hardy, Dan Gaulin, and Bill Drummond. Comments from Thierry Noyelle and anonymous JAPA reviewers proved very helpful in revising this essay.

5 Cyclical Startups and Closures in Key Industries of America's Cities and Suburbs

Marie Howland

A severe national recession in 1973–75, followed by a weak expansion from 1975 to 1979, and another recession in 1979–82 have left many local governments with persistent unemployment and budgetary problems. While these problems are especially acute for central cities adversely affected by sectoral shifts in the national economy and a deteriorating employment base, previously healthy suburban areas have not been immune. Communities have responded to these problems with accelerated economic development efforts that center on advertising campaigns, site selection assistance, financial incentives, tax abatements, and employment training programs. The expressed purpose of these programs is to attract new businesses and retain existing ones, increasing or stabilizing the local tax base and providing jobs to unemployed residents.

In many places, however, these efforts are not as effective as they could be because they do not take into account the effects of national business cycles on local employment. This essay analyzes those effects and suggests how localities can adapt their economic development strategies to be more successful. One thing we have learned from the experience of the 1970s and 1980s is that swings in the business cycle are frequent. Thus, an understanding of local responses to national cycles will continue to be relevant for improving and guiding future local development efforts.

Employment growth is determined by rates of job creation resulting from births of new establishments, job dissolution resulting from establishment closings, employment changes stemming from expansions or contractions in continuing plants, and employment changes resulting from the net migration of establishments. Local development programs are based on a similar framework: specific development strategies are formulated to generate births of new firms, to encourage expansions of existing firms, to encourage the in-migration of establishments, to discourage local closings, to discourage contractions of existing firms, and to discourage the out-migration of establishments.

The availability of Dun and Bradstreet data on annual employment totals and locations for individual establishments permits us to analyze local employment changes on a disaggregated basis. This study combined four years of Dun and Bradstreet data to creat employment histories for more than 53,000 establishments in three important manufacturing industries: machine tools, electronic components, and motor vehicles.

The results indicate two findings of immediate interest. One is that cyclical fluctuations in metropolitan employment are explained not by expansions and contractions in employment in continuing establishments, but by fluctuations in births and closings of establishments. Employment in continuing establishments, which was expected to contract during recessions and expand during recoveries, was found to be stable over the cycle or to behave countercyclically. Instead, fluctuations in establishment births and closings explain employment growth and decline over the cycle. During expansions in the national economy, local growth occurs because of a high establishment birthrate and a low establishment failure rate. During downswings in the national economy a rising failure rate and falling birthrate are responsible for employment decline.

Second, each industry's cyclical pattern is different in central cities and in suburbs; an industry experiences greater cyclical variability in the area where it is growing most rapidly. A strong expansion in a healthy region, which is explained primarily by high birthrates, turns into a relatively severe recession when the newly created firms fail at high rates during a downswing in the national economy.

These findings have important implications for local development planning. Development strategies in a local agency's portfolio should adjust to the phase of the business cycle. During expansions in the national economy, rates of business formation are high, and local development efforts should emphasize creating firms and attracting branches. However, during periods of national economic decline, strategies to attract new establishments will be less effective, and a larger share of development efforts should be devoted to helping struggling firms maintain their foothold. The results of this study show that many potentially viable businesses created during the expansion fail during the subsequent recession because newly created firms lack adequate capital and established markets to see them through periods of slack demand (see, for example, Litvak and Daniels 1979; U.S. Small Business Administration 1983). The local development portfolio, therefore, should include short-term working capital loans to aid promising businesses threatened with failure, and this focus should sharpen during downswings in the national economy. Expansions in continuing firms occur throughout the cycle—during recessions as well as expansions. Thus, programs designed to aid these establishments need not be adjusted over the cycle.

Previous Literature

Struyk and James (1975) studied employment changes in all manufacturing industries within four Standard Metropolitan Statistical Areas. Their study covered the growth period from 1965 to 1968 and concluded that the manufacturing industry was decentralizing. The authors found that the most important component of metropolitan employment growth was in establishments that remained stationary throughout the observation period; they also found that natural increase—births minus closings—played a secondary role. The spatial pattern of births greatly favored areas outside the central city; closings were, in general, as high in suburbs as in central cities. Our data on all SMSAS and three industries in the growth period from 1973 to 1979 are consistent with these findings.

Birch (1979) used the Dun and Bradstreet data to analyze the components of regional employment change. Birch studied the periods from 1972 to 1974 and 1974 to 1976. Both periods include one year of economic expansion and one year of contraction. Birch's analysis shows that the sequential closing and migration of establishments plays a small role in regional differences in growth rates, particularly in the growth of the Sunbelt. He found high establishment birthrates and on-site expansions to be the most important components of change and the primary factors in the shift of employment from Frostbelt to Sunbelt; finally, he noted that plant closing rates are similar in all regions.

A local economy's industrial composition has been found to be an important determinant of its response to national cycles (Borts 1969; Browne 1978). Industries vary in their responsiveness to the business cycle, and local economies composed of a high proportion of cyclically sensitive industries will experience greater exposure to national cycles. In a study of the cyclical variability of central-city and suburban economies, Manson (1983) found central-city economies to be more stable over the business cycle than suburban economies. The major reason was that both durable goods manufacturing income and construction income are sensitive to the business cycles, and a lower proportion of central-city income is generated in these industries than is true for the suburbs.

Other authors, such as Borts (1960), Engerman (1965), and Howland (1984), have hypothesized that a local economy's rate of growth influences its cyclical variability. Borts correlated manufacturing growth rates in thirty-three states with the states' cyclical amplitude and found that strong-growth states were more variable than weak-growth states. The findings from the Engerman study were similar. In a study using state level data Howland develops a model that holds industrial composition and a number of other variables constant. She found that employment in states with new capital was more cyclically variable than employment in states with an old capital stock. We would expect a state's rate of secular growth to be highly and negatively correlated with the age of its capital stock. The study reported here uses data that are disaggregated by industry and establishments and finds results consistent with those just reported.

Another hypothesis holds that employment in headquarters is less vulnerable to economic cycles than employment in branch locations. In this interpretation cities can be divided into "command and control" centers and "production" centers (Noyelle and Stanback 1983). The former have a high concentration of service and management activities that should insulate them from cyclical fluctuations. Firms are more reluctant to lay off managerial and administrative employees during recessions than production workers.

All three hypotheses suggest that employment fluctuations in suburbs should be greater than those of central cities. A favorable industrial composition, slow economic growth, and a large proportion of employment in administrative rather than productive tasks should mitigate employment swings in central cities.

This study controls for city-suburb differences in industry structure by considering three industries rather than metropolitan economies in total. The results will shed light on the second hypothesis by comparing long-run rates of industry growth in metropolitan areas with the local economy's cyclical variability. Unfortunately, the Dun and Bradstreet data will not permit a testing of the third hypothesis because the data do not distinguish between administrative and production employees by establishment.

Methodology

All establishments in three industries were drawn from the D&B Duns Market Identifiers (DMI) files for 1973, 1975, 1979, and 1982. The data set includes 27,014 machine tool establishments, 14,067 electronic component establishments, and 11,909 motor vehicle establishments.[1] Because the sum of employment in each industry is equal to 100 percent of total employment as reported by the *Country Business Patterns* (U.S. Bureau of the Census, 1973; 1975; 1979), the data are treated as a census rather than a sample.

These industries represent an average-growth industry, machine tools, which grew at a national annual average rate of 2.2 percent from 1973 to 1979; a fast-growth industry, electronic components, which grew at a national annual average rate of 4.7 percent over the same period; and a stagnating industry, motor vehicles, which grew at a national annual average rate of 0.9 percent over the period. The long-run growth pattern of machine tools is similar to that of all manufacturing employment, which grew at an annual average rate of 2.5 percent from 1973 to 1979. Total employment in the three industries represented 3 percent of all manufacturing employment in 1979 (U.S. Bureau of Labor Statistics 1983).

D&B assigns a unique Duns number to each establishment. The four DMI data sets (one for each year) were merged by combining all data for each establishment under one Duns number. The merger of the four DMI files permitted an analysis of employment changes in individual establishments for two recessions, 1973–75 and 1979–82, and one expansion, 1975 to 1979. If an establishment existed in the file in an earlier year but not in a later year, the establishment was registered as a closing. If the establishment was absent from the file in an earlier year and appeared in a later year and had a date of birth

that corresponded to an interim year, the establishment was registered as a birth. If the establishment relocated, it was tagged as a
mover. The merged data set then was merged again with the U.S.
Bureau of the Census City Reference File. This second merger used
Zip Codes to identify each metropolitan establishment as having
either a central-city or suburban location, using 1977 central-city
and suburban boundaries throughout the period studied.

One adjustment had to be made in the estimation of jobs created
as a result of new business formations. Our work with the D&B data
suggests that the DMI file accounts for 13.7 percent of all new employment in the machine tool and electronic components industries that
results from establishment births in a given year. By comparison, the
DMI file appears to account for a much higher proportion of all new
activity in the motor vehicles industry, primarily because there are
fewer new establishments to record. To correct for the underreport-
ing of new establishments in machine tool and electronic components industries, employment gains resulting from births of new
firms were extracted from the file and scaled upward by 1/0.137.
Birthrates in motor vehicles are unchanged. Total employment
changes in central cities and suburbs reflect this adjustment.[2]

Findings

The central-city and suburban growth rates (peak to peak), disaggregated by components of change, are shown in table 5.1. Machine
tools and motor vehicles are seen to be decentralizing, whereas the
electronic components industry is becoming more centralized. For
example, the average annual growth rate for central-city machine
tool firms was −2.4 percent, whereas the suburban growth rate was 4
percent. Electronic components employment grew at an annual average rate of 2.2 percent in the central cities and only 0.5 percent in the
suburbs. Motor vehicles employment declined by 3.7 percent in the
suburbs and declined by even more in central cities at 6.5 percent.

Unfortunately, data are not yet available on the relative growth
rates of central-city and suburban manufacturing for all nonagricultural employment for the period from 1970 to 1980. Census employment data are available, however, for one hundred cities in 1960 and
1970; those data show that central-city employment grew by 2 percent over the decade. In ninety Standard Metropolitan Statistical

Table 5.1 Peak-to-peak growth rates in central cities and suburbs, subdivided into components of change, for machine tools, electronic components, and motor vehicles (percentages), 1973–79

Industry and components of change	Location	
	Central city	Suburbs
Machine tools		
Births	4.3	7.1
Closings	7.0	5.4
Net expansion	0.5	1.9
Migration	−0.2	0.4
Total	−2.4	4.0
Electronic components		
Births	6.9	5.9
Closings	7.3	8.1
Net expansion	3.5	2.3
Migration	−0.9	0.4
Total	2.2	0.5
Motor vehicles		
Births	0.3	0.5
Closings	5.7	5.2
Net expansion	−0.9	0.7
Migration	−0.2	0.3
Total	−6.5	−3.7

Source: Urban Institute Analysis of the Dun and Bradstreet Duns Market Indicator files.

Areas 1970 employment could be calculated for the part of the area that was within its 1960 boundaries; the growth rate for those SMSAS was 13.7 percent, indicating that suburban employment exceeded that of central cities (Bradbury et al. 1982, 32). While the data are not completely comparable, due to differences in the definition of employment by place of residence in the census and by place of work in the Dun and Bradstreet file, these data do suggest that the pattern identified for machine tools and motor vehicles is typical for most employment. Data on central counties' share of SMSA income in manufacturing is consistent with these data on the suburbanization trend. Manson (1983, 108) found that, in 1969, 74 percent of SMSAS' manufacturing income was generated in central counties. By 1980 the figure had fallen to 71 percent. The tendency for electronic components to centralize indicates that innovative manufacturing industries still find central cities the most profitable location for new investment, but that this is not the general pattern for all manufacturing. It should be noted, moreover, that manufacturing employment is not growing in all suburbs and declining in all central cities. There are clear regional variations in these patterns (see Bradbury et al. 1982).

As expected, the data indicate that uneven metropolitan growth is explained by uneven birth- and expansion rates. For example, suburban machine tool employment grew faster than central-city employment because suburban areas experienced higher birthrates of new establishments and greater expansion rates in continuing firms (see table 5.1). There is some tendency for closings to be higher in the slow-growth area. For example, employment losses in machine tools due to closings were 7.0 percent in central cities and only 5.4 percent in the suburbs. The net migration of establishments in and out of central cities and suburbs plays a small but positive role in the decentralization of employment.[3] For example, the net out-migration of plants from central cities explains only 8 percent of the 2.4 percent employment loss in the machine tool industry during the period 1973–79. Net in-migration of establishments to suburbs explains only 10 percent of the 4.0 percent employment growth in the machine tool industry.

These data indicate that central-city and suburban differences in growth result primarily from uneven birth- and expansion rates. Local areas capture a disproportionate share of aggregate employment growth through high rates of new business formations and expansions in continuing establishments. In the long run spatial differences in closing rates and the net migration of establishments also appear to play a role in the suburbanization of metropolitan employment.

It was expected that this general pattern would explain employment fluctuations over the business cycle. Employment declines during recessions were expected to be caused by contractions in existing establishments, rising establishment closing rates, and falling rates of establishment formation. Expansions in existing establishments, falling establishment closing rates, and rising rates of new business formation were expected to explain employment growth during the economic recovery. This pattern was not found.

Table 5.2 shows the annual average employment rates over the

Table 5.2   Annual average rates of central-city and suburban employment change over the business cycle, by component of change (percentages)

Industry and location	1973–75	1975–79	1979–82
Machine tools			
Central city			
Births	2.36	4.59	3.82
Closings	7.96	5.60	9.14
Net expansion	0.39	0.53	1.54
Net migration	−0.32	−0.16	−0.42
Total	−5.53	−0.64	−4.19
Suburbs			
Births	4.92	7.82	5.34
Closings	8.27	4.18	7.05
Net expansion	3.17	1.38	1.19
Net migration	0.43	0.36	0.54
Total	0.25	5.38	0.02
Electronic components			
Central city			
Births	2.95	8.43	4.91
Closings	9.74	6.16	7.09
Net expansion	3.26	3.52	1.65
Net migration	−0.42	−0.04	0.09
Total	−3.95	5.75	−0.44
Suburbs			
Births	3.71	6.57	6.85
Closings	10.85	6.45	6.65
Net expansion	3.24	1.71	2.34
Net migration	0.52	0.34	0.01
Total	−3.33	2.17	2.55
Motor vehicles			
Central cities			
Births	0.11	0.32	0.28
Closings	3.67	5.41	5.50
Net expansion	3.62	−2.94	4.62
Net migration	−0.23	−0.13	−0.06
Total	−.17	−8.16	−9.90
Suburbs			
Births	0.28	0.66	0.76
Closings	4.60	5.48	8.94
Net expansion	−7.15	4.72	−0.37
Net migration	0.46	0.25	0.23
Total	−11.01	0.15	−8.32

Source: Urban Institute Analysis of the Dun and Bradstreet Duns Market Indicators files.

business cycle in the three industries. These rates are presented for central cities and suburbs. Table 5.2 further disaggregates the growth rates into components of employment change resulting from births, closings, net expansions, and migration.

Aggregate growth rates show the expected cyclical pattern; that is, growth rates rise during the expansions and fall during the recessions. This cyclical employment pattern appears to be explained primarily by fluctuations in establishment births and deaths rather than by expansions and contractions in employment at existing plants. Establishment birthrates rise during expansions and fall during recessions (see table 5.2). Closing rates also show the expected pattern of rising during recessions and falling during expansions. However, employment in continuing establishments rarely coincides with the cycle and frequently behaves countercyclically. For example, growth in central-city machine tool employment in continuing establishments was positive during both recessions as well as during the expansion. Employment growth in these establishments was greater during the 1979–82 recession (1.5) than during the expansion (0.5). That pattern is exhibited in several cases for all three industries. One explanation for this countercyclical employment pattern in ongoing operations is that these establishments are hardy survivors that not only maintain established markets and contracts during recessions, but also pick up contracts and production from establishments that fail during national slack periods. Another explanation is that work subcontracted during good economic times must be conducted in-house when subcontractors fail during the recession. A clear exception to this countercyclical pattern is suburban motor vehicles employment, where numbers of jobs in continuing establishments declined during the two recessions and rose during the expansion.

We suspected that the migration of establishments would slow during recessions and rise during expansions. Establishments were expected to delay relocation plans during periods of uncertain demand and unused capacity at existing plants and to proceed with plans to relocate when the economy recovered. That, however, does not appear to be the case. There is no evidence that relocation patterns are influenced by national business cycles. Central-city employment losses resulting from the net out-migration of establishments are as likely to increase during recessions as they are to fall.

A second set of results compares cyclical fluctuations in central-

Table 5.3 Differences between average annual growth rates during expansions and recessions

	Location	
Industry and period	Central city	Suburbs
Machine tools		
1973–79	4.89	5.13
1975–82	3.55	5.36
Electronic components		
1973–79	9.70	5.49
1975–82	6.19	−0.38
Motor vehicles		
1973–79	−8.0	11.16
1979–82	1.84	8.47

Source: Calculated from the data presented in table 5.2

city employment with fluctuations in suburban employment. Because of the absence of a quarterly or monthly employment series for central cities and suburbs, the amplitude of local business cycles is measured as the annual average growth rate during the expansion minus the growth rate during the recession. The larger the difference in annual growth rate between the recessions and the expansions, the larger the swings in local employment. A negative value signifies that a growth rate rose during the recession and fell during the expansion; in other words, the local economy behaved counter-cyclically. This method of measuring the amplitude of local cycles is similar to that of Friedenberg and Bretzfelder (1980).

The differences between average annual growth rates during expansions and recessions are displayed in table 5.3. These results indicate that, for all industries, employment levels are most volatile where jobs are growing most rapidly. Machine tool and motor vehicles employment is more variable in suburbs, and electronic components employment is more variable in central cities.

To determine which components of employment change are responsible for an industry's greater cyclical variability where it grows most rapidly, differences in central-city and suburb establishment birth- and closing rates during the recession and expansion were calculated. Establishment birthrates during the expansion minus establishment birthrates during the recession and establishment closing rates dur-

Table 5.4 Variability of birthrates and closing rates

	Central city		Suburbs	
	Births	Closings	Births	Closings
Machine tools				
1973–79	2.2	−2.4	2.9	−4.1
1975–82	−0.8	−3.5	2.5	−2.9
Electronic components				
1973–79	5.5	−3.5	2.9	−4.4
1975–82	3.6	−0.9	−0.3	−0.1
Motor vehicles				
1973–79	0.2	1.7	0.4	0.9
1975–82	0.0	−0.1	−0.1	−3.5

Source: Calculated from the data presented in table 5.2

ing expansion minus establishment closing rates during the recession indicate the amplitude of swings in establishment formations and dissolutions over the business cycle. The results, shown in table 5.4, generally show that both establishment birthrates and closing rates are more variable where the industry is growing most rapidly. For machine tools and motor vehicles, establishment births and closings are more cyclically variable in suburbs. For electronic components, establishment births are more cyclically variable in central cities, whereas fluctuations in closing rates for this industry are similar in both central cities and suburbs. This pattern indicates that the greater cyclical variability of both establishment birth- and closing rates explains the greater employment variability of fast-growth local economies.

Closing rates are more variable in fast-growth areas because employment in new firms is a higher proportion of total employment in fast-growth areas, and these new firms are susceptible to failure during recessions. Our analysis of the Dun and Bradstreet data confirms the view that new firms close at higher rates than well-established firms. For example, machine tool firms aged zero to four years represented 32 percent of all closings in the United States between 1979 and 1982 and only 24 percent of all machine tool firms. Firms aged twenty to twenty-nine years accounted for only 12 percent of all closings in the United States from 1979 to 1982 and yet represented 15 percent of all firms. This pattern for machine tools holds for electronic components and motor vehicles as well as for firms in general. The U.S. Small Business Administration found that 53.6 percent of all business failures in 1980 were firms aged zero to five years. Only 18.3 percent of failures were in firms aged eleven years and older (U.S. Small Business Administration 1983, 238). Thus fast-growth economies experience high rates of plant closings during recessions because these economies have a concentration of new firms that fail at high rates during the downturn in the economy.

Variability in establishment birthrates also contributes to the cyclical sensitivity of fast-growth areas. One reason why a locality experiences strong economic growth is because new firms and branches find it attractive. Establishment birthrates have further to fall in these fast-growth areas than they do in slow-growth areas where the establishment birthrate is already low.

Summary of Findings and Implications for Economic Development

The data indicate that the pattern of long-run growth differs from that of short-run fluctuations. Metropolitan areas exhibiting strong long-run growth do so because of high rates of new business formations, high net expansions and low closing rates. The net migration of establishments from central cities to suburbs plays a positive but minor role in the suburbanization of manufacturing employment.

That pattern of long-run growth does not, however, hold for short-run fluctuations in local employment. Fluctuations in birth- and death rates (rather than fluctuations in employment in continuing firms or migration patterns) explain growth and decline in local employment over the business cycle. One implication is that fast-growth economies also tend to be more cyclically variable than slow-growth economies. The high proportion of mature firms in the area where establishment birthrates are low promotes cyclical stability since mature firms are more likely than new firms to have the retained earnings, established credit ratings, and/or secure markets to survive recessions (U.S. Small Business Administration 1983, 160–63).

This pattern of short-run employment growth and decline suggests new possibilities for increasing the effectiveness of local economic development strategies, especially in fast-growth economies. Local development programs include a package or portfolio of tools and techniques. Some of these tools and techniques are loan guarantees, grants, capital subsidies, industrial revenue bonds, equity financing, tax abatements, site selection assistance, streamlining of regulations, advertising campaigns, labor force training programs, and public infrastructure development. The relative emphasis on many of these tools should shift with the business cycle.

During periods of national economic expansion, when new business formations are high and branches are being established at high rates, local development strategies should emphasize the attraction of branch plants and the incubation of new firms. Site selection assistance, acceleration of the permit approval process, use of loan guarantees and industrial revenue bonds for plant and equipment for small firms, and customized training for potential employees are especially appropriate strategies during this phase of the cycle. Human and financial resources should be shifted toward these strategies. During periods of rapid national growth and high rates of establishment formation, development strategies designed to compete for and encourage new firms are more likely to yield success. As the national and local economies move into a period of economic decline, however, the locale should shift emphasis from incubating new firms and attracting their branches to retaining potentially failing firms.

A large proportion of the establishment failures in the recessionary phase of the business cycle are firms created in the most recent expansion. Many of these firms are viable in the long run but have had the misfortune to be hit by a recession before sufficient profits are generated to provide retained earnings, before a credit rating with lenders and suppliers is established, and before markets are secured. During periods of cutbacks, purchasers are more likely to continue agreements with long-term trading partners. To maximize local job growth or to minimize job loss, the local development portfolio should shift its emphasis to the retention of jobs. Financial resources and personnel should focus on identifying and evaluating viable establishments with financial problems and negotiating and providing short-term working capital loans or loan guarantees to carry fledgling firms through the recession.

A pool of working capital funds could be generated through general tax revenues, general obligation bonds repaid through tax revenues, cooperative agreements among private banks to pool funds and diversify the risk, or through loan guarantees. Loans do not necessarily need to be provided at below the market rate for this type of "risky" firm. Earlier work has shown that it is access to capital, not the cost of capital, that is the most severe constraint and cause of failure for small firms (Litvak and Daniels 1979). Therefore, a job retention strategy, such as that proposed here, need not be a costly addition to local development programs. Moreover, offering loans at market interest rates would discourage firms that are adequately served by private capital markets from applying for government assistance and would weed out marginal applicants for loans.

For most localities this responsive strategy to business cycles would require few alterations in current programs. One policy change would have to be the provision of working capital loans or loan guarantees. Most local governments that provide capital to private businesses do so only for the acquisition of plant and capital equipment. The strategy suggested here requires the release of funds for working capital as well.

In addition, the strategy proposed here would require a less specialized staff. Economic development officials would have to be able to shift functions with changes in external economic conditions.

Local development efforts to attract new firms and branches should not completely halt during recessions. Rather, scarce economic development resources should be reallocated so the relative importance of job creation strategies declines during recessions when the number of new business formations is low and the competition and cost of attracting these establishments rises.

Development tools and techniques designed to promote business expansions in ongoing establishments or to court firms considering relocation do not require adjustment over the cycle. The data in table 5.2 show that expansion and relocation plans for many establishments continue throughout recessions as well as during the recovery. Development strategies that promote expansions in existing plants include financing for new capital, technical and administrative assistance, zoning and regulatory relief, and public infrastructure investment. These strategies are as likely to be as effective in recessionary periods as in growth periods. Strategies designed to attract relocating establishments include advertising at trade meetings and in trade magazines, making contacts with businesses likely to be relocating, and financial incentives. Since relocation plans continue throughout all phases of the business cycle these strategies also do not need to be reduced or augmented over the cycle.

This business-cycle-sensitive strategy can be applied to economies or to particular "target" industries. While the strategy is applicable to all local economies, or to specific industries, it is especially appropriate for those that are fast-growth. As indicated by the data analysis above, it is fast-growth economies and industries with their high proportion of young firms that are particularly susceptible to business failures during the recession. As shown in table 5.2, however, slow-growth industries exhibit a pattern similar to but less dramatic than fast-growth industries. For these slow-growth industries, failure rates also rise during the recession and fall during the expansion. Establishment birthrates show the reverse of the expected pattern. Thus, the proposed strategy also would be appropriate for, and would improve development planning in, slow-growth industries and economies as well as those that are fast-growth.

There are limited data requirements to implementing a cyclically adjusted development program. A locale must be able to determine whether rising business failure rates are a sign of secular or cyclical decline. Empirical research on local business cycles has shown that the magnitude and timing of a local cycle cannot be predicted by the national cycle. The local response to the national cycle is not consistent over time (Vernez et al. 1977; Dunn 1982). Therefore, the local cycle will have to be carefully monitored. Fortunately, the U.S. Bureau of Labor Statistics provides monthly employment totals for the states as well as for most of the metropolitan areas that are also available in considerable industry detail. Another source of data is the unemployment rate, which also is available monthly by state and for some labor market areas. These data are collected by the Census Bureau for the Bureau of Labor Statistics.

Stabilization of Local Employment

To my knowledge there are no local development policies that adjust strategies to phases of the business cycle. However, one side effect of the business-cycle-sensitive development strategy proposed here would be the stabilization of local employment over the business cycle. Several local stabilization policies that have been implemented widely either have been initiated by the federal government or are side effects of other federal, state, or local programs. Federal support for local stabilization programs has greatly diminished, and recent evidence shows that persistently high interest rates and budgetary problems have reduced the stabilizing effects of local government expenditures.

The federal government set up a program to promote cyclical stability in local economies with the "Economic Stimulus Package of 1977." This legislation provided revenue-sharing assistance and earmarked grant monies for local public works or public service employment to state and local governments in times of recession. In both cases the funding amount was tied to the economic condition of the local economy. Empirical evidence indicated that such attempts to stabilize local economies, and ultimately the national economy, would be ineffective, and that may be one reason the program was never extended. Gramlich (1979) estimated the response of state and local expenditures to the types of federal aid included in the Economic Stimulus Program. His estimates indicated that in the short run, federal subventions to states and localities did not result in either an increase in local or state expenditure or a reduction in taxes. Instead, local governments used the money to increase budget surpluses. Clearly, it is the short-run response that is important for reducing local recessionary unemployment. Over the longer run, federal subventions did result in increased state and local expenditures or reduced taxes, which often meant state and local expenditure increases or tax cuts coincided with the recovery, possibly creating inflationary pressure. The changes in local development policy proposed in this chapter should not encounter similar problems since the local development agency initiating the program also would be the implementing agency.

Other studies have found that current local government expenditure patterns have, until the recent recessions, mitigated cyclical employment declines and promoted economic recoveries in the process of meeting other goals. In prior recessions, tax receipts fell, but local government expenditures tended to rise or be stable throughout the downturn for any of several reasons: capital improvements were undertaken as interest rates fell and projects could be carried out at lower costs; budget surpluses acquired during the expansionary phase of the cycle were reduced; and government transfer payments, such as unemployment insurance and welfare, rose (Advisory Commission on Intergovernmental Relations 1978). This pattern was not characteristic of the 1973–80 cycle (Manson 1983, 39–40) and for

128

similar reasons did not stabilize local employment during the 1979–83 cycle. Persistently high interest rates plus slow population growth have discouraged capital investments during the most recent downturns, and two recessions in rapid succession eliminated the budgetary surpluses that locales usually acquired during economic recovery and spent during downturns. The program proposed in this chapter would promote two goals. While designed to promote another goal (in this case, long-run growth), it would have the side effect of stabilizing local economies at a time when other local stabilization programs have become weak and ineffective.

Author's Note: This research was conducted while the author was a consultant to the Public Finance Division at The Urban Institute. The work was funded by a grant from the U.S. Department of Housing and Urban Development to the Urban Institute. The author is grateful to George Peterson for his support, to Terry Whitehouse for her research assistance, and to Melvin R. Levin, Edward Bergman, Mike Luger, and an anonymous referee for their helpful comments.

6 High-Technology Sectors and Local Economic Development
Edward J. Malecki

High technology is now a common term in economic development promotion. The high-tech phenomenon is actually quite recent, having been stimulated by the negative effects of the economic recessions of the past decade and by emerging structural changes in regional and local economies (Bergman and Goldstein 1983a). To a certain extent, the recent recessions exposed the shortcomings of specialized regional economies, as seen in the massive employment reductions in steel, auto, and heavy equipment manufacturing centers of the industrial Midwest. In addition, there has been a growing awareness among planners that technological change is occurring rapidly, but that its effects on local and regional economies are complex and not understood fully (Malecki 1983a). As a result, economic development planners have built their programs on the expectation that regional economies based on high-technology industry, rather than on old-line manufacturing, are less vulnerable to the vicissitudes of the business cycle. Consequently, efforts to transform state and local economies into high-technology areas now pervade industrial development and economic growth policies (Mier 1983). Slogans such as Oklahoma's "High-Tech Triangle," Tennessee's "Technological Corridor," New Mexico's "Rio Grande Research Corridor," and the "solid states" of New Jersey and Tennessee are becoming commonplace in state and local promotions to create employment and attract industry (Banschick 1982; *Business Week* 1983; Farrell 1983).

Nearly all such policies are modeled after the phenomenal growth of a few regions where high technology was an important factor: Silicon Valley (Santa Clara County) in California, Route 128 surrounding Boston, and, to a lesser extent, the Research Triangle area (Raleigh–Durham–Chapel Hill metropolitan area) in North Carolina.

The conditions that generated these prominent examples, however, are unlikely to be replicated in many other locations. There has been little attempt to standardize the definition of "high technology," and local economic development promoters use liberal interpretations to make their areas more attractive to high-tech and other industries. In a local context the most useful definition of "high technology" is based on the activities of local firms, not on the products or services they ultimately produce. Routine manufacturing, even of high-tech products like computers, does not rely on the technical or scientific skills of workers. More often it is concerned mainly with the manual dexterity demanded of, and low wages commanded by, its workers. Innovation and nonroutine production activities—such as research and development, experimental and prototype manufacturing, and small-volume production of new and changing products—are more appropriately regarded as high technology. These criteria are similar to those expressed nearly twenty years ago by Thompson (1965), who said the true economic base of a city was not its manufacturing activity, but the innovative activity located there and the city's ability to generate new firms and activities in the urban area as economic and technological conditions changed. Thus, emerging technologies and unstandardized activities that require skill-intensive labor should be considered the only real high-tech industries. When viewed that way, it is evident that there is relatively little high-technology employment to go around and that high-tech activities' needs are specialized and cannot be manipulated easily over the short term. Instead of being unduly pessimistic, planners need to identify and develop local and regional assets that are related to corporate innovation, including local air service and the professional and technical labor pools associated with local universities.

What Is High Technology?

The definition of high technology is one of the fundamental stumbling blocks in the study of current economic change and the design of local economic development policy. A common interpretation simply includes any industry that has been growing or is likely to grow in employment, but that sort of classification is not very meaningful. Greene, Harrington, and Vinson (1983) note that some discernible technical sophistication is desired in defining high technology, but that this lends itself too easily to subjective judgments.

This section considers two categories of definitions of high technology. The first category represents an attempt to classify industrial sectors of the economy using readily available data. Averages of the amount of research and development or of the percentages of scientific, engineering, and technical occupations in an industry are used to identify sectors that are above average in those areas and, thereby, high technology relative to other sectors (Riche, Hecker, and Burgan 1983; U.S. International Trade Administration 1983). When all above-average sectors are considered high technology, however, a number of rather routine, standardized, and large-volume industries are included that would not be considered "emerging" or knowledge-based, such as petroleum refining, some chemical sectors, and construction machinery. These industries conduct little R&D but have relatively high percentages of technical employees (Armington, Harris, and Odle 1983; Greene, Harrington, and Vinson 1983).

Table 6.1 lists several high-technology sectors that meet the stricter criterion of R&D intensity (the ratio of R&D expenditures to net sales) that is significantly above the average for all industries. It is, therefore, more restrictive than other lists that are based merely on above-average figures.[1] The industries in table 6.1 represented only 5.3 million jobs in 1981 (about five percent of total U.S. employment). The organizational status of high-tech jobs (e.g., whether an establishment is a branch of a large corporation or is an independent firm) also allows planners to evaluate the effectiveness of focusing area promotion on large firms or small enterprises. The evidence on this provides mixed signals. The high-tech jobs tend to be in large firms and large establishments; despite the publicity about small high-tech firms, most high-technology activity takes place within units of the nation's large corporations or large multinational firms (Armington, Harris, and Odle 1983; *Business Week* 1983; Greene, Harrington, and Vinson 1983). That has serious implications for local economies, since branch plants and establishments of large firms tend to have fewer local linkages and are generally less able to generate innovations and new jobs locally (Bergman and Goldstein 1983a; Watts 1981). For example, a common expectation is that high-tech activity will produce new, related spinoff firms and ventures, a

Table 6.1 High-technology sectors of the U.S. economy

Sector	Standard industrial classification	1981 employment (thousands)
Manufacturing		
Guided missiles and spacecraft	376	121.7
Radio and TV receiving equipment	365	142.6
Communications equipment	366	551.8
Electronic components	367	559.2
Aircraft and parts	372	648.9
Office and computing machines	357	463.8
Ordnance and accessories	348	69.1
Drugs and medicines	283	199.2
Industrial inorganic chemicals	281	161.1
Professional and scientific instruments	38	693.2
Engines and turbines	351	133.6
Plastic materials and synthetics	282	195.0
Services		
Computer programming, data processing, and other services	737	334.8
Research and development laboratories	7,391	315.0
Management consulting	7,392	661.7
Commercial testing laboratories	7,397	61.5
Total		5,312.2

Source: The manufacturing sectors in the table are significantly above the national average in R&D intensity (R&D expenditures as a percentage of net sales) and are taken from U.S. International Trade Administration (1983, 37). Service sectors added are above-average in both R&D intensity and in their proportion of scientific, engineering, and technical workers in the industry's labor force. See Armington, Harris, and Odle (1983), Browne (1983), and Greene, Harrington, and Vinson (forthcoming). Employment data are from Greene, Harrington, and Vinson (forthcoming), except for service sectors, which are from Armington, Harris, and Odle (1983).

phenomenon that has been fairly widespread in the Boston and Silicon Valley areas. What is known about such spinoffs, however, suggests that they are likely to occur only when an industry is new, unstandardized, and not yet dominated by large firms. Promoting local growth through spinoffs would require area promoters to shift their emphasis away from attracting branches of large firms.

Until recently, most lists of high-tech industries concentrated exclusively on manufacturing sectors and omitted services entirely, despite the growing importance of many advanced business services (Noyelle 1983a; Stanback and Noyelle 1982). Table 6.1 includes a few service sectors that are clearly high technology, based on their occupational structure, new-product orientation, and linkage with innovative manufacturing: computer programming, data processing, and research and testing laboratories (Armington, Harris, and Odle 1983). Browne (1983) adds management consulting to that list. Including services, despite some shortcomings in data collection at the federal level, allows us to assess local economic potential more meaningfully.

A second category of definitions of high technology focuses on science-based, emerging products, processes, and firms that operate based on state-of-the-art knowledge (Botkin, Dimancescu, and Stata 1982). This strict perspective would include the research and development activity of a firm like Procter and Gamble but not its manufacture of various soap, food, or paper products. Similarly, a firm like General Electric produces not only light bulbs, which are not high tech, but also jet engines and electronic defense systems, which are. This definition of high technology, therefore, distinguishes among the activities related to the various product lines of individual firms. Large corporations and small local firms would have equal effects on the local economy, based on their employment of skilled professional and technical workers. They can be grouped to describe the *activity mix* of local and regional economies, in contrast to the conventional concept of industry mix (Malecki 1981). Nonroutine functions such as R&D, prototype manufacturing, and small-volume production of products such as medical diagnostic scanners and cruise missiles are readily seen as high technology. Routine standardized manufacturing, whether of microelectronic chips, personal computers, or textile products, is not high tech. Abernathy and Utterback (1978) and Porter (1980) emphasize, from a management perspective, the fundamental difference between a focus on new products and a primary concern with low-cost, standardized production. The skilled technical and professional workers needed in the nonroutine activities are the greatest single location factor for new products and high technology (Browning 1980). By contrast, standardized production activity is increasingly mobile—strikingly and globally in the case of electronics—being attracted primarily to low-wage labor, whether in rural areas of the United States or in Mexico, Taiwan, or other Third World nations (Bluestone and Harrison 1982; Hanson 1982; Phillips and Vidal 1983).[2] The global context of economic competition, the topic of the next section, has implications for local economies that have been recognized only recently.

High Technology: From the Global to the Local Context

The effects of technological change have recently come home to many corporations, communities, and individuals as fierce international competition for world markets has reduced employment (and company profits). Several books have stressed the need for American firms to increase R&D, adopt innovations more quickly, and use greater numbers of scientists and technicians to meet and beat the foreign competition (Botkin, Dimancescu, and Stata 1982; Lewis and Allison 1982; Reich 1983). Especially from a national or industrial policy perspective, one of the best ways to reverse losses of markets to foreign producers is for the United States to concentrate on products in which we have a comparative advantage—technology-intensive products and those not amenable to standardized production—since our industries cannot compete in low-cost manufacturing. For example, as computers and semiconductors have become large-volume, standardized products, the advantage has shifted to foreign producers whose low-cost production is either more highly automated or able to use workers in low-wage areas, such as Asia. The recent announcement that Atari, a firm often associated with American high technology, would move all of its video game production from California to Hong Kong and Taiwan tangibly demonstrated that point to many Americans. In both high-tech and low-tech industries, the global mobility of standardized production and its attraction to low labor costs have been the primary factors in industrial location since about 1970 (Bluestone and Harrison 1982).

In some ways, the pressure of foreign competition merely adds another dimension to the traditional problems of industrial specialization of regions. Lower-cost foreign producers have been making inroads for several years into some sectors, such as steel, automobiles, and apparel. Other sectors, such as electronics, computers, and communication equipment, have stood up to competition fairly well. In addition, the prospect of a postindustrial society includes employment growth in services and the sectors that supply them and continued decline in traditional manufacturing or smokestack sectors. Consequently, state and local development groups have learned (belatedly in many cases) that not all jobs are created equal. Some industries will face not only cyclical employment patterns but also continuing pressure for lower costs that will eliminate jobs in some locations entirely, as in many steel towns. High-technology industries are perceived to be less vulnerable to both cyclical and structural changes in the economy and are the objects of nearly all economic development efforts (*Business Week* 1983). This perception of differences among industrial sectors represents a useful improvement for economic development planners, who generally have attempted to attract routine production jobs regardless of the technological level of the industry.

Diversification among sectors, however, does not capture all the benefits of employment diversity. There is another important way in which local economic development strategies need to seek diversity: by type of job activity. A regional economy that is diverse by product but limited to manufacturing and local service jobs is vulnerable both to cyclical and to structural or competitive effects. Empirical studies of capital mobility have found capital to be mobile almost exclusively in relation to routine production activity, rather than to nonroutine functions such as administration and R&D, which show considerable stability in location (Friedmann and Wolff 1982). Diversification to include not only manufacturing and services but also administration and R&D, therefore, would make a local economy far less vulnerable to those influences.

For example, recent research by Hekman (1980a) on the computer industry suggests that computer firms have kept their R&D and administrative activities in places like California, Massachusetts, Minnesota, and New Jersey, while they moved their production facilities to the southeastern states to take advantage of lower labor costs. Koch et al. (1983) assert that high-technology growth in the Southeast is illusory—it consists almost entirely of standardized production and assembly operations that have moved into small towns and rural areas (Park and Wheeler 1983). It might not be long before the production facilities are moved to sites outside the United States where labor costs are even lower than in the rural Southeast. In contrast, Hekman (1980b) also looked at the medical instruments industry, which is characterized by relatively small production volumes. Since most production in that industry cannot be standardized in large plants, most manufacturing takes place near medical research centers, such as Boston and Chicago, where the industry's R&D also is concentrated. It is in sectors such as instruments, communications equipment, and custom electronic equipment that American industry and employment are least threatened. These two industries illustrate that high-technology sectors are not all alike; they should be classified, at least in part, according to whether their production is standardized. That also applies to high-tech services. Recent work by Hall et al. (1983) on the computer software industry in California shows that, even in that sector, the work tasks are becoming polarized into two groups: "supertech" professional jobs, which are likely to remain concentrated in the Los Angeles and San Francisco urban regions; and paraprofessional jobs for more standardized programming tasks, which are being spread out to other parts of the country and, if they follow the pattern of many manufacturing industries, to low-wage foreign locations as well.

Local and regional economies, like national economies, stand to lose routine production jobs to areas whose low wages or automated operations allow competitive pricing in global markets. This seems inevitable in industries that produce products in large volume. Employment in these large-volume sectors has been large historically but is now relatively dispersed around the world, often with devastating impact on local areas. On the other hand, products with small-volume markets, especially new, innovative products and those that continually incorporate technological advances, are more likely to be able to resist competition. Although employment in such sectors will not be large, it is likely to be a relatively reliable economic base both locally and nationally.

High-tech Economic Growth Policies

Policies to attract high-tech employment tend to be only a subset of the policies and programs for industrial development that are common to nearly all states and localities. Traditionally, the top priorities of these programs have been to create jobs and to improve incomes.[3] Achieving those goals, in turn, helps the local tax base and increases demand for goods and services from local business (Levy 1981).

Unfortunately, a very short-term perspective pervades industrial development, and many localities are forced to constantly attract new industry to replace a firm that just left the area for a new location. The roster of available buildings and sites in small towns throughout the United States is tangible evidence of the temporary nature of the employment attracted to many localities.

Industrial development, as we now know it, began in the South in the 1930s, when states were aggressively promoting themselves as attractive locations for industrial plants. The strengths of southern locations were their low-wage and nonunion labor forces, advantages bolstered by industrial revenue bonds and other subsidies (Cobb 1982). Northern states began to counter the South's promotions in the 1950s, emphasizing their relative strengths, such as easy access to transportation, large nearby markets, and skilled labor forces. As long as manufacturing employment was growing generally, the northern states could replace their losses and not be overly concerned about the gains in the southern states. But as employment in manufacturing has declined in absolute terms since the early 1970s, nearly all state and local development agencies have used subsidies and the ready availability of low-wage labor as enticements to industry (Cobb 1982; Goodman 1979; Harrison and Kanter 1978). Still, manufacturing jobs alone have not been plentiful enough to go around in the United States; many have left for foreign locations, so industrial growth promotions have focused recently on services and high technology.

Industrial developers, however, have been slow to discern the very different factors that affect the location decisions that are made for administration, R&D, and small-volume production facilities in any industry. The South's traditional strengths—low-wage labor, low taxes, and subsidies—actually make it difficult to attract skilled professional personnel. Harrison (1982) in New England and Hall et al. (1983), Markusen (1983), and Weiss (1983) in Silicon Valley have identified the "vanishing middle" range of skilled manufacturing jobs in high-tech manufacturing and services. These growing sectors of the dual labor market are characterized at one end by high proportions of clerical and service workers and at the other end by high proportions of professional and technical workers; but they employ few in the kinds of skilled, blue-collar jobs that most state and local programs and training are geared for.

Standard surveys of location factors common in industrial development are of little use across or within manufacturing sectors, because
each industry has different locational needs (e.g., McGraw-Hill 1980;
Vaughan 1977, 41–45). The variation in locational factors relevant to
the various activities of specific firms, rather than to whole industrial sectors, is receiving attention in the corporate location literature (Browning 1980; Lund 1979). Briefly, the most important factors
for a firm's R&D facility or headquarters are the availability (not the
cost) of professional personnel and accessibility to air transportation
—not the market, freight transportation, and raw materials that
remain dominant for the same firm's production facilities (Browning
1980, 58). The importance for nonroutine activities of scientific and
engineering talent presents a different context for development planning from that common for branch production plants.

Skilled Labor, Quality of Life, and Corporate Location

The term quality of life invariably enters into any account of high-
tech growth and location, but the phrase remains very fuzzy in
practice. It is typically used to embrace the set of attractive climatic,
recreational, and cultural attributes found in high-tech areas but not
in most older industrial cities. An urban environment of some threshold size seems most critical since nearly all R&D and headquarters
activities are found in metropolitan areas (Malecki 1980). Generally,
an urban milieu with excellent universities, abundant urban social
and cultural activities, and a job market that allows individuals (and
spouses) to switch jobs without relocating is the type of place where
high-tech activities are found. Several prominent examples in the
United States—Boston, the Los Angeles area, San Francisco Bay, and
northern New Jersey—historically have been centers of research and
headquarters activities, despite high labor costs and high taxes,
because they are attractive to the scientific, engineering, and administrative personnel whom firms must attract and retain for their
nonroutine functions (Malecki 1980). Surveys of scientists and engineers show that they prefer an urban area that has large universities
nearby, good local schools, and well-maintained public facilities
(McElyea 1974).

The reputation of an area as "the right place to be" for R&D personnel may be more important than objective measures of quality of life

(Oakey 1983). Relatively high housing costs may even be an attraction, since they are associated with growing, dynamic cities, rather than static or declining ones (Carruthers and Pinder 1983). That point was made recently by Thomas A. Vanderslice of GTE Corporation, who spoke of the move of a facility from suburban Chicago to Phoenix:

> We went through hell in Northlake [a suburb of Chicago] trying to recruit software people. You can locate in Boston, in spite of its high taxes, because it has a nice ambience. You can do it in parts of Dallas or Houston, but you sure can't do it out in the boonies. (*Business Week* 1983, 87)

Although "the boonies" are typically thought to be small, isolated towns, recruitment difficulties in a large urban area like Chicago show that subjective factors related to the "ambience" and high-tech reputation of an area also enter into the locational preferences of skilled personnel. In short, the traditional checklists of location factors (markets, transportation, labor costs, taxes) fail to be very relevant in the light of a professional labor force that largely determines which sites succeed or fail as high-tech regions.

Universities traditionally are cited as an important locational factor in high-tech economic growth (Clark 1972). Universities train new personnel, allow professionals to improve their skills, and have academic experts whose research can create or interact with commercial technology. One can even consider universities a restrictive factor, as Gurwitz (1982) does, concluding that most regional economies lack the leading technical university necessary to develop a high-tech industrial base. He considers only Stanford, MIT, "and possibly Caltech" as schools important enough to confer a "special competitive advantage" on their regions. A more liberal definition of the quality of universities, employing state levels of per-capita federal R&D at universities and colleges, shows that only seventeen states (nearly all in the Northeast and the West) are above the national average.[4] Texas is on record as trying to put both its major institutions into "first-class" status (Norman 1983). The levels of funding required to put a university into a leading rank is beyond the reach of most states. With the exception of Texas, however, schools away from the Northeast or the West Coast have scarcely been included in the large research programs and arrangements initiated by corporations with universities.

Bollinger, Hope, and Utterback (1983, 7) point out that there is no single set of attributes necessary for a region to be a high-tech region, and they emphasize the "level of interest and enthusiasm of the area's citizens and merchants." Such interest in support of an area's advantages occurs for nonroutine facilities just as it does for production plants, but fewer places are likely to be chosen as R&D or headquarters locations. For example, the Microelectronics and Computer Technology Corporation recently selected a location for its single facility, where four hundred engineers and computer scientists will work. Among the site selection committee's priorities was that the location be "a place where it isn't too expensive to do business and one that will help attract workers. But most important, Microelectronics wants to locate near universities with graduate-level technical programs that produce a pool of potential employees" (Ingrassia 1983, 27). The four finalists favored by engineers and their employers were all Sunbelt cities: Atlanta, Austin, San Diego, and Raleigh-Durham. Austin was selected, in part because of state and local commitment to supporting the university research demanded by high-tech firms.

Conclusions

Two patterns are evident in the location of high-technology activity. First, attracting and keeping professional workers is the highest priority of high-tech employers, who depend on scarce skills needed for research and development and low-quantity production work. Scientists and engineers are more reluctant to relocate than in the past, and that is a factor in favor of locations with existing concentrations of high-tech firms. Housing concerns (including price, availability, and difficulty of selling) are an important factor in the increased inertia of those workers (Wolff 1982). For firms, that translates into a greater need to locate in existing high-tech regions or in places with university, cultural, and employment opportunities. That tends to reinforce the agglomeration economies already present in those areas, and it cumulatively adds to their attraction for future high-tech enterprises, despite high housing prices (Hall et al. 1983; Markusen 1983). Other cities have the disadvantages of both less widespread alternative job opportunities and the inability to create, in the short run, a high-tech aura that would attract technical workers. Pennings (1982) also associates those factors with new firm startups.

The second pattern contrasts with the continued concentration of high-tech employment. Agglomeration economies may operate at a lower size threshold or in different ways than they traditionally have for manufacturing. Examples of small- or medium-sized urban areas attracting significant high-tech activity are Austin, Dayton, Raleigh-Durham, and Tucson. Thus, it would seem that innovative activity can continue to be dispersed to areas outside the historic technological core regions of Boston, Los Angeles, San Francisco, and New Jersey.

Although "there will be only a few new Silicon Valleys," long-term local and national competitiveness would be enhanced by improvements in education, research, urban and rural infrastructure, and cooperation among the private, public, and nonprofit sectors (Denny 1982). In education and research in particular, the very dispersed nature of higher education in the United States suggests that there is potential to generate more widespread local high-tech activity using universities as the foundation for growth. The strong universities of many states often are export industries, producing scientists, engineers, and other professionals for employment elsewhere. At the same time state and local industrial developers seek out manufacturing operations that do not need the skills associated with universities. Having increased employment via new manufacturing plants, developers typically fail to see that a scarce local resource has left the area or the state (often involuntarily) and boosted other regions' attractiveness to high-tech industries.

A problem many regions face is the local economies' inability to provide a variety of job opportunities for their residents. If the local employment mix consists mainly of routine, unskilled manufacturing, retail, and service jobs, the area will fail to retain its university graduates, who will be forced to seek jobs elsewhere. At the same time the absence of local examples of success in nonroutine activities (and the ready availability of jobs for those with few skills and no university education) discourages many from seeking an education that would qualify them for jobs other than in routine activities. Finally, high-tech activity is a product of research, and many state legislators belittle the value of the research component of state universities in comparison with classroom teaching. The schools associated with high-technology locations in California, Massachusetts, and North Carolina are important research institutions, where both undergraduate and graduate students can encounter new ideas and methods as they are developed.

The infrastructure aspects that attract high-technology employees and industries are of three types. First, local airline service is the most important location factor for corporate offices and is second (after professional labor) for R&D (Browning 1980, 58). If areas can improve their airline service, the payoff in employment growth can be significant (Brueckner 1983). Second, cultural and social activities that make up an area's "quality of life" include symphony orchestras, opera and dance companies, theaters, museums, and libraries. To provide and upgrade these aspects of urban life requires cooperation between the public and private sectors. Third, the good schools and well-maintained public facilities demanded by professional employees can be supported generally only by communities with relatively large tax bases. High-tech firms and their employees are less interested in the traditional industrial tax incentives than in the facilities provided by public expenditures.

Perhaps what is needed most is a change in the perspective of politicians and local business communities away from the idea that short-term growth in employment is good, even if long-term potential for more and higher-quality growth is sacrificed. For example, in order to take advantage of local university research, a capital fund could assist businesses started by local research-based entrepreneurs. Research-oriented firms would have a longer-term local impact for the same cost as the tax breaks, infrastructure costs, and industrial development bonds.[5] High technology arises from companies' concern that they remain competitive in the face of rapid change and international competition. Local and regional economic development can succeed only if responsible officials understand that concern and respond by paying attention to the difference between routine and nonroutine activity and to the local conditions that support high technology. Even if few high-technology jobs emerge in some regions, those places will have improved their attractiveness as sites for economic activities that grow less spectacularly than high tech but that use human skills in nonroutine ways. Responding to high technology presents a challenge and opportunity to improve local economies in response to rapid economic and regional change.

Author's Note: The author would like to thank Professors Wilbur R. Maki and Charles R. Adelberg of the University of Minnesota for their comments on an earlier version of this essay and Eleanor M. Thomas of the National Science Foundation for helpful discussions. This research was supported by the National Science Foundation's Division of Policy Research and Analysis.

7 Advanced Services in the System of Cities
Thierry J. Noyelle

The postwar era has witnessed a major transformation of the U.S. economy. At times heralded as the advent of the service economy, this transformation has involved at once reduced employment growth in manufacturing and major changes in the geography of production, major increases in the number of white-collar and service worker jobs, and the rise of new service activities. Despite its importance, considerable confusion remains in explaining the nature of this transformation, both empirically and conceptually. To a large extent "postindustrial" or "service" theoreticians have either overlooked the critical distinction between services to consumers and services to businesses and organizations or obfuscated the nature of the linkages among white-collar work and manufacturing production (Bell 1976; Fuchs 1968 and 1977). In so doing they also have underemphasized or ignored the role that services to producers have played in recent urban development. There are exceptions, of course: Singelmann's 1979 work on services or Pred's 1977 work on urban development, for example.

The postwar decades have seen major shifts in the location of manufacturing assets to the South, away from major urban centers and, more recently, abroad (Bluestone and Harrison 1982). These shifts have been accompanied by a reversal of earlier migration flows (from the South to the North and from the countryside to the cities during the thirties and forties, into their opposites during the sixties and seventies) and by a decreasing need for labor in manufacturing and blue-collar occupations, thus permitting expanded employment in white-collar occupations and the new service activities (Noyelle 1983b). These changes in the geography of production and in the use of labor have occurred largely because major productivity gains have been achieved in the manufacturing sector, mostly as a result of changes in transportation, the introduction of new technologies, and the growth of a whole range of new services and new servicelike activities carried out within manufacturing corporations themselves. The latter are aimed at both complementing production work (e.g., engineering, drafting, testing) and managing, planning, and developing manufacturing resources (e.g., accounting, inventory control, research and development, finance). Within this complex shift of people and resources into the development of these relatively newer or "advanced" services, we see a fundamental feature of the current transformation of American cities.

The Rise of Advanced Services in the Postwar Period

Of the many changes underlying the postwar transformation of the U.S. economy, at least four are of paramount importance: the increasing size of the market, changes in transportation and technology, the growing importance of government and nonprofit institutions, and the rise of the large corporation (Stanback et al. 1981).

Forces of Change

Increasing size of the market. By any measure the U.S. market has grown enormously during the postwar years. Between 1950 and 1980 population grew from 152 to 222 million, the civilian labor force from 62 to 102 million, and disposable income from $362 billion to over $1,000 billion (1972 prices) (U.S. Bureau of Census 1981). There also have been major changes in the character of consumer markets, involving a breakdown of regional barriers and the development of nationwide markets.

In recent years, however, this has led not so much to the development of broad homogeneous markets but to the creation of sales potentials permitting the exploitation of a large number of specialized markets—for the most part nationwide—in which products are specifically designed and advertised to cater to the interests of well-defined segments of the population: the teenager, the hobbyist, the ethnic group, and so on. The result has been a proliferation of products and services and an increased emphasis on product differentiation, branding, styling, and promotion—all combined with an intensified effort to introduce new products and redesign old ones (Toffler 1970).

Changes in transportation and technology. The importance of the changes that have occurred in transportation and technology can hardly be overstated. In terms of transportation, the putting in place of the interstate highway system alongside extensive state road systems and the resulting shift from rail to trucks have permitted a dramatic decentralization of manufacturing facilities away from the oldest and largest metropolitan centers (President's Commission for a National Agenda for the Eighties 1980).

With respect to technology, the postwar period has seen the growth and greater dispersion of assembly line production, which has made a much wider distribution of cheap consumer goods possible. In addition, the development of computer and communications technologies has pushed forward tremendously the capacity of management to control large and widely dispersed operations.

The growing importance of government and nonprofit institutions. Government and nonprofit sectors have contributed large shares of employment expansion during the postwar decades. This rapid expansion, which has slowed somewhat in recent years, has occurred in a number of ways.

At the federal level, government has been heavily committed to enlarging and modernizing the defense establishments (including extensive R&D), to expanding the scope and size of public services, and to increasing the scope of regulatory and administrative action. At the state and local levels, governments have been responsive to widespread demand for service expansion and for attention to the new requirements incident to suburbanization and other population shifts. In both the public and nonprofit areas there has been a major growth of health, education (especially higher education), and research and development (R&D).

In part, then, the expansion of nonprofit and public services has reflected at once the growth of publicly supported consumer services, greater investment in research, and the development of a better-trained labor force needed by an ever more technologically and institutionally complex society (Abramovitz 1972).

The rise of the large corporation. Perhaps more important, however, in determining the pace and direction of the postwar transformation has been the rise of the large "multilocational" corporation (Bergman and Goldstein 1983). While the existence of the large corporation dates back to the rise of the railroads, the extent of its control over a variety of markets and product lines, the scale of its operations, as well as the complexity of its organization have all increased dramatically during the postwar period (Blumberg 1975).

The success of the large corporation in both producing for and distributing to nationwide markets has stemmed largely in its ability to manage profitably large numbers of plants or consumer outlets through the centralization of many of the service functions once performed or purchased at the plant or establishment level in the central offices of the firm (accounting, advertising, inventory control, etc.), thereby permitting it to achieve firm-level scale economies. The emergence of the multiproduct, multiregional corporation characterized by a well-developed structure of divisional offices, regional sales headquarters, and servicelike establishments (R&D labs, account processing offices, foreign trade offices), in addition to its national headquarters, is a hallmark of the postwar period (Chandler 1977). As this chapter attempts to demonstrate, the differential impact of the growth of the central offices of the large corporation on cities has been fundamental for urban development.

The Rise of Advanced Services

The aforementioned changes are indicative of a dual transformation: a transformation in *what* and in *how* the economy produces (Stanback et al. 1981; *Forbes* 1983).

In terms of what the economy produces, there has been a shift to services, although not so much in terms of an increase in free-standing consumer services (barbershops, cleaners, etc.) as in terms of services either provided along with goods (e.g., payment plans, warranty plans, and specialized retailing services) or embodied within goods (e.g., advertising, styling, and customizing) (Stanback 1980).

In terms of how the economy produces, the importance of services to producers and producer servicelike activities carried within the central offices of the large corporations itself has grown tremendously, reflecting the need of large business organizations to devote greater resources to research and development, to the planning of the different phases of the product cycle, to engineering, branding, customizing and styling, and to the management of the corporate institution's growing complexity (Chandler 1977; Stanback et al. 1981).

To highlight these changes, Noyelle and Stanback (1984) make use of a classification of industries that distinguishes among six major groups of services based on the type of outputs (intermediate or final outputs) and the institutional setting under which services are provided (private, public, or nonprofit sectors). They are the distributive services, the complex or corporate activities, the retail services, the mainly consumer services, the nonprofit services, and the public sector services, as shown in table 7.1.[1]

Distributive services include transportation, communications, utilities, and wholesale trade. These are activities that, for the most part, involve the distribution of goods and services among producers or from producer to retailers. Activities of the corporate complex include service functions carried out in the central offices of the corporation and services such as finance, accounting, advertising, or management consulting that assist firms in carrying out administrative and developmental functions. For the most part, distributive services and activities of the corporate complex are intermediate outputs by nature.

Retailing and mainly consumer services (hotels, auto repairs, movie theaters, and so on) constitute two industry groupings most readily identifiable as final outputs.

The last two groups—nonprofit services (mostly health and higher education) and public sector services—are the least easy to classify. Conventional economic theory and National Income Accounting practices view such services as final outputs. Indeed, as noted earlier, the growth of public and nonprofit sector services has been, in large part, associated wtih consumer demand. At the same time, however, many of the functions fulfilled by the public and nonprofit sectors represent important contributions to the development of the economy's stock of capital such as infrastructure works, higher education, R&D, and the like, and as such are more similar to activities encompassed by the corporate complex.

Table 7.2 presents changes in the shares of employment and GNP (Gross National Product) in major service and nonservice sectors of the economy in 1947 and 1977. In employment terms, what is clear is that retailing and mainly consumer services—often regarded as

Table 7.1   Classification of sectors for GNP and employment analysis

Agriculture, extractive and transformative industries	
1 Agriculture	SIC 01, 02, 07, 08, 09
2 Extractive and transformative	
Mining	SIC 10, 11, 12, 13, 14
Construction	SIC 15, 16, 17
Manufacturing	SIC 20 to 39
Services	
3 Distributive services	
Transportation, communications,	
and utilities	SIC 40 to 49
Wholesale	SIC 50, 51
4 Complex of corporate activities	
Central administrative offices	CAO&A of each 1-digit SIC group
Producer services	
Finance, insurance, and real estate	SIC 60 to 67
Business services	SIC 73
Legal services	SIC 81
Membership organizations	SIC 86
Miscellaneous professional services	SIC 89
Social services	SIC 83*
5 Nonprofit services	
Health	SIC 80
Education	SIC 82
6 Retail services	SIC 52 to 59
7 Mainly consumer services	
Hotel and other lodging places	SIC 70
Personal services	SIC 72
Auto repair, services, and garages	SIC 75
Miscellaneous repair services	SIC 76
Motion pictures	SIC 78
Amusements & recreation services	SIC 79, 84
Private households	SIC 88
8 Government and government	
enterprises	SIC 91 to 97

*After 1974.
Source: From Noyelle and Stanback (1983). Adapted from J. Singlemann, *From Agriculture to Services*, Beverly Hills: Sage Publications, 1979. Based on U.S. Office of Management and Budget *Standard Industrial Classification Manual* (Washington, D.C., U.S. Government Printing Office, 1976).

the most important activities involved in the rise of services (Fuchs 1968 and 1977)—have not grown rapidly, whereas the complex of corporate activities, the nonprofit and the public sector services have made impressive employment gains. In GNP terms, one finding stands out: the share of national product originating from the two groups of services most readily identifiable as intermediate outputs—distributive services and complex of corporate activities—grew from 29 percent in 1947 to over 36 percent in 1977. (The data used in table 7.2 do not permit one to break out the share of GNP originating from the central offices of corporations. In accordance with the indus-

Table 7.2 Percentage distribution of full-time equivalent employment and GNP (in 1972 dollars) by industries: 1947 and 1977

	1947		1977	
	Employment	GNP	Employment	GNP
Agriculture extractive and transformative	43.39	37.38	31.60	32.81
Agriculture	4.31	5.57	1.90	2.87
Extractive and transformative[a]	39.08	31.81	29.70	29.94
Manufacturing	32.27	24.53	24.10	24.18
Services	56.61	62.68	68.40	66.09
Distributive services	13.54	13.36	11.36	16.51
Retailing services	12.57	11.06	14.18	9.89
Nonprofit services	2.61	2.67	6.34	4.04
Complex of corporate activities[b]	6.06	15.50	11.96	20.12
Mainly consumer services	7.67	5.47	4.99	3.11
Government and government enterprises	14.16	14.62	19.57	12.43
	100.00	100.00	100.00	100.00

a Includes mining and construction (not shown).
b Because of data limitations, this grouping includes only the producer services (see table 5.1). Employment and GNP originating from the Central Administrative Offices are not disaggregated and are included in their respective category: e.g., distributive services, retailing services, manufacturing.
Source: From Noyelle and Stanback, 1983; from U.S. Department of Commerce, Bureau of Economic Analysis, *The National Income and Product Accounts of the United States, 1929–74 Statistical Tables* and *Survey of Current Business*, July 1978.

try classification scheme presented in table 7.1, this share should properly be counted in the complex of corporate activities grouping. Stanback et al. [1981] have estimated that the central offices of corporations contributed, at least, an additional 5 percent share of GNP in 1977, making the share of intermediate outputs even bigger.)

Advanced Services and U.S. Cities

To evaluate the impact of the rise of advanced services on U.S. cities, Noyelle and Stanback (1983) have developed a typology of the 140 largest Standard Metropolitan Statistical Areas (SMSAs), based on their 1976 employment structure, and analyzed their recent economic transformation. Their analysis indicates that the rise of advanced services has affected cities unevenly, resulting in the emergence of a four-tiered urban system comprising: (1) diversified advanced service centers, (2) specialized advanced service centers, (3) production centers, and (4) consumer-oriented centers, with characteristics of economic structure and recent experience of transformation differing widely from type to type. These major types of cities are shown in table 7.3 and are described briefly in the following paragraphs.[2]

The diversified advanced service centers. This first major class of cities includes places ranging from New York, Chicago, Los Angeles, and San Francisco, to Charlotte and Omaha, by way of Philadelphia, Boston, Houston, or Atlanta. These SMSAs are characterized by large shares of their employment in the distributive services, in the complex of corporate activities, and somewhat more selectively in universities, hospitals, and public sector services. In other words, they are both centers of distribution for hinterland markets and strong centers of advanced services.

The national centers—New York, Chicago, Los Angeles, and San Francisco—stand at the apex. Nearly one-third of the nation's 1,150 largest corporations[3] and nearly one-fourth of the industrial divisions of the largest American corporations[4] are headquartered in one of these four centers. About one out of every two large U.S. corporations maintains regional sales headquarters in each of these four places.[5] New York has a special place as the dominant American urban center. Nearly two-thirds of the area's labor force is employed in firms of the complex of corporate activities, in nonprofit institutions, or in public sector organizations. One out of every five

"Fortune 1000" firms are headquartered in the New York SMSA. Close to 30 percent of the nation's commercial banking assets are controlled by New York banks. This is where the very large investment banks are headquartered and where most of the nation's advertising industry operates.

More generally speaking, the four national centers are places characterized by enormous banking resources, great depth in many business service areas such as accounting, advertising, legal counsel, or investment banking, and a capacity to provide specialized expertise to firms engaged in international operations unmatched anywhere else. Many a large U.S. corporation not headquartered in one of these four cities finds it necessary to maintain its financial offices, foreign trade/investment facilities, or like establishments in one of them to draw on the very special resources they offer. Likewise, it is there that foreign multinational corporations and transnational banks have located their North American headquarters as they moved forcefully into U.S. markets during the late 1970s (Cohen 1979a; Sears and Hawkins 1979).

The next subgroup of cities, the regional centers, includes places ranging from Philadelphia, Boston, and Dallas to New Orleans, Portland, and Columbus. These nineteen places account for another one-fourth of the headquarters of the nation's 1,150 largest firms and a roughly similar percentage of the headquarters of the industrial divisions of the largest firms. Large corporations headquartered in those centers tend to be somewhat smaller and less international in orientation than those found in the very large national centers (Cohen 1979b). For the most part, they retain closer ties to their surrounding regional markets. For example, many large food, retail, transportation, and utilities companies are headquartered in such centers.

The producer service base of the regional centers remains extensive but is somewhat less sophisticated than that found in the national centers. With almost one out of every two large U.S. corporations locating regional sales headquarters in each of these regional centers, one of their key roles is clearly that of providing a base from which large corporations can oversee their commercial operations in major U.S. regional markets. This is also reflected in the fact that most of these places tend to have well-developed warehousing and shipping facilities and airports with extensive air connections.

The subregional centers—e.g., Memphis, Omaha, or Charlotte

Table 7.3 140 largest SMSAS classified by type and size, 1976

Diversified advanced service centers

National

1[a]	New York	1[b]	32	Indianapolis	2
2	Los Angeles	1	33	New Orleans	2
3	Chicago	1	34	Portland	2
7	San Francisco	1	35	Columbus	2

Regional / Subregional

4	Philadelphia	1	41	Memphis	3
6	Boston	1	45	Salt Lake City	3
10	Dallas	1	46	Birmingham	3
11	Houston	1	52	Nashville	3
12	St. Louis	1	53	Oklahoma City	3
14	Baltimore	1	56	Jacksonville	3
15	Minneapolis	1	58	Syracuse	3
17	Cleveland	1	65	Richmond	3
18	Atlanta	2	69	Omaha	3
21	Miami	2	91	Mobile	4
22	Denver	2	101	Little Rock	4
23	Seattle	2	106	Shreveport	4
26	Cincinnati	2	110	Des Moines	4
28	Kansas City	2	114	Spokane	4
30	Phoenix	2	120	Jackson, MS	4

Specialized advanced service centers

Functional nodal / Government and education

5	Detroit	1	8	Washington, D.C.	1
13	Pittsburgh	1	39	Sacramento	3
16	Newark	1	48	Albany	3
24	Milwaukee	2	54	New Haven	3
31	San Jose	2	64	Springfield, MA	3
36	Hartford	2	77	Raleigh-Durham	4
38	Rochester	3	81	Fresno	4
40	Louisville	3	82	Austin	4
44	Dayton	3	84	Lansing	4
47	Bridgeport	3	85	Oxnard-Ventura	4
50	Toledo	3	88	Harrisburg	4
51	Greensboro	3	89	Baton Rouge	4
57	Akron	3	90	Tacoma	4
62	Allentown	3	99	Columbia, SC	4
63	Tulsa	3	111	Utica	4

Table 7.3 (continued)

Specialized advanced service centers

Functional nodal			Government and education		
67	New Brunswick	3	112	Trenton	4
70	Jersey City	3	113	Madison	4
75	Wilmington	3	117	Stockton	4
78	Paterson	4	130	South Bend	4
86	Knoxville	4	140	Ann Arbor	4
96	Wichita	4			
100	Fort Wayne	4			
103	Peoria	4			
137	Kalamazoo	4			

Production centers

Manufacturing					
27	Buffalo	2	116	Reading	4
42	Providence	3	119	Huntington	4
59	Worcester	3	124	Evansville	4
60	Gary	3	125	Appleton	4
61	N.E. Pennsylvania	3	131	Erie	4
71	Grand Rapids	3	134	Rockford	4
72	Youngstown	3	136	Lorain	4
73	Greenville	3			
74	Flint	3	Industrial-military		
80	New Bedford	4	20	San Diego	2
92	Canton	4	37	San Antonio	3
93	Johnson City	4	49	Norfolk	3
94	Chattanooga	4	87	El Paso	4
98	Davenport	4	97	Charleston, SC	4
104	Beaumont	4	102	Newport News	4
107	York	4	121	Lexington	4
109	Lancaster	4			
115	Binghamton	4			

Consumer oriented centers

			Residential		
23	Huntsville	4	9	Nassau	1
26	Augusta	4	19	Anaheim	2
27	Vallejo	4	76	Long Branch	3
28	Colorado Springs	4			
32	Pensacola	4			
33	Salinas	4			

Table 7.3 (continued)

Consumer oriented centers

Mining-industrial			Resort-retirement		
83	Tucson	4	25	Tampa	2
105	Bakersfield	4	29	Riverside	2
118	Corpus Christi	4	43	Ft. Lauderdale	3
129	Lakeland	4	55	Honolulu	3
135	Johnstown, PA	4	68	Orlando	3
138	Duluth	4	79	West Palm Beach	4
139	Charleston, WV	4	95	Albuquerque	4
			108	Las Vegas	4
			122	Santa Barbara	4

a 1976 population rank.
b 1976 population size group. Size 1: over 2 million population; size 2: between
1 and 2 million population; size 3: between 0.5 and 1 million population; size 4:
between 0.25 and 0.5 million population
Source: From Noyelle and Stanback, 1983; from U.S. Bureau of the Census, *Current Population Report*, Series P-25.

—have clearly a less diversified base of advanced services than their larger counterparts, but they do stand out by their strong involvement in the distributive services (particularly wholesaling and trucking).

National and regional diversified advanced service centers have usually been characterized both by strong losses in their once-important manufacturing sector and considerable rebuilding of their economic base in the advanced service sectors. In terms of overall growth, Sunbelt centers have typically performed better than their northern counterparts, if only because they had smaller manufacturing sectors to begin with or because their manufacturing base has not yet been subject to the wrenching adjustments that have occurred in many older cities. Subregional centers have typically grown rapidly, although they appear to have been somewhat restricted in their development of advanced service activities both by their size and function in the overall urban hierarchy. For example, few have been successful in bringing about the development of strong educational or research complexes, or in attracting large numbers of headquarters and divisional offices of major firms (e.g., see Stanback's and Noyelle's 1982 discussion of some of the limits to development in Charlotte).

The specialized advanced service centers. This second major class of centers includes two groups of places. The first group (the functional nodal centers) is exemplified by places like Detroit, San Jose, Rochester, or Akron, which are characterized by large numbers of central offices of large industrial corporations (primarily national headquarters and divisional head offices)[6] and by strong concentrations of production establishments, usually in highly specialized complexes of industries: Detroit in automobile, San Jose in electronics, Rochester in scientific and office equipment, Akron in tires. The second group (government and education centers) is characterized by cities with strong concentrations of public sector facilities (e.g., state capitals), universities, and other nonprofit institutions.

Specialized service centers are highly specialized in the range of advanced services they offer, tend to be weak financial or business service centers, have limited involvement in regional consumer markets outside their immediate hinterland, but also tend to be well-oriented toward higher education and research. Two consequences follow: corporations headquartered in specialized service centers must typically obtain the financial and business service assistance lacking in their locale from organizations located in the diversified advanced service centers; because of their orientation toward R&D and higher education, specialized service centers are likely to provide fertile grounds for developing new firms and new industries (Joint Economic Committee 1982; chapter 8 of this volume).

Among this class of cities, the functional nodal centers have usually experienced low growth due to large losses of production jobs (depending, of course, on their industry of specialization) that they have barely managed to balance by employment gains in central offices of industrial firms or in other advanced services. Their more restricted economic base has obviously made for a more difficult process of transition. Government and education centers have usually fared better, if only because of the lesser weight of manufacturing in their economic base and the surge of employment in the public and nonprofit sectors during the 1960s and 1970s.

The production centers. This third major class includes three groups of places—the manufacturing, industrial-military, and mining-industrial centers—characterized, respectively, by an overconcentration of employment in manufacturing, government (mostly military-related installations, such as bases, arsenals, and shipyards), or mining.

Industrial-military places (e.g., San Diego, Norfolk, or Newport News) enjoyed fairly rapid development from the 1940s through the 1960s because of their direct linkage to the various war efforts (ordnance, shipbuilding, aerospace). Although the largest ones, particularly San Diego and San Antonio, seem to have succeeded in bringing some diversity to their economic base, most remain highly dependent upon the flow of federal funds for military or related projects.

Mining-industrial centers (e.g., Bakersfield or Charleston, West Virginia) enjoyed a certain vitality in the late 1970s, if only because of the nation's growing concern with domestic energy and mineral resources at that time. Their short-term future does not appear as bright as it did.[7]

Among manufacturing centers (e.g., Buffalo, Youngstown, Reading, etc.), the record has been, for the most part, dismal. This has been so not simply because many are specialized in older manufacturing industries, but because of a key feature of their structure. Compared to the functional nodal centers, manufacturing centers (and to a similar extent, military-industrial and mining-industrial places) have more likely been traditionally engaged in standardized production work—mostly assembly work. Furthermore, as a result of the accelerated process of corporate concentration characteristic of the 1960s and 1970s, they have tended to lose what little involvement they may have had in the planning, administration, or research and development functions of their industry. As a result, they have tended to be the most vulnerable to adverse development affecting their particular industry and to the widespread shrinking of blue-collar jobs (Bluestone and Harrison 1982; Committee on Small Business 1980). These centers have demonstrated very limited ability to dissociate themselves from their blue-collar image and have found very little relief other than through developing local public sector jobs or consumer-oriented services to fill the gap of plant shutdowns (see Stanback's and Noyelle's 1982 discussion of Buffalo).

The consumer-oriented centers. The last and smallest group of places (only twelve) includes two sets of cities: residential centers that are metropolitan areas at the periphery of the national metropolises (Nassau – Suffolk and Long Branch – Asbury Park near New York, Anaheim near Los Angeles) and resort retirement cities (e.g., Orlando, West Palm Beach, or Las Vegas) that have sprung up in the postwar era under the combined effects of residential suburbanization, rising consumerism, and widespread retirement benefits.

In general, these places have been characterized by trends in population settlement that have made for substantial growth. But, with the exception of the few largest ones (Nassau-Suffolk, Anaheim, Orlando, and possibly Tampa), the orientation of their economic growth and employment expansion toward providing consumer services has tended to work against agglomerations of activities that draw upon high level corporate, public, and nonprofit services. The only consistent departure in their pattern of development has come, thus far, through limited growth in the area of manufacturing assembly.

Developmental Dynamics

The presentation, thus far, suggests that the postwar transformation of the urban system has resulted in the emergence of a functional dichotomy between urban centers that are by now well positioned in terms of the production and export of advanced services (the diversified and specialized advanced service centers) and those that are not (the production and consumer-oriented centers). The implications of this dichotomy for the developmental dynamics of the urban system are important to assess.

Intermetropolitan Linkages and Advanced Services

Until recently, manufacturing had been a principal component of the export base of many of the current diversified and specialized service centers. Increasingly, however, it is advanced services that constitute the vital sector of their economies. Obviously, this development does not mean that goods-producing activities are altogether losing their place in urban economies. Many diversified or specialized advanced service centers will continue to carry out some form of goods production, whether it be for local markets or even for export (see in particular, the case of the functional nodal centers among the specialized advanced service centers). More important, manufacturing is likely to remain a major, if not the principal, component of the economic base of many production centers and possibly grow in importance in some of the consumer-oriented centers. Still, the current concentration of advanced services in the economies of the diversified and specialized advanced service centers does reflect changes in the nature of intermetropolitan linkages and, ultimately, changes in the way in which growth impulses are being diffused throughout the entire urban system.

Since final outputs (whether manufactured goods or consumer services) and advanced services are highly interdependent, growth of places that specialize in advanced services remains fundamentally linked to the growth of places that specialize in the production of final goods or consumer services. In an economy that is more and more dominated by large multilocational organizations, growth increments are increasingly transmitted from these lower-ranking cities to the advanced service centers. This may occur either through direct intra-firm linkages between remote plants and consumer-serving outlets and central offices or through inter-firm linkages as growth of activity in remote facilities necessitates the purchase of expertise from producer service firms located in advanced service centers (Pred 1977; Noyelle and Stanback 1984). Conversely, demand generated in advanced service cities flows back to production- or consumer-oriented centers for the goods produced there or as local expenditures by commuters, vacationers, and retirees.

These processes of growth transmission are biased, however, in two fundamental ways. First, if the past is any indication of the future, it is reasonable to assume that, on balance, advanced service centers enjoy the most favorable position since economic growth creates increasingly fewer jobs and less GNP in production establishments or consumer-serving establishments and increasingly more in the advanced services (as discussed above). Second, this tendency is aggravated by the fact that, directly through the headquarters of large firms and more indirectly through the community of business service firms that assist corporations in decisionmaking, advanced service centers hold increasingly greater control over the diffusion of innovation, the flows of investment, and the creation of jobs in the lower-ranking production- and consumer-oriented centers (Pred 1977; Committee on Small Business 1980; Bluestone and Harrison 1982; Noyelle and Stanback 1983).

These important observations lead us directly to what, I believe, ought to be a central concern of current urban policy. The issue is whether or not production and consumer-oriented cities are, or can be, properly equipped to regain better control over both their economic destiny and future sources of growth through the retention, local development, or even attraction (via relocation) of advanced service activities, which have, thus far, tended to escape them. Here, a cursory look at the record of decentralization among advanced services sheds additional—albeit mostly unpromising—light on the immediate future.

Is Decentralization of Advanced Services in the Offing?

In answer to the question raised in the above heading, the Noyelle and Stanback study (1984) suggests that while there is no straightforward answer, it is likely that, if left to market forces alone, advanced services will continue to concentrate most vigorously in the upper tier of the urban system. Their study shows instances where centralizing tendencies are at work, where decentralizing tendencies are at work, and instances where the record is ambivalent. The study further tends to suggest that the limited decentralization that has occurred largely passed by the production- and consumer-oriented centers. On balance, decentralization of advanced services has been largely restricted to a trend away from the largest diversified advanced service centers toward the smallest ones or toward the specialized advanced service centers. The following examples illustrate some of the various trends at work.

Centralization. Among producer services, trends seem to favor strong centralization. In banking, for example, concentration of assets in the few largest banking centers has been increasing throughout the postwar period, and it appears that deregulation is bringing about even further centralization rather than decentralization of high-level financial resources. Between the early 1960s and the early 1980s the share of the deposits in the top 250 commercial banks controlled by the nation's money centers has grown from roughly 30 percent to over 50 percent.

In advertising, Noyelle and Stanback (1984) find little evidence of movement out of New York City. In management consulting, Noyelle (1983c) observes the increasing domination of New York City since the mid-1970s. In air transportation, Noyelle and Stanback (1983) find that the smallest diversified service centers and many among the specialized service centers have lost rather than gained air connections and traffic as a result of higher fuel costs and industry deregulation, while the largest diversified service centers consolidated their leadership.

Ambivalence. Among national headquarters and divisional offices of large firms, the trends have been somewhat ambivalent. During the 1960s and early 1970s a number of large corporations did display some tendencies toward decentralizing their national headquarters. However, the great majority of the changes that took place were of the following nature: (1) New York–based corporations relocating to the Stamford–Greenwich–Bridgeport area or to some of the large regional diversified centers—namely, Dallas, Houston, Atlanta, and Minneapolis; (2) a few large corporations reshuffling their headquarters from one regional diversified center to another; or (3) some local gains and losses associated with rank upgrading or downgrading of local corporations—a phenomenon that has always been going on and will likely continue. Overall, there was practically no change between 1960 and 1980 in the total number of the nation's largest corporations (Fortune 1,150) headquartered in the diversified and specialized service center (roughly 85 percent), and there remains compelling evidence that when large corporations take over smaller ones headquartered in other than the advanced service centers, they will pull critical managerial or developmental functions back into some of their more centrally located offices (Committee on Small Business 1980).

Another ambivalent case is that of the divisional headquarters of large firms. On the one hand, the Noyelle and Stanback study (1983) points to strong evidence of increasingly tighter relationships among divisional headquarters of firms, specialized production establishments (batch or short-run production as opposed to assembly work), and research and higher educational facilities, if only because divisional offices and high-level production establishments require the employment of increasingly larger numbers of highly skilled and highly trained personnel (engineers, draftsmen, technicians, computer specialists). On the other hand, the same study suggests that the decentralization of research and higher educational facilities, which has occurred over the past two decades or so, has permitted the development of new technology-oriented firms and has resulted in the attraction of key divisional offices or production facilities of established firms to places previously marginally affected by industrial development (see also Joint Economic Committee 1982). San Jose in the fifties or Raleigh–Durham–Chapel Hill in the seventies seem good examples of such a process of development. Research and higher education are still often dependent on federal dollars, however, and in the face of current retrenchment on this front there may not be much room for change in the near future.

Decentralization. Nonetheless, there are some examples of decentralization. Data processing facilities of large businesses (e.g., insurance, banks) appear to be attracted to certain, relatively off-centered locations, in part because advances in communications permit such facilities to operate from a distance and because advances in electronic data processing technology have somewhat changed the nature of labor force requirements. Our more recent research, however, may also suggest that the potential for decentralization of data processing facilities is not as extensive as is often assumed (Noyelle 1984a).

Likewise, warehousing and trucking have been moving away from the largest centers, primarily because the completion of the interstate highway system and the rise of large-scale containerization has made it increasingly possible and even profitable to operate large warehousing and shipping facilities in locations at a distance from the largest, often more congested, places.

Policy Implications

What does this analysis imply for urban planners and policymakers? A few lessons can be drawn that may help local development planners and urban policymakers think their way through some of the implications of the current transformation.

The postwar period has been characterized by a marked shift to the services, but services have not grown independent from manufacturing. Rather, the services that have grown the most are those that have tended to be closely associated with manufacturing itself. These services have grown because, in a sense, production has become increasingly "service-intensive." Two consequences follow: that the vitality of many of the service sectors remains, in large part, dependent upon the vitality of manufacturing itself, but also that restored dynamism in industry will not necessarily translate into large numbers of jobs in plants and factories. More likely, this dynamism will be felt in the growth of white-collar occupations in service organizations and central offices of industrial firms. In general, this may mean that economic development efforts call for a major shift in focus, away from traditional incentives for capital formation and job creation in factories, toward incentives geared at promoting growth and development in advanced service firms and service establishments. This does not mean, however, that local planners ought to turn their backs on the more traditional areas of employment.

If anything, almost every city must deal with some problems of employment contraction in manufacturing, although, admittedly, problems are being felt more acutely in some than in others. The resulting displacement effect cannot be overlooked. At the same time to conclude from the above that, for instance, the solution to unemployment among steelworkers lies in their retraining and reemployment as office workers—some would have them become computer programmers—is simply ludicrous. Most studies of displacement indicate that the majority of older blue-collar workers (those past their late forties) permanently laid off from their industry of employment end up drifting away from stable employment and steady income through much of the remainder of their working years, largely because social and cultural commitments to an earlier, blue-collar way of life are often hard to break in these older generations (Bluestone and Harrison 1982; Gilchrist and Shenkin 1980; Hanson 1983). Most likely, the realistic approach lies in a strategy based partly on reinvestment to modernize faltering sectors and partly on planned factory employment retrenchment so that older workers are eased out of blue-collar employment as they retire, thereby alleviating the personal suffering and the overall cost to society associated with rising welfare costs and lost human capital. This obviously begs the question as to the conditions under which factory employment should be left to contract and reinvestment take place.

Equally important is the fact that advanced services—which have provided important sources of new employment in recent years—have developed highly unevenly among metropolitan economies. This suggests that different types of cities are facing very different challenges in effecting their transition and are thus calling for very different developmental strategies. A few hints may be helpful in suggesting what may lie in store.

Among diversified service centers, which have thus far been the most successful at transforming themselves, local development planners may need to become more attuned to the implications of the relationships that are developing between the service base of their economies and the wider regional or national markets that these are meant to serve. As Bergman and Goldstein (1983) suggest, their general performance is likely to become increasingly related to that of the macroeconomy, and it is rather unlikely that their service orientation will somehow shield them from either cyclical or structural adjustments in the future.

Among specialized service centers, local development planners need to wrestle with the problem that the narrow specialization of their advanced service base makes these places highly susceptible to negative developments in the economic areas that their service base is meant to serve. Thus, retrenchment in the public sector, in higher education, or particularly in manufacturing industries may wreak havoc with some of these economies. Here, local development planners probably need to look for ways to both stabilize the current economic base and build on local resources—especially, advanced services—to diversify the local economy.

Overall, however, it is in the production centers that the greatest challenges seem to lie.[9] Thus far, large corporations have been left to move capital, jobs, and innovation in and out of these areas pretty much as they pleased, while market forces have left them with very little means to retain, let alone develop or attract, some advanced service activities. As a result, these places have typically been caught in a vicious circle of development in which the only alternative to decline has often meant intense competition for low-level manufacturing work with lower wage areas in both this country and abroad, at the cost of high subsidies and decline in real wages. In the absence of an industrial policy very different from the policy of free market adjustment that has been exercised through much of the past decade or so, it is hard to see how most of these cities will ever get out of their current bind. While I do not mean to suggest that, given the proper set of policies, the Youngstowns and Flints of this country can suddenly be turned into New Yorks or San Joses, I believe that a reasonable policy apparatus has to be developed that will permit them to stabilize their traditional manufacturing base and give them a crack at some of the new jobs and new activities.

Because of the persistent tendency for many of these places to repeatedly lose the tenuous involvement they may have gained earlier in high-value added production (i.e., "service-intensive") or in the advanced services, largely as a result of the locational decisions taken by large corporations, I have to conclude that this new policy apparatus must include substantial changes in the rule exercised by large corporations. At a minimum, what may be called for are restrictions on capital mobility, safeguards on industrial sector adjustments, and strong incentives for the decentralization of advanced service activities. Ultimately what may truly be called for is an industrial planning apparatus that permits both a more evenly distributed economic development process and a fairer measurement and distribution of the social costs of transition.

Author's Note: This chapter is a slightly edited version of a paper published in the Summer 1983 issue of the Journal of the American Planning Association. The author would like to thank Ed Bergman, Harvey Goldstein, Tom Stanback, and three anonymous JAPA readers for their comments and suggestions on a first draft of this essay.

8 Establishing High-Technology Enterprises in Metropolitan Areas

Candee S. Harris

The context of domestic business activity has undergone some fundamental changes in the past few decades. Recently the United States has witnessed the convergence of several factors—a secular decline in the rate of growth, intensifying cyclical fluctuations, and accelerating processes of structural change. Policymakers at all levels of government are trying to understand and anticipate these changes in order to guide their communities through these economically turbulent times. In the search for cures for various economic ills, the high-technology prescription has recently gained popularity. Despite a proliferation of new state and local programs to encourage high-tech development, the fundamental processes of business activity underlying development remain poorly understood. The development of effective policies hinges on the availability of suitable information on the composition and growth behavior of firms in the high-technology sector.

This study provides some empirical evidence with which to assess the basic assumptions of two general approaches to promoting high-technology development. Using a newly available business data base, the size and structure of the high-technology sector, as well as the sector's recent growth performance, are examined.[1] Within a conceptual framework drawn from the existing literature on industrial location theory and entrepreneurship, metropolitan variations in formation rates of new high-technology business establishments are analyzed in the context of differences in several economic and social characteristics.

The High-Technology Sector[2]

Much of the interest in high-technology industries has centered largely on their potential for generating new employment opportunities. Indeed, employment in that sector grew more than 19 percent between 1976 and 1980, in contrast to only 6 percent growth in non-high-technology manufacturing industries. Their disproportionately high growth enabled high-technology manufacturing industries to contribute 42 percent of the net new jobs in manufacturing. Growth performance aside, high-technology industries comprise only 2 percent of all private sector business establishments and account for only 7 percent of employment. Over the next ten years, they are expected to contribute less than 10 percent of the net new jobs created.[3]

Furthermore, patterns of recent employment change vary widely for industries within this sector. Some industries experienced mercurial employment growth (e.g., computer programming grew more than 75 percent in the four years) and others dramatic shrinkage (e.g., electronic capacitor manufacturing reduced employment by more than 50 percent). Technological advance is not necessarily associated with employment generation in the high-technology sector nor in other industries. Rapid gains in labor productivity and constant turnover in product lines can actually reduce the number of jobs provided by a technologically intensive industry (Freeman et al. 1982). These constraints on the potential employment contribution of high-technology industries should be borne in mind by policymakers.

A popular conception of the high-technology sector links its rapid expansion of employment to successful small independent firms (Koch et al. 1983). In fact, independent firms in all industrial sectors did have much higher growth rates than affiliates of larger firms between 1976 and 1980. Despite their dynamism, independent firms (single establishment) still account for only 12 percent of the high-technology sector's employment; almost 90 percent is in firms with more than one hundred employees. Independent firms may contribute disproportionately to innovation and the competitive stimulus in high-technology industries, but appreciable increments in employment are realized later in the product-business life cycle. Consequently, most high-technology employment growth (71 percent between 1976 and 1980) takes place in branch and subsidiary establishments of larger firms. Formations by existing firms of branch and subsidiary establishments accounted for more than 85 percent of high-technology employment in new establishments between 1976 and 1980.[4]

Though the regional distribution of higher-technology employment roughly parallels that of overall employment, the Northeast and the West have slightly higher proportions of high-technology employment, while the South's proportion is relatively low. Organizational aspects of the regional distribution of high-technology activity lend some credence to the regional product life cycle theory, which states that certain stages of the production process have different locational requirements (U.S. Office of Technology Assessment 1983). For instance, the high-technology sectors in the Northeast and the West have larger proportions of independents (around 13 percent) and above average net formation rates for independents. The greater presence of independents in these regions in which high-technology industries were historically conceived and concentrated could be evidence of the "seedbed," or incubator, effect often discussed in connection with the high-technology sector. In the research and development phase of the product cycle, firms would be more likely to benefit from the clustering of highly trained research and technical personnel and support facilities that exist in these regions (Freeman 1982). On the other hand, the South's high proportion of large production facilities owned by out-of-state firms (68 percent) and its higher rates of growth in such establishments probably reflects the firms' decisions to locate large, standardized production facilities in areas with lower operating costs. The following analysis of metropolitan differences in formation rates of independent and branch establishments of high-technology firms provides further evidence concerning these growth patterns.

High-Technology Development: The Conceptual Framework

The combination of structural changes taking place in metropolitan areas and repeated cyclical economic distress has prompted local and state governments to institute programs to encourage growth of high-technology industries. With the common objective of getting "their fair share of these environmentally clean industries that bring tremendous growth, profitability, and resilience to the business cycle" (Koch et al. 1983, 4–16), two approaches to high-technology development predominate. Paralleling earlier "smokestack-chasing" programs, the most popular approach tries to attract relocations or new branch plants of existing high-technology firms. The more immediate and visible benefits of a new large branch plant, especially in terms of job generation, often obscure the development potential of the second approach, which focuses on local business initiative in high-technology fields (Philips and Vidal 1983, 292). Both approaches are predicated on assumptions about the factors that influence business decisions and the degree to which those factors are subject to policy manipulation. What are these factors and their supposed relationship to the formation and growth of high-technology firms? How do the factors thought to affect branch location decisions of large businesses differ from those influencing local entrepreneurship in the high-technology sector? After examining the relevant literature, we formulated two models relating business formations to several characteristics of metropolitan areas, one for formations of new branch operations and one for formations of new independent firms.

Branch Location Decisions of High-Technology Firms

As a variation on an earlier theme, programs to recruit high-technology operations from established firms outside the area draw upon a well-developed body of industrial location theory and experience. Simply, firms identify alternative sites for new facilities based on the availability of necessary resources, such as a material input or trained labor force, then select the site that minimizes annual operating costs that are spatially variable, e.g., wages, energy costs, taxes. Some cost factors are obviously more important than others. Labor-related costs are usually the bulk of variable operating costs and are consequently thought to be a major factor in location decisions. Other cost factors important in traditional manufacturing industries are frequently less relevant for high-technology firms. For instance, the high value-to-volume ratio of many high-technology products reduces the importance of shipping costs.

Two noncost factors considered of particular concern in locating some high-technology establishments are the availability of a large pool of scientific, engineering, and technical workers and the existence of a concentration of firms in related industries, which together comprise a technological infrastructure providing agglomeration economies.

Clearly, the availability of an appropriately skilled work force is necessary for establishing business operations. According to recent surveys, high-technology managers consider an ample pool of technical workers more important than a local supply of engineers and scientists (Joint Economic Committee 1982).[5] A majority of the operations subject to branch location are production facilities or service offices. Firms tend to retain research and development facilities near their headquarters. Therefore, there are a limited number of positions at most branch plants requiring personnel from these highest skill categories. These can usually be filled from other locations, provided the area offers a sufficiently attractive quality of life, such as cultural facilities, good schools, lower rates of crime and pollution, and affordable housing.

Traditional industrial location theory has emphasized the importance of externalities that can accrue to a firm locating at a plexus of similar industrial activity. New firms can lock into an existing network of supplier-customer relationships and auxiliary support services, reducing tactical problems for the management. Given the human capital-intensive nature of much high-technology production, the most attractive aspect of locating near an existing high-technology center is access to a large labor pool capable of providing the broad range of skills required. The larger the network of related industrial activity, and therefore the size of relevant supplier and customer markets, the greater the opportunity for each subsector and firm to benefit from economies of scale.

Although the importance of such agglomeration economies to new independent firms is clear, the argument weakens with reference to branch operations of existing firms. As Bergman and Goldstein (1983, 265) point out, the increasing predominance of large, vertically integrated and conglomerate firms is probably eroding the importance of such agglomeration economies. In many high-technology industries shipping costs are relatively low, so intrafirm sourcing to geographically dispersed subsidiaries or branch plants is feasible and cost-effective. Consequently, agglomeration economies are probably much less important to high-technology branch establishments than they are to new independent firms, which do not have a ready-made corporate support structure.

In sum, the rate of formation of high-technology branch plants should vary across metropolitan areas in direct relation to variations in the availability of skilled labor and the potential for recruiting high-level expertise (quality of life) and should vary inversely with respect to differences in operating costs. Although some relationship to the existence of a high-technology center might be found, agglomeration factors should have limited effect on branch location decisions, especially relative to their impact on formations of new high-technology firms.

High-Technology Entrepreneurship

An alternative to the "branch plant" route to high-technology development is the encouragement of local entrepreneurship in promising industries. This has been the less-taken path in local and state high-technology programs for several reasons. Programs aimed at attracting high-technology branch plants have a well-defined objective and a limited number of large companies to contact. In addition, their success is easily measured by the large parcels of jobs they can deliver. On the other hand, the processes determining the incidence, the form, and the success of new entrepreneurial efforts are not well-defined or understood, making the formulation of effective policies difficult. While the value of branch plant development may be questioned, industrial location theory at least contains a consistent, predominant set of assumptions with relatively clear policy implications. There is no such consensus regarding the underlying causes and consequences of initiatives by or for local businessmen. However, the potential benefits of developing an indigenous sector of high-technology entrepreneurs merit further investigation of factors influencing that process.

Entrepreneurism begins with the decisions of individuals to undertake economic activities entailing a great deal of uncertainty. Consequently, much of the analysis of entrepreneurship focuses on the characteristics of the individuals involved in successful ventures. Nonetheless, the decision to start a business, the selection of the business activity to be pursued, and the prospect for the business's success are all qualified by a number of environmental factors. The decision made by the individual is seminal, but the individual's abilities and the local environment are gestational. The interaction of these elements determines the economic outcome of entrepreneurial endeavors. In this study the focus is on the factors in the economic and social context of metropolitan business activity that are responsive to policy efforts. Together, these might be called the "opportunity structure" (Greenfield and Strickon 1979, 329–50).

In general, the ingredients essential for spawning a high level of entrepreneurial activity are three: (1) a supply of potential entrepreneurs, (2) a range of products or services in demand, and (3) ample and accessible sources of investment capital. Broadly defined, these prerequisites are common to all new ventures, not just high-technology firms. Their translation into operational terms specific to the high-technology sector reveals some constraints on the short-term potential of this development tack for some areas.

For initial entry into the market, independent firms generally locate in the proximity of the owner's residence, rarely considering distant alternative sites. Therefore, intermetropolitan differences in spatially variable operating costs should be irrelevant to formation rates of independent high-technology firms. Costs are, of course, variable within metropolitan areas and do affect intrametropolitan location decisions, but our data confine this analysis to variations across different metropolitan areas.

As with branch location decisions of large high-tech firms, formations of new independent firms are most sensitive to the presence of a highly trained labor force. The pool of engineers and scientists represents both a source of potential entrepreneurs and highly skilled employees. Lacking the extensive communication and financial resources necessary to recruit professionals and technical workers from outside the area, small firms are more dependent than large corporations on the local labor supply.

Reliance on the local labor market is simply one aspect of the greater overall dependence of independent high-technology firms on existing technological and financial infrastructure. As discussed earlier, the broadening geographic and industrial scope of large corporations has eroded the importance of agglomeration economies for their branches and subsidiaries. The complementary effect has been to intensify the importance of such economies for independent firms.

Locating near an established high-technology center offers many advantages to new small firms, in addition to the aforementioned abundance of potential employees spanning a wide range of needed skills (Dorfman 1983). For example, a concentration of high-technology activity provides timely access to essential components or services for production equipment (including business equipment and testing laboratories). New enterprises can benefit from existing support industries, such as advertising or marketing firms familiar with high-technology products and their markets.

The high-technology sector includes many innovative, rapidly evolving industries. In such a competitive environment it is essential for new firms seeking a market niche or greater market share to keep abreast of new product developments, new production processes, and new supplier and customer markets. Corporate headquarters and centralized research and development units provide this service to their geographically dispersed affiliates. Independent firms must rely on their own resources, increasing the benefits of proximity.

Furthermore, there is the benefit of example. Entrepreneurs, particularly in new or innovative industries, are instigators of change. They are individuals employing a similar path in pursuit of a variety of goals—economic success, fame, or making a contribution to progress in their field. Whatever the objective, the path entails risk and uncertainty. As the success rate of the trailblazing high-technology entrepreneurs increases, so should the propensity of others to follow the same path. An established concentration of high-technology activity furnishes reassuring examples of success, which should prompt higher rates of new ventures. Related to this factor, the literature on high-technology development devotes much attention to "spinoff," that is, the tendency for employees of an established high-technology firm to break off and form their own business, usually in the same locale. In a study of the Massachusetts high-technology sector (Roberts and Wainer 1968), one large firm was found responsible for spawning thirty-nine new high-technology enterprises. Although there has been no comprehensive study of this phenomenon, numerous case studies of particular regions or industries support its existence.

The model provided by successful high-technology endeavors affects not only the willingness and ability of individuals to enter the high-technology field, but also the willingness of other individuals and financial institutions to provide the necessary investment capital. In general, financing is more readily available in areas experiencing healthy economic growth, but the supply of venture capital seems to migrate to locations with concentrations of successful entrepreneurs (Dorfman 1983, 307). This suggests a circular pattern of behavior reinforcing growth and entrepreneurship in established high-technology centers. The ventures of several entrepreneurs are successful, and their example is followed by others, drawing on increased sources of investment capital attracted to the areas.

Thus, the expected behavior of new independent enterprises in high-technology industries differs from that of new branches of large high-technology firms. Independent firms should not be responsive to differences in operating costs across metropolitan areas. Entrepreneurial activity in a high-technology sector, as indicated by formations of new independent firms, should be a function of the pool of potential entrepreneurs, the supply of appropriately skilled labor, the availability of investment capital, and the presence of a healthy, extant high-technology sector. There are undoubtedly numerous other important factors that have not yet been identified. These hypothesized relationships affecting formations of independent high-technology firms and those described earlier for formations of high-technology branch establishments were evaluated empirically.

High-Technology Development in
Metropolitan Areas: The Evidence

Data Sources and Model Specification

To assess the validity of these hypothesized processes of high-tech development, an aggregate data base recording entry, exit, and growth of high tech establishments by various geographic and organizational characteristics was used. The data were available for thirty-five SMSAS, covering the period from 1976 to 1980.[6] A list of these SMSAS and of the metropolitan characteristics used in the model can be found in appendix tables 8A.1 and 8A.2. Though geographically dispersed, these SMSAS tend to be older and larger than the national average. We anticipate further research with a broader sample will strengthen our findings.

The conceptual frameworks provided in the discussion above were translated into two equations that were tested through regression analysis. The outcome of location decisions of multiestablishment high-technology firms was expressed as the formation rate of branches and subsidiaries, that is, the number of new branch and subsidiary establishments in the high-technology sector per one thousand employees in the SMSA as a whole. Likewise, high-technology entrepreneurship was measured by the number of newly formed independent firms per thousand employees in the SMSA.[7] The variation in these formation rates was analyzed with respect to variations in the characteristics of the metropolitan areas, as indicated by the independent variables discussed below.

For the availability of appropriately skilled labor, two measures were included: (1) the proportion of the labor force employed in scientific, engineering, and technical occupations in 1976, indicating labor quality, and (2) the size of the population in 1975, indicating the size of the labor force. The attractiveness of an area (and implied ease of attracting talented scientists, engineers, and upper-level managers) was measured by population growth in the previous five-year period (1970–75).

Three business cost items were included—average hourly wages for manufacturing production workers in 1976, average monthly commercial electricity bills in 1976, and an index of per capita local taxes in 1977. Overall employment growth between 1976 and 1980 was included as a measure of general economic health and availability of investment capital.

Finally, the relative size of the high-technology sector in 1976—the ratio of the high-technology share of the SMSAs' employment to that sector's share of total national employment—was included to measure the importance of agglomeration economies. It should be noted that this measure of the proportion of employment in high-technology industries is very different from the measure of the proportion of employees in technology-oriented occupations. Employment within a high-technology industry and even within a single high-technology firm spans a wide range of skill requirements, with only a small percentage qualifying as "technology-oriented jobs" (Dorfman 1983, 301). Similarly, non-high-technology industries also employ technology-oriented workers, but these represent a small portion of their work force. It is possible that the benefits of agglomeration supposed to accrue to high-technology firms are better derived from concentrations of the research and development facilities of all industries than from concentrations of employment of all categories in high-technology industries.[8]

Using these variables as proxies for the metropolitan characteristics of interest, the model proposed to explain branch formations in metropolitan areas (F_b) is presented in the first equation below.[9] Local entrepreneurial activity, as reflected in the formation rate of independent firms (F_i), was regressed on components of the opportunity structures of the thirty-five metropolitan areas, specified in the second equation below.[10]

$$F_b = a + b_1(L) + b_2(P) + b_3(PG) - b_4(W) - b_5(E) - b_6(T) + e$$
$$F_i = c + d_1(L) + d_2(EG) + d_3(AG) + d_4(P) + d_5(I) + f$$

where

F_b = number of branch formations per 1,000 employees

F_i = number of independent formations per 1,000 employees

a,c = constant

L = percent of workers in technology-oriented jobs (1975)

P = population (1975)

PG = population growth (1970–75)

W = hourly wages of mfg. production workers in 1976

E = average commercial electricity bill in 1976

T = index of local taxes (personal & business, 1976)

EG = private sector employment growth (1976–80)

I = median family income (1975)

AG = agglomeration indicator

e,f = error terms

Analytic Findings

The original formulation of the model for branch location decisions performed well overall. As shown in table 8.1a, 53 percent of the variation in branch formations was explained by the six independent variables. However, only three of the variables were statistically significant—the proportion of workers in technology-oriented jobs, population size, and population growth. None of the business cost factors were significantly related to branch formation rate, with local taxes showing the least association.

Two alternative formulations of the branch formation equation were constructed and tested. In the first, an agglomeration indicator,

Table 8.1a High-technology branch formations: First formulation

Variable	Coefficient	t-statistic	Elasticity
R-squared: 0.534			
Constant (a)	−1.23	−3.41	—
Population growth	0.86	3.71	4.09
Tech-oriented jobs	0.02	4.43	1.71
Population size	0.03	2.49	0.21
Wage level	0.02	1.08	0.58
Electricity cost	−0.01	−1.04	−0.29
Local taxes	0.03	0.55	0.12

the proportion of the SMSA's employment in high-technology industries relative to the national average was added, and two of the business cost variables were dropped—average manufacturing wage in 1976 and local taxes in 1977. A moderate positive relationship with the agglomeration variable was evident, and the energy cost variable became statistically significant. The proportion of variation explained by the second version of the equation increased to 64 percent (see table 8.1b). Suspicion of the dominance of the population growth variable led to the third version of the equation for branch establishments. Elimination of the population growth variable reduced the amount of explained variation but caused the wage-level factor to approach significance.

The relative strength of the associations between the metropolitan characteristics and the rate of formations of high-technology branch establishments was consistent through all three versions of the equations. The availability of a skilled work force was the most

Table 8.1b High-technology branch formations

Variable	Coefficient	t-statistic	Elasticity
R-squared: 0.640			
Constant (a)	−0.81	−4.36	—
Population growth	0.75	4.67	3.54
Agglomeration	0.06	3.03	0.30
Tech-oriented jobs	0.01	2.21	0.94
Population size	0.03	2.77	0.20
Electricity cost	−0.13	−1.96	−0.42

important positive factor influencing branch formations, followed by an existing concentration of high-technology activity. Though a rather strong relationship with the wage level was indicated, it was not statistically significant. Of the business cost variables, only the energy cost measure showed a significant negative association with branch formation rates in high-technology industries. The importance of these business cost variables would, of course, vary across specific high-technology industries. Further, the sample of SMSAs may lead to an understatement of the importance of cost variables. There is considerably less variance in the cost measures within the sample than within the population at large. Using a larger, more representative sample, a study of location behavior in the computer industry found significant association with cost measures (Hekman 1983).

The model describing the overall formation behavior of independent high-technology firms also was statistically strong. Over 65 percent of the variation in formation rates of independent high-technology firms was explained, but only three of the five variables were significant — overall employment growth, proportion of technology-oriented workers, and the agglomeration indicator (see table 8.2). Neither the city size (population in 1975) nor the family income variable was significant in explaining metropolitan differences in appearances of new high-technology firms.

Several alternative formulations of the equation were tested, but no consistent, significant relationship was found for any of the other metropolitan characteristics. Exclusion of the general employment growth variable simply increased the strength of the labor quality and agglomeration indicators. However, one modification of the origi-

Table 8.2 Formations of independent high-technology firms: Form 1

Variable	Coefficient	t-statistic	Elasticity
R-squared: 0.652			
Constant	−0.88	−2.41	—
Employment growth	0.62	3.21	2.15
Tech-oriented jobs	0.02	1.96	1.15
Agglomeration	0.15	3.32	0.52
Population	0.003	0.16	0.02
Family income	*	−0.30	−0.28

*less than 0.001.

nal equation, which excluded the two insignificant variables (median family income and population size), increased the strength of the remaining variables and also increased the explained variation to more than 67 percent.

The availability of a skilled, technology-oriented labor force was extremely important in explaining high-technology formations. The indicator of the importance of agglomeration economies was much stronger for new independent enterprises than it was for the branch formations.

The results of the models for the two types of formations strongly supported most of the relationships anticipated. The key role of labor quality and availability was firmly supported in the analysis of both branch and independent formations. Agglomeration tendencies, though an influence on branch formations, were far more important for new high-technology enterprise development. Finally, one business cost variable (electricity costs) was negatively associated with branch location decisions but appeared to be irrelevant to rates of new enterprise formation, as expected.[11] Both the statistical indicators of general metropolitan well-being and attractiveness (previous period population growth and overall employment growth) performed well. However, their overwhelming strength suggests that they are capturing the effects of factors beyond those intended.

Finally, an equation for all formations of new business establishments was tested for both the high-technology sector and for the non-high-technology manufacturing and business service industries.[12] (See table 8.3.) Of those factors that were significant in explaining differences in all high-technology formations across metropolitan areas, the most important was again the availability of a skilled, technology-oriented work force.[13] The elasticity of the labor quality measure was twice as strong for high-technology industries as for non-high-technology industries. Agglomeration economies also were a factor encouraging high-technology development, while relatively high wage levels apparently discouraged new establishments. High-technology formations did not show a significant negative reaction to local taxes, but non-high-technology formations did.

Total formations in the non-high-technology manufacturing and business service sector behaved much as predicted by traditional industrial location theory. They were negatively associated with variations in all three business cost measures and positively responsive to

Table 8.3   Formations of all new establishments

Variable	High technology			Other Mfg. and Bus. Serv.		
	co-efficient	t-statistic	elas-ticity	co-efficient	t-statistic	elas-ticity
Constant	0.63	1.18	—	6.91	2.98	—
Wage level	−0.11	−1.91	−1.08	−0.55	−1.91	−0.91
Electricity costs	−0.01	−2.35	−0.76	−0.02	−1.97	−0.56
Local taxes	−0.19	−1.30	−0.31	−1.71	−2.28	−0.49
Technology-oriented jobs	0.05	2.66	1.52	0.15	1.96	0.77
Population size	0.06	1.66	0.16	0.25	1.43	0.12
Agglomeration	0.19	2.74	0.38	—	—	—
	R-squared: 0.549			R-squared: 0.320		

labor force quality. The elasticities indicate that wage levels were the strongest factor associated with non-high-tech formations, followed by labor quality, electricity costs, and local taxes.

If previous period population growth is added to either equation, the R-squareds increase to more than 0.60. However, this obscures the relationships to other variables; only labor quality, agglomeration economies, and energy costs retain their significance. This pattern held for all four dependent variables, although formation rates of independent high-technology firms were much less sensitive to this factor than the other formation rates. Clearly, the measure is capturing far more than the ability to attract technical and professional expertise. The high correlation between the regional location of a metropolitan area and its population growth rate suggests that business formation rates reflect in part the general shift of population toward the regions of the West and South (Bradbury et al. 1982). There were distinct differences in the employment growth performance of metropolitan areas in various regions of the country during the 1970s. While large metropolitan areas in the Northeast and North Central suffered absolute declines in manufacturing employment between 1967 and 1977, regions in the South and West experienced healthy economic expansion in most industrial sectors (Philips and Vidal 1983, 297–299). Though hardly amenable to policy manipulation, this trend should inform the development of program alternatives.

Conclusion and Policy Implications

Faced with an increasingly cyclical national economy and secular decline in many local economies, policymakers and planners are anxiously trying to devise new approaches to spur development. Two different policy strategies for pursuing high-technology development were considered in this analysis—programs to attract locations of new branches of existing high-technology firms and programs to encourage local entrepreneurship in high-technology industries. Before reviewing the results of this analysis of factors influencing high-technology formations, let us consider the potential costs and benefits of such development.

The branch plant approach offers several benefits. First, new branches are often production facilities that will offer a large number of new jobs. Large increments of employment provide obvious benefits, especially to regions with floundering employment rates. Furthermore, capturing this secondary level of high-technology activity could facilitate the development of local labor skills and other factors, increasing the local capacity to attract additional similar facilities or to generate its own high-technology firms.

Of course, there also are drawbacks to this type of development. Primary among them is that the locus of corporate control is often geographically distant. This can affect the local economy in several ways. Metropolitan economies are being progressively incorporated into the national and even international economic system. Branching and acquisition of independent businesses are a manifestation of this geographic decentralization of the activities of firms with national and multinational scopes of operation. If such branch plants are important sources of local employment, the local economy can become more vulnerable to the exigencies of corporate decisions made outside the community. For example, during recessions it is often more economical to a firm to close one or more entire plants than to reduce production at several sites. Furthermore, the "footloose" nature of branches that qualifies them as targets for local developers makes them candidates for future relocations—for example, to offshore sites with lower wages, taxes, or pollution standards. In small communities or those dependent on single industries or employers, this could produce short-term or even long-term distress (Harris 1984).

Reliance on local entrepreneurship as the primary engine of growth also has its shortcomings. The economic activities of the nation and the world are increasingly dominated by relatively few corporations of immense size (Bergman and Goldstein 1983, 265). Locales failing to recognize this fact risk the negative side effects of balkanization of their economies. With more than two-thirds of all private sector economic activity concentrated in less than one thousand firms, development efforts restricted to small- and medium-scale entrepreneurism seriously limit their potential payoff (Bergman and Goldstein 1983, 265). Initial employment gains from new enterprises are relatively small, though their long-run potential, like that of large firms, is almost unlimited. The entrepreneurial route also is fraught with uncertainties and a high risk of failure.

As with the branch plant approach, new enterprise development has its offsetting benefits. First, it has the appeal of being indigenous. New small and mid-sized businesses would tend to define "what's good for the firm" in local terms. Second, a good base of locally owned independent businesses can act as a buffer to cyclical fluctuations. Small businesses tend to retain employees and remain in business during recessions, somewhat moderating wide fluctuations in large firms during economic downturns (Gray and Phillips 1983 and Harris 1983b).

Finally, in terms of continued development and structural change, the role of local entrepreneurs is proactive. Entrepreneurs are often on the front line of economic change. Individuals seeking new paths to "success" are important sources of innovation and adaptation to new technological and economic realities. Encouraging entrepreneurial activity can facilitate a community's transition from declining or outmoded forms of economic activity to progressive forms.

The results of this analysis indicate several factors that significantly affect an area's ability to stimulate high-technology development. Both forms of high-technology development have in common their reliance on a skilled, technology-oriented labor force. The priority placed on the quality of the available work force is consistent with the findings of other surveys and regional case studies of high-technology firms. Formation and expansion of high-technology businesses in an area can be constrained by the lack of qualified entrepreneurs and technicians. A mismatch between the skills of local job-seekers, including new entrants to the labor market and displaced workers, and the demands of the labor market is clearly a potential bottleneck that might inhibit development. In the longer run the availability of a flexible, well-educated work force is amenable to public policy. In the shorter run, however, many high-technology facilities require only a few highly skilled persons (who often can be relocated from outside the area) and a large number of production workers.

Further, new enterprise development in the high-technology sector is strongly associated with the presence of an existing concentration of similar economic activity.[14] Not surprisingly, this tendency toward clustering of new independent high-technology firms lends support to the anecdotal evidence suggesting that spinoffs of individuals from existing firms are an important source of new independent businesses. Easier access to venture capital is another possible benefit of entering business near an existing high-technology center (Dorfman 1983). In addition, the relatively concentrated structure of the high-technology sector and the rapid pace of its technological evolution would suggest further agglomeration benefits for small firms.

Branch formations, on the other hand, are more responsive to business cost factors associated with traditional industrial location decisions, such as wage and energy costs. Variations in the rate of personal and business taxes across locales had little effect on high-technology formations of either type. Lacking evidence that such incentives affect the formation rates of new establishments, community planners should consider the forgone revenue possibly associated with such policies.

Considerable overlap in the factors affecting these two types of high-technology growth suggests that they represent complementary rather than competing policy alternatives. Simultaneous pursuit of both forms of development meets several needs of metropolitan areas seeking revitalization or continued growth. Capturing some of the economic activity in expanding national and multinational corporations provides immediate rewards in terms of jobs and income. It also contributes to the development of the infrastructure conducive to further high-technology growth. Nurturing local entrepreneurs fulfills the complementary functions of lessening dependence on externally controlled firms, providing some insulation from national business cycles, and facilitating local adaptation to the continuing process of structural change. Despite the fact that the high-technology sector is expected to provide less than 10 percent of the new jobs created between 1982 and 1995 (Riche et al. 1983, 54), the approaches described in this study to encourage high-technology development can be modified for application in other growth sectors, such as financial or educational services. Developing the capacity to anticipate and adapt to changes in the broad context of economic activity is essential to the vitality of metropolitan areas.

High Technology Industries

1311	Crude petroleum & natural gas	3533	Oil machinery
1321	Natural gas liquids	3534	Elevators & moving stairways
2812	Alkalies & chlorine	3535	Conveyors
2813	Industrial gases	3536	Hoists, industrial cranes
2816	Inorganic pigments	3537	Industrial trucks, tractors, trailers, stackers
2821	Plastic materials, synthetic resins, & nonvulcanizable elastomers	3561	Pumps & pumping equipment
2822	Synthetic rubber	3562	Ball & roller bearings
2823	Cellulosic man-made fibers	3563	Air & gas compressors
2824	Synthetic organic fibers	3564	Blowers & exhaust & ventilation fans
2831	Biological products	3565	Industrial patterns
2833	Medicinal chemicals & botanical products	3566	Speed changers, industrial high-speed gears
2834	Pharmaceutical preparations	3567	Industrial process furnace & ovens
2861	Gum & wood chemicals		
2865	Coal tar, crudes & intermediates, dyes & organic pigments	3568	Mechanical power transmission equipment
2891	Adhesives & sealants	3569	General industrial machinery
2892	Explosives	3572	Typewriters
2893	Printing ink	3573	Electronic computing equipment
2895	Carbon black		
2899	Chemicals & chemical preparation n.e.c.	3574	Calculating & accounting machines
2911	Petroleum refining	3576	Scales & balances
3482	Small arms ammunition	3579	Office machines
3483	Ammunition	3622	Industrial controls
3484	Small arms	3623	Welding apparatus
3489	Ordnance & accessories	3624	Carbon & graphite products
3511	Steam, gas, hydraulic turbines	3629	Electrical industrial apparatus
3519	Internal combustion engines	3651	Radio & TV receivers
3531	Construction machinery & equipment	3652	Phonograph records & tapes
3532	Mining machinery	3661	Telephone & telegraph apparatus

3662 Radio-TV transmitting
3671 Radio & TV electron tubes
3672 Cathode ray TV picture tubes
3673 Transmitting, industrial electron tubes
3674 Semi-conductors
3675 Electronic capacitors
3676 Resistors for electronic apparatus
3677 Electronic coils, transformers
3678 Connectors for electronics
3679 Electronic components, n.e.c.
3721 Aircraft
3724 Aircraft engines & engine parts
3728 Aircraft parts & equipment n.e.c.
3761 Guided missiles & space vehicles
3764 Guided missiles & space propulsion units
3769 Guided missiles & space parts & equipment n.e.c.
3811 Engineering, lab, science research instruments
3822 Automatic controls for regulating residential & commercial environment

3823 Industrial instruments for measuring and control of process variables
3824 Totalizing fluid meters & counting devices
3829 Measuring & controlling devices
3832 Optical instruments & lenses
3841 Surgical and medical instruments
3842 Orthopedic & surgical supplies
3843 Dental equipment
3851 Ophthalmic goods
3861 Photographic equipment
3873 Watches, clocks

Business Services

7372 Computer programming & other services
7374 Data processing equipment
7379 Computer related service n.e.c.
7391 Research & development labs
7397 Commercial testing labs
8922 Non-commercial educational & science research organizations

Author's Note: The views expressed are those of the author and should not be attributed to the Brookings Institution. The author is grateful for thoughtful criticism provided by Edward Bergman, Nancy Dorfman, Dennis Carlton, and others.

9 City Venture Corporation: Initiatives in U.S. Cities

Calvin Bradford and Mihailo Temali

In a sense, what the city did was give a charter to City Venture to go out and plan and then to implement. Neither the city nor the neighborhood found itself defining what was to be done.[1]

This statement from Donald Fraser, the mayor of Minneapolis, catches the essence of the general lesson to be learned from this case study of City Venture Corporation. Public/private partnerships offer new economic development potentials for sharing community, government, and private sector resources. However, to the extent that the private sector sees these partnerships as profitable business opportunities, governments and community residents will have to respond as consumers and clients rather than as partners.

This report on a study of City Venture Corporation indicates that many governments and their agencies often have difficulty defining their own roles in such partnerships. In some cases this led governments to give up some of the functions that are essential to the governing role. In addition, some governments did not approach these partnerships in a businesslike way. Therefore, they often failed to hold the private sector accountable for its performance. The conclusion is that the most critical issue in these partnerships is to define the appropriate role of the government, without which the other roles also are confused.

This study of City Venture Corporation cannot be assumed to embody all the larger issues of the world of public/private partnerships from which it is taken. Due to its size and scope, however, and because it includes failures as well as successes, City Venture does offer some experiences that help to inform us in an area where the body of existing research is small and generally superficial. (There are case studies by Fosler and Berger [1982] and Sekera [1982], and the survey by Clarke and Rich [1982a].)

City Venture Corporation

It was during the Carter administration that the reduction in the direct role of the government and the increased dependence on the private sector to help solve our economic development problems became conceptualized as a movement toward "public/private partnerships." But under the Reagan administration, a new term, "private sector initiatives" has emerged to replace this original concept. The change is more than semantic. It indicates a move beyond a concept of shared roles to a position that depends upon the private sector to initiate the proposals, programs, and policies (see Berger et al. 1982). City Venture Corporation is a paradigm of the private sector initiatives' version of public/private partnerships.

City Venture Corporation (CVC) was created by William Norris, chairman of the board and founder of Control Data Corporation (CDC). It was formed in 1978 as a for-profit company by thirteen companies and two church organizations.[2] Control Data Corporation is the largest stockholder, and William Norris is the driving force behind City Venture. William Norris's philosophy and the high-technology products and services of Control Data Corporation are the essence of the City Venture concept. Excerpts from a series of City Venture statements express the concept:

> City Venture functions as a catalyst. . . . Our basic belief is that the private sector must take the lead role previously left to government in initiating and managing urban revitalization.[3]

> City Venture's leadership is rooted in the private sector. City Venture has assembled unprecedented resources to bring large-scale management skills to the inner city. City Venture assembles the critical management know-how and private financing, and the full range of new and emerging technology from both the physical and social sciences necessary for holistic solutions to urban problems.[4]

> In a typical City Venture project, a minimum of 2,000 new jobs are targeted. The primary strategy for this job creation is the

> start-up and growth of new and small businesses. . . . Programs pioneered by Control Data form the basis of these efforts.[5]

> City Venture's strength is in . . . its ability to formulate specific strategies to address problems, and its capability to manage the implementation of development for an entire community's benefit.[6]

City Venture gains its income from contracts to "design a community revitalization strategy" and contracts for the "long-term implementation of the strategy."[7] This strategy (usually called a plan) integrates a specific set of City Venture elements into existing local plans, proposals, and projects. Each element is subsidized or funded through its own separate contract. The five basic elements of City Venture projects are:

1. A Business and Technology Center (BTC) containing "manufacturing, laboratory and office space on very flexible terms, centrally shared model rooms, accounting, purchasing and legal services, and a complete range of computer services and computer-based management education programs."[8] The prototypes are in St. Paul and Minneapolis.

2. A Fair Break Program, which is part of Control Data's computer-based education program, called PLATO. Fair Break uses the PLATO system to make clients "job ready." This includes computer courses for a high school equivalence degree, along with computer programs and counseling on employment attitudes, self-image, and behavior —but not specific job skills training.[9]

3. The establishment of a Cooperation Office, based on the original Minnesota Cooperation Office (MCO) opened in Minnesota in 1979. It is funded through private grants. Businesses draw on panels of experts from the private sector and universities to help entrepreneurs in high-technology areas develop business ideas by providing assistance in planning, research and development, and identifying sources of financing. By mid-1982 MCO had started eight companies and produced eighty-five jobs.[10]

4. Establishment of a Seed Capital Fund, based on the Minnesota Seed Capital Fund that Control Data began early in 1980. In Minnesota this fund comes from private corporations that take equity positions in the high-technology companies they support with seed

capital. The Seed Capital Fund often works to finance companies receiving planning aid from the Cooperation Office.[11]

5. City Venture projects may include a production plant, typically a Magnetic Peripherals plant (a company in which Control Data owns controlling stock) or, for part-time jobs, a bindery (started by, and often owned by, Control Data companies) that uses unskilled labor for the assembly of manuals and other printed materials.[12] City Venture clients are routinely given tours of the prototypes for these plants—Control Data's own computer peripherals assembly plant constructed in the Northside community of Minneapolis after the area was torn by riots in 1967 and the Selby bindery in a low-income, minority section of St. Paul. The Fair Break program was first used in the Northside plant. It is Control Data's original inner-city plant, employing a large percentage of minority residents in its semi-skilled assembly jobs.

In addition, all City Venture projects include some other Control Data programs, usually developed from the PLATO system. For example, versions of these PLATO-based products and services are included in at least two or more of the City Venture plans, proposals, and contracts: computer-based business management programs; ACET (a job skills training program for computer-related jobs); STAY-WELL (a health care training program); EAR (an employee counseling program); HOMEWORK or TAP (job training and job readiness programs for the disabled); SKILTECH (a computer job-matching program); and several versions of computer-based education programs from Adult Learning Centers to Career Readiness Programs for high school students.

The Study

This study is based on a review of all twenty-one of the City Venture proposals and projects initiated by March 1982. These include activities in Akron, Buffalo, Boston, Cleveland, Denver, Detroit, Oakland, Richmond, Virginia, and St. Louis, where City Venture made proposals that were either turned down or remained pending. The study reviewed ongoing City Venture projects in Baltimore, Charleston, South Carolina, Duluth, Philadelphia, San Antonio, and Toledo, as well as projects that have now been discontinued in Benton Harbor, Michigan, Miami, and Minneapolis. Reviews of the Business and

Technology Center projects in the southwest Bronx, Omaha, and St. Paul were undertaken to enrich the limited number of cases of full City Venture projects.

The Minneapolis and St. Paul Business and Technology Centers, the Minnesota Cooperation Office, the Minnesota Seed Capital Fund, Control Data's Northside assembly plant, and the St. Paul Bindery are all included in the study. Data also were collected on five other business incubators to compare costs, services, and job production with the Business and Technology Centers. Because the study was based in Minnesota, field observations of the Minneapolis City Venture project were made on more than thirty occasions. Field observations also were made in Baltimore, Benton Harbor, Boston, Charleston, Miami, Philadelphia, Richmond, San Antonio, and Toledo.

Data collection included an analysis of City Venture proposals, contracts, progress reports to contractors, speeches, public relations and promotional materials produced by Control Data and City Venture Corporation, articles in major newspapers in cities with City Venture projects, articles in national newspapers, newsmagazines, and relevant trade publications, government documents and memoranda obtained through Freedom of Information act requests, and transcripts, tapes, and notes from field observations and interviews.

The members of the research team conducted 168 interviews with the development professionals, community residents, and other public and private figures identified as major actors in each City Venture project. These include forty-eight interviews with members of community organizations in City Venture areas, thirty-four professionals directly involved in negotiating and monitoring City Venture and Control Data contracts, twenty-six other government officials, eighteen members of City Venture staffs (including the directors of all the City Venture projects), sixteen other personnel (board members or officers) at Control Data and City Venture, and twenty-six independent business people involved in City Venture projects or engaged in alternative projects in inner-city job creation.[13] These data were collected from fall 1979 to spring 1983. The study method was designed to be open-ended in order to define critical issues rather than to test hypotheses. Therefore, many of the field data are qualitative. This may not be satisfying to readers used to quantitative analysis. But these methods are appropriate in new areas to develop the issues for more discrete testing in the future.

City Venture's Economic Development Performance

Fifteen cities made decisions for or against contracting with City Venture for its economic development package. In six cases (Buffalo, Boston, Cleveland, Denver, Oakland, and Richmond) the cities did not feel that City Venture was an improvement over their own resources or potentials. The evaluation of City Venture's performance is based primarily on seven of the nine cities where City Venture projects are ongoing or were terminated after initial contracts (Baltimore, Benton Harbor, Charleston, Miami, Minneapolis, Philadelphia, and Toledo). San Antonio and Duluth projects are just beginning but are included where appropriate.

The City Venture Planning Process

Table 9.1 displays the various elements, their status, and the dates of the initial contracts for the nine City Venture plans. All plans contain a BTC. All but one project contain a Fair Break program. All but two contain a bindery or similar facility. Four projects include a Control Data (Magnetic Peripherals, Inc.) plant. All but the Toledo project have plans for Cooperation Offices and Seed Capital Funds. Finally, the City Venture plans each included some of the Control Data educational and human service programs detailed above.

With the exception of Charleston, where the mayor felt that the city lacked City Venture's planning skills, the interviews with public officials and economic development professionals indicated that there was universal dissatisfaction with the City Venture plans. In Philadelphia the Private Industry Council, which paid for part of the initial plan, required that it be done again.

The most common complaint was that City Venture simply delivered to the city a cut-and-paste version of existing city plans. However, the City Venture plans did bring together some existing plans and projects into a single process. Second, as was expected, City Venture worked selected elements of the City Venture package into this integrated plan. But it was the inclusion of a range of the other Control Data educational and human service programs that most upset local officials and agency professionals. As one development professional in Florida put it, "We all resented the management plan pushing

Table 9.1   Elements of City Venture projects through December 1982[1]

City	First contract date	BTC	Fair Break	Bindery	CDC plant	Seed capital fund	Cooperation office
Minneapolis[2]	3/79	C	C	C	C	C	C
Toledo	4/79	C	C	C	C	—	—
Baltimore	6/80	C	P	C	—	P	P
Philadelphia	10/79	P	C	—	—	P	P
Miami	9/80	P	C	P	—	P	P
Charleston	3/81	C	C	P	—	P	C
Benton Harbor	10/81	P	P	C	—	P	P
San Antonio	3/82	P	C	—	C	P	P
Duluth	10/82	P	—	—[3]	—	P	P

P: Proposed in CVC contract or plan, to be studied or implemented by City Venture or Control Data.
C: Completed or in progress.
—: Not proposed.
Notes:
1 The data are taken from City Venture proposals and contracts. Elements are occasionally added or dropped from City Venture projects after contracts and plans have been issued.
2 While all of these elements have existed in the Minneapolis CVC project area subsequent to the CVC project beginning, the CVC project as such ended after the planning contract was completed.
3 City Venture will start one business, according to the contract, one option for this being a bindery.

Control Data Corporation products. Virtually everything they came up with (in the plan) had a Control Data product."

While some public officials and agency professionals were concerned with the extent of these products in the plans, they did not delete them from the implementation contracts. In the interviews most officials reported that they considered these products part of the price of the job commitments expected from City Venture. For its part, Control Data was clear in its aims. As William Norris said, "The main benefit derived from City Venture by corporate stockholders is in the identification of new markets in their fields of interest."

As an example, the March-April (1982) issue of *CONTACT*, Control Data's internal newsletter, highlights the City Venture project in

Toledo. The article quotes Herbert Trader (then president of City Venture) as saying, "The effort to attack Toledo's social need for urban revitalization has created several business opportunities for Control Data." He added, "In fact there is quite a list of Control Data activities." These include a Control Data Business and Technology Center, a Magnetic Peripherals plant, a Fair Break contract, a CETA contract, a contract for Control Data's Career Readiness program, a contract for the Control Data Institute (computer-based training in computer repair and electronics), a Control Data Learning Center (PLATO), a contract with Commercial Credit Corporation (Control Data's financial subsidiary), and business for Control Data Temps (a temporary help business).

Mark Twain is credited with once saying, "If the only tool you have is a hammer, all problems look like nails." Control Data Corporation is a high-technology computer corporation. It is not surprising that in expressing the corporate philosophy on social problem-solving William Norris would say, "Technology is the keystone of our economic system. . . . Financing and management are important but not as fundamental as technology."

Those whose complaints centered on these additional computer-based products did not share Control Data's commitment to computer-based education as the solution to so many economic and social problems.

City Venture's disagreements with some of the community organizations in the project areas escalated to public confrontations. City Venture officials often became frustrated when the opposition persisted after many presentations of their plans at meetings in the community. For two projects, this frustration was expressed by William Norris as a belief that radical community activists were exploiting the City Venture process. Norris described it this way:

> At times it appears as if there is a conspiracy to undermine the private enterprise system . . . at least two years are required to show tangible evidence of progress—much longer to reach job creation goals. This allows time for those in opposition to create doubts—and in two City Venture projects, in Minneapolis and Miami, to prevent them from progressing beyond the planning stage.

There was some political opposition to City Venture in Minneapolis and Miami due to Control Data's business involvements in South Africa. However, Norris's view does not explain the considerable variations in City Venture's relationships with the existing community organizations to which they had to respond in their target areas in Boston, Baltimore, Philadelphia, and Toledo, as well as Miami and Minneapolis. Rather, it appears that the nature of these relationships was defined by the difference between a community group's beliefs about its capacity to participate in economic development projects and the *advisory* role offered to it by City Venture.

In Toledo and Philadelphia the community groups in the City Venture neighborhoods reported that the advisory role they were given was an improvement over their previous roles of activism, trying with little success to get the cities to respond to their concerns. But in Minneapolis and Miami, where the community organizations involved with City Venture had considerable experience in either housing or economic development, these organizations expected to be included as *partners*, not advisers. Community groups in both cities produced position papers that pointed to community-based programs and capacities that were not included in the City Venture plans, questioned the costs and value of City Venture programs, and criticized City Venture for not including the community as a full partner, with veto powers and a share of the profits.[14]

In both Boston and Baltimore the proposed City Venture projects were complements to the industrial park projects of community-based developers. The Community Development Corporation of Boston had experience in an industrial park development with Digital Corporation, and it controlled the land and EDA funds for a business incubator site. City Venture was asked to play the limited role of assessing the feasibility of the BTC for this site. City Venture insisted on an entire planning and management package and withdrew rather than play this limited role.[15] On the other hand, the Park Heights Community Development Corporation in Baltimore accepted City Venture, hoping that the BTC and bindery projects would free the Development Corporation for other tasks. But in the implementation stage the partnership broke down when City Venture delays held up the local development schedule, and City Venture received Community Development Block Grant funds while the Development Corporation's CDBG funds were cut.[16]

Except in Benton Harbor and Charleston, city officials and develop-

Table 9.2 City Venture contracts—summary[1]

City	Date	Amount	Source
Minneapolis	3/79	$ 205,000	Tax increment financing (planning contract)
Toledo	4/79	50,000	Economic Development Administration (EDA)
	3/80	300,000	Community Development Block Grant (CDBG)
	2/81	90,000	CDBG
	7/81	145,000	CDBG
	1/82	80,000	CETA (job bank operations)
	7/82	145,000	CDBG
	total	810,000	
Philadelphia	10/79	67,500	Private Industry Council (PIC) ($40,000) and general city funds ($27,500)
	5/80	316,500	EDA, State grant to city
	7/81	150,000	CDBG
	7/82	110,000	CDBG (1-month extension of existing contract)
	total	644,000	
Baltimore	6/80	320,000	PIC/CETA (planning contract)
	3/81	327,500	PIC/CETA
	3/82	276,000	CETA ($100,000), CDBG (approx. $176,000)
	total	923,500	
Miami	9/80	42,500	Chamber of Commerce, Burger King (planning)
	4/81	380,000	PIC/CETA (planning contract)
	total	422,500	
Charleston	3/81	285,000	State PIC/CETA Title 7 (planning contract)
	2/82	200,000	CETA and CDBG ($100,000 from each)
	total	485,000	

Table 9.2 (continued)

Benton Harbor	10/81	375,000	State Department of Labor/ CETA (CVC actually began work here in May 1981)
	3/82	200,000	State Department of Labor
	total	575,000	
San Antonio	3/82	422,501	CDBG (discretionary)
Duluth	10/82	187,000	EDA
Total		$4,694,501	
Total by source			
Total PIC/CETA		$2,007,500	(42.8%)
Total CDBG		$1,658,501	(35.3%)
Total EDA		$ 553,500	(11.8%)
Total State and Local		$ 475,000	(10.1%)

1 These figures represent the best estimate. In some cases precise data were not available or were, at times, contradictory.

ment professionals tended to see City Venture as just one, among several, development projects. City Venture identified federal funds beyond present city allocations for many of its programs. This, coupled with the promise of so many jobs, made it easier for the cities to accept City Venture plans with the Control Data products.

Table 9.2 shows the amounts and sources of funds for each City Venture contract. The largest source is from Comprehensive Employment Training Act (CETA) funds, followed by CDBG funds. Separate Fair Break and Career Readiness contracts from the U.S. Department of Labor (mostly CETA funds) supported over $3 million of training in Minneapolis, Miami, Philadelphia, Charleston, and Toledo, with an additional $3 million committed for the San Antonio project. The BTCs, on the other hand, often required locally generated subsidies as in Minneapolis ($2.4 million in tax increment financing), Baltimore ($3.5 million in industrial revenue bonds), or Toledo ($8.25 million in industrial revenue bonds). Production plants all draw on the Fair Break subsidies for workers. Some use the BTC space or resources, and others use additional subsidies, such as the $5 million in site preparation costs and an estimated $24 million in rent subsidies over the life of the land lease for the Control Data plant in San Antonio.[17]

Community organizations with development experience, especially in Minneapolis and Miami where their own plans were not included in the City Venture strategy, were more concerned than the local governments about the costs of these contracts, the control of the development process, and the issue of whether by contracting with City Venture the community and the city had both become consumers of Control Data products rather than partners in development. One issue was the size of the direct cash payments to City Venture's central office ("Corporate Cost and Contribution") above the direct expenses and overhead budgeted to complete local contract obligations. For example, this was 32 percent of the $442,501 contract in San Antonio, and 34 percent of a $360,000 contract request in Philadelphia.[18]

Job Creation

For officials in all the cities, the promise of job creation was the essential reason for contracting with City Venture. Table 9.3 indicates City Venture's performance on short-term job goals. Performance is measured against the goals and by the definitions set by City Venture. In Minneapolis, Philadelphia, Baltimore, and Benton Harbor the term "new creations" is used. In Charleston and Toledo the job goals combine "new creations" and "job placements." In Miami the goal was for "job placements" only. Neither City Venture nor the cities differentiated between part-time and full-time jobs, nor between actual new jobs and jobs that moved in from other, often nearby, locations. No clear reporting was required to distinguish job placements from job creations.

City Venture projected 1,610 jobs in the short term. Measured against these goals City Venture produced 749 jobs and placements, 46.5 percent of its goal. But City Venture reached 72.9 percent of its goals in cities with Magnetic Peripherals plants and/or binderies (Minneapolis, Toledo, Baltimore, and Benton Harbor).[19] In Minneapolis, Baltimore, and Benton Harbor over 95 percent of the jobs produced were in these plants. Overwhelmingly, the location of production plants was the primary source of job creation. There is, however, a caution. Huge subsidies for plants may actually reduce corporate costs to a point where they can easily move to another location where wages are lower or subsidies are higher.

Table 9.3 City Venture job creations and placements[1]

City	Job goals[2] Long-term	Short-term	Jobs produced
Minneapolis	3,000 by 1984	150 by 3/81	164 by 3/81
Toledo	2,000 by 1984	550 by 7/82	423 new/Pl. by 8/82
Philadelphia	2,500 by 1986	200 by 7/82	2 new[3]
Baltimore	2,500 by 1985	170 by 3/82	47[4] by 4/82
Miami	4,000 by 1985	250 Pl. by 1/82	approx. 50 Pl. by 3/82[5]
Charleston	1,500 by 1986	250 by 3/83	approx. 34, most Pl., by 10/82
Benton Harbor	1,200 by 1986	40 by 12/82	29 by 12/82
Total		1610	749

1 These figures represent our best estimate after reviewing City Venture reports, interviewing City Venture staff, and, in some cases, calling the individual businesses.
2 "Pl." refers to placements; all other figures refer to new job creations.
3 City Venture quarterly reports indicate creation or placement of sixty-nine jobs, but interviews with businesses and with others at the site indicate that these jobs already existed or were located independently of City Venture. Others of these jobs were placements, which are not counted because the contract calls for creation of new jobs.
4 City Venture claimed one hundred jobs, but interviews with the business involved indicated that only forty-seven were created as a result of City Venture. The others were created as a result of the efforts of the Park Heights Community Development Corporation, a community-based organization.
5 City Venture was originally credited with reaching its goal of 250 placements, but interviews with the staffs of the Private Industry Council and the local CETA agency revealed that all but about fifty of these placements were actually made by other CETA sponsors.

Since the publication of David Birch's (1979) study of the job creation potential for small businesses, there has been an increased interest in generating jobs through the creation and growth of small businesses. The Control Data Business and Technology Centers (BTCS) are designed as incubators for small businesses, especially high-technology businesses. The prototype BTC in St. Paul opened in 1979, and the other City Venture BTCS in Toledo, Charleston, and Minneapolis are in their early stages of operating. In the course of the study two independent high-technology incubators were identified and surveyed, the Rensselaer Polytechnic Institute's Incubator Program in

Troy, New York, and the University City Science Center in Philadelphia. Three inner-city industrial incubators also were identified and surveyed, the City of Buffalo incubator, the incubator of the City of Chester, Pennsylvania, and the Fulton-Carroll Center for Industry in Chicago.[20]

Staff at the Rensselaer program estimate that seventy jobs have been created since it opened in 1980, while the Science Center estimates put job creation at over 1,140 since 1963. Both incubators report that few of these jobs are classified as less than highly skilled.[21] Site visits to the St. Paul and Minneapolis BTCs, which are predominantly oriented toward professional and high-technology firms, indicated that, aside from some custodial and clerical jobs, these incubators also house highly skilled and professional jobs. The City Venture job plan for Baltimore indicates that this BTC also will provide few jobs that are not highly skilled.[22]

When these businesses move into the production stage that might provide lower-skilled jobs, they may be expected to seek locations where labor costs are low. One high-technology firm assisted by the Minnesota Cooperation Office moved to Florida for the final development and production phase.[23] In a larger example the proposed Magnetic Peripherals plant for San Antonio, where wages are very low, will employ more people than all other City Venture computer-assembly plants combined. On an even larger scale we have the decision of Atari to move its major production plants out of the country to Taiwan.

Industrial incubators appear to provide more of the kinds of jobs that inner-city community residents might secure. Since their creation in 1978 the Buffalo incubator estimated creating "about thirty" jobs, and the Chester incubator estimated creating 135. The Fulton-Carroll incubator reported creating or saving 263 jobs since starting in 1980. Very few of the jobs in these incubators were highly skilled.[24] The managers of these incubators also indicated that low rents, assistance in locating financing, and some *very simple* shared resources, such as a receptionist, a photocopying machine, or a conference room, were the key ingredients of success. Rents during 1982 ranged from a low of $1.35 per square foot in the Fulton-Carroll incubator to $2.50 in the Buffalo incubator.

During 1982 office space rental in the Control Data BTCs ranged from $9.50 in the Charleston Center to $12.00 in the Minneapolis

Center. In the BTCs where some raw industrial space was available at much lower rents (an annex of the St. Paul BTC and space in the Charleston BTC at $3.50, and 50,000 square feet in the Toledo Center starting at $1.50), this space housed some businesses with lower-skilled jobs. These include a children's clothing manufacturer in Charleston, a sheet metal fabrication plant in Toledo, and a Laotian furniture manufacturer in St. Paul. This issue needs more study. But this initial exploration suggests that in spite of the overall growth of high-technology businesses, industrial incubators hold more potential for inner-city job production, at least in the short run.

Finally, City Venture is based on an assumed need for job preparedness training through Fair Break and other PLATO programs. The quality of the data is not sufficient for definite conclusions. But the initial pattern indicates difficulty placing Fair Break participants unless jobs were already committed for them. The Fair Break systems in Minneapolis and Toledo achieved high placement rates by expressly placing participants in the Magnetic Peripherals plants and in the binderies. On the other hand, in Philadelphia, which lacked either of these plants or a BTC, the CETA contractor reported that the Fair Break program placed only 23 percent of its graduates in the first year, compared to a typical placement rate of 60 percent for the Philadelphia CETA agency. The first year City Venture contract in Philadelphia linked Fair Break placements to private sector job commitments that never materialized.[25]

Management and Accountability

In addition to Control Data's belief in technology as the key to economic problems, City Venture evolved from a conviction that the skills developed to manage complex weapons systems and space programs in the 1960s could be transferred to the problems of urban economic development (see Gregory 1968a, 1968b; Bradford et al. 1982). As to the application of this philosophy, City Venture's experience suggests some caution about the direct transferability of these private sector management styles and skills.

With the exception of those in Duluth and San Antonio, three of the remaining seven projects were terminated when City Venture could not complete some of its tasks. In Minneapolis, City Venture had twice failed to produce an industrial park UDAG that met the minimum HUD requirements for the leveraging of private funds. City Venture withdrew from Minneapolis in February 1981 because the city would not give it a management contract until there was an acceptable UDAG application.[26] In Benton Harbor, after failing to reach all the goals of its first contract, City Venture was unable to raise all the funds necessary for its second contract.[27]

In Miami, where the City Venture contract was being administered by the Private Industry Council, a staff report recommended termination of the contract for lack of performance on several tasks. After an additional extension, it became clear that City Venture could not meet its obligations, including 250 job placements. In April 1982 the PIC took over these obligations, and City Venture's contract was not renewed.[28] Sylvan Meyer, chair of the PIC, reflected, "They were excellent at turning out paper and showing what their proposals were going to be, but they didn't know how to implement what they were doing." These problems indicate a need to have the substantive knowledge for particular tasks as well as the process skills of management.

Some of the other problems City Venture had may be indicative of more general characteristics of the private sector management style. First, in mass production fashion, City Venture tried to apply its prepackaged programs to local settings that varied considerably. The failure to modify these programs caused the loss of the Boston contract and delayed the BTC developments in Miami and Philadelphia, where neither the city nor Control Data had secured site control over the planned location. Second, City Venture's centralized management system, making all decisions at the central office in Minneapolis, replicated, rather than replaced, the familiar red tape and delays characteristic of government management. Third, in many cases problems between community groups and governments were not due to lack of coordination but to political differences about goals, plans, and control. Being itself an advocate of a particular plan, and Control Data products, City Venture was not in a position to play the role of mediator.

Edward Dirkswager, deputy to the mayor of Minneapolis, described City Venture's overall management style this way:

> They did planning more like they would do it in a corporation, which is a little bit more closed and the decision making a little

more centralized, and on a tighter time frame than we're used to. . . . And they were misinterpreted in the community as trying to ram things down their throats; and the corporation, for its part, not being used to that slowness and that deliberation and that democracy, if you will, misunderstood that as chaos and anarchy.

On the other side of the coin the agencies funding City Venture failed to draft contracts that held City Venture accountable for its performance. Philadelphia, Minneapolis, and San Antonio offer three good examples.

All the Philadelphia contracts revolve around City Venture securing an investment by Control Data in a BTC. The first contract states "CVC shall deliver to City a commitment from Control Data . . . to implement a business and technology center." But this is made "contingent on other commitments public and private" that must be "made sufficient to meet Control Data's needs," which are left unspecified in the contract. Failing in this first contract, the second contract included a letter of intent from Control Data to invest in a BTC, but the letter indicated that it was not legally binding. The third contract required City Venture to produce a financing package for a BTC, but it failed to require that Control Data be an investor, as the city wanted. The fourth contract specifically required Control Data to inform the city of the amount of the investment it would make, but all commitments were still contingent upon obtaining a site and other investors. Meanwhile, the city, the state, and the Private Industry Council paid City Venture a total of $644,000 and had to fulfill their own contractual obligations, including helping to secure funding for Control Data programs and granting City Venture "exclusive development rights" to sections of the project area.[29]

In Minneapolis the City Venture management plan indicated that Magnetic Peripherals had made a commitment to locate its plant in the BTC, when completed, but there was no contract for this.[30] A few months after City Venture failed to get its contract renewed, the Magnetic Peripherals plant relocated out of Minneapolis.

In San Antonio, Control Data wanted a City Venture contract as a condition for expanding an existing Magnetic Peripherals plant to accommodate a thousand employees. Control Data got an estimated total of $34 million in construction and rental subsidies, and Fair

Break got contracts for $15 million in building commitments, yet the contract does not require Control Data to occupy the site or to actually employ any local residents.[31]

As a general practice, partnership agreements include all the participants and define clear obligations. The holistic City Venture plans identify many participants. City Venture claims that "accountability is established in the terms of the contract(s)" and that "this accountability is further insured by the participation of local business, neighborhood, and government officials in establishing project goals and carrying out implementation."[32] City Venture, however, never had contractual authority over Control Data or any other participant. Since the contracts make City Venture's performance contingent upon the performance of each and every one of these other participants, the City Venture contracts provide no effective accountability at all. An accountable management agent would need central contractual authority over the elements of the plan. Funders and actual equity investors could have this authority, but, as a grantee, City Venture was not in the appropriate position.

Conditions of Success and Failure

Where City Venture succeeded, the following conditions tended to prevail:

1. The goals and programs to reach those goals were commonly accepted by all involved parties.

2. In implementing the programs, the community, government, and other private sector actors all played *active*, cooperating parts that were *consistent with their own images of their roles and capacities.*

3. There were no delays in gaining control of necessary land and access to required government subsidies and grants.

4. The primary source of job creation was through the location of production plants, in the familiar tradition of smokestack chasing or in the modified version of incubators with an industrial and manufacturing focus.

The one project that exemplified these characteristics was the Toledo project. Here the city had established plans for an industrial park and shopping center. The community was given an advisory role that was an improvement over its previous defensive, activist

role. Control Data created new jobs through the location of a Magnetic Peripherals plant and offered assistance in the creation of a
bindery and a business incubator that had substantial, low-cost
industrial space. Finally, there was a local business leader, the president of Toledo Trust, who not only supported the project verbally,
but who personally opened doors in the local business community
for Control Data and who beat the bushes looking for businesses for
the industrial park. Toledo was the only place where City Venture
actually fulfilled the catalyst role of attracting other major businesses through the location of a box fabrication plant of the Owens-
Illinois Corporation. Lacking one or more of these critical conditions,
City Venture encountered significant, and even fatal, obstacles in
other cities.

Where City Venture failed, in whole or in part, it lacked one or
more of the four conditions above. Failures also appeared to be the
result of the following conditions:

1. The government agencies that contracted with City Venture
transferred their own public planning and management functions to
a private corporation. The private sector initiative defined both the
ends and means, thus co-opting the public planning processes.

2. Confusion in roles resulted from City Venture and Control Data
assuming parts of so many roles, from planning to the provision of
social services. As a result, local governments and community residents became clients and consumers of programs rather than partners.

3. City Venture did not recognize and appreciate the *different* self-
interests of the participants nor did it create a forum to seek compromises and to negotiate acceptable joint efforts. In their study of
seven successful public/private partnerships, Fosler and Berger (1982)
define this merging of self-interest and common action as the essence
of working partnerships.

4. There was no process for accountability nor were there clear
measures of success or reporting mechanisms to gauge progress. For
most Control Data programs, success was defined simply as having
the program.

Some Concluding Remarks

All of the conditions of success and failure could be translated into
recommendations and hypotheses for more research. But these con-

clusions need to be tempered with some practical considerations. First, in severely depressed areas the promise of jobs moves people to give away some of the accountability they might normally require. As Bernardo Eureste, city councilman in San Antonio, said, "We'll give them [Control Data] half the city for the jobs." Many of the officials and professionals interviewed expressed anxiety about not knowing what accountability could be required or what would drive away job producers. These officials were like tourists in a Middle Eastern bazaar who didn't know enough about the market to haggle effectively over the price or the requirement that they also buy some extra items that they didn't care about.

Second, interviews indicated several political pressures to accept City Venture. In Baltimore, where there are notable development projects in the central business district, the city seemed to want City Venture to show that the city could do economic development in the neighborhoods as well. In Philadelphia a new mayor wanted to use City Venture as a symbol of his administration's concern for minority neighborhood development. In Miami a powerful business leader saw City Venture as a way of getting the private sector to initiate its own plan for the revitalization of Liberty City. In San Antonio, Control Data held the City Venture contract hostage as part of the deal for a plant location that the city needed to complete a UDAG and avoid the pending forfeit of some of these federal funds.

Appropriately, private sector initiatives may be designed to make profits. This focus, however, is not adequate to protect the public interest, to set public goals, or to guarantee public accountability. These are government functions. Solutions to the problem of proper roles must take account of the political realities of development projects and the tremendous power contained in the promise of jobs. The fundamental issue is how local governments can hold prospective private sector job producers accountable in a job sellers' market.

Author's Note: We would like to thank Edward Bergman and Jean Marc Choukroun for their extensive and valuable editorial comments, and Karen Branan for her extensive assistance in the research. This chapter was first published in the *American Planning Association Journal* 1983 (Summer): 326–35.

When an industrial sewing company on Chicago's west side moved
its business to Mississippi in 1981, workers with twenty and
twenty-five years of seniority were thrown on the streets without any
severance pay or pension rights. For a few of them, however, the
period since then has been one of renewed hope and enormous personal growth as they helped start a community-sponsored industrial
sewing cooperative of their own, which grossed $125,000 in its first
year. All over the country not-for-profit organizations are starting, or
talking about starting, new businesses designed to fight unemployment, generate income to overcome budget cutbacks, or respond to
the parent organizations' own internal growth needs. Some are setting up construction companies as outgrowths of housing rehabilitation training programs; others are starting supermarkets because
chain stores have left their areas; still others are involved in auto
repair, millwork, television repair, and a myriad of other likely and
unlikely enterprises.[1] Although organizations ranging from museums to mental health centers are involved in these kinds of activities,
this essay focuses on community organizations since they are of
most relevance to planners.

This phenomenon is important to planners for several reasons.
The first has to do with the effect of these business activities on the
low- and moderate-income neighborhoods in which most of them
are being set up, as well as on the parent community organizations
themselves. Community organizations first became involved in business activities through the Community Development Corporations
(cDCs) originally sponsored in the late 1960s by the Ford Foundation
and the federal Office of Economic Opportunity. However, even dur-

ing the heyday of federal intervention, there were only forty relatively well-financed CDCs nationwide. Are the new, smaller scale, and more widespread bootstrap efforts likely to have any significant community impact? What does it take for them to be successful, however success may be defined?

The second reason that these new businesses are important to planners is that they reflect an important new policy trend, away from governmental intervention and toward a reliance on the market. President Reagan's policies have necessitated a trend toward self-sufficiency, popularly defined as freedom from external subsidies (Mier 1982b). This notion has traditionally connoted grassroots self-help efforts, but the Reagan-inspired variation puts particular emphasis on the market as a source of revenues. A specific example of this is the proposed role of community organizations in enterprise zones, where they are expected to take over many services previously rendered by government and to provide them on a for-profit basis (Butler 1981). Is "privatization" a rationale shared by the people engaged in implementing these new activities, or do they act out of different political and social beliefs? Do these new initiatives, as Boyte (1980) suggests, represent the conviction of community organizations that without control over productive enterprises they will always remain at the mercy of philanthropy and be reduced to irrelevance? Or, at the opposite extreme, do these initiatives indicate a renewed romance with free enterprise, an attempt, as Butler (1981) urges, to reinvigorate small-scale capitalism in areas thought to be forsaken by the market and most investors? Understanding more about the trend of neighborhood organizations setting up businesses will provide insight into both the potential for neighborhood development and the role of planning vis-à-vis that development.

From a policy perspective, then, the questions addressed in this chapter concern whether these new approaches can be used to plan and implement economic development efforts; what their political and ideological content is likely to be; and what impact they will have on the neighborhoods. These questions are intertwined for us; at the same time we realize that other planners may be interested in the implementation questions without concern for their political context.

Background

The ambiguous political content of business development efforts by community organizations reflects a similar ambiguity in the neighborhood movement itself. The neighborhood movement has popularly been cast as progressive, and its internal differences perceived mostly as ones of style or political tactics (E. Schwartz 1979). However, the movement has an equally important conservative and racist aspect (Philpot 1978; Goering 1979). On the progressive side, the diverse neighborhood movements of the 1960s frequently fought for community control and autonomy as solutions to social distress and powerlessness (Levy 1979; Hampden-Turner 1975). The federally sponsored Community Development Corporations were a major result of these movements.[2] A significant aspect of such efforts was a focus on job generation within the community and control over the production process. Although such efforts became less visible during the latter part of the 1970s, they by no means lost their intensity (Boyte 1980).

On the other hand, local organizing efforts with their roots in neighborhood homeowners' associations, the church, and long-standing voluntary organizations, have often been effective vehicles for preserving the fundamental institutions and values of modern industrial society.[3] As has been demonstrated by the anti-ERA (Equal Rights Amendment) movement and tax revolts, community-based organizations have often supported a conservative political agenda.[4] The latest evidence of the neighborhood movement's confused political agenda is its relatively weak opposition to President Reagan's urban policy of extensive cutbacks in social support programs, a yet-to-be-passed experimental enterprise zone program as an alternative to them, and a call for greater self-sufficiency through the market.[5]

Like the neighborhood movement itself, the practice of neighborhood-oriented planning also has had a multifaceted nature. Traditional forms of community planning are rooted, in theory and practice, in the same ideological soil as the homeowners' associations themselves. Our own premise in working with neighborhood organizations that attempt to set up small businesses, one shared by many of the organizations, is the belief that the organizations must begin to experiment with more democratically controlled and socially responsible forms of economic activity. Like Katznelson (1981) and Friedmann (1982), we believe that such activity is one important way for community organizations to work toward attaining political control over the process of production and distribution.

The tension between political and economic purposes also existed in the federally sponsored Community Development Corporations started in the early 1970s. What lessons do their experiences hold for the current attempt? Did their business development efforts prove a viable route for progressive community development?

Originally, many of their proponents saw Community Development Corporations as political institutions as much as economic ones, arguing that the condition of poor neighborhoods was a question of powerlessness, not just poverty, and that economic and political development had to proceed apace (Goldsmith 1974). Evaluations of CDCs have always been hampered by the vagueness of the organizations' mandates, the magnitude of the problems they were expected to address, and the relative paucity of their resources. By private sector standards, CDCs have not been very successful. Michelson (1979) analyzed 136 for-profit ventures owned by CDCs that existed at some point during 1975 and found that at least 70 percent suffered losses. His conclusion was that the ventures may have been a relatively cheap way of creating jobs but that as profit centers for CDCs they were not very successful.

An early evaluation by Abt Associates (1973) was generally positive as far as employment and training benefits were concerned. Of all people employed in the ventures, 29 percent had previously been unemployed or underemployed. Their total wages increased after hiring by 17 percent over what they had received before. Similarly, employees were generally satisfied and felt they were learning new skills (Stein 1973). However, in the absence of comparative data from other firms, the significance of these findings is unclear.

None of the various evaluations of the CDCs provides any systematic information about their possible indirect effects. There is no assessment of the type of products or services they have produced, whether there is any increase in the local multiplier, or whether these considerations even played any role in the selections of enterprises. Nor has the issue been addressed of whether the CDC ventures have helped foster community power. In an interesting modeling of factors affecting these ventures' profitability, Cromwell and Merrill (1973) found that the more representative the staff and board are of the community, the more likely the CDC businesses are to be profitable. However, others have found that CDC boards are largely self-perpetuating (Kelly 1977); one describes them as "the new rulers of the ghetto" (Berndt 1977).

Whatever the emphasis on noneconomic factors in the early years of CDC experience may have been, it became totally secondary as the Community Services Administration began to cut back its funding in the late 1970s. Profitability became an increasingly important criterion. Under the Reagan administration, the Community Services Administration has been terminated altogether, so that the CDCs now have joined the legion of other community-based organizations seeking funding from public and private institutions while showing, to a greater or lesser degree, an ability to support themselves from business-derived revenues.

Generally speaking, the CDCs' efforts to develop business activities clearly show the problems of trying to establish profitable enterprises in poor neighborhoods. At the same time their history suggests that there is a strong tendency to establish profitability as the main yardstick of success because it is much easier to measure than any other type of benefit. Finally, the same history suggests that as profitability becomes the yardstick, the political and social significance of the organization and its ventures decreases (Tabb 1979; Michelson 1979).

Current Community Business Ventures

In 1979, through our work with the Center for Urban Economic Development at the University of Illinois at Chicago (UICUED),[6] we began to work with several community-based organizations that were thinking of establishing profit-earning subsidiaries. The organizations were engaged in housing rehabilitation, construction, and job training and were interested in the business ventures for several reasons. They felt that their training programs had been fairly successful in developing marketable individual and institutional skills but were having trouble obtaining agreements with building and construction trade unions to enroll their graduates in apprenticeship programs, partially because the construction industry was not robust.

As a consequence, these organizations began several efforts to generate their own employment opportunities for their graduates.

Around the same time the Department of Housing and Urban Development (HUD) Self-Help Development Program was begun. Eventually, three of the rehabilitation employment and training organizations with which we worked (Voice of the People in Uptown, Bickerdike Redevelopment Corporation, and the Eighteenth Street Development Corporation) received HUD Self-Help Development Grants to set up subsidiaries.

To help the organizations sort out the complex relationships that develop between a profit-seeking subsidiary and its nonprofit, socially oriented parent organization, we looked with them at the various organizational structures that might be adopted by the parent or the subsidiary in order to minimize potential conflicts. In the course of doing this we surveyed six other Chicago organizations that had set up subsidiaries as well as six organizations from outside Chicago (Wiewel et al. 1982).

Then, in 1980, we worked with a local foundation and a public interest group based in Washington, D.C., both of which were trying to promote enterprises that employ significant numbers of youths as well as provide ownership opportunities to employees via employee stock ownership plans. The two organizations were looking for Chicago community organizations in which they could invest and located about ten youth groups that had some interest in establishing profit-making subsidiaries.

Since then, based on these early experiences, UICUED has expanded its efforts to help community organizations set up businesses. The organizations worked with or surveyed, which are listed in table 10.1, include the following types of subsidiaries: construction companies engaged in housing rehabilitation, a mill shop, home repair services, development companies, a housing insulation and general energy conservation service, an office supply store, a bookstore, a restaurant-bakery, a bulk mailing and distribution service, an industrial sewing contractor, housing management firms, a printshop, and auto repair shops.

Some of the efforts are off and running, others remain a dream, and most fall in between. None is "high-tech" (although, we *did* discover the world's greatest onion peeler). Few depart very far from the basic services their parent community organizations were already providing.

Based on what is known of experiences elsewhere, the cases involved are thought to be representative of similar efforts nationwide (Williams 1982; Cagnon 1982). Before general conclusions are discussed, three of the cases will be presented in greater detail.

South Shore Energy Store

Chicago's South Shore community is a black working- and middle-class neighborhood, attractively situated along Lake Michigan about seven miles south of the Loop. Most of its housing stock consists of large multiunit buildings that are increasingly showing the negative effects of the disinvestment that has been taking place since blacks began moving in in the late 1960s.[7] One of the area's main community development institutions is the South Shore Bank, which has gained national prominence as a model of community-oriented banking (Grzywinski and Marino 1981). It is owned by the Illinois Development Corporation, which also has another subsidiary, The Neighborhood Institute (TNI). This not-for-profit organization implements social service and economic development projects in South Shore. Early in 1981, hurt by cutbacks in social service programs, the TNI staff began to look around for a potential profit-making enterprise that would still be compatible with its main social purposes. Having already set up TNI's construction training program as a for-profit construction company, they decided to try the same approach with their weatherization program. This program had previously been funded by the City of Chicago, which paid for labor and materials for weatherizing the homes of low-income residents. TNI's program coordinator had previously worked at an "energy store" in another city where energy-saving devices, weatherization materials, and installation services were sold to the general public. TNI asked the Center for Urban Economic Development to prepare a feasibility study for a similar business in South Shore.

The study found that interest in energy conservation existed in the community, but that few homeowners were ready to buy any of the equipment or services. In any case, the market of owner-occupied homes in the community was too small to sustain a business. On the other hand, the managers and owners of the large apartment buildings, potentially a significant market, were even more reluctant to invest any money. They were already embarked on a course of disinvestment, or at best a course of trying to hold the line in what many of them perceived as an area with little future. They also were being approached frequently by companies from all over the metropolitan area who were marketing energy-saving devices and were thus well-served, in contrast to the homeowners who tend to be poorly informed about how to save energy.

These findings were disappointing to the TNI staff, and they temporarily shelved the idea of the energy store. They later concluded that energy conservation was a worthwhile purpose to pursue since it could potentially improve the cash flow of investor-owned buildings in the area and increased the buildings' chances of survival. Second, they saw energy conservation as worthwhile because, if implemented, it might help low-income residents save money. Since the feasibility study had shown a basic interest in energy conservation but a lack of knowledge, the TNI staff decided to develop an educational program that would develop the market and ultimately allow a business to be set up. The program would offer information on energy conservation, materials, and equipment and act as a referral source to the weatherization crew, which would continue to work in the city's program. The selling of materials and installation services would meet some of the costs of the total program, although it would not be a money-maker and, in fact, not break even. Rather than being totally dependent on grants, this valuable community program would meet some of its own expenses and hold out to funding sources the promise of increasing self-sufficiency.

Whether the business will succeed or not has yet to be determined. It is clearly based on substantial current organizational experience in a particular programmatic field that has allowed a fairly rapid assessment of market potential and a timely reassessment of community needs rather than a total abandonment of the initial idea. This flexibility was helped by the fact that energy conservation complemented the overall program of the organization. This example illustrates the approach of a mixed-model enterprise, straddling the gap between business and social service. In addition, it illustrates the importance of preliminary market research to avoid costly mistakes.

Spread The News

Spread The News is a fledgling mailing and distribution service operated as a not-for-profit enterprise by the Jane Addams Center of the Hull House Association, a multibranch social service agency in Chicago. It is located in Lakeview, a gentrifying neighborhood on the city's fashionable north side, but which still contains a substantial low-income population of many different ethnic backgrounds. The Jane Addams Center operates a job readiness program that takes in about forty young persons every month. It includes basic skills training, interviewing skills, and assistance in finding employment.

Frequently the gap between what the program teaches and the demands of a real job has been too wide, and the staff looked for a program that would create a bridge. Since they already received numerous requests from local businesses for help from their program participants in distributing advertising flyers, a mailing and distribution service looked like a good business opportunity. They already had much of the necessary machinery used for the center's own mailings, so they could immediately start attracting customers. Through Hull House contacts, they landed a contract with a Holiday Inn for monthly mass mailings. This gave them a foot in the door of the industry. Simultaneously, the program participants conducted a telephone survey of businesses in the neighborhood to find out what kinds of services were needed, who currently provided them, and at what rates. Contrary to their expectations, they found out that there was a greater demand for door-to-door leaflet distribution than for mass mailings; this fit the program's purpose well since the former is more labor-intensive. The program's staff person was taking business courses at a university and was able to use her newly acquired skills to analyze the venture. Along with the youths, she collected and analyzed information on competitors in the neighborhood and elsewhere, gathered basic industry information, and prepared a three-year business plan. The whole enterprise was helped along by an advisory board that had more business expertise than the social service-oriented board of the Jane Addams Center itself.

The business now operates marginally on revenues from the big Holiday Inn contract and from occasional smaller contracts with area firms. To get more customers, the business needs to expand its handling capabilities; this requires more machinery. From charitable sources the directors are raising some of the money needed to buy it, and they also may borrow from a financial institution. Once they have the machinery, they expect to nearly double their volume each year for the first three years and break even by the third.

Like the first case, this enterprise, even though it developed from ongoing activities, required a fair amount of market and organizational analysis before it was ready to be launched. Fortunately, a promising niche in the market was found. Unlike The Neighborhood Institute, the Jane Addams Center did most of the research itself. In the process, the program's staff person developed her understanding of the business and her business skills and now has access to a new career ladder within the organization.

The Fastest Peeler in the West

The previous two cases hardly look like they will make anyone rich. One way in which a business *can* become a big money-maker is by the use of a new, highly efficient technical development. The third case falls into this category and concerns a new machine that can peel onions with only about 7 percent waste instead of the customary 25 percent.

An entrepreneur on Chicago's west side who was already running a food-processing business was interested in purchasing this machine and starting a new company to process onions for the food industry. He needed help raising capital and training employees, and he was working with a business organization and the Center for Urban Economic Development. He was interested in funding from the special sources of capital for employee-owned new businesses mentioned earlier and was willing to invest $50,000 of his own to obtain a minority position. As he pointed out, reducing waste as much as the new machine did would allow very competitive prices and large profits. He would manage the company because he had extensive background in the food industry, especially with onions.

The enterprise was never implemented because the expected special funds never materialized. It is mentioned here because it is one of the few examples seen that appeared to hold the potential for significant profits. This business, unlike the others, would not have been a spinoff by a community organization. It would have taken the form of a joint venture of some type, in this respect resembling many of the projects that have been undertaken by the Community Development Corporations and sponsored by the Ford Foundation and the Community Services Administration.

Analysis

By examining the cases listed in table 10.1, some common features of which were highlighted in the detailed descriptions above, four areas of analysis can be identified as important: the meaning of success, which relates to the impact of these ventures; the catalytic elements and the question of how they may be used to organize an economic development program; the nature of the start-up process and the role of planning assistance; and organizational and political questions.

Success

If success is defined as the generation of significant profits (the most common criterion), the chances of achieving it are very slim. This is not surprising; most small businesses do not generate large cash flows. Their profits are only a few percent of sales, with much of it going to finance the working capital needed for expansion. In addition, their managerial salaries tend to be a greater than the average proportion of operating costs (Robert Morris Associates 1981).

If success is more modestly defined as breaking even, i.e., having market-derived revenues cover costs rather than generate profits, then the odds get better. (Of course, which costs are included as being covered is itself a complex question.) Finally, in mixed models such as the South Shore energy program, where revenues are partially derived from subsidies and partially from the market, there will be even more opportunities for financial success, which in this sense simply means being less financially dependent on charitable funding than traditional social service programs are. In sum, there are revenue opportunities in the market for community-based organizations, and some of the businesses listed in table 10.1 are operating successfully by one of these three standards.

While this emphasis on financial success is perhaps inevitable at the present time when community organizations are being forced to

Table 10.1 Business activities by not-for-profit organizations

Organization	Business activity
Alternatives, Chicago (social service)	Printing shop (not implemented)
Bethel Housing, Inc., Chicago (housing development and social service)	Stitches Unlimited, industrial sewing contractors (producers' cooperative); New Life Unlimited, housing management company (not-for-profit wholly controlled company)
Bickerdike Redevelopment Corporation, Chicago (housing development)	Humboldt Construction Company (wholly owned for-profit subsidiary)
Blue Gargoyle, Chicago (social service)	Blue Gargoyle Bakery and Restaurant (not-for-profit program)
Eighteenth Street Development Corporation, Chicago (housing development)	CALACCO, Construction Company (wholly owned for-profit subsidiary)
Fifth City Industrial Promotion Corporation, Chicago (commercial development)	Fifth City Auto, auto repair shop and car wash (wholly owned for-profit subsidiary)
Greater West Side Development Corporation, Chicago (business development organization)	Onion Peeling Company (not implemented)
Inquilinos Borincuas en Accion, Boston (social service)	Emergency Tenants Council (wholly owned for-profit development corporation)
Jane Addams Center of Hull House, Chicago (social service)	Spread the News, mailing and distribution service (not-for-profit program)
Jeff-Vander-Lou, St. Louis (community development)	JVL, Inc. Development Corporation (50 percent controlled not-for-profit organization)
Lakeview Citizens' Council, Chicago (community organizing)	Building Lakeview's Urban Environment (BLUE), housing development free-standing not-for-profit organization)
Latino Youth, Chicago (social service)	Latino Youth Home Remodelling (not-for-profit program)
Native American Educational Services (NAES), Chicago (college)	NAES Bookstore (not-for-profit program)

Table 10.1 (continued)

South Side United Development Corporation (Los Sures), Brooklyn (community development corporation)	Housing Management Co., and Construction Co. (both wholly owned for-profit subsidiaries)
The Neighborhood Institute, Chicago	The Neighborhood Crew, construction company (wholly owned for-profit subsidiary) South Shore Energy Store (not implemented) South Side Auto Co-op, auto repair shop (user-owned cooperative)
The Woodlawn Community Development Corporation, Chicago (community development corporation)	The Woodlawn Home Improvement Corporation, Inc. (wholly owned for-profit subsidiary)
Tri-City Citizens Union for Progress, Newark (community organization)	Housing Management Company and Maintenance Co. (wholly controlled not-for-profit subsidiaries)
Union Sarah Community Organization, St. Louis (community organization)	Union Sarah Economic Development Corporation (51 percent owned for-profit development corporation, which in turn owns majority interests in other for-profit corporations)
Voice of the People of Uptown, Inc., Chicago (housing development corporation)	Voice Millshop (never implemented)

try to survive with less (or no) outside government help, it nevertheless obscures more important concerns about their reasons for being. For all but three of the seventeen Chicago cases, job creation rather than profits was the primary reason for contemplating the development of a business activity. In over half, the need to create jobs was linked directly to the fact that funds for training programs were running out and the organizations hoped to support the trainees through business operations. In other cases, job creation was the main economic development strategy the organization had pursued from its inception. In these cases the organization often had to come up with a business idea with which it had no previous experience. Examples are the onion-slicing operation, Fifth City's auto shop, and Bethel's industrial sewing operation.

Exceptions to the primacy of job creation included the American Indian college, which was interested in its bookstore for the sake of promoting Indian culture, and the auto repair cooperative planned by The Neighborhood Institute. In both cases the primary consideration was the desire to serve the community. Although community service was not the primary rationale in the other cases, it was generally an important consideration. For instance, most of the organizations that entered construction-related businesses argued that reliable contractors were scarce in their areas. They planned to focus marketing within their neighborhoods rather than seeking construction work in higher-income areas of the city, even though there might be more business to be gained outside. Such considerations were unimportant only in the cases of the sewing contractor, the onion-slicing operation, and the mailing and distribution service, all of which of necessity had to rely on much larger markets than their own neighborhoods.

The importance of these organizations' desire to serve their neighborhoods' needs is also reflected in the fact that most of them used their ongoing operations as the basis for launching their businesses by converting into businesses programs they already thought of as worthwhile. An important further advantage of doing this, of course, was that their personnel were already experienced in some aspect of the business and did not need to start from scratch.

Only in the case of the energy store was the initial motivation the wish to generate extra cash for the parent organization, although in most other situations it entered into people's considerations at some point. However, even in the case of the energy store it soon became clear that such an expectation was unrealistic. Thus, most organizations saw business development as a way to survive the New Federalism rather than to generate profits that could be used for not-for-profit purposes. In short, they pursued in the marketplace what no longer could be pursued on a fully subsidized basis.

In evaluating businesses begun by community organizations, it should be pointed out that some failure is to be anticipated. Public and philanthropic organizations, after all, often apply a double standard when evaluating community groups. They demand a virtually 100 percent success rate among new small businesses sponsored by community organizations while readily accepting an 80 percent failure rate among new small private sector businesses. We think that among the seventeen Chicago cases looked at, three or four (20 percent) will indeed be successful by private sector standards.[8] An additional six or seven are expected eventually to operate successfully, if judged by the other standards discussed.

Catalyst

A second issue concerns the spark or catalyst that gets community enterprises going. One catalyst is confidence on the part of a community-based organization that it has a good handle on its operations and the ability to try to do new and different things. This was clearly the case with the construction-related companies that emerged from the rehabilitation employment training programs. A second catalyst is the availability of equity capital. This was particularly noticeable in our work in trying to stimulate the formation of youth-oriented businesses and suggests that the formation of an equity pool could be an important vehicle by which public bodies, or public-private partnerships, could stimulate new business generation. Such efforts are currently under way in Lincoln, Nebraska, and in Wisconsin, with planners playing important roles in initiating them.

Start-up

A third issue concerns the business start-up process. It was found that a significant nurturing period is required to develop a revenue-generating venture. This period generally lasts from one to four years and is required for a variety of reasons. First, organizations need to increase significantly the scale and complexity of their operations. For instance, the Jane Addams Center youth training program, precursor to Spread The News, Inc., had an annual budget of approximately $50,000, only $2,500 of which was generated by sales of mailing and distribution services. The minimum sales needed by a financially self-sufficient business was found to be $150,000. In addition to obvious increases in scale, entirely new administrative functions such as marketing and management of accounts receivable were required. In every situation that we have observed, this problem inevitably necessitates reconsideration of every aspect of the existing organization and its proposed business. Everything from the relationship to the constituency to employee qualifications and pay scales becomes an object of scrutiny.

Another reason for a nurturing period is the need to find or develop a niche in the market. There may be a need for a product or service but little initial actual demand. People may not be ready or able to spend money on energy conservation products, important as they may be. In other cases it is necessary to gain an understanding of the actual and potential market. In the Jane Addams case the would-be entrepreneurs had to sort out where they were going to be positioned in a market that already existed and was reasonably competitive. This required a comparison of direct mailing versus door-to-door distribution services and evaluation of the relative advantages of serving one neighborhood or developing a citywide clientele.

A final reason why a nurturing period is needed is because it takes time to transform social service management skills into business management skills. For instance, in the social services a clientele can often be assumed and customers do not need to be actively recruited. Since performance is hard to measure, individual and collective inefficiencies also show up less than in a business. While social service agencies frequently experience the same cash flow problems that businesses do, overall margins for error appear wider. Although it may be possible to hire new staff who already possess the needed business skills, it may well be worthwhile for an organization to invest in helping its own staff make the transition because it may offer them a new career path.

Organizational Questions

Finally, the important organizational and political questions need to be resolved during the kind of nurturing period identified above. It takes time to resolve organizational questions surrounding the relationship between the parent organization and the business activity. This also is often the ground for political debate. Should the business be operated in-house or as a separate entity? If the second, how much control should be retained and for how long? Might the different missions of the organizations cause friction between the respective staffs and board members? Should the new activity be operated on a for-profit basis, or can not-for-profit status be justified? If not, how will that affect the parent organization's legal status, image, and mode of operation? These are not just legal problems but concern the image and self-image of the organization. Consequently, it will take considerable effort from staff and board members to resolve them.[9]

The organizational formats contemplated for the new ventures reflect their varied origins and purposes. In some cases extensive analysis of a wide variety of organizational structures and variations was pursued (Wiewel et al. 1982). Only four were seriously considered: operation of the venture as a regular program of the parent organization; operation as a wholly owned for-profit subsidiary; operation as a workers' or consumers' cooperative; and operation as a business with an Employee Stock Ownership Plan (ESOP). (A number of organizations looked at the idea of a youth-run ESOP because such an organizational form was required by one of the potential funding sources.) Some of the other organizations also considered the ESOP approach but were put off by the effort and expense of setting one up, especially for a fledgling business. An even more important reason for organizations' reluctance to pursue it was their desire to maintain control of the enterprise. The parent organizations of the construction companies in particular were concerned about the possibility of employees, or outside board members, deciding that the companies should work in more profitable neighborhoods or participate in large gentrification projects. Therefore, they set up wholly owned for-profit companies.

The two cooperatives studied were initiated with the assistance of a local philanthropic organization with a special interest in co-ops. This was one instance among many of the enormous influence funding sources have on the decision to start an enterprise and on its format.

Retaining a business activity as a program of the parent organization can serve the purpose of giving the venture more time to find its place in the market or to develop a market where none exists. This was the course taken for the mill shop, the bookstore, and the home remodeling business. The mailing and distribution service also was maintained as a program because the board of the parent social service agency was uneasy about the idea of a profit-making business and wanted to emphasize the primacy of job training and job creation.

Finally, throughout this entire nurturing period,[10] technical assistance may often be helpful or even necessary. In many cases, planning and management assistance is required to sort things out and assist in the process of thinking through complex decisions. Technical aspects of the process include market and financial feasibility studies, organizational planning and the development of management systems, physical planning and design, and education about the nature and impact of the new ventures. Because the organizations starting the businesses are not solely driven by the profit motive, but rather by complex social and political motives, traditional business consulting has limited applicability. Often the organizations assemble teams of technical assistance providers from diverse sources such as their own boards, local law and accounting firms, financial institutions, and local universities.

How the cooperation between planners and community organizations in this process gets structured reflects both the technical and organizational sophistication of the organization and its political direction. For a less sophisticated organization, a close, continuous relationship, where the planners raise questions as much as they answer them, is appropriate. A sophisticated group may be able to ascertain its needs quite specifically and may be interested only in a short-term, traditional client-consultant relationship. However, the more interested the organization is in the political implications of its entering the economic arena, the more planners will have to deal with the political implications of their analytical contributions. This, in turn, requires a close involvement and extensive discussions of goals and means.

Conclusion

What follows is a summary of our views on the agenda set out at the beginning of this chapter: the impact of these business activities on the neighborhoods, their political content, and how they relate to work of planners. Clearly, the business activities discussed are being used by the organizations as part of their overall attempts to have an impact on their neighborhoods. These attempts are often very political in nature. As such, the business activities emphasize not only some combination of job creation and service for the neighborhood, but also a particular approach to community politics. This approach more directly confronts economic issues through the local, small business or neighborhood economy.

When organizations first consider this strategy, the revenue motive also is often considered, and sometimes it is paramount. However, in many cases it soon takes on a theoretical character, aimed at potential funders and investors. The greatest limitation on the profitability of community businesses is that low-income neighborhood people simply may not be able to purchase needed goods and services. Nevertheless, some opportunities still exist for organizations to achieve their social purposes with less dependence on subsidization and more reliance on the market. It has been shown above that expectations must be very modest in this regard: in most cases other good reasons must be present to justify the large effort involved.

Some of these good reasons may relate to the social benefits. The more organizations and businesses are created in a neighborhood, the more and better the communication and information coming into the neighborhood will be. As a result, more diverse and creative approaches to community problems might emerge (Galaskiewicz 1979). Also, a multiplication of community-oriented institutions provides more career paths for organizational staff. Many good people coming into the community movement burn out in five years and move on. We would prefer to see them stay on and become, for example, president of Neighborhood Construction, Inc., rather than move on to become public relations officer for an oil company.

Venturing into business also has progressive political connotations. Business activities provide an interesting alternative to other organization-building strategies such as direct action and community organizing. They provide a much clearer link to the economy, the sector where most of the problems originate that community organizations typically address. The business activities by community organizations could be useful for changing these sectors, eventually bringing a greater proportion under community control. In addition, they might serve as a model for others of how economic activity could be conducted differently. In this respect, these activities play much the same political role as producer and consumer cooperatives and worker-owned enterprises (Cornoy and Shearer 1981).

The development of business skills also makes them more competent counterparts in their dealings with governments and businesses, a valuable asset in an era of increasing privatization and emphasis on public-private partnerships.

Several caveats are in order. Involvement in business activities requires community organizations to become increasingly sophisticated. Without conscious and continuous effort, they can become strikingly similar to other businesses (witness the history of large Community Development Corporations such as The Woodlawn Organization, which retained one of the nation's foremost antiunion law firms to break a strike by its security guards) (Thomas and Forrester 1982; Park 1982). Beyond the level of the individual organization, there exists another type of risk: what is politically progressive on a very small scale may not be so on a larger scale. The Chicago mayoral campaign of Harold Washington included a commitment to start a citywide waste recycling program (*The Washington Papers* 1983). If implemented, one result would be substitution of close to minimum wage recycling jobs for well-paying, unionized sanitation department jobs.

The progressive aspects of the politics of community-controlled businesses are unlikely to fit with the economic development plans of local, state, or federal agencies. However, at the current scale, the quite moderate goals are not at odds with the privatization pursued by the current administration. In the short run, then, opportunities exist for planners to work with these efforts. As they expand in scale and become more political, it may be necessary for planners to work on a volunteer basis or out of relatively sheltered environments, such as universities.

Another problem may be posed by the faddish appeal of business activities by not-for-profit organizations. As soon as this method of revenue generation began to receive publicity, foundations and other funding sources started to urge applicants to consider this option and to strive toward often illusory self-sufficiency. In our own work we have found many organizations that became so focused on the idea of setting up their own business that they ignored other, more viable strategies. In response, the Center for Urban Economic Development now only assists in business spinoff ventures if they result from a strategic planning process in which a variety of economic development strategies are considered. More jobs for community residents may be obtained by working with (or pressuring) local businesses than by establishing one's own; or investing in a full-time fund-raiser may do more for organizational revenues than investing in a business.

As this analysis has shown, there are several roles that planners can play in voluntary or formal capacities. First, there may be the possibility of playing a Freirian or Habermasian role, participating with groups in thinking through their decisions. Indeed, this process of goals' clarification and strategic assessment may well lead to the decision that business activities are not the best strategy to pursue. Second, at a number of stages in the development process, there is a need for technical analysis, market and financial feasibility analyses, and organizational development plans. Finally, there are additional opportunities for planners emerging in the implementation stage. It is at that stage that progressive formulations about new ways of conducting the economy have to be given concrete shape. How a new business activity is controlled, how it operates, and whom it responds to determine whether it will meet any of the political and social considerations presented above, such as providing a model for economic democracy, considering community needs before profits, or training community leaders. Obviously the experiences are still limited, but they allow a guarded optimism that the political potential is quite real.

11 Local Economic Development and Job Targeting
Carl E. Van Horn, Robert A. Beauregard, and David S. Ford

Economic development programs often offer attractive benefits and sometimes powerful incentives to private firms. Federal, state, and local governments annually invest millions of dollars in subsidized low-interest loans and grants, property tax abatements, tax credits, site preparation assistance, marketing studies, and a host of other economic development tactics. The avowed purpose is to retain and create jobs, improve and diversify the economy, and stabilize and strengthen the tax base.[1] In return for public investments in economic development, governmental officials and the public expect tangible social benefits to result.

Despite the enormous public investment in economic development activities, disadvantaged individuals and small and minority businesses have received only limited benefits. For example, an exhaustive study of the Urban Development Action Grant (UDAG) program found that only one in ten of the new permanent jobs created by these investments were filled by people who qualified for assistance under the now-defunct Comprehensive Employment and Training Act (U.S. Department of Housing and Urban Development 1982, 65). Though UDAGs were intended to benefit disadvantaged people in distressed communities, few who obtained jobs came from the ranks of the low-income and long-term unemployed. The evidence of benefits to small and minority businesses, moreover, is generally anecdotal, indicating the lack of regard for this goal.

In fact, the relationship between various economic development programs and either federally funded job training programs or governmental programs assisting small and minority businesses has been a tenuous one. Such programs were not coordinated at the federal level, and several federally initiated demonstrations aimed at overcoming local impediments to closer linkage were disappointing.[2] Seldom did economic development agencies work with employment and training agencies and small and minority business agencies to target jobs for the long-term unemployed and economically disadvantaged or to identify business opportunities for small and minority business enterprises. Rarely were the graduates of job training programs placed in private sector jobs produced through public economic development investments. Infrequently did small and minority entrepreneurs benefit from local economic development activity engendered through local government.

The purpose of this essay is to probe the obstacles and opportunities facing local governments as they attempt, through their economic development agencies, to link economic development assistance with job placement for the economically disadvantaged and business opportunities for small and minority businesses. Additionally, we wish to identify those tactics and strategies most effective for achieving these outcomes. The focus of our study is the Targeted Jobs Demonstration Program (TJDP), a national demonstration project in operation between 1980 and 1983. Its intent was to develop these linkages through targeting strategies.[3]

The Targeted Jobs Demonstration

The Targeted Jobs Demonstration Program was designed to capture a portion of the public benefits that flow from economic development projects and to direct them toward the least advantaged segments of the community—low income, unemployed residents, and small, minority, and women-owned enterprises (Peters 1983; Van Horn et al. 1984). Fourteen communities each were awarded approximately $200,000 from the federal government to answer a novel question: Can local government officials increase the number of jobs and business opportunities that disadvantaged segments of the community obtain from federally assisted economic development projects?[4]

While the central rationale for job and business targeting was *equity*, the central concept underlying targeting strategies was *leverage*. In theory, local officials would use the provision of economic development aid as a lever to negotiate on behalf of the disadvantaged for jobs and on behalf of small, minority, and women's businesses for contracts. All economic development assistance is given conditionally. Firms are frequently required to repay their loans, hire a certain number of people, remain in the community, or contribute to some public objective, such as providing monies for upgrading local transit stops. Jobs and business targeting would add another condition—aid would be given only to private employers willing to make commitments to targeted groups. If the firm were unwilling to accept the conditions, then governmental assistance would not be forthcoming.

This experimental job and business targeting strategy emerged from President Carter's National Urban Policy of 1978. Its central goals were to coordinate federal assistance, increase private sector employment in urban areas, and direct more jobs and business opportunities to minorities and low-income people. In April 1979 the president's Interagency Coordinating Council announced a nationwide "Employment Initiatives" effort designed to link federal economic and community development programs with federal employment and training efforts.[5] Several federal agencies made a commitment to increase employment opportunities for low-income citizens. For example, the Economic Development Administration (EDA) agreed to a 10 to 15 percent target for all appropriate job-producing projects. As part of the overall Employment Initiatives strategy, applicants for project funding under the Department of Housing and Urban Development's UDAG program and EDA's public works programs, among others, were required to submit an Employment Plan detailing how many CETA eligibles would be placed in permanent jobs due to the investment. Federal Regional Coordinating Councils were responsible for reviewing pending applications and for monitoring progress. TJDP was to be part of this effort.

The Employment Initiatives Program, however, was never fully implemented. Procedures for implementing interagency agreements were delayed for over a year after the initial program announcement, Federal Regional Councils did not begin training sessions for local officials until near the end of the Carter administration, and, according to the U.S. Conference of Mayors, local officials were neither adequately informed about Employment Initiatives nor notified on a timely basis of pending economic development projects.

During the Reagan administration, concern for the Carter administration's Employment Initiatives program vanished, but TJDP continued. Thus, at no time during the TJDP did local officials enjoy the full support of participating federal agencies. TJDP staffs were left to follow their own paths. They could not expect and did not receive explicit support from federal agencies for the demonstration's central objectives. TJDP was therefore not an important component of a nationwide job and business targeting strategy—as had been envisioned—but rather an isolated demonstration program. Nonetheless, it yields important lessons for understanding the strategies of economic development targeting and leveraging.

Job Targeting under TJDP

The fundamental purpose of TJDP—and the one to which most TJDP grantees devoted the bulk of their energies—was to develop strategies and techniques through which employers who benefit from economic development programs would be induced to hire economically disadvantaged people. Given that economic development projects produce some private sector jobs, it was hoped that TJDP would increase the flow of low-income people into those positions.

Though the idea of negotiating with private employers to obtain benefits for low-income groups seems simple, accomplishing positive results is difficult. With the national Employment Initiatives policy a dim memory, the TJDP sites were left to determine their own strategies. Ten of the fourteen sites attempted to develop new policies and practices emphasizing job targeting. These ranged from mere exhortations that employers should cooperate with employment and training agencies to city council ordinances mandating agreements between publicly assisted private employers and the employment and training organizations.

In most of the demonstration sites TJDP was interpreted to mean that local employment and training agencies should somehow *link* their programs and services with economic development assistance. In short, most sites had no intention of negotiating with firms to obtain *legally binding agreements* through which firms would hire the disadvantaged. Rather, almost all of the agencies *jointly packaged* economic development incentives with employment and training incentives. Economic development programs were used as a means for getting the low-income, unemployed participant's "feet in the door." The weakest of these approaches could be characterized as "little carrot and no stick."

An equally significant finding from the research was that four of the sites did not even attempt to carry out the TJDP concept. Instead, the demonstration funds were absorbed into programs providing general employment and training services. TJDP was virtually indistinguishable from the organization in which it was located.

The grantees developed divergent strategies, and several grantees did not even attempt to target jobs from economic development projects. Moreover, the demonstration sites deliberately chose different yardsticks for themselves. Some sites concentrated on developing enduring mechanisms that would produce high quality jobs; others tried to rapidly generate a large number of jobs in the "secondary" labor market. The sites that did not target jobs maintained that job leveraging was inappropriate for their community because they could not afford to anger potential employers with additional requirements. Uniform criteria for comparing and evaluating TJDP performance were needed.

The sites were evaluated in terms of the central policy questions in TJDP: does job targeting work and, if so, what are the most effective approaches? Progress toward the goal of job targeting was indicated by:

the development of effective job targeting strategies;

the number of jobs obtained by low-income, long-term unemployed people;

the quality of jobs obtained by those individuals;

the extent to which the job targeting strategy altered the normal hiring patterns of private firms or the flow of job opportunities for the economically disadvantaged.[6]

Developing Effective Job Targeting Strategies

The first criterion for assessing the job targeting objective is the extent to which the community implemented an effective strategy for obtaining jobs for the economically disadvantaged from economic development projects. Because many economic development projects take years to complete, an exclusive focus on "jobs produced during the demonstration period" is unfair and shortsighted. A thorough assessment must consider the potential for long-term change by examining the extent to which procedures for job targeting were established and institutionalized.

An effective job targeting strategy must contain the following six elements:[7]

a policy supporting job targeting through mandated hiring agreements;
agency procedures that support job targeting;
direct negotiations between the employer and the city/county agency at an early stage in the economic development project;
careful employee screening and timely referrals;
monitoring procedures for hiring agreements;
enforcement mechanisms that can be used if private firms fail to carry out the terms of the hiring agreements.

These six criteria constitute a comprehensive strategy that any community wishing to increase the number of jobs allocated to low-income people would have to approximate. The criteria are demanding and require political support and administrative adroitness. Additionally, the process is lengthy and complicated. As a result, there are many opportunities for missteps.

To evaluate the site performance we first considered whether the job targeting criterion was present—e.g., did the site have a job targeting policy or not? Four sites had no job targeting strategy as we defined it: Buffalo/Erie County, Metcalfe, Milwaukee, and Paterson. For the remaining sites we considered how well each element of the ideal strategy was functioning—e.g., was the element strong, moderate, or weak? Based on this analysis the sites were allocated to one of four categories: excellent, good, fair, or poor. Portland (Oregon) had the only excellent job targeting strategy. Lynn, New York City, Portland (Maine), and Montanawide had good strategies. Fair strategies existed in Genesee County and Seattle. Last, Philadelphia, San Antonio, and Wilmington had poor strategies.

Because the strategy of Portland, Oregon, was the only one judged as excellent, it deserves further comment. This city government fully implemented and institutionalized the original job targeting concept embodied in TJDP. The provision of economic development assistance was used by the city's staff to lever job opportunities for long-term unemployed and low-income city residents. Portland's efforts began as far back as 1979 when it pioneered the use of a technique known as the First Source Agreement, which is a legally binding agreement between the city and the private companies that obtain public assistance for economic development. In these contracts companies agree to use the city's Training and Employment Division as their first source for recruiting employees for all jobs covered by the contracts. Only if the city is unable to supply adequate and qualified labor can the employer seek employees elsewhere. The final hiring decision, in any case, rests with the employer.

Portland's job targeting strategy was promulgated in various city planning documents and supported by two mayoral administrations. Moreover, each agreement between the city and private firms was endorsed by city council ordinance. Strong agency procedures to carry out the policy were initially developed and subsequently strengthened. Monitoring was accomplished through quarterly hiring reports submitted by employers. Enforcement procedures were available (though never invoked) whereby the city or the employer could request arbitration to resolve disputes; loan revocation or other penalties were to function as remedies in cases where firms refused to honor their commitments. In sum, Portland's First Source strategy met all the requirements for effective job targeting.

With this notable exception, the overall record of the demonstration sites was disappointing. Of the remaining sites, four were judged to be good, and the rest were either fair, poor, or nonexistent. Several factors account for this varied performance. First, the absence of encouragement or pressure from the national government was critical. Because the concept of job targeting lacked legal or regulatory authority from the federal level, local officials were put in the awkward position of adding requirements to the use of federal funds that were not imposed by Congress or the executive departments.[8]

Second, given the absence of federal support, the degree of local political support for using economic development projects as an opportunity to garner jobs for low-income residents became the fundamental determinant of local strategies. In those sites where job targeting processes were well developed and effective, political leaders publicly and privately endorsed the job targeting concept. In less successful communities, political leaders were usually openly opposed to the idea.

Third, the attitudes of local professionals toward job targeting were a principal explanation for progress on targeting strategies. The notion of leveraging jobs for the economically disadvantaged from economic development projects divided many staffs along philosophical lines.

Key agency officials in Paterson, Milwaukee, and Buffalo, for example, did not believe it appropriate for the city to negotiate with private firms on behalf of low-income, unemployed individuals. Clearly, officials in Portland, Oregon, decided that legally binding hiring agreements were appropriate and potentially useful for getting low-income people into jobs created by economic development investments. A middle-of-the-road view was held in such communities as New York City, Lynn, and Portland, Maine, where senior staff thought that low-income clients should be given access to economic development jobs but that private firms should not be required to use city employment agencies as an exclusive source for entry-level employees.

The staff and agency directors who opposed job targeting approaches tended to view themselves as advocates for the private sector. Therefore, they resisted any efforts to further "hamstring" their employer clients. They also feared that hiring agreements would render their city or county less competitive with adjacent communities and create perceptions of an antibusiness climate. However, the way that staff interpreted the economy depended more upon administrative values than on empirical realities. Staff members and agency heads in Portland, Oregon—where the unemployment rate doubled during the demonstration period—did not regard their troubled economy as a hindrance to job targeting. Rather, they maintained that unfavorable economic conditions enhanced the value of economic development tools and thus strengthened their negotiating position.

Interestingly, support for this latter view comes from our survey of private employers. Two-thirds of the eighty-one employers interviewed agreed that it was appropriate for city or county government to seek agreements whereby employers are required to hire low-income people in return for economic development assistance. Private employers indicated that they were willing to enter into any reasonable agreement to obtain the favorable loan rates offered by economic development agencies.

Finally, two other factors deserve brief mention. The administrative environment of TJDP was an important determinant of success. Instability in the agencies housing the demonstration, including staff turnover, agency reorganization, and staff confusion, hindered TJDP in several communities. The location of staff also fostered or thwarted progress. Staff in more successful sites had access to key decisionmakers and obtained timely information from both employment and training as well as economic development agencies. In contrast, staff in less successful sites suffered from their relatively low position in the city's bureaucracy and the accompanying lack of access to agency directors and city policymakers.

The Number of Jobs Obtained

A second and obvious criterion for evaluating the job opportunities' goal is the actual number of jobs obtained by low-income unemployed people due to TJDP staff efforts. Before analyzing the data, several caveats must be entered. The data reported here were submitted by local staff but not verified independently. Moreover, no data were collected on the duration of job placements. Finally, many of the reported job placements were neither located with firms that had received economic development assistance nor were they produced via formal or informal hiring agreements. Thus, for example, none of Paterson's 144 jobs were generated through hiring agreements, but all seventy-five jobs in Portland, Oregon, and most of New York City's 131 placements were obtained through agreements negotiated with economic development–assisted employers.

Table 11.1 presents information gathered from the final field visits near the completion of the formal demonstration period. Overall, more than a thousand jobs were obtained for low-income individuals through the efforts of TJDP staff. Among those sites practicing a targeted jobs strategy, Lynn was clearly the leader at 196 jobs. San Antonio, with only forty placements, produced the fewest number of jobs among those sites reporting data (although its project had been under way for less than a year at the time of reporting).

Several sites anticipated that additional placements for low-income unemployed people on economic development projects would result from efforts undertaken during the demonstration. For example, as of late 1982, Portland, Oregon, had signed more than twenty First Source Agreements that could lead to approximately four hundred entry-level jobs during the next three to five years, New York City had obtained tentative commitments for over 2,500 jobs from seventy-nine employers, and Portland, Maine, expected another 250 placements from projects already under way.

Table 11.1 also compares the jobs reported by TJDP sites with the number of jobs projected in their funding proposals. The ten sites

Table 11.1   Comparison of the number of jobs originally projected
with the actual number of jobs obtained for CETA eligibles

Sites	Planned number of jobs	Actual number of jobs	Percent of planned jobs achieved
Buffalo/Erie County[a]	2,700	No estimates	Not applicable
Genesee	300	90	30
Lynn	800	196	25
Metcalfe[a]	467	No estimates	Not applicable
Milwaukee[c]	400	66	17
Montanawide[a]	787	No estimates	Not applicable
New York City	2,490	131	5
Paterson[b,c]	325	144	44
Philadelphia[c]	100	45	45
Portland, ME	250	155	62
Portland, OR	Did not propose a specific number	75	Not applicable
San Antonio	200	40	20
Seattle	238	50	21
Wilmington	384	72	19
Subtotal	5,487	989	18
Total[e]	9,441	1,064	Not applicable

Sources: Quarterly jobs-related activity reports submitted by TJDP staff and estimates
provided to Rutgers Field Research Associates by TJDP staff
a Quarterly reports were either not submitted or not usable.
b Includes all placements made by the Private Industry Council whose staff was
largely funded by TJDP. The totals include placements from the PIC's machine tool
operators program, on-the-job training placements, and direct placements into private-
sector jobs.
c Includes a number of placements in firms that did not receive economic development assistance.
d For sites with planned *and* actual job placement data only.
e For all sites.

where we can make comparisons achieved only 18 percent of their
projections. Portland, Maine, came close to matching its planned
performance level, whereas New York City achieved only 5 percent
of its planned placements.

Several conditions account for the wide variations in progress
among the fourteen demonstration sites and for the gaps between
planned and actual performance. Clearly, the job targeting strategy

chosen by the local staff profoundly influenced the number of jobs obtained during the demonstration period. Significant differences in strategies explain, for example, why Portland, Oregon, with an effective targeting strategy, reported considerably fewer placements during the demonstration period than a site like Paterson, which had no job targeting strategy. Portland (Oregon), New York City, Portland (Maine), Seattle, and Lynn chose a complex and protracted process, restricted the number of businesses with which they dealt, and tied their placement rates to the timetable and progress of economic development projects. We would expect the sites not using formal hiring agreements to show more rapid progress because *all* firms in those communities were potential sources of jobs for their clients.

The communities using a job targeting approach added their efforts to traditional methods for helping the economically disadvantaged obtain jobs. The other communities merely folded their TJDP staff into the existing job development strategies of employment and training agencies. In the long run the sites with effective job targeting strategies should realize substantially more jobs for the targeted groups. Not only were the jobs obtained through their efforts additive rather than substitutive of other efforts, but agreements reached during the demonstration may yield additional placements for several years.

Within sites that attempted to target jobs, the quality of their approach made an important difference. In particular, the quality of screening, referral, and monitoring processes explained underperformance in several sites. For instance, New York City's performance could have increased substantially had the staff developed a better procedure for referring qualified job applicants to firms in a timely manner. Other sites simply lacked basic policies and procedures to support their job targeting efforts. Thus, TJDP staff in Wilmington, Seattle, and Genesee County were not involved in the economic development process at a sufficiently early stage to take advantage of job opportunities.

A principal impediment to additional job placements in most sites was the economic recession of 1981–83. Poor economic conditions delayed or canceled over half of the economic development projects identified in the sites' initial proposals. The clients of many TJDP projects were slated to fill positions created through expansion, but many firms were either not hiring, laying off employees, or going out of business entirely.

The influx of unemployed but experienced workers into the labor market allowed employers to be more selective and less interested in hiring unproven workers. An example of this phenomenon is provided by a UDAG-funded Hyatt Hotel in Flint, Michigan, located in Genesee County. The hotel's management agreed to hire eighty-six low- or moderate-income people for its staff of 215. The employment and training agency screened potential employees and funded a restaurant and hotel management training program using the Hyatt Corporation's training procedures. When the hotel announced its intention to hire, thousands of applications were filed by hopeful unemployed residents. The hotel's personnel department had no trouble finding a full supply of experienced workers. The bottom line: only twenty-six of the 215 workers were trained or even referred by the Genesee County employment and training agency.

One particularly devastating problem caused by the slack economy was the failure to generate construction jobs for low-income, unemployed people. Most TJDP proposals anticipated numerous construction jobs, but these simply did not materialize because there were too many qualified and unemployed union members who were called to work when construction activities began. Many TJDP proposals also substantially overestimated the number of nonconstruction jobs that could be obtained. TJDP staffs discovered that many economic development projects either create no new "permanent" jobs or create far fewer nonconstruction jobs than anticipated.

The Quality of Jobs Obtained

Another criterion for assessing TJDP is the quality of jobs obtained by low-income unemployed people. In theory, linkage with economic development projects through hiring agreements could be used to obtain better-than-average jobs for the client population. Traditional employment and training strategies have used such inducements as on-the-job training wage subsidies or the Targeted Jobs Tax Credits to convince employers to hire low-income unemployed workers for entry-level positions. Perhaps the leverage afforded by the hiring agreement could be a more powerful incentive.

238

Table 11.2 The quality of TJDP jobs

Sites[a]	Average entering wage[b]	Most common occupations	Percentage Construction	Compared to CETA/PIC
Genesee	$3.64	Fast food worker, metal fabricator, shipping clerk, aligner, parts manufacturer	0	Some same, others better
Lynn	$3.50	Extruder trainee, stitchers, assemblers, shoe laborers, factory workers	0	Worse
Milwaukee	$4.22	Hotel service workers, laundry workers, production workers, machine operators, clerks, auto mechanics	0	Same[c]
Montana-wide	$7.00	Oil rig laborer, seismic tester, surveyors, truck drivers, laborers	No estimate available	No estimate available
New York City	$3.95	Production machinists, data processors, bakery workers, electrician helpers, clerks, truck drivers	0	Some better, others worse
Paterson	$4.30	Machine operators, bench assemblers, clerks, warehouse laborer, management trainee, restaurant worker	0	Same
Philadelphia	$4.44	Secretaries, clerks, machinists, shippers, security guards, hotel workers	0	Same
Portland, ME	$5.13	Construction laborers, carpenters, ironworkers, clerks, restaurant workers	50	Construction better; "permanent" jobs worse
Portland, OR	$4.49	Truck drivers, production workers, custodial, clerks, maintenance	0	Some same, others better

Table 11.2   (continued)

Sites[a]	Average entering wage[b]	Most common occupations	Percentage Construction	Compared to CETA/PIC
		mechanic, materials handler		
San Antonio	No estimate available	Construction workers, restaurant workers, maintenance workers, hotel workers	5	Same
Seattle	$4.61	Fast food worker, laborer, assembler, clerk, construction laborer	8	Same
Wilmington	$3.75	Retail sales, restaurant help, textile worker	0	No estimate available

Source: Quarterly jobs-related activity reports submitted by TJDP staff.
a Data on job quality were unavailable for Buffalo and Metcalfe.
b Average wages were calculated from the latest available data submitted by the sites. In several cases data on wages were not included in the final job placement report.
c Since the TJDP program and the CETA/PIC programs were indistinguishable in Milwaukee, it follows that placements from TJDP and the CETA/PIC would be the same.

The evidence indicates that TJDP job targeting strategies were largely ineffective in improving the quality of jobs available to low-income people. Table 11.2 presents three rough measures of performance —the average entering wages of TJDP-placed individuals, their modal occupations, and a comparison with jobs obtained through the regular CETA system in each community. The average entering wage was $4.45 per hour, and most of the jobs were above the minimum wage; however, two sites reported many jobs at or below the federal minimum wage. Almost all of the jobs fell into the unskilled, entry-level category, including general laborers, restaurant workers, factory assembly workers, and low-skilled clerical positions.[9] In six of the eight sites where comparisons are meaningful, TJDP jobs were judged to be of about the same quality as jobs obtained by low-income unemployed people through regular employment and training programs.

Only a few jobs in Portland, Oregon, New York City, and Genesee County represented improvements over the typical opportunities available to the client population.

It is not surprising that the types of jobs obtained through TJDP were similar to the types of jobs obtained through CETA since the same client population was being served. This finding undermines the claim that job targeting can be used to enhance job quality. More important, perhaps, is what it reveals about economic development projects. Economic development investments often create (1) low-paying, unskilled, and high-turnover positions, (2) higher-paying construction jobs that are not available to the vast majority of the client population, or (3) jobs that are obviously beyond the immediate grasp of CETA program graduates. This problem is not unique to economic development projects but is one that frequently plagues federal job training programs (Baumer and Van Horn, 1985).

Altering the Hiring Patterns of Private Firms

The last of our four criteria for evaluating job placement performance is clearly the most demanding. Did TJDP targeting strategies alter the normal hiring patterns of employers who entered into hiring agreements? Did job targeting efforts increase the flow of job opportunities for low-income unemployed individuals over what they would have gotten otherwise? Unfortunately, systematic information about people hired by employers on economic development projects prior to TJDP was not available. Therefore, we asked employers to tell us whether the types of people they hired or would hire under TJDP were different from those they had already hired.

Our interviews with 136 employers suggested that job targeting strategies did not affect hiring patterns in most communities. In fact, we estimate that TJDP hiring agreements systematically changed hiring patterns in only three of the ten sites where job targeting strategies were attempted. Some of the *individuals* would have remained unemployed or on welfare without the assistance they received from TJDP, but the overall record does not reflect much change in the *types* of people hired by employers under TJDP hiring agreements.

Approximately half of the employers in our survey indicated that the individuals hired were similar to those people they normally hire; only one-third reported changes. The employers that had entered into TJDP agreements but had not yet hired people made similar responses—about half felt there would be no change; one-third anticipated some differences. Two comments made by employers during the interviews reflect the majority. One employer remarked: "We usually hire minorities and low-income people, anyway. These workers will just come from a different source." Another businessperson pointed out: "Minorities and low-income workers are the most available workers. The city doesn't have to ask you to hire them. They are just there."

Although most TJDP job targeting strategies were not effective in altering hiring patterns, there is strong evidence that hiring patterns were affected in three sites. This occurred most dramatically in Portland, Oregon. Interviews with TJDP employers in that city confirm that a greater percentage of minorities and women had been hired than would have been employed in the absence of TJDP. Minorities and women were employed in firms that previously had all-male or all-white work forces. While an effective job targeting strategy can bring about systematic changes in the hiring patterns of employers, such results are not automatically attained.

The TJDP record also compares favorably with the hiring patterns of firms under the UDAG program where TJDP hiring agreements were not in force. According to a systematic analysis of the characteristics of people employed on eighty UDAG projects in seventy cities, "about one in ten of the new permanent jobs created thus far are filled by those who were part of or qualified for training under the CETA program (U.S. Department of Housing and Urban Development 1982, 65). Our survey of twenty-five employers with hiring agreements in six TJDP sites found that the CETA-eligible people already hired represented 6 percent of the firm's *total work force*, and that if all the jobs contained in the agreements were filled, disadvantaged individuals would constitute over 25 percent of the *total work force* of those firms.

Once again, the experience of Portland, Oregon, is significant. The city's First Source Agreement strategy was designed to capture all entry-level jobs for disadvantaged clientele. Ideally, low-income, unemployed residents of the city would receive most if not all of the new permanent positions created by economic development investments. Evidence from employer interviews in Portland suggest that low-income people obtained a substantially larger share of the new permanent entry-level positions than the national pattern reported in HUD's UDAG study. For example, one of the largest First Source employers—a major printing firm—indicated that 75 percent of the 114 jobs created through its UDAG would be filled by disadvantaged individuals referred by the city's Training and Employment Division.

Capturing Spin-off Business Opportunities

Economic development projects create more than jobs; they also generate business opportunities. In designing TJDP, the federal government urged local communities to target governmentally induced contracts, subcontracts, and investment opportunities to small, minority, and women-owned enterprises (hereinafter S/M/WBES). The rationale for targeting business opportunities was twofold: first, local governments could prevent the benefits of economic development from leaking out of the community; and, second, "disadvantaged" entrepreneurs would be better able to compete more effectively for business opportunities. In short, both efficiency and equity concerns were considered in the business targeting objective (Chen 1984; Clark and Gertler 1983).

S/M/WBES typically find it more difficult to compete for contracts or to establish themselves and expand relative to "majority-owned" businesses. S/M/WBES are at a disadvantage even when they receive government financial assistance. Moreover, small businesses in general—most minority and women-owned businesses are small —have higher failure rates than larger ones. Yet small businesses are significant job generators and provide a supportive environment in which disadvantaged individuals may become acquainted with the worlds of employment and entrepreneurship (U.S. Department of Commerce 1982; Bates and Osborne 1979; Birch 1979).

In sum, the inclusion of a business targeting objective under the general rubric of Employment Initiatives and TJDP was consistent with the Carter administration's philosophical and political principles. In designing the demonstration, selecting the demonstration sites, and overseeing the demonstration, however, the federal government gave relatively little emphasis to the goal of capturing spin-off business opportunities.

Business Assistance Activities

Few of the TJDP sites attempted to aid S/M/WBES in any manner or with any vigor. Those communities that did mount business assistance programs for S/M/WBES generally disregarded the concept of capturing and redistributing spin-off business opportunities to disadvantaged entrepreneurs. Four communities totally ignored this aspect of TJDP; five sites offered business assistance on an ad hoc and highly diffused basis; and five made serious, sustained attempts to implement a business assistance strategy. In communities with minimal business assistance programs, activities that were inexpensive, politically innocuous, and therefore easy to perform were undertaken: public relations, conferences and seminars, research and market analyses, and information dissemination. Sites with significant business programs were more likely to tackle politically difficult tasks with larger resource commitments and to focus on a major project. Five sites made this substantial commitment.

In Lynn the TJDP-funded business assistance program was viewed as a necessary prelude to economic development and job growth. Business and employment goals were viewed as interdependent: firms receiving economic development assistance might have other business-related needs and also desire employment and training aid. Given this underlying premise, the staff initiated several related activities, including technical assistance to firms, the development of a revolving loan fund from which low-interest loans could be dispersed, a set-aside of construction contracts for minority firms, a newsletter on minority employment and investment issues, a business affirmative action plan for city government, and the general linkage of economic development and employment and training programs.

San Antonio's TJDP staff focused its energies on pursuing spin-off business opportunities for S/M/WBES. During approximately a year of operation, the TJDP staff helped minority firms obtain construction subcontracts, aided small and minority retailers in bids for space in a new downtown hotel, and assisted S/M/WBES in their efforts to obtain contracts for hotel equipment and furnishings. These activities were augmented by efforts designed to increase the participation of S/M/WBES in local government contracting: the conduct of surveys and bidders' conferences, the development of an affirmative action plan for city government, and the establishment of S/M/WBE utilization goals.

Montanawide's TJDP program had goals similar to those in San Antonio. Staff worked with Indian contractors to identify subcontracting opportunities, helped them develop bids, and in some instances, provided technical assistance so that they could fulfill their contracts. All of Montanawide's activities were designed to enable Indian contractors to take advantage of laws that give Indian workers and contractors preferences in economic development projects undertaken with private or government funds on reservations.

In Seattle the TJDP effort engaged in several activities to assist women-owned and minority business enterprises, with an emphasis on women's businesses. After viable economic development projects were identified, the TJDP staff and other city agencies attempted to establish minimum commitment levels for the use of women-owned businesses. Additionally, information about Seattle's S/M/WBES was gathered through a survey distributed to city agencies and major firms and drawn upon for matching business opportunities to S/M/WBES' capabilities. TJDP staff also provided technical assistance to targeted firms, held workshops and conferences, and worked to increase the city's commitment to using S/M/WBES in governmental contracts.

Although Portland, Maine, devoted much of its TJDP staff time to the business assistance goal, the activities yielded few tangible products for S/M/WBES. There were attempts to help small entrepreneurs obtain retail space in large developments, tangential involvement in a revolving loan fund, aid to a fledgling cooperative, and the development of planning and market analysis. The bulk of the staff efforts, however, was devoted to the Neighborhood Job Development Project, a study of investment opportunities for new and existing small businesses. Economic development projects were not targeted, and no spin-off business opportunities were obtained for S/M/WBES.

Assessing the Business Targeting Goal

To a large extent the paucity of interest and attention to business targeting objectives can be explained by the original design of the demonstration. Business assistance was given little emphasis, and job targeting dominated. But there were other factors that undermined effective business targeting. To capture business opportunities for S/M/WBES, government officials must contend with the uncertainty surrounding economic development projects, the limitations of S/M/WBES, and the political opposition to policies that suggest automatic quotas or set-asides for any single constituency. As with affirmative action in hiring, the concept of aiding one group of businesses in competition with another, without regard to cost or quality, rankles many in political office and a large segment of the public. As with the job targeting objective, few communities had the political will to undertake such a controversial strategy, especially without federal government support.

San Antonio's modest success, however, demonstrates what can be accomplished in a short period of time with an aggressive negotiation strategy and a firm political commitment. Thus, while the evidence on the business targeting objective of TJDP is disappointing, it does suggest that a city-directed business assistance strategy is neither impossible nor detrimental to the overall economic development of a community.

Assessing the TJDP Experiment

In our judgment TJDP was a partial success. While several sites either made no attempt or were unsuccessful in carrying out the demonstration's objectives, significant accomplishments were realized in a few communities. Most important, the success of Portland, Oregon, with its First Source Agreement strategy for targeting jobs from economic development projects to low-income people strongly suggests the potential value of this approach for other cities and counties. Given the problems and obstacles that beset the demonstration, the achievements of the more effective communities are indeed noteworthy, and the poor performance of the other sites is not surprising.

Is job targeting an effective tool for helping the disadvantaged obtain unsubsidized employment from private firms assisted by economic development investments? The Portland, Oregon, experience strongly suggests that a strategy designed to increase job opportunities for low-income people through negotiated agreements can be effective. Political officials and agency administrators in the city supported the strategy. Employers with hiring agreements bought the idea in principle and expressed satisfaction with the results. According to local staff, Portland's strategy was at least as efficient, and probably more so, than traditional approaches to helping the disadvantaged obtain jobs. Finally, the job targeting strategy altered the hiring pattern of employers in the city, directing substantially larger shares of the new permanent entry-level positions to low-income unemployed individuals than they otherwise would have received.

Whether the positive experience in Portland, Oregon, can be replicated elsewhere is dependent on the will and capacity of a community. Initiative and support for job targeting must come from elected officials and senior agency administrators. Once the will to undertake hiring agreements exists, their success rests with the ability of economic development and employment and training agencies to deliver on their commitments. Complex agreements involving cooperation among many agencies over a long period of time are not likely to work unless the responsible agencies already function effectively in carrying out their normal tasks. In short, job targeting is a strategy more suited to mature and well-functioning agencies than to those plagued with mundane administrative problems.

In our view a mandated job targeting policy is essential. Private employers who benefit from low-interest loans and other government aid ought to be required to reserve a substantial portion of the entry-level jobs created by those investments for the disadvantaged and long-term unemployed residents of their communities. Such a policy enhances the value of the investment by aiding people who would otherwise be dependent on governmental assistance. Without a firm policy on job targeting, private employers will be reluctant to grant such conditions. Yet the overwhelming majority of the employers who signed hiring agreements were satisfied with the services made available to them during TJDP. While agreements should be mandated, government agencies must be flexible concerning which jobs should be covered by the agreements and the time period during which they must be fulfilled.

Our overall evaluation of business targeting can be less specific. The strategy has yet to be implemented on a wide basis. Much is still not known about how to aid small, minority, and women-owned businesses and about how economic development investments generate direct contractual opportunities for local businesses. Yet there were some successes under TJDP, and they give confidence that the linkage of economic development assistance and s/m/wBES can prove mutually beneficial.

In summary, under the conditions noted above, hiring agreements can be an effective tool for helping low-income unemployed people attain productive jobs, and business targeting can be developed without strain upon overall economic development success. Therefore, even though many TJDP sites did not successfully implement a job targeting strategy and none of the sites effectively captured spin-off business opportunities, the notable success of one community's job targeting strategy and the substantial accomplishments of a few others underscore the value of TJDP. An innovative approach for directing jobs to the economically disadvantaged was demonstrated to be effective. State and local officials concerned with economic development, employment and training, and small and minority business development should carefully consider adopting similar strategies in their communities.

Authors' Note: The studies forming the basis for this essay were conducted pursuant to a contract with the U.S. Department of Housing and Urban Development. The authors are solely responsible for the accuracy of statements or interpretations contained herein. The authors wish to thank Dr. Judith V. May, chairperson of the TJDP Interagency Monitoring Board, for her assistance. The authors also wish to thank the other individuals who prepared excellent case studies of TJDP sites: Donald Baumer, Edward Dement, Grace Franklin, Peter Kobrak, Michelle Lamar, Robert McPherson, Patti Moeller, Randall Ripley, Donald Rosenthal, Ken Ryan, and Lance de Haven-Smith.

12　Urban Growth, Subemployment, and Mobility

Patricia Wilson Salinas

Introduction

A useful concept for analyzing the nature of low-income urban employment is "subemployment." The urban unrest of the 1960s underscored the inability of conventional labor market analysis to grasp the nature of center-city employment problems. Even in growing periods of relatively low unemployment, center-city workers manifested their discontent. It was found that a lack of jobs was only part of the problem. Another serious problem was the kind of jobs available to inner-city residents. To measure this larger problem, an index of subemployment, more formally called labor force underutilization, was created and quantified based on a survey of inner-city workers (Manpower Report to the President 1968, 34). The subemployment index measures not only how many people do not have any job at a particular time, but also how many have bad jobs—i.e., jobs that do not afford a decent annual income because of low pay, part-time work, or intermittent work.

Labor economists of the human capital school attribute subemployment primarily to the low skills, education, and experience—i.e., the human capital—of the subemployed and adopt the neoclassical assumption that low wages reflect low productivity on the part of the worker. This model relates investment in human capital —particularly education and experience—to earnings, showing that the return on investment (i.e., earnings) increases with the amount of investment in human capital.

The segmented labor market framework[1] posits the major causes of subemployment to be the structure of the labor market and the job generation process rather than the characteristics of the workers.

Subemployment—like unemployment—stems from the fact that the country's productive structure requires fewer workers than are available. A surplus population is created that is willing to offer its labor for less than culturally defined subsistence earnings. These people take the economy's marginal jobs—jobs that are punctuated with repeated periods of unemployment—and often have to supplement their earnings with public assistance. The amount of subemployment varies cyclically but does not disappear. For some, subemployment is a temporary phenomenon. These people will return to better-paying jobs when there is sufficient demand. For others, subemployment is long-term or permanent.

The marginal jobs typical of subemployment provide only intermittent, seasonal, or part-time work, or they are jobs whose low pay provides little incentive for staying with them. Thus, the nature of the work produces repeated periods of unemployment. These jobs produce inadequate annual incomes—i.e., incomes that do not permit the individual (or family) to live at culturally defined subsistence levels without assistance from either other family members or public transfer payments (welfare). These marginal jobs belong to what the segmented or dual labor market literature calls the secondary sector: those firms or occupations with low productivity, high turnover, low capital/labor ratios, and a low percentage of unionized labor. While the permanently subemployed remain in the secondary sector, the temporarily subemployed have access to the better-paying, more stable primary sector jobs. Structural barriers to mobility between labor market segments produce a pool of permanent or long-term subemployed workers—what many call the "urban underclass" (Schurmann and Close 1979; Salinas 1980).

Regardless of high-visibility concentrations of the subemployed urban underclass in "pockets of poverty" in growing Sunbelt cities, much urban economic development policy is based on the assumption that growth will reduce subemployment. This common belief has spawned policy suggestions to help relocate the urban poor from the Northeast to growing Sunbelt cities[2] and to minimize federal economic development funds going to cities with growth rates above a certain threshold.[3] The theoretical and empirical support for this trickle-down[4] belief is strong: whether an urban Kuznets curve, a Keynesian aggregate demand analysis, or a queue concept is used, most urban and regional growth theorists would posit that in devel-

oped economies a city or region's growth will provide job opportunities and upward earnings mobility to the low-income subemployed
labor force (e.g., Williamson 1965; Harris and Todaro 1970). Moreover,
post–World War II data (up to 1970) show the proportion of low-
income urban workers to total urban labor force declining in the
United States as a whole, as well as in Sunbelt cities.

In the following analysis I argue, using an historically informed
segmented labor market framework, that growth is not significantly
reducing the barriers between labor market segments in large Sunbelt
cities and, in fact, is creating secondary sector jobs that reinforce
low-income employment. The result is no significant economic
improvement for the low-income subemployed labor force. I derive
three testable hypotheses based on this argument and test them with
longitudinal data from the Social Security Continuous Work History
1% Sample by comparing twenty-five Sunbelt metropolitan areas to
a nationwide sample of over fifty metropolitan areas. The results,
while they do not prove the argument, are consistent with the
argument: post-1970 metropolitan employment growth—which is
concentrated in the Sunbelt—is statistically associated with very
little change in the proportion of low-income subemployed workers,
no reduction in the longevity of individual subemployment, and no
improvement in immediate upward mobility for the subemployed
whether they reside in, or migrate to, growing metropolitan areas.
The last part of the chapter weaves these findings into an evaluation
of policy alternatives for addressing urban subemployment. The overall conclusion is that trickle-down policies even with migration assistance will not solve the problem of urban subemployment.

Hypothesizing the Relationship between
Urban Growth and Subemployment

Empirical examinations of the distributive implications of growth
have been done largely at a national level (between income groups
[Kuznets 1955] and between regions [Williamson 1965]). Their
findings are similar: years of increasing inequality and growth, followed by a period of growth and no change in inequality, and finally
slow convergence between disparate income and regional groups.
Most researchers using data that go through the 1960s have found
the United States to be in the third phase. Some urban growth theo-

rists would apply the third phase of the Kuznets curve to metropolitan areas in the United States, as well, and hypothesize that metropolitan growth would tend to reduce the proportion of the labor force that is subemployed or low-income.

A simplistic Keynesian analysis would posit a similar inverse relationship between metropolitan growth and subemployment. A Keynesian explanation would attribute subemployment—like employment—largely to a lack of aggregate demand for labor. A surplus population is created that is willing to offer its labor for less than culturally defined subsistence earnings. With sufficient growth in demand for labor, subemployment will tend to disappear.

Queue theorists point out that this inverse relationship between growth and subemployment may not hold for metropolitan economies due to their openness to in-migration. The in-migration of poor—particularly rural poor—in response to urban growth can cause increasing income inequality within a growing city. The in-migrants simply enter a queue waiting for the income and employment benefits of the growth to trickle down to them. The poor will continue to migrate to the growing city until the present value of expected income is equal between places.[5] The implication is that the queue moves faster in growing places than in nongrowing places, even though at any point in time the queue may be longer in growing places (i.e., there may be a higher percentage of poor, but their rate of upward mobility is higher than in nongrowing cities). Whether an urban Kuznets curve, a Keynesian aggregate demand analysis, or the queue concept is adopted, the poor are assumed to benefit from urban growth.

The segmented labor market literature posits that growth may slightly weaken some of the barriers between labor market segments, such as race, gender, and age discrimination by employers. Nevertheless, growth will not tend to eliminate the barriers (Bluestone et al. 1973, 31). Furthermore, the growth itself will produce some proportion of secondary sector jobs, which reinforces subemployment. But even growth in the better-paying, more stable primary sector jobs may not benefit secondary sector workers because of mobility barriers between segments of the labor market.

Adding an historical dimension to the segmented labor market theory reinforces the hypothesis that urban growth will not significantly ameliorate urban subemployment. In response to increasing competition in world markets since the late 1960s, multinational corporations have been reorganizing the process of production on a world scale. In this new international division of labor, the pivotal competitive factor is labor costs (Storper and Walker 1983). To minimize labor costs, many industries are either relocating to cheaper labor sites or changing the technology of production to require less skilled labor or both. In the United States those cities able to capture the high-growth sectors of corporate headquarter functions, producer services, and high-tech industry are likely to develop an increasingly bifurcated labor market in which the growth of high-level primary sector jobs and low-level secondary sector jobs outpaces the growth of intermediate-level jobs. In the growing number of lower-tiered specialized production centers characterized by the importance of consumer services, retailing, or assembly industry, secondary sector jobs are likely to predominate. In both cases the intermediate-level jobs—the major channel of upward mobility for labor and the fruits of the crumbling big labor/big business alliance—are likely to be underrepresented.[6]

On the basis of this historical analysis in combination with the segmented labor market framework, I hypothesize that current urban growth in the United States is likely to provide a significant source of upward mobility for secondary sector workers and therefore is not associated with a significant decline in subemployment.

Operationalizing the Hypotheses

To test these hypotheses relating growth to subemployment requires measuring not only the net or aggregate relationship between urban growth and subemployment, but also the longitudinal work histories of individual subemployed workers by metropolitan area. Only by tracing individual workers over time (and space) can rates of upward mobility and movements of the employment queue in growing vs. nongrowing cities be assessed.

The only nationwide data base permitting such longitudinal analysis is the Social Security Continuous Work History Sample—a 1 percent sample of the social security–covered work force (which includes 88 percent of the entire U.S. work force). The CWHS is a sample of workers' earnings recorded from employers' quarterly reports to the Social Security Administration. The sample is based on specific digits in workers' social security numbers. Because the same social security numbers are included in the sample for each period, work histories for workers in the sample can be assembled by linking the data files for successive periods.[7] Work histories include data on sex, race, year of birth and, for each time period, the state, county,[8] and three-digit classification of industrial employment, as well as an estimate of earnings from each social security–covered job.

Because the CWHS data base does not include information on education, training, experience, or family income, it permits only an individual earnings cutoff to define and measure subemployment. For the following empirical analysis, then, a subemployed individual is defined as a member of the labor force who—because of low wages, intermittent work, or part-time work—receives annual earnings that are inadequate to support a family of four. This definition is a reflection of the income structure of jobs—not a measure of whether a person is working in the most productive capacity that his/her skills permit, whether the person is voluntarily subemployed,[9] or whether she/he needs such a job to support a family.[10]

The Social Security Administration publishes (and updates yearly) figures on what is considered a poverty level income for families of different sizes. Critics argue that this indicator is too low. In fact, similar data issued by the Bureau of Labor Statistics for a "lower standard of living" are consistently higher. The Social Security poverty level for a family of four was equal to $5,038 in 1974, as compared to $9,198 for the Bureau of Labor Statistics "lower budget." Applied to the CWHS data, the poverty level cutoff produced a sample that was too small for much detailed analysis by Standard Metropolitan Statistical Area (SMSA) and industrial sector. It was decided therefore to define a subemployed worker as one earning less than 125 percent of the poverty level for a family of four for the year in question. For 1974 this meant that workers earning less than $6,300 during that year were considered to be subemployed.[11]

An hourly wage cutoff, as opposed to an annual earnings cutoff, is often used to define subemployment. Most of the attempts in the dual labor market literature to reach an operating definition of the secondary sector (Andrisani 1973, Bluestone et al. 1973, O'Connor 1973, Harrison and Hill 1978) have concentrated on wage levels and/or hours worked. In theory, a wage cutoff alone would not get at the problem of jobs that permit or foster only intermittent or part-time work. The annual earnings definition bridges that gap.[12]

Table 12.1 Classification of sample SMSAS based on 1970–77 employment growth rate

Group 1: Fast-growing

Albuquerque	46.1	Nashville	25.9
Atlanta	22.2	Norfolk	24.8
Austin	68.7	Oklahoma City	26.1
Billings	53.4	Phoenix	42.2
Birmingham	21.6	Portland	25.3
Boise	70.0	Reno	60.3
Dallas–Fort Worth	23.0	Sacramento	41.9
Denver–Boulder	40.6	Salt Lake City	48.1
(Des Moines)	(24.4)	San Antonio	35.2
Fort Lauderdale	46.8	San Diego	37.1
Fresno	42.5	San Jose	44.3
Houston	49.4	Spokane	30.4
Memphis	19.7	Tampa	36.1

Group 2: Declining

Albany	0.8	Hartford	2.5
Baltimore	3.9	New York	−13.9
Boston	1.0	Newark	− 0.6
Buffalo	− 2.8	Philadelphia	− 0.3
Cleveland	0.5	Pittsburgh	1.3
Detroit	4.3	St. Louis	3.9

Group 3: Intermediate

Chicago	5.1	Milwaukee	7.8
Cincinnati	10.4	Minneapolis–St. Paul	14.4
Greensboro	13.6	New Orleans	17.6
Indianapolis	11.0	Providence	5.9
Kansas City	7.5	Rochester	11.6
Los Angeles	6.2	San Francisco–Oakland	15.8
Louisville	6.3	Seattle	17.1
Miami	13.8		

Source: U.S. Bureau of the Census, *County Business Patterns.* 1970 and 1977, U. S. Summary, tables.

Methodology

Out of the approximately 1.5 million records per year available from the 1 percent Social Security sample, data for fifty-three SMSAS were used. The fifty-three SMSAS included thirty-six of the largest SMSAS plus other medium and small SMSAS added to provide adequate representation from all regions. Twenty-five of the SMSAS are in the Sunbelt—i.e., the South, Southeast, and West census regions (table 12.1). The data covered the years 1970–75. Starting in 1974, all subemployed individuals in the sample of fifty-three SMSAS were traced four years back (to 1970) and one year forward (to 1975).

With these data it was possible to divide the subemployed—i.e., those earning less than 1.25 times the national poverty level—into the long-term subemployed—those subemployed for at least five continuous years—and the short-term subemployed—those subemployed for four continuous years or less.[13] Various socioeconomic subdivisions also were possible. Minimum sample cell size was one hundred (representing a population of 10,000) in order to have a standard error of no more than 10 percent (Cartwright et al. 1976, 74). For SMSA employment growth rates, two different sources were used. The Bureau of Labor Statistics' *Employment and Earnings* was used for change in SMSA employment, 1970–74. *County Business Patterns* provided the percentage change in the labor force, 1970–77. In some cases the figures had to be adjusted to compensate for changes in SMSA boundaries over time.

Test 1: The Sensitivity of Subemployment to Growth

The first test deals with total subemployment (long-term plus short-term). A simple linear regression was estimated to test the sensitivity of subemployment to growth, i.e., to determine the net or aggregate relationship between urban growth and subemployment. The following relationship was specified:

$$Y = a_0 + a_1 X$$

where

Y = change in the percentage of the subemployed metropolitan labor force, 1970–74 and

> X = percentage change in metropolitan employment, 1970–74

Social Security CWHS was used for subemployment rates. Bureau of Labor Statistics' *Employment and Earnings* was used for growth rates. Of the fifty-three SMSAS sampled, forty-eight were used (Austin, Nashville, Boise, Hartford, and Albany were omitted for lack of BLS data).

The analysis yielded the following results:

$$Y_x = 0.52 - 0.16X$$
$$\bar{Y} = 12.7 \quad s^2_y = 116.2$$
$$\bar{X} = -1.1 \quad s^2_x = 12.7$$

The t score is 3.1, making the estimate for coefficient a_1 significant at the .01 level. The coefficient of determination R^2, which shows the proportion of variance in Y determined by X, is .17.

The results point to several interesting conclusions: (1) the low value of the coefficient (a_1) shows a low sensitivity of subemployment to growth rates; (2) the relationship between growth rates and subemployment is negative—i.e., growth is associated with a decline in subemployment; (3) however, the relationship is so weak that an extraordinarily high growth rate would produce a slight drop in subemployment—e.g., a 10 percent annual growth rate (or 46.4 percent for four years) would produce an annual drop in the percentage of the labor force that is subemployed of only 1.7;[14] (4) put in other terms, a large increase in a metropolitan area's growth rate (for example, from 10 to 14 percent over the four years) would produce an unimportant drop in the subemployment rate of .64 over the four years (i.e., from the mean subemployment rate of 54.99 percent to 54.35 percent, for example);[15] (5) the low percentage of variance in subemployment explained by growth rates indicates that factors other than growth are the major determinants of subemployment.

To test the difference in sensitivity of subemployment to growth between growing and nongrowing SMSAS, two similar linear regressions were estimated for the set of growing SMSAS (i.e., those with average annual growth rates greater than the entire sample average of 1.75 percent) and the set of nongrowing SMSAS (i.e., those with average annual growth rates of less than 1.75 percent).

Using the same specification as above, analysis for the growing SMSAS yielded the following results:

$$Y_X = 0.36 - 0.15X$$

The t score is 1.6, making the coefficient a_1 significant only at the .10 level. The coefficient of determination R^2 is .08.

The analysis of the nongrowing SMSAS, using the same specification as above, yielded the following results:

$$Y_X = 1.05 - 0.39X$$

The t score is 2.8, making the coefficient a_1 significant at the .01 level. The coefficient of determination R^2 is .32.

These results indicate that subemployment rates are much more sensitive to growth rates in nongrowing SMSAS than in growing SMSAS. In fact, growth rates for the nongrowing SMSAS explain one-third of the variance in subemployment rates. While this may indicate that in cities not subject to much in-migration of low-income workers — such as declining northeastern cities — subemployment rates are more sensitive to growth rates, the relationship is still weak. An increase in the growth rate of a nongrowing SMSA of 1 percent (an extremely sizable increase) would decrease the percentage of the labor force that is subemployed by only .4.[16] Even in rapidly growing SMSAS such an increase would reduce the subemployment rate by a negligible .15.

Test 2: Longevity of Subemployment in Growing and Declining Metropolitan Areas

While test 1 shows an overall very weak relationship between growth and subemployment, these results could still be consistent with the queue hypothesis that even though the line may not be shorter, it moves more rapidly in growing places. Test 2 (Salinas 1982) quantifies how long subemployed workers residing in a SMSA are subemployed and compares the longevity between growing and declining SMSAS.

The Continuous Work History Sample was crucial to performing this test, since individual workers had to be followed over time. Workers subemployed in each SMSA in 1974 were traced back to 1970 to see which ones had been continuously subemployed for all five years. With this information a ratio of long-term subemployed to total subemployed was calculated for each SMSA sampled.

For this test the sample of fifty-three SMSAS was divided into growing and declining cities. The measure of growth for each SMSA was given by the percentage change in the labor force between 1970 and 1977. Data on employment were derived from the 1970 and 1977 issues of *County Business Patterns*.

The average rate of growth in employment for the fifty-three SMSA sample was calculated to be 9 percent for the 1970–77 period. Consequently, metropolitan areas whose growth rate was higher than twice the sample average (or 18 percent) were defined as "fast-growing." SMSAS with a growth rate of less than one-half the sample average (or 4.5 percent) were considered "declining," while the remaining ones were labeled as "intermediate" (see table 12.1).

All but one of the twenty-five cities that met the "fast-growing" criterion are located in the South and West census regions. All but one of the twelve "declining" cities are located in the Northeast and North Central regions. In fact, ten of them are concentrated in the Northeast and East North Central divisions. In terms of employment covered by the 1 percent Social Security data, the two regional samples created for the study are approximately similar in size: 100,960 workers in the twenty-five growing SMSAS and 130,741 workers in the twelve declining ones. The results show that the average percentage of long-term subemployed is actually higher in the growing metropolitan areas: 37.7 percent, compared to the declining cities' average of 34.7 percent.

The longevity data also was analyzed by census region and cohort: prime age males, prime age females, and youth, each divided into blacks and nonblacks (see table 12.2). The results reinforce the finding that subemployment is longer-term in growing areas; the ratio of long-term subemployment to total subemployment is slightly higher in the South/Southwest than the North East/East North Central region for males, youth, and black females, with the largest regional difference appearing for prime-age black males. (Only white prime-age females experience a slightly lower proportion of long-term subemployment in the Sunbelt, perhaps due to their slower incorporation into the labor force in the South than in the North.) These data show that, on the whole, growth is not associated with shorter duration of individual subemployment.

Table 12.2. Duration of individual subemployment,[1] by cohort and region[2]

Race & Region	Males, 25–55			Females, 25–55			Youth, 17–24		
	1 year %	2–4 years %	5+ years %	1 year %	2–4 years %	5+ years %	1 year %	2–4 years %	5+ years %
Black	20.1	36.9	43.0	9.0	33.0	57.9	3.2	65.1	31.7
NE/ENC	22.7	38.0	39.3	11.3	36.3	52.4	3.7	66.9	29.4
WNC	23.2	33.6	43.2	10.0	35.6	54.4	2.2	59.6	38.2
WEST	18.3	47.4	34.3	12.1	35.9	52.0	4.3	70.8	24.9
S/SW	17.6	32.4	50.0	5.6	28.3	66.1	2.4	62.8	34.8
White[3]	26.7	43.5	29.8	10.6	42.3	47.1	4.6	68.7	26.7
NE/ENC	30.5	42.5	27.0	10.7	41.8	47.5	5.1	67.9	27.0
WNC	28.6	40.3	31.1	12.5	35.7	51.8	3.1	66.2	30.7
WEST	24.5	45.2	30.3	9.8	44.8	45.4	4.4	74.7	20.9
S/SW	24.1	43.6	32.3	10.5	43.0	46.5	3.5	67.4	29.1

Source: Social Security CWHC, using data on subemployed individuals in 53 SMSAS in 1974, tracing their work histories back to 1970.
1 defined as having annual earnings less than 1.25 × poverty level and greater than zero.
2 Regionalization based on modified census regions, shown in table 12.2.
3 Whites defined as non-blacks.

Test 3: Upward Mobility and Growth

While test 2 indicates the queue does not move more rapidly for the subemployed in growing as opposed to declining SMSAS (and the regions where they are located), the question remains whether the waiting in the queue is more worthwhile in the growing metropolitan areas. In other words, is the rate of upward mobility of the long-term subemployed higher in growing than declining SMSAS?

The Continuous Work History Sample data were crucial to this test, as well, in order to follow individual workers over time. A long-term subemployed worker—i.e., one subemployed continuously from 1970 through 1974—was considered to be upwardly mobile if in 1975 he or she earned more than 125 percent of the poverty level for that year.

For this analysis SMSAS were grouped by census region and upward mobility rates compared between region. Table 12.3 (see "total" column) shows that metropolitan areas in growing regions provide no consistent advantage in upward mobility for the long-term subemployed. For the growing regions the rate of upward mobility is 11 percent in the South/Southwest and 13 percent in the West. For the declining Northeast/East North Central the rate of upward mobility is 12 percent.

Table 12.3   Upward mobility of the long-term subemployed by region, 1974–75

Long-term subemployed workers, 1974[1,2]

Region[4]	Total			Nonmovers (same region, same SMSA)			Moved to NE/ENC		
	Number fully employed in 1975[3]	Total number of workers	Percentage fully employed in 1975	Number fully employed in 1975	Total number of workers	Percentage fully employed in 1975	Number fully employed in 1975	Total number of workers	Percentage fully employed in 1975
NE/ENC	2,509	21,551	11.6	2,058	17,167	12.0	356	3,166	11.2
WNC	476	4,352	10.9	419	3,651	11.5	19	189	10.1
WEST	1,570	11,877	13.2	1,242	8,560	14.5	31	345	9.0
S/SW	1,785	16,855	10.6	1,172	11,355	10.3	53	651	8.1
Total	6,340	54,635	11.6	4,891	40,733	12.0	459	4,351	10.5

Moved to WNC			Moved to WEST			Moved to S/SW		
Number fully employed in 1975	Total number of workers	Percentage fully employed in 1975	Number fully employed in 1975	Total number of workers	Percentage fully employed in 1975	Number fully employed in 1975	Total number of workers	Percentage fully employed in 1975
16	156	10.3	28	305	9.2	51	757	6.7
19	267	7.1	5	99	5.1	16	146	9.6
4	124	3.2	265	2,452	10.8	28	396	7.1
14	128	10.9	41	376	10.9	505	4,345	11.6
53	675	7.9	339	3,232	10.5	598	5,644	10.6

Source: Social Security CWHS for 53 SMSAS.
1 Number of workers who in 1974 had earned less than 1.25 × poverty level since 1970.
2 In thousands.
3 Fully employed in 1975: earned more than 1.25 × poverty level for 1975.
4 See table 12.2 for regionalization.

The queue theorist could still claim that while the *average* upward mobility rate for the long-term subemployed does not appear to be influenced by growth rates, growing SMSAS may still offer relatively more opportunity to the in-migrating long-term subemployed worker than if she or he stays behind in a lagging SMSA. In fact, this is a major assumption in one of the panel reports of the President's Commission for a National Agenda for the Eighties (1980, 57–62), which recommends a package of migration assistance to the urban underclass in distressed cities similar to that done in Europe. However, strong empirical justification of this policy recommendation has not been forthcoming. The President's Commission's report cites a series of demonstration projects using relocation allowances conducted by the Department of Labor between 1965 and 1969 in which the "vast majority" of the 14,000 unemployed and underemployed who relocated were "satisfied" with their moves (p. 60). James and Blair (1983) have cited an unpublished cross-sectional study imputing the economic well-being of origin and destination communities (mainly states) to individual migrants, concluding that migrants (except black males and white females with eleven years of education) would face a lower probability of poverty after migration.

An adequate test of the relocation hypothesis requires longitudinal data on individual migrants using metropolitan areas (not states) for origin and destination communities. The yearly location data on each individual in the CWHS file of fifty-three SMSAS provided such evidence. A regional origin and destination matrix was determined for all the long-term subemployed in the sample for 1974–75. Nonmovers were considered those who stayed in the same SMSA between 1974 and 1975 (even though they may have moved within the SMSA). Upward mobility rates were compared for nonmovers and movers (see table 12.3). Note that two cells report a population size of less than 10,000 and are therefore subject to a standard error of more than 10 percent.)

The results show that moving to the booming South/Southwest from another region actually reduces the probability of at least immediate upward mobility compared to not moving. Moving to the West from any other region except the South/Southwest also reduces the probability of upward mobility (moving from the South/Southwest to the West raises the probability of upward mobility by an insignificant .3 percent).[17] For example, if you lived in the Frostbelt

(NE/ENC) and were subemployed from 1970 to 1974, and you stayed there in 1975, your immediate chances of moving out of subemployment were about one in eight. If you moved to the Sunbelt (s/sw) to try to escape subemployment — that is, to find a job paying a nonpoverty income — your chances in 1975 fell to one in fifteen. This is even lower than the odds facing someone who stayed in the Sunbelt all along. A long-term subemployed southerner who remained within the region in 1975 (either in the same SMSA or another within the s/sw) had between a one in eight and a one in ten chance of escaping subemployment. It would seem that subemployed migrants from the Frostbelt were getting disproportionately tracked into low-wage jobs.[18] These findings are consistent with Bartel's findings (1979, 785) that the unemployed (he examined only those who had been laid off) are better off if they do not migrate.[19]

While this analysis indicates that living in or migrating to growing metropolitan areas is not a panacea for subemployment, the bivariate regression used here can lead to specification error that biases the a_1 coefficient in an unknown direction. Future researchers will want to specify a more complete model, taking into account structural characteristics of the local economies such as the amount and kind of growth industries that are present.

Policy Implications

All subemployment is not a problem requiring public intervention. Subemployment — i.e., the existence of a labor force willing to offer its labor for less than a culturally defined subsistence income — is beneficial to the economy in several ways:

(1) It provides a reserve pool of labor willing to enter the better-paid primary sector when demand requires.

(2) It provides another reserve pool of labor available for the low-paid high-turnover jobs in the secondary sector.

(3) The lower wages accepted by the subemployed in competitive sector jobs mean cheaper goods and services are available to businesses and consumers in the rest of the economy.

Subemployment is detrimental to the economy in two ways:

(1) Many of the permanently subemployed contribute to a heavy tax burden because of their continual need for welfare and unemployment insurance to supplement their inadequate earnings.

(2) The permanently subemployed who are geographically concentrated in the inner cities pose the threat of social unrest (e.g., Watts in the 1960s, Miami in 1980) and related costs (e.g., crime).

The portion of the subemployed labor force whose costs far outweigh its benefits to the economy is composed of the permanently subemployed of the inner cities who rely on government transfer payments to supplement their inadequate earnings. Public policy on urban subemployment, often called underemployment,[20] need concern itself only with these long-term or permanently subemployed who are concentrated in inner-city neighborhoods—i.e., the urban underclass. A range of policy options, varying by the kind of targeting, can be considered for improving the employment prospects of the urban underclass.

The Do-Nothing Alternative
(or Why Do We Need Any of These Programs, Anyway?)

First, the alternative of no public intervention into the problem of subemployment must be addressed. The do-nothing argument typically rests on two legs. The first is that subemployment is a short-term phenomenon—either a problem experienced by youth before they become stably linked to the job market or a cyclical problem affecting otherwise stable workers at the trough of a recession. In either case, government intervention is not appropriate if subemployment is a short-term individual problem that will clear up with age or the end of the recession.

The other leg of the argument is that even if subemployment is a long-term problem for many people, the proportion of the labor force experiencing long-term subemployment is declining over time. Since the gradual expansion—however slow—of the nation's economy is absorbing more and more of the subemployed, no public sector intervention is necessary.[21]

Data are available that question both these arguments. Census data for the fifty-three metropolitan areas studied show that the proportion of subemployed to the total work force indeed declined dramatically in all regions throughout the fifties and sixties. However, the decline came to a stop in the seventies. The end of the long postwar boom, the onset of a general economic slowdown throughout the seventies, and a gradual restructuring of industry that has reinforced secondary sector employment (Noyelle 1983a) brought a halt to the decline in subemployment in the South, Southwest, and West. In the troubled Northeast the proportion of subemployed even grew. All the regions experienced absolute increases in urban subemployment. Given the bleak economic projections for the 1980s, there is no basis for assuming that the subemployed urban underclass will disappear. On the contrary, it is likely to present a growing problem requiring decisive public sector intervention.

The other leg of the nonintervention hypothesis—i.e., the argument that subemployment is largely a short-term cyclical phenomenon—is addressed by the CWHS data in table 12.2, which follow individuals from 1970 to 1974, right through the business cycle that peaked in 1971. It was found that a substantial proportion of those subemployed adults (ages twenty-five to fifty-five) in 1974 had been continuously subemployed since 1970 (30 percent of white males, 43 percent of black males, 47 percent of white females, and 58 percent of black females), thus indicating that subemployment is not just a cyclical phenomenon. Moreover, a breakdown of the long-term subemployed by age in 1974 shows that less than 40 percent of them were young workers between the ages of sixteen and twenty-four. Thus, long-term subemployment is not just a passing phenomenon of youth or business cycles.

The fact that subemployment is not disappearing over time and that it is not just a short-term phenomenon related to age or business cycles leads many to reject the do-nothing hypothesis.

The Untargeted Approach: Macrostimulus

The basic untargeted approach is macrostimulus, i.e., monetary or fiscal policies to boost the national economy under the assumption that a general increase in economic activity will provide—directly or indirectly—increased economic opportunity for the nation's poor. The ineffectiveness of macrostimulus policy in improving the employment prospects of the urban underclass is well documented (e.g., Feldstein 1973). While the Keynesian policy of stimulating demand to create more jobs and reduce unemployment may assist certain sectors of the population—specifically, unemployed primary sector workers—it provides little help to the target group.

Unemployment and subemployment rates for the urban underclass are not very responsive to changes in the aggregate demand for labor. Feldstein calculates that a 1 percent fall in the unemployment rate for adult males would lower the black youth unemployment rate by .26 percent. In 1971 if the adult male unemployment rate had been reduced to an unprecedented 1.5 percent, the black youth unemployment rate would have fallen from 32 percent to a still unacceptably high 25 percent (Feldstein 1973, p. 7).

Place Targeting: Microstimulus

Some federal agencies—e.g., U.S. Department of Housing and Urban Development (HUD), the Economic Development Administration (EDA), and the now defunct Community Services Agency (CSA) —concentrate their economic development funds on those urban or rural places that evidence a high degree of unemployment or subemployment. Since the approach is to stimulate the depressed local economy to produce more private sector jobs, it may be called a microstimulus approach. It is based on the fundamental assumption that an increase in the number of permanent jobs, regardless of their type or location within the eligible city or county, will directly or indirectly benefit the local subemployed and unemployed. EDA infrastructure grants and business loans, for example, are targeted to qualifying places on this assumption.

The longitudinal evidence from the three CWHS tests presented earlier challenges the growth/trickle-down hypothesis: these data indicate that (1) metropolitan employment growth produces a negligible decrease in subemployment in growing metropolitan areas; (2) growth is not associated with increased probability of upward mobility for the long-term subemployed residents or in-migrants; and (3) neither is growth associated with shorter spells of individual subemployment. Thus, exclusive reliance on a microstimulus or place targeting approach is questionable.

A more focused form of place targeting restricts economic development incentives to depressed zones or neighborhoods within metropolitan areas that may or may not qualify as a whole. This approach to place targeting assumes that to benefit the permanently subemployed in a qualifying metropolitan area, the jobs created must be physically accessible to them. Incentives to locate new jobs in or near the inner city are the primary focus of this approach.

EDA's Special Impact Area program is an example of this approach. By concentrating investments in specially designated low-income inner-city neighborhoods, it is assumed that the local low-income residents will have access to these jobs. Another example may be HUD's efforts to facilitate downtown revitalization in qualifying cities. The hotel, office, and retail jobs created in the central business districts are within easy access of the inner-city neighborhoods. Another example would be enterprise zones as proposed in the Kemp-Garcia bill (Sternlieb and Listokin 1981). This bill would offer automatic tax breaks to firms locating within the designated neighborhoods. While neighborhood targeting would indeed be more likely than citywide targeting to provide jobs that are physically accessible to the urban underclass, the question remains to what point is physical accessibility the main barrier. (See Goldsmith 1982 for other arguments against enterprise zones.)

Industry Targeting

Another policy approach to economic development aimed at reducing subemployment is to promote those industries that tend to provide the most opportunity for upward mobility to the urban underclass. As segmented labor market theory points out, most jobs readily accessible to the long-term subemployed are low-productivity low-pay secondary sector jobs. An economic development strategy that emphasized the creation of secondary sector jobs would to a great extent reinforce the subemployment of the urban underclass. Yet a policy to promote primary sector jobs may not benefit the subemployed because of labor market barriers impeding their access to those jobs. A policy of industry targeting, therefore, would have to favor those industries that are both accessible to the subemployed and provide a significant probability of earnings mobility and reject the industries that provide neither.

The CWHS provided a data base for determining which three-digit SICs (Standard Industrial Classification sectors) offer both accessibility and upward mobility to the long-term subemployed and which offer neither. Using the CWHS data for fifty-three SMSAs, I traced long-term subemployed workers in 1974 to 1975 and analyzed the SIC composition of the 11.8 percent of those workers who were

Table 12.4 SICs affording greater than average accessibility and mobility for the long-term subemployed

SIC	name of industry	SIC	name of industry
(Construction)		(Retail trade)	
154	Nonresidential buildings	541	Grocery stores
162	Heavy construction	551	Motor vehicle dealers
171	Plumbing, heating, a/c	571	Furniture stores
179	Miscellaneous special trades		
		(Manufacturing, insurance and real estate)	
(Manufacturing)			
271	Newspaper publishing and printing	612	Savings and loan associations
275	Commercial printing	631	Life insurance
344	Fabricated structural metal products	633	Fire, marine and casualty insurance
357	Office machines	641	Insurance agents, brokers, and service
366	Communication equipment		
367	Electrical components and accessories	653	Real estate agents and managers
(Transportation, communication, utilities)		(Other services)	
421	Trucking	753	Automotive repair shops
481	Telephone communication	806	Hospitals
(Wholesale trade)		811	Legal services
501	Motor vehicles, parts, and supplies	821	Elementary and secondary schools
506	Electrical goods	822	Colleges, universities, professional schools
508	Machinery, equipment, and supplies	891	Engineering, architectural and surveying services
514	Groceries and related products	893	Accounting, auditing, and bookkeeping services
		(Public administration)	
		901	Public administration

Source: CWHS, 53 SMSAS, 1975

upwardly mobile—i.e., who were earning over 1.25 times the poverty level in 1975.

The results show that less than 10 percent of the 347 three-digit SICs afforded both above-average accessibility *and* mobility (see table 12.4). High-tech manufacturing producer services (e.g., transportation, communications, wholesale trade, financial, legal, and engineering services) and health and education figure prominently among them. Most of the industries, however, showed either high mobility and low accessibility or low mobility and high accessibility. A policy that relied on less than 10 percent of all industries to absorb the subemployed would not only be economically implausible but also politically unfeasible. Moreover, specific industry characterizations may not be stable over time. There is mounting evidence that high-tech manufacturing employment, for example, is becoming increasingly polarized into good jobs and bad (Harris 1983a).

People Targeting

People targeting traditionally refers to a human capital approach to improving the supply of labor, rather than stimulating the demand for labor. People-targeting programs emphasize skills training to make unemployed and subemployed individuals more attractive to employers. However, lack of adequate jobs and labor market barriers often prevent even trained, potentially productive workers from getting decent jobs. Some proof of the existence of this labor market segmentation is the fact that the return on investment (i.e., earnings) in human capital (formal and on-the-job training) varies by race and sex.[22]

Another people-targeting measure often talked about is public assistance in relocating the unemployed and subemployed from lagging or declining regions to growing areas (e.g., President's Commission for a National Agenda for the Eighties 1980; James and Blair 1983; Kasarda 1982, 1983). This policy prescription is based on the idea that growing areas may offer relatively greater opportunities to the in-migrating long-term subemployed worker than if she or he stayed behind in a lagging area. However, the regional origin and destination matrix using the longitudinal CWHS data (see table 12.3) indicates that moving to the booming South/Southwest from another region may actually reduce the immediate probability of upward mobility compared to not moving. If this is the case, providing migration assistance at the cost of reducing in-place assistance may not be justifiable.[23]

Another type of people targeting is the building up of entrepreneurial skills (and access to capital) among minorities and women—i.e., two demographic groups that together account for over half of the long-term subemployed—either to help them directly by starting or expanding businesses or indirectly through increasing the opportunity of being hired by minority or female entrepreneurs who presumably would not discriminate in hiring practices. Two questions come to mind with respect to this strategy: to what extent is the urban underclass—as opposed to the minority/female middle class—served by these measures? Also, how much and what kind of employment is created by the small businesses typically generated?

Community-Based Economic Development: The Bottom-Up Approach

Popularized and made official in the 1960s with federal OEO (Office of Economic Opportunity) funding for community development corporations, this approach rests on the assumption that the economic situation of the urban underclass can change significantly only if the members of the underclass work together to change it by building their own economic (and political) organizational capacity (National Economic Development Law Project [NEDLP] 1974). Federal support for this approach (through, for example, HUD's Office of Neighborhood Assistance, EDA's Office of Special Projects, and CSA) has dropped off sharply in recent years, and evaluations of CDC's ability to establish and operate firms that provide good jobs for the low-income community have been mixed (Abt Associates 1973; Stein 1973; Perlman 1976; Daniels, Barbe, and Seigal 1981). Nevertheless, grassroots efforts at community economic development have continued, often with state and local government support. Moreover, new strategies of community-based economic development are being tried. Not yet adequately evaluated, for instance, are CDC efforts to pursue joint ventures with private firms that are rediscovering the benefits of inner-city locations (Salinas 1981; Pierce 1981). While community-based economic development has not been an effective policy tool on a large scale in the past, its potential has not been adequately tested.

Conclusions

While this survey is not exhaustive, most economic development approaches used in the United States fall under one of the six categories discussed. As pointed out, none of the approaches offers a panacea for subemployment. The most effective local economic development strategies for alleviating subemployment *combine* the approaches surveyed to offset the limitations of each: e.g., trickle-down with bottom-up approaches, labor supply with labor demand approaches,[24] place targeting with people targeting, and general growth stimulus with industry-specific growth stimulus. Today's economic development slogans—e.g., investment leveraging, enterprise zones, private-public partnerships—reflect a trickle-down stimulus strategy that by itself cannot be expected to significantly benefit the urban subemployed.

Author's Note: The research for this paper was part of a larger study funded by the Economic Development Administration, Division of Economic Research. Analysis and findings do not necessarily reflect the views of the Economic Development Administration. Thanks go to Ken Horrowitz of the Bureau of Economic Analysis for the computer work; to Allen Olson, project monitor at EDA; and to Sandro Pio, Research Assistant.

13 Labor Mobility in National Policy and Local Economies

Franklin J. James and John P. Blair

The federal government has tried for several years to articulate and implement national urban policies capable of ameliorating the fiscal distress of declining cities and the economic distress of people living in these places (see, for example, *President's National Urban Policy Report 1980*; Joint Economic Committee 1984). National urban programs have offered fiscal assistance to state and local governments, training and income supports to disadvantaged people, and job creation, both in the public sector (e.g., CETA public service employment) and in the private sector (e.g., economic development programs of HUD and the Economic Development Administration).

The urban policy of the Carter administration emphasized targeted economic development programs for their promise to create jobs in distressed communities (a "jobs to people" strategy) and to strengthen local tax bases. The Reagan administration has greatly deemphasized such programs. It has argued for reliance on market economic forces to ameliorate the problems of cities. Nevertheless, some effective economic development programs have received administration support (Bingham and Blair 1984; Palmer and Sawhill 1984). The current administration's proposal for urban enterprise zones reflects a continued interest in economic development as a means to alleviate joblessness and fiscal strain in distressed places.

Economic development efforts have been criticized by some observers as hopeless efforts to prop up obsolete economies, and thus efforts that are inimical to national economic progress (President's Commission 1980). Supporters of economic development efforts argue that they create jobs and tax base most effectively when they foster adaptation of troubled economies to current economic realities (*President's National Urban Policy Report 1980*). Supporters also point out that taxation, transportation, and other policies of the federal government have hastened the shift of business and industry from declining cities and regions to growing places. Targeted economic development programs can help compensate distressed communities for such economic damage.[1]

Prominent by their absence in past urban policies have been efforts to foster geographic mobility of disadvantaged people. Fostering mobility means deliberate government efforts to increase migration of poor people or minority persons from distressed communities to places where jobs and economic opportunity may be available, i.e., a "people to jobs" strategy. One reason for the absence of mobility programs is that they lack a clear political constituency.[2]

This essay will show that a second and damaging impediment to the implementation of mobility programs is that available evidence is not sufficient to show that such a program would have a significant impact. Much more research is needed to determine the degree to which public programs can shape the migration decisions of disadvantaged persons.

However, available evidence does show that there are sizable potential economic gains to disadvantaged people who migrate from distressed communities to economically healthy places. Evidence also shows that a number of federal programs currently impede such migration. It makes sense to begin immediately to dismantle such barriers, not as a substitute for current urban programs but rather as a complement to them. A number of examples of such barriers are identified in this chapter.[3]

Geographic Differences in Economic Opportunity

Amazingly little evidence has been compiled to measure the degree to which economic opportunities for disadvantaged people differ among communities or regions. Such differences are necessary to justify a mobility policy aimed at fostering migration. They also are a key element for justifying targeted economic development efforts. That such differences exist and are significant should not be taken as self-evident. Unemployment is higher in distressed communities than elsewhere. However, minorities, unskilled people, and households headed by women make up significantly greater proportions of the populations of distressed cities than of most economically healthy places. Wherever they live, these groups all suffer greater employment and poverty problems than others. Conceivably, the large-scale migrations of young, relatively skilled persons in the 1970s reduced or eliminated the incentives of less mobile disadvantaged workers to migrate.

Much of the existing literature that has attempted to measure and describe the potential economic returns to migration is old and focuses on the rural-to-urban migrants of the 1950s and 1960s (see Bowles 1970; Greenwood 1975). Since 1970 migration has been predominantly between urban places.

Evidence from the Current Population Survey

An unpublished study by Frank Levy (1981) used the March 1979 Current Population Survey of the U.S. Bureau of the Census to assess three hypotheses:

(1) that significant geographic differences exist among states or metropolitan areas in the rates of employment and earnings of disadvantaged people;

(2) that these differences appear to be in part a function of the strength of the economies of the places; and

(3) that migrants to places with stronger economies share in the economic opportunities of the places.

The third hypothesis is important because new migrants to a place are unlikely to have the same access to economic opportunity that long-term residents do.

Levy's research verified each hypothesis.[4] Regression techniques were used to estimate relationships among the indicators of the strength of area and economies and indicators of the economic achievements of working-age persons in the areas. These relationships took into account age, sex, education, and race.[5]

Levy provides several simulations of the effects of economic conditions and migration on individuals' economic achievements. These simulations compare the expected achievements of working-age persons in a hypothetical "origin" area with a relatively weak economy and the expected achievements of migrants to a hypothetical place with a stronger economy. The characteristics of the hypothetical origin and destination places are described in table 13.1.[6]

Table 13.2 presents Levy's simulations of the effects of migration on the expected economic achievements of males. As can be seen, Levy's results suggest that black males have significant incentives to migrate between the hypothetical communities. Black men with some college education are estimated to be twice as likely to be unemployed in the origin community as they are in the destination place. The estimated probability of poverty is also lower in the destination community. Black men with eleven years of education are also estimated to benefit from the move in terms of both earnings

Table 13.1 Simulated economic conditions in migrants' origin and destination

	Origin place	Destination place
Unemployment rate (1979)	6.5%	5.5%
1972–1977 job growth	10.0%	15.0%
1969 poverty rate	16.5%	11.5%

Source: Levy, 1981.

Table 13.2 Estimated economic indicators for male nonmigrant and male intraregional migrants with various characteristics (all men assumed to be thirty-five years old)

	Black men with thirteen to fifteen years of education		Black men with eleven years of education		White men with eleven years of education	
	Origin	Destination[1]	Origin	Destination	Origin	Destination
Estimated probability of employment	.88	.94	.73	.75	.86	.87
Estimated annual earnings	$12,931	$13,711	$8,472	$9,128	$11,459	$11,594
Estimated probability of poverty	.073	.051	.211	.229	.142	.136

Note: Area economic statistics taken from table 13.1. Origin calculations are based on equations for all men developed in section III of Levy. Destination calculations are based on equations for migrants developed in section V of Levy.
Source: Levy, 1981, table 45.

and the probability of employment, though their probability of living in poverty is high in both places. The returns from the hypothetical migration for white men with eleven years of education are estimated to be uniformly positive, though very small in absolute magnitude.

Table 13.3 presents comparable results for women. The analysis of the economic achievement of women is made more complex by interactions of migration, the strength of a community's economy, and the strength of the black family. Levy focused on women heading households with children, and married women (with or without children). Unmarried women without children were omitted from his analysis.

Among black female heads of households, Levy found that migra-

Table 13.3 Estimated economic indicators for female nonmigrants and female migrants with various characteristics (all women assumed to be age thirty-five)

	Black women with thirteen to fifteen years of education		Black women with eleven years of education		White women with eleven years of education	
	Origin	Destination[1]	Origin	Destination	Origin	Destination
Estimated probability of being a female household head rather than married	.33	.37	.47	.54	.09	.07
Estimated annual earnings, 1978						
Female household heads	$6,225	$7,158	$2,306	$2,977	$3,243	$3,537
Married women	$6,983	$7,352	$3,372	$3,473	$2,496	$2,890
Estimated probability of living in a poverty household, 1978						
Female household heads	.43	.29	.75	.68	.56	.57
Married women	.08	.10	.21	.21	.13	.18

Note: Area economic statistics taken from table 13.1. Where AFDC payments are required, they were assumed by Levy to equal $3,922. Origin calculations are based on equations for all women estimated in section III of Levy. Destination calculations are based on equations for migrants estimated in section V of Levy.
Source: Levy, 1981, table 46.

tion substantially increased expected earnings and reduced the probability of improverishment. The estimated effects of migration on earnings also are positive but much smaller for black married women. Migration has no apparent impacts on the probability that black married women will live in poverty.

For white women (in this case, women with eleven years of education), migration had little effect on their household living arrangements. Migration is estimated to have improved substantially their expected annual earnings.

It should be emphasized that data restrictions made it impossible for Levy to compare the economic well-being of migrants per se in their origin and destination communities. In addition, Levy's results are sometimes of marginal statistical significance. Data restrictions doubtlessly contributed to the relatively low levels of statistical significance.[7]

Given these caveats, Levy concluded that geographic disparities in the strength of area economies were reflected in significant disparities in people's economic opportunities. In some cases, measures of the effects of area economies on achievement were of the same order of magnitude as the effects of a high school diploma.

Levy's recent findings are corroborated by two earlier studies that used longitudinal data from the Panel Study on Income Dynamics. The first study, again by Levy, focused on the probability that a person would live in poverty.[8] His analysis found that the probability of living in poverty significantly increased, other things being equal, in communities with higher unemployment rates. This was found to be true for households headed by both white and nonwhite males, and for households headed by women both with and without children.

The second study, by Bennett Harrison (1978), examined the probability of welfare dependency during the same period. Harrison found that the probability of dependence upon welfare was significantly higher in areas where unemployment rates were higher or where the number of unskilled jobs were fewer than the number of potential applicants for such jobs.

The Effectiveness of Employment
and Training Programs

Additional evidence for significant geographic differences in economic opportunities of the disadvantaged comes from evaluations of federal employment and training programs. Recent evaluations suggest that these programs are less successful in placing disadvantaged people in jobs in communities with weak economies than in places with strong economies.

Until its dismantling, the CETA (Comprehensive Employment and Training Act) program was the biggest of the federal employment and training programs. A study by Randall Ripley (1978) concluded that local labor market conditions were an important, though not paramount, determinant of the effectiveness of CETA programs.[9] Local unemployment rates were found to be inversely (and significantly) related to a variety of indicators of the effectiveness of the training programs managed by CETA prime sponsors. However, other factors were found to be of greater importance.[10]

A second recent study by the Department of Labor, Office of Employment and Training, concluded that areas with high unemployment rates and low employment growth rates had significantly lower placement rates for CETA enrollees. The influence of the local economy remained statistically significant even when other important determinants of success (such as characteristics of clients and the type of training) were held constant.

In quantitative terms the effects were small. The study concluded that a difference of 1 percentage point in the unemployment rates of two communities would be associated with a 1.6 percent difference in placement rates for CETA trainees. A difference of 5 percentage points in the rate of job growth over a decade in a community would be associated with a 1.5 percent difference in placement rates.

The Work Incentive Program (WIN) of the U.S. government provided employment and training assistance for all AFDC (Aid to Families with Dependent Children) beneficiaries sixteen years old or older who are not aged, incapacitated, ill, or caretakers of young children. Over $360 million was spent on this program in 1978. Evidence from a study by Mitchell (1980) verifies that local economic conditions have a significant impact on the success rates of WIN enrollees in getting or holding jobs.[11]

Conclusion

At base, available evidence leaves no doubt that there are significant differences between places with strong economies and places with weak economies in the job opportunities they offer disadvantaged persons. Although the absolute magnitude and importance of such differences cannot yet be estimated with confidence, the evidence satisfies one critical element of the case for a mobility policy.

Barriers to the Mobility of the Disadvantaged

That some places offer greater economic opportunities for the disadvantaged than others is not alone a strong argument for public efforts to foster mobility. Another necessary condition is that the potential benefits to migrants (and to communities) exceed the costs of migration. A direct comparison of the benefits and costs of migration is impossible because so many of the costs and benefits are intangible. Nevertheless, simple evidence suggests that a number of barriers to mobility exist that make the costs of migration needlessly high for the disadvantaged. These barriers present a prima facie case that migration makes good economic sense for a number of people who are not choosing to migrate because of unnecessary impediments in current programs.

To state the conclusion before the evidence, the mobility of disadvantaged people is impeded by a large number of federal programs, including public assistance programs for poor people and the unemployed, housing subsidy programs, and the U.S. tax system. These programs merely illustrate the effects of federal activities. The large array of federal government programs that deliver services for disadvantaged people through state and local governments also impede mobility because the quality and scope of federally financed services vary greatly among communities.

Mobility, Information, and Education

There is little doubt that the primary barriers to mobility are not created by government programs. Such barriers are community ties, both personal and economic; the sometimes substantial out-of-pocket costs of migration; lack of information about opportunities in other places; and for poorly educated or unskilled people, limited capacity to discover opportunities in other places.

Reflecting the importance of information, virtually every study of migration over long distances has found that the probability of movement is inversely related to age and directly related to education (Greenwood 1975). Levy (1981), for example, showed that a black man with eleven or fewer years of education was 4 percent less likely to move among counties than was an "otherwise similar" black man with a high school education and 14 percent less likely to make such a move than was a black man with a college education.

Research with a more behavioral focus adds more insight into the effects of limited education or skills on mobility. Da Vanzo (1978) has used longitudinal data files to examine mobility of disadvantaged people. She followed people's mobility from year to year and found that low-skilled persons who moved among communities moved back to their places of origin more frequently than did other people. Put another way, the migration efforts of low-skilled migrants appear to fail more commonly than do those of higher-skilled people. These failures were attributed by da Vanzo to factors such as an inability to adjust to the new community or a mistaken view of the opportunities actually available in the new community.

Welfare Programs and Mobility

Welfare programs in the United States raise additional barriers to mobility. In the AFDC program, for example, recipients lose their eligibility for payments when they move to another state for purposes of obtaining employment or when the move is part of a permanent change in residence. Moreover, AFDC benefit levels and qualifications for eligibility vary greatly among states. Often, informal barriers impede people's registration for the program even when they meet formal eligibility standards. The result is that migration in search of economic opportunity is made more risky and costly for AFDC recipients than it needs to be.[12]

Table 13.4 provides an indication of variations in AFDC benefit levels among selected states with both rapid and slow employment growth. The benefit levels are about one-third higher in states with sluggish employment growth than in rapidly growing states. Benefits are particularly low in South Carolina, North Carolina, Georgia, and Texas. During the 1950s and part of the 1960s the higher welfare payments in northern states were accompanied by high levels of economic opportunity for people moving from the South to the North. Today, such benefit differences encourage poor people to move to or

Table 13.4 Employment growth and AFDC programs in selected states

	1970–77 Employment growth	1976[a] Average mean monthly AFDC payment per case	Leniency[a] restrictive ness rank	Unemployed[a] parents program
Slow employment growth states				
Massachusetts	4.5	278	2	Yes
New York	−4.6	399	3	Yes
New Jersey	9.0	274	3	Yes
Pennsylvania	4.7	283	6	Yes
Michigan	13.5	287	8	Yes
Ohio	8.6	201	7	Yes
Unweighted average	5.9	2,876	4.8	
Fast employment growth states				
South Carolina	28.1	86	11	No
North Carolina	19.3	155	8	No
Georgia	21.3	96	7	No
Texas	33.9	105	13	No
Colorado	33.5	200	7	Yes
Washington	24.3	240	9	Yes
California	22.6	261	3	Yes
Unweighted average	26.1	163	8.2	

a From Campbell and Bendick 1977.

remain in regions experiencing little or no economic growth.[13]

Potential payment disruptions and differences among states in welfare eligibility requirements would hinder mobility even if benefits were equal among states. Among the qualification variations among states are limits on the value of real and personal property, the extent of income exclusions, "man-in-the-house" rules, and age limitations for dependent children. The same regulations may be administered differently even within a state. Until a family actually applies for

AFDC in a particular place, it is extremely difficult for it to know whether it will be eligible.

A leniency-restrictiveness scale developed by Cunningham indicates the extent to which eligibility rules vary among states (Campbell and Bendick 1977). The index compares eight eligibility factors on a zero (least restrictive) to two (most restrictive) scale. For any one state, the highest possible score, indicating the most restrictive eligibility practices, would be sixteen (two points on all eight factors). The index is shown for selected slow and rapid employment growth states in table 13.4. The mean value of the index for slow employment growth states was 4.8, compared to 8.2 for fast employment growth areas. This means that it is easier to qualify for AFDC in the slow growth states.

The unemployed parents' program allows families to receive welfare payments even when both parents are in the household. As shown in table 13.4, many of the growing states do not have an unemployed parents' program, but most of the slow growth states do. Thus, husband-wife families on welfare moving from a state that has the unemployed parent program to one that does not risk either foregoing the AFDC benefits or splitting up the family.

Time delays associated with processing even routine applications arc a third source of potential disruptions. The average amount of time that it takes for a family to be declared eligible for AFDC is slightly less than thirty days. The average delay, however, does not reflect the variations that are possible. Many states require longer than the thirty-day average, and even within a state there is substantial variation. This additional uncertainty contributes to immobility.

Subsidized Housing Programs

Other barriers to the mobility of the poor are apparent in the nation's housing subsidy programs for low-income people. Approximately 3.5 million low- and moderate-income households receive federal housing assistance, or about one-quarter of eligible households (U.S. Congressional Budget Office 1980). Long waiting lines provide dramatic evidence of the competition for housing assistance. The Section 8 program is the principal mechanism through which housing assistance is provided to poor people. The households fortunate enough to receive assistance under this program receive an average annual subsidy of about $2,300 (U.S. Congressional Budget Office 1980). The other three-fourths of the eligible households receive nothing.

Two principal types of Section 8 housing assistance are the new construction and existing housing programs. The new construction program subsidizes construction of units to be provided at below-market rents to low- and moderate-income families. The Section 8 existing program is designed to provide housing assistance through the existing housing stock. The existing program provides recipients some mobility because when a Secton 8 existing certificate is issued the recipient may shop for housing anywhere within the local juris-diction (usually a city or county).[14] Families receiving assistance in Section 8 new or rehabilitated units have less choice because the subsidy is tied to the unit.

The mobility disincentives in Section 8 may be even greater than the AFDC program because eligibility for housing assistance in a new area does not mean that a migrant will actually receive assistance. In fact, in light of the small proportion of income-eligible families that receive assistance, a new migrant into an area will probably not receive housing assistance even if the family is eligible.

The Federal Tax System

As a practical matter the current tax system offers greater incentives for affluent people to migrate than it does for lower-income people. Under current tax laws, persons are entitled to deduct moving costs from their gross income when moving is related to a job change or (for unemployed persons) a new job.[15] In 1979 about 1 million house-holds claimed deductions for moving costs. More than half of the overall deductions were claimed by taxpayers reporting adjusted gross incomes of $20,000 or more. Taxpayers in this income class were several times more likely to claim moving expenses as were taxpay-ers reporting incomes less than $10,000. When deductions were claimed, reported costs were substantially greater among higher-income persons.

These tax breaks reduce the costs of relocation for higher-income persons to a greater extent than for lower-income persons, as is shown in table 13.5. In 1979 taxpayers receiving incomes less than $5,000

Table 13.5 Estimated tax savings resulting from moving expenses in 1975, under prevailing law and under a tax credit

Adjusted gross income	Average moving expenses claimed by movers, 1975	Estimated tax savings under current typical law		
		Marginal tax rate	Tax savings	Assuming a 25 percent tax credit
Less than $5,000	$1,060	14%	$148	$265
$5,000 to $9,999	$1,024	19%	$229	$301
$10,000 to $14,999	$1,390	23%	$334	$347
$15,000 to $19,999	$1,831	30%	$549	$458
$20,000 or more	$2,975	39%	$1,160	$744
Mean	$2,128	24%	$511	$532

Source: Commerce Clearinghouse, 1979: U.S. Master Tax Guide; and Internal Revenue Service, *Statistics of Income: Individuals.*

were generally in the 14 percent tax bracket when their income generated tax liabilities. A typical household in this income group that was fully able to take advantage of the deductions received a tax subsidy amounting to $150, or 14 percent of its moving costs. By contrast, a typical taxpayer with income in excess of $20,000 received a tax break of almost $1,200, or 39 percent of his moving costs.

Policy Options

That the relative immobility of minorities and the poor exacerbated the economic and fiscal problems of declining cities and regions during the 1970s is beyond doubt. That enhancing the mobility of these groups could improve the groups' access to economic opportunity also seems likely on the basis of the evidence. Enhanced mobility options for disadvantaged people also would improve the effectiveness of federal employment and training programs. Because a number of important barriers to mobility have been created unintentionally by the federal government, the nation has opportunities for action that are clearly beneficial and can be implemented at practically no cost.

Actions for Reducing Barriers to Mobility

There are four obvious steps the federal government could take to reduce needless barriers to the migration of disadvantaged people among communities, states, and regions.

First, a promising solution that could be introduced within the current welfare system would be to permit AFDC beneficiaries to maintain their benefits for a time following relocation among states, so as to reduce the risks to them from relocation and to give them sufficient time in their new communities to settle down and search for work.

Second, the Section 8 existing program (or the experimental "certificate" program implemented by the Reagan administration) could be readily altered to make benefits portable anywhere within the United States on a permanent basis.[16]

Third, federal employment and training programs have not been shown to be highly effective. Expenditures under these programs have been cut deeply in recent years. The evidence presented above suggests that both the mobility of disadvantaged people and the effectiveness of the programs could be enhanced if the persons trained and assisted in the programs were offered the opportunity for national job referrals upon the completion of their training or offered vouchers for training assistance that could be used anywhere within the United States that the trainees chose. Alternatively, both programs could be ended and a national program offering training or wage subsidy vouchers implemented in their place.

Finally, the U.S. Employment Service could offer national job referral services for all unemployed people. The concept of a national job bank has received vigorous support for many years but has yet to be implemented except on an experimental basis.

The preceding options are a partial and incomplete list of actions that could be taken to reduce barriers to mobility, but they give an idea of the potential for action.

Incentives for Mobility

Subsidies toward the costs of voluntary relocation for disadvantaged people may be appropriate, given the potential benefits to society from greater mobility of these groups. For example, relocation assistance could readily be made a part of federal training programs. Unfortunately, available evidence does not provide a firm basis for affirmative public subsidies or direct assistance to disadvantaged persons seeking to migrate in search of work. Past experimental efforts of this kind have yielded mixed results (Bart 1979). At present there is no way to project the effects of subsidies or assistance on the rates and patterns of migration by disadvantaged persons and, therefore, on their economic opportunities or achievement.

Conclusions

The United States has chosen an eclectic approach to dealing with urban problems of joblessness and poverty. Targeted economic development aid, employment and training assistance, and labor mobility programs all can contribute to improving the economic opportunities of disadvantaged persons in distressed communities.

It would be naive to claim that mobility initiatives could by themselves solve urban problems associated with poverty, joblessness, and dependence. However, they can make a useful difference. High priority should be placed on eliminating needless barriers to migration of disadvantaged persons in search of work. High priority also should be placed on doing the research required to identify desirable ways more affirmative assistance could be provided to foster mobility.

14　Transforming Cities and Employment Policy for Displaced Workers

John D. Kasarda

America's cities always have performed and will continue to perform valuable social and economic functions. Yet changing technological and industrial conditions (both nationally and internationally) alter these functions over time. Historically, recall that cities performed the functions of assimilation and socioeconomic upgrading of mass numbers of disadvantaged persons most effectively in an industrial and transportation era that no longer exists. During the late nineteenth and early twentieth centuries America's industrial revolution fostered dramatic national economic development creating millions of low-skill jobs, while prevailing transportation technologies restricted the vast bulk of national employment growth to our urban centers (Hawley 1981; Norton 1979). As a result, our early industrial cities were characterized by entry-level job *surpluses* compared to the entry-level job *deficits* that characterize their employment bases today (Kovaleff 1974; Bradbury et al. 1982). It was these job surpluses, with few requisites for entry, that attracted waves of migrants and offered them a foothold in the urban economy. The rapidly expanding job base accompanying national economic growth, in turn, provided ladders of opportunity and social mobility for the migrants, most of whom were escaping areas of economic distress (Bodner et al. 1982; Fleigstein 1981; Vinyard 1976; Zunz 1982).

The access to opportunity and social mobility that our industrial cities provided was obtained at significant human costs, however. Prejudice, discrimination, hostility, and, frequently, physical violence greeted the new arrivals (Hauser 1960). Lacking financial resources, unaccustomed to city ways, and often without English language skills, immigrants were ascribed the lowest status and were residentially segregated in overcrowded dwellings in the least desirable sections of cities. A polluted, unsanitary physical environment contributed to high morbidity and mortality rates, as did the hazardous working conditions found in the factories (Mohl 1976). Political corruption and exploitation were common, working hours long, and there was no such thing as a minimum wage. In the rubric of dual labor market theory, virtually all immigrants held dead-end jobs (Berg 1981).

Nonetheless, there was an abundance of these jobs for which the only requisites were a person's desire and physical ability to work. The surplus of low-skill jobs and overall economic growth provided our older industrial cities with a unique role in our nation's history as developers of manpower and springboards for social mobility.

During the first half of the twentieth century a number of advances occurred in transportation, communications, and production-distribution technologies (e.g., shifts from rail and barge to truck transport, the spread of peripheral highways and public utilities, automated assembly-line production and warehousing techniques). These advances markedly reduced the previous locational advantages that older, compactly structured cities had held for manufacturing, processing, and distributive activities; they also made uncongested suburban sites more cost-effective. By 1960 further advances in transportation and communication technologies and growing industrial competition from nonmetropolitan areas and abroad all but made our older, densely settled cities obsolete as locations for large-scale manufacturing, material processing, and warehousing facilities (Kasarda 1980; Hicks 1982). A massive exodus of blue-collar jobs from the cities began—an exodus that has accelerated to the present.

There are, however, significant countertrends occurring in certain retail and service sectors as businesses and institutions offering highly specialized goods and services continue to be attracted to downtown areas. The specialized nature of these establishments still makes it advantageous for many to locate at centralized nodes that maximize their accessibility to the largest number of people and firms in the metropolitan area. Such establishments as advertising agencies, brokerage houses, consulting firms, financial institutions, luxury goods shops, and legal, accounting, and professional complexes have been accumulating in the central business districts, replacing traditional department stores and many other standardized retail goods and consumer service establishments that were unable to compete effectively or afford the skyrocketing rents of a central location (Perloff 1978; Stanback and Noyelle 1982).

The past two decades also witnessed remarkable growth of high-rise administrative office buildings in the central business districts of our largest cities. Even with major advances in telecommunications technology, many administrative headquarters continuously rely on a complement of legal, financial, public relations, and other specialized business services that are most readily available in central business districts. Moreover, unlike manufacturing, wholesale trade, and retail trade, which typically have large space-per-employee requirements, most managerial, clerical, professional, and business service functions are highly space-intensive. In addition, persons performing these service functions can be stacked vertically, layer upon layer, in downtown high-rise office buildings with no loss in productivity (Porter 1976). Indeed, vertical stack and resulting spatial proximity often enhance the productivity of those whose activities entail extensive, nonroutinized face-to-face interaction. The outcome has been a central business district office building boom.

From Springboard to Anchor

The growth of administrative, financial, professional, and related "knowledge class" jobs in central business districts along with their substantial losses of blue-collar jobs have altered the important role these cities once played as opportunity ladders for disadvantaged persons. Aggravating problems engendered by deterioration of their historic blue-collar job bases have been the flight of middle-income population and traditional retail trade and consumer service establishments from much of the remainder of the city (Zimmer 1975; Bradbury, Downs, and Small 1982). These movements have combined to further erode city tax bases, weaken secondary labor markets, and spatially isolate many disadvantaged persons in economically distressed subareas where opportunities for employment are minimal (Lowry 1980; Wilson 1983).

Our larger, older central cities in the Northern industrial belt have been particularly hard hit by post–World War II declines of middle-income population and blue-collar jobs (Sternlieb and Hughes 1975, 1977; Suttles 1978). Unfortunately, it is many of these same cities that experienced the largest postwar migration flows of persons whose educational backgrounds and skills are ill-suited for the white-collar information-processing jobs that have partially replaced blue-collar job losses. As a result, their, and their children's, unemployment rates are well above the national average and especially high among disadvantaged minorities left behind in inner-city areas of decline.

Transforming Urban Employment Bases

An empirical snapshot of transformations occurring in the employment bases of our oldest and largest cities since the mid-1950s is provided in table 14.1. The economies of New York City, Philadelphia, and Boston show marked employment declines in their traditional production (manufacturing and construction) and goods processing (retail and wholesale) industries, with corresponding rapid employment gains in their information-processing industries. Information-processing industries are defined as those service industries (excluding government) wherein more than one-half of the employees are classified in executive, managerial, professional, and clerical occupations.

Observe that New York City gained more than 650,000 jobs in its information-processing industries between 1953 and 1980 while losing more than 525,000 jobs in its manufacturing and construction industries. Notice further the selective nature of service employment expansion, especially during the seventies. From 1970 to 1980 employment in information-processing industries continued to mushroom in New York, Philadelphia, and Boston, whereas employment in other (predominantly blue-collar) service industries (e.g., barbershops, car washes, and domestic services) declined considerably in each city. In just ten years, New York City lost more than 100,000 jobs in its predominantly blue-collar service industries, Philadelphia lost nearly 30,000 such jobs, and Boston nearly 10,000. All three cities experienced even larger absolute employment declines in their traditional retail and wholesale industries.

The extent of this transformation is highlighted by the proportional changes in these cities' industrial employment bases between 1953 and 1980. In 1953, 50 percent of Philadelphia's private sector employment was in manufacturing and construction industries. For Boston and New York City the corresponding percentages that year were 32 and 40. By 1980 employment in these predominantly blue-

Table 14.1 Central-city employment, by industry, derived from *County Business Patterns*, selected years 1953–80.

| | 1953 | | 1970 | | 1980 | |
	Number	% of Total	Number	% of Total	Number	% of Total
Total employment (classified)*	2,976,591	100	3,350,257	100	2,866,462	100
Agriculture and mining	5,030	<1	4,591	<1	4,515	<1
Manufacturing and construction	1,176,221	40	970,924	29	649,970	23
Retail and wholesale	805,226	27	779,387	23	596,062	20
Selected services Information Processing**	646,044	22	1,171,849	35	1,302,372	45
Other services	344,070	12	423,506	13	313,543	11
Philadelphia Total employment (classified)*	787,865	100	772,045	100	628,260	100
Agriculture and mining	705	<1	675	<1	515	<1
Manufacturing and construction	397,823	50	290,845	38	171,366	27
Retail and wholesale	205,540	26	179,736	23	133,731	22
Selected services Information Processing**	98,335	12	219,778	28	270,509	43
Other services	85,462	12	81,011	10	52,139	8
Boston (Suffolk Co.) Total employment (classified)*	402,272	100	464,908	100	437,239	100
Agriculture and mining	2,029	<1	950	<1	522	<1
Manufacturing and construction	129,914	32	104,599	22	76,872	17

Table 14.1 (continued)

	1953		1970		1980	
	Number	% of Total	Number	% of Total	Number	% of Total
Retail and wholesale Selected services	132,051	32	111,231	24	81,943	19
Information Processing**	87,453	22	193,558	42	232,061	53
Other services	50,825	13	54,570	12	45,841	10

* Total classified employment and industry subcategories excluding government employees and sole proprietors.

** Information processing industries are those service industries (excluding government, retail, and wholesale) wherein more than one-half the employees are classified as executive, managerial, professional, or clerical occupations in U.S. Bureau of the Census 1970 occupation by industry cross-classifications.

collar industries had dropped to 27 percent of private sector employment in Philadelphia, to 23 percent in New York City, and to 17 percent in Boston. During the same period employment in predominantly white-collar information-processing industries as a proportion of total private sector employment expanded from 22 to 45 percent in New York City, from 12 to 43 percent in Philadelphia, and from 22 to 53 percent in Boston. By 1980 New York City and Boston each had more employees in its information-processing industries than in its manufacturing, construction, retail, and wholesale industries combined. This represents a dramatic metamorphosis since 1953 when employment in these more traditional urban industries outnumbered employment in information-processing industries in each city by at least a three-to-one margin.

Educational Requirements for Urban Employment

To determine the extent to which inner-city unemployment is structural in nature necessitates going beyond descriptions of industrial sector job changes in cities. One must assess educational prerequisites for employment in their transforming economies. Although much has been said during the past five years about declines in entry-level jobs in our major cities, there has been remarkably little empirical grounding of the phenomenon. This subsection works toward such grounding by documenting changes in numbers of jobs in cities during the past ten years in terms of their average educational requirements for employment.

Job changes by educational requirements were estimated by synthesizing individual level data on the schooling completed by jobholders in detailed classified industries with *County Business Patterns* data on aggregate job changes that have occurred within each industry in each city. The March 1982 *Current Population Survey* was used to compute the mean years of schooling completed by central-city residents who were employed in two-, three-, and four-digit SIC coded industries (see Kasarda 1982). Education levels were then assigned to each industry designation in *County Business Patterns*. Industries whose employees had completed a mean schooling of less than twelve years were classified as entry-level. Industries whose employees had, on the average, completed more than 14 years of schooling were classified as knowledge-intensive. In other words, entry-level industries are those with mean jobholder education levels below high school completed, whereas knowledge-intensive industries employ persons whose average education levels are above two years of college completed. Aggregate job changes within each educationally classified industry were then traced between 1970 and 1980 for nine cities whose boundaries are either identical to or closely approximate those for which place-specific industrial employment data are available in *County Business Patterns*.

Table 14.2 presents entry-level and knowledge-intensive industry employment changes between 1970 and 1980 for the three cities shown in table 14.1 plus Baltimore, St. Louis, Atlanta, Houston, Denver, and San Francisco. These cities were added to provide regional representation as well as for comparative analysis of clearly declining vs. expanding urban job bases.

Changing education requisites for urban employment are strikingly apparent in the four large northeastern cities. Between 1970 and 1980 New York City lost nearly 500,000 jobs in entry-level industries, whereas Philadelphia lost over 100,000 such jobs, Baltimore over 50,000, and Boston over 33,000. Conversely, during the same decade employment in industries whose average jobholder education levels exceed two years of college expanded by at least 20 percent in each of the four cities.

St. Louis, like a number of other declining industrial cities in the Midwest, suffered employment contraction in its knowledge-intensive as well as its entry-level industries. In aggregate terms, however, entry-level industry employment declines substantially exceeded declines in St. Louis' knowledge-intensive industries.

Atlanta's experience is consistent with that of major cities in the Northeast. Rather substantial employment declines are occurring in its entry-level industries, while employment growth is taking place in its knowledge-intensive industries. Percentage changes in entry-level industry employment in Atlanta, compared with those of the four northeastern cities, reveal that Atlanta's low education requisite employment declines have not been quite as severe.

Houston, Denver, and San Francisco depart rather sharply from the patterns of other cities shown in table 14.2. All three exhibit employment growth in their entry-level industries as well as in their knowledge-intensive industries. Take particular note of Houston (Harris County) where industries having mean employee education levels below twelve years of schooling expanded by nearly 200,000 jobs between 1970 and 1980. Individual city analysis of changing minority unemployment rates and rates of minority labor force participation during the decade revealed that minorities residing in Houston fared much better than those in other central cities (see Kasarda 1982).

Educational Distributions of Central-City Whites and Blacks

Analysis thus far documents precipitous employment declines in Northern central-city industries that traditionally sustained large numbers of lesser-educated persons. These job losses have been only partially replaced by growth in white-collar service industries with substantially higher educational requisites. In another essay (Kasarda 1985) the substantial expansion of minority populations in a number of these cities during the 1970s was documented. For example, despite large overall population declines, the non-Hispanic black populations of New York City, Chicago, and Detroit each increased by more than 100,000 during the seventies. Such racial minorities

Table 14.2 Numbers of jobs and employment change in entry-level industries (mean schooling completed by industry employees is less than 12 years) and in knowledge-intensive industries (mean schooling completed by industry employees is more than 14 years) for selected cities, 1970 and 1980.

City and industry characteristic	Year and numbers of employees			
	1970	1980	Change 1970–80	% change 1970–80
New York City				
Entry-level industries (schooling mean < 12 years)	1,234,338	762,661	−471,677	−38.2
Knowledge-intensive industries (schooling mean > 14 years)	370,243	462,334	92,091	24.9
Philadelphia City				
Entry-level industries (schooling mean < 12 years)	309,656	207,653	−102,003	−32.9
Knowledge-intensive industries (schooling mean > 14 years)	65,849	90,753	24,904	37.8
Baltimore City				
Entry-level industries (schooling mean < 12 years)	160,128	108,279	−51,849	−32.4
Knowledge-intensive industries (schooling mean > 14 years)	26,132	31,530	5,398	20.6
Boston (Suffolk County)				
Entry-level industries (schooling mean < 12 years)	148,874	115,192	−33,682	−22.6
Knowledge-intensive industries (schooling mean > 14 years)	56,449	75,237	18,788	33.3
St. Louis				
Entry-level industries (schooling mean < 12 years)	126,252	103,275	−22,977	−18.2
Knowledge-intensive industries (schooling mean > 14 years)	28,647	21,100	−7,547	−26.3
Atlanta (Fulton County)				
Entry-level industries (schooling mean < 12 years)	154,242	135,548	−18,694	−12.1
Knowledge-intensive industries (schooling mean > 14 years)	30,162	40,895	10,733	35.6
Houston (Harris County)				
Entry-level industries				

Table 14.2 (continued)

City and industry characteristic	Year and numbers of employees			
	1970	1980	Change 1970–80	% change 1970–80
(schooling mean < 12 years)	263,035	457,180	194,145	73.8
Knowledge-intensive industries				
(schooling mean > 14 years)	69,378	152,250	82,872	119.4
Denver				
Entry-level industries				
(schooling mean < 12 years)	95,962	109,888	13,926	14.5
Knowledge-intensive industries				
(schooling mean > 14 years)	22,914	43,846	20,932	91.4
San Francisco				
Entry-level industries				
(schooling mean < 12 years)	129,304	142,487	13,183	10.2
Knowledge-intensive industries				
(schooling mean > 14 years)	44,238	64,934	20,696	46.8

Sources: Current Population Survey Tapes (1982) and *County Business Patterns*, 1970 and 1980.

are at a structural disadvantage in cities losing entry-level jobs because substantially larger proportions of these minorities lack the necessary schooling to take advantage of information-processing industries. To illustrate this structural disadvantage, table 14.3 presents data on years of schooling completed by white and black central-city residents (aged sixteen to sixty-four) by sex and region.

The data show that the modal education category for central-city black males and black females in the Northeast, the North Central region, and the South is "Did Not Complete High School." Conversely, for white male central-city residents in these three regions, the modal education category is "Attended College for at Least One Year." For white females in cities in the Northeast, North Central region, and the South, high school completed is the modal category. The statistics of note, however, relate to the much smaller proportion of black central-city residents with schooling levels appropriate to expanding industries in Northern cities and higher proportions with education levels appropriate primarily to those industries undergoing severe employment contraction.

Table 14.3 Number of central-city residents aged 16–64 by race, sex, and years of school completed, 1982

	Northeast	North Central	South	West
White males				
Did not complete high school	1,042,422	816,363	1,007,731	613,391
Completed high school only	1,136,990	1,109,219	1,159,796	915,672
Attended college 1 year +	1,138,162	1,187,494	1,760,943	1,626,176
White females				
Did not complete high school	1,116,545	766,283	1,108,272	711,926
Completed high school only	1,404,561	1,454,969	1,591,838	1,109,256
Attended college 1 year +	975,912	1,117,948	1,589,654	1,319,875
Black males				
Did not complete high school	399,239	424,832	618,037	142,989
Completed high school only	321,736	417,421	492,533	132,226
Attended college 1 year +	225,699	246,908	349,545	160,476
Black females				
Did not complete high school	534,395	516,439	713,599	146,079
Completed high school only	517,730	494,121	650,528	171,594
Attended college 1 year +	283,422	278,903	383,383	190,000

Source: U.S. Bureau of the Census, Current Population Survey, 1982.

Black residents in Western cities, however, have more favorable education distributions to take advantage of new urban growth industries. In 1982 the number of blacks in Western central cities who attended college for at least one year was greater than the number who did not complete high school. The education distribution for whites shows Western cities to have, by far, the most educated nonminority populations of the four regions. Nearly one-half of the white male and female central-city residents (aged sixteen to sixty-four) in the West have attended college for at least one year.

In sum, we see that large proportions of black central-city residents still do not possess the education to participate in information-processing industries. As entry-level jobs disappear (particularly from large Northeastern and North Central region cities), blacks, as a group, are especially disadvantaged.

Rising Central-City Unemployment

Table 14.4 displays the rates of central city unemployment for black and white males by region and years of schooling completed. These rates were computed from the 1969, 1977, and 1982 Current Population Survey tapes. For all regions one observes steadily rising central-city unemployment rates over time for both races, with the exception of better-educated white males. The importance of education for urban employment can be observed by reading down the columns from "did not complete high school" to "attended college for at least one full year." Within racial groups, those who did not complete high school have substantially higher unemployment rates, with the absolute gap in unemployment rates between the lowest and highest schooling completed categories widening between 1969 and 1982. The disproportionate concentration of central-city black males in the lowest schooling completed category in every region but the West, no doubt, contributes to the widening gap over time in overall white-black urban unemployment rates. For white male central-city residents as a whole (i.e., all education levels), unemployment rates rose from 2.6 percent in 1969 to 9.5 percent in 1982, whereas, overall, black male central-city unemployment rates rose from 5.4 to 23.4 percent during this period.

It is important to note, however, that substantial racial differences in central-city unemployment rates remain even when controlling for schooling completed. Indeed, observe that black male central-city residents in the North Central and Southern regions who have attended college had higher rates of unemployment in 1982 than did white central-city residents in these same regions who did not complete high school. Putting aside issues of possible racial differences in quality of schooling received, such discrepancies imply that problems of racial discrimination may be compounding the structural disadvantage central-city blacks face given their overall education distributions in transforming city economies.

Table 14.4 Unemployment rates of central-city males aged 16–64 by race, region, and years of schooling completed, 1969, 1977, and 1982

All regions	White males			Black males		
	1969	1977	1982	1969	1977	1982
Did not complete high school	4.3	12.2	17.7	6.6	19.8	29.7
Completed high school only	1.7	8.0	11.0	4.1	16.2	23.5
Attended college 1 year +	1.6	4.7	4.4	3.7	10.7	16.1
All education levels	2.6	7.7	9.5	5.4	16.5	23.4
Northeast						
Did not complete high school	3.7	13.9	17.2	7.6	20.9	26.2
Completed high school only	1.7	9.4	10.3	3.4	18.2	21.9
Attended college 1 year +	1.4	6.0	4.8	7.1	13.9	18.6
All education levels	2.4	9.6	10.2	6.1	18.6	22.6
North Central						
Did not complete high school	4.9	12.8	24.3	8.3	26.2	34.8
Completed high school only	1.1	8.0	14.5	3.3	18.0	35.8
Attended college 1 year +	1.3	3.5	3.8	1.4	12.3	22.2
All education levels	2.6	7.6	12.2	6.0	20.6	32.0
South						
Did not complete high school	3.4	9.9	13.2	3.8	14.5	28.2
Completed high school only	.8	5.9	6.8	3.6	13.5	16.6
Attended college 1 year +	1.7	3.1	2.9	3.6	6.2	13.6
All education levels	2.0	5.7	6.4	3.7	12.6	19.9
West						
Did not complete high school	6.4	12.0	17.3	11.6	22.2	32.9
Completed high school only	4.2	8.6	13.4	9.6	17.7	15.9
Attended college 1 year +	1.9	6.4	6.0	2.9	13.2	9.9
All education levels	3.9	8.2	10.1	8.3	17.0	16.5

Source: Computed from Current Population Survey Tapes, 1969, 1977, and 1982.

Discouraged Workers and Other Labor Force Dropouts

Because central-city unemployment rates cover only persons who have actively sought employment during the four weeks prior to their being surveyed, these rates illustrate only a portion of the problem of urban economic displacement. Excluded entirely from the labor force and unemployment statistics are those who have simply given up looking for work because they believe no jobs are available (discouraged workers), disabled persons, and those who want to work but cannot hold employment for a variety of personal reasons.

To tap changing labor force nonparticipation rates among central-city blacks and whites, a statistic was computed from the 1969 and 1982 Current Population Surveys measuring the proportion of each city's males not in the school population (aged sixteen to sixty-four) who also are not in the labor force. The numerator of this statistic is the number of city resident males classified as being neither employed, unemployed, nor in school. The denominator is the total number of males classified as employed, unemployed, and not in the labor force (excluding those in school). In other words, the "in school" population has been simultaneously subtracted from the "not in labor force" numerator and from the "labor force" plus "not in labor force" denominator.

Table 14.5 provides the labor force nonparticipation rates by race, age, and region for black and white males in 1969 and 1982. These rates clearly show that unemployment figures do not fully reveal the extent of racial differences in formal participation in central-city economies. For every region and age group, black males have markedly higher rates than white males of labor force nonparticipation. Moreover, whereas central-city white male labor force nonparticipation rates increased modestly between 1969 and 1982, labor force nonparticipation rates for black males climbed substantially. Take particular note of the rising rates of black labor force nonparticipation in central cities in the industrially declining North Central region. By 1982 these rates were more than three times larger than those of white males. Just as the central-city racial gap in unemployment rates is widening, so is the racial gap in urban labor force nonparticipation.

Table 14.5 Proportion of male central-city residents not in school who are not in the labor force, by region, race, and age, 1969 and 1982.

All regions	1969	1982
White males		
Age 16–24	4.5	5.4
Age 25–64	5.8	9.2
Black males		
Age 16–24	8.2	16.5
Age 25–64	10.3	17.1
Northeast		
White males		
Age 16–24	6.9	6.8
Age 25–64	6.9	10.8
Black males		
Age 16–24	12.2	20.1
Age 25–64	10.7	18.4
North Central		
White males		
Age 16–24	3.2	6.1
Age 25–64	5.1	9.3
Black males		
Age 16–24	7.2	24.5
Age 25–64	9.9	19.3
South		
White males		
Age 16–24	4.0	4.2
Age 25–64	5.0	8.2
Black males		
Age 16–24	6.9	17.0
Age 25–64	10.6	14.5
West		
White males		
Age 16–24	4.5	4.6
Age 25–64	6.0	8.7
Black males		
Age 16–24	6.0	16.1
Age 25–64	9.3	18.1

Source: U.S. Bureau of the Census, Current Population Survey Tapes, 1969 and 1982.

Urban Employment Decline and Subsistence Surrogates

It was noted initially that America's largest and oldest cities once had surpluses of entry-level jobs that served to attract and sustain large numbers of low-skill residents. As these cities have structurally transformed, many have experienced dramatic declines in blue-collar and other entry-level jobs. Yet it also was pointed out that the minority populations in many of these cities have continued to expand during the past decade, even as their rates of unemployment and labor force nonparticipation rise.

Such circumstances raise fundamental policy questions. What continues to attract and hold minority and other disadvantaged persons in central cities undergoing severe blue-collar employment decline? How are economically displaced inner-city residents able to survive? What, in brief, has replaced traditional blue-collar jobs as a means of economic subsistence for urban minority unemployed and labor force dropouts?

Answers to the above are provided, in part, by the data presented in table 14.6, which displays computations from the 1982 Current Population Survey on welfare recipiency rates of central-city householders (aged sixteen to sixty-four) by race, sex, and labor force status. These data show the absolute numbers of central-city household heads in each labor force category along with the respective proportion who receive assistance from at least one of three major welfare programs: (1) public or subsidized housing, (2) AFDC and other cash assistance, and (3) food stamps.

The differentially high rates of welfare dependency of unemployed and not-in-labor-force minority householders are clearly revealed. This is especially so for black female household heads. Moreover, consistent with analysis presented in tables 14.4 and 14.5, black householders of both sexes have far greater proportions unemployed and not in the labor force than their white counterparts. Indeed, cities in the Northeast and North Central regions have more black female household heads who are unemployed or not in the labor force than who are employed. Compare this to white female heads of households in cities in the same regions where those employed outnumber the combined unemployed and not in labor force by more than a two-to-one margin.

Regional differences in proportions of male household heads

Table 14.6 Welfare recipiency of central-city householders age 16–64 by region, race, sex, and labor force status, 1982

Region	Employed	Unemployed	Not in labor force
Northeast			
White householders			
Male	1,780,721	133,437	250,124
% receiving welfare	5	19	21
Female	661,414	46,965	372,857
% receiving welfare	9	23	58
Black householders			
Male	321,460	47,911	71,701
% receiving welfare	12	41	39
Female	290,170	53,443	312,714
% receiving welfare	29	75	84
North Central			
White householders			
Male	1,844,638	173,930	204,694
% receiving welfare	4	27	15
Female	676,752	55,236	219,332
% receiving welfare	8	42	48
Black householders			
Male	329,641	98,748	98,337
% receiving welfare	9	52	35
Female	254,824	90,206	240,679
% receiving welfare	27	72	82
South			
White householders			
Male	2,501,673	92,020	239,869
% receiving welfare	4	16	16
Female	843,015	44,480	214,877
% receiving welfare	7	26	35
Black householders			
Male	605,206	63,080	89,943
% receiving welfare	8	19	50
Female	452,362	57,629	267,596
% receiving welfare	30	76	79
West			
White householders			
Male	1,841,616	136,150	206,716

Table 14.6   (continued)

Region	Employed	Unemployed	Not in labor force
% receiving welfare	3	20	11
Female	653,245	43,314	208,054
% receiving welfare	8	20	35
Black householders			
Male	178,056	19,592	45,594
% receiving welfare	4	32	38
Female	123,656	26,110	78,970
% receiving welfare	18	63	86

Source: U.S. Current Population Survey Tape, March 1982.

employed are also striking. For example, in cities in the North Central region only 63 percent of black male household heads were employed in 1982 compared to 80 percent of black male household heads in cities in the South. To understand better how large portions of black male unemployed householders are surviving in economically transforming Northern cities, contrast the welfare recipiency rates of those who are unemployed and residing in the Northeast and North Central regions with those unemployed black male central-city householders residing in the South. In the North Central region, for example, more than 50 percent of unemployed black male householders were on welfare compared to less than 20 percent of those in Southern central cities. These welfare rates, along with the much larger proportions of central-city black male householders who are unemployed in Northern cities compared to those in the South and West, illustrate the differential scope of welfare economies in Northern cities that serve as partial subsistence surrogates for their declining (blue-collar) production economies.

Targeting, Anchoring, and Demographic Disequilibria

From a policy perspective it is important to realize that while the expanding urban production economies of the past offered mass numbers of disadvantaged residents entry into the mainstream economy and opportunities for mobility, today's urban welfare economies often have the opposite effects—limiting options and reinforcing the concentration of those without access to the economic mainstream. Many well-intentioned welfare programs, for example, have been specifically targeted to inner-city areas of greatest economic distress, thereby providing the subsistence infrastructure that keeps disadvantaged people there. Dependent on place-oriented public housing, nutritional care, health care, income maintenance, and other public assistance programs, a large minority underclass has become anchored in localities of severe employment decline. Racial discrimination and insufficient low-cost housing in areas of employment growth further seriously obstruct mobility and job acquisition by this underclass as do their frequent deficiencies in technical and interpersonal skills so necessary to obtain and hold jobs. The outcome is that increasing numbers of potentially productive minorities find themselves isolated in distressed localities where they subsist, in absence of job opportunities, on a combination of government handouts and their own informal economies.

I do not wish to imply that targeted government aid to people and places in distress is unnecessary or without merit. Most urban welfare programs have had important palliative effects, temporarily relieving some very painful symptoms associated with the departure of blue-collar jobs (e.g., poor housing, inadequate nutrition and health care). However, while some success has been achieved in relieving such pains, the disequilibrium grows worse between low-skill labor availability in distressed cities and local labor needs.

It must be recognized that this demographic disequilibrium, increasingly sustained by well-meaning government subsidies, works against the long-term economic health of distressed cities and their structurally unemployed residents. Imagine, for instance, what would have happened in the first half of this century if the great numbers of structurally displaced Southerners who migrated to economically expanding Northern cities in search of jobs and a better life had been sustained in their distressed localities by targeted government subsidies. It is possible that most never would have moved and that the significant advances in income levels and living standards that both the South and their out-migrants experienced would not have occurred.

Circumstances today are analogous, but regionally the reverse. Our economically transforming Northern cities are now characterized by growing surpluses of structurally displaced labor as their blue-collar job bases wither. Addressing this problem, some have suggested that through a National Development Bank, a Reconstruction Finance Corporation, enterprise zones, or government-business-labor partnerships, we can "reindustrialize" these cities or otherwise rebuild their historic blue-collar employment bases (see Butler 1981; Hanson 1983; Rohatyn 1979, 1981; U.S. Department of Housing and Urban Development 1978, 1980, 1982). Such suggestions are as unrealistic as they are economically nostalgic. In an increasingly cost-competitive world economy, the comparative locational disadvantages of large Northern cities for labor-intensive blue-collar industries must be faced.

New urban realities dictate that politically popular (but ineffective) jobs-to-people strategies and necessary stopgap welfare programs must be complemented with serious efforts to upgrade the education and skills of disadvantaged city residents *and* with people-to-jobs strategies that would facilitate the migration of structurally unemployed to places where jobs appropriate to their skills are still expanding. Contrary to conventional wisdom, there have been major increases in entry-level jobs nationwide during the past decade (see Kasarda 1985). However, this form of job growth has occurred primarily in the suburbs, exurbs, and nonmetropolitan areas far removed from concentrations of inner-city minorities.

The inability of most urban minorities to follow deconcentrating entry-level jobs (either because of racial discrimination, lack of knowledge, or subsidized anchoring) is among the chief reasons for the widening gap in black-white rates of unemployment and labor force nonparticipation. It also is a major contributor to rising demographic disequilibria in transforming cities and their correspondingly high social overhead burdens.

Summary and Policy Options

This essay has documented the functional transformation of our larger older cities from centers of material goods production to centers of information exchange and higher-order service provision. In the process of urban functional transformation, many blue-collar industries that once constituted the economic backbone of cities and provided ready employment for less-educated residents have vanished. These blue-collar industries have been replaced, in part, by knowledge-intensive white-collar industries whose requisites for employment entry entail substantial education or technical training and, hence, are unavailable to large segments of minority populations residing in these cities. The outcome has been simultaneously rising rates of unemployment, labor force nonparticipation, and welfare dependency among central-city minority residents.

There seems little doubt that the disproportionately high levels of minority unemployment, labor force nonparticipation, and resulting welfare dependency will remain in larger, older cities as long as their demographic and job opportunity structures conflict. Government subsidies, tax incentives, and regulatory relief contained in existing and proposed urban policies are not nearly sufficient to overcome technological and market-driven forces redistributing jobs and shaping the economies of our largest and oldest cities.

Cities that are able to exploit their emerging service sector roles may well experience renewed economic vitality and net job increases in the years ahead. However, lacking appropriate skills for advanced service sector jobs, those on the bottom rungs of the socioeconomic ladder are unlikely to benefit. Indeed, their employment prospects could further deteriorate. For example, New York City, capitalizing on its strength as an international financial and administrative center, experienced a net increase of 167,000 jobs between 1977 and 1982. Yet, while the city's total employment base was expanding, its overall minority unemployment rates continued to climb. This is because virtually all of New York's employment expansion was concentrated in white-collar service industries whereas manufacturing employment dropped by 55,000 jobs, and wholesale and retail trade employment declined by an additional 9,000 jobs during the four-year period. These figures suggest that the urban residential composition – job opportunity mismatch and corresponding minority unemployment rates can worsen even under conditions of overall central-city employment gains.

The stark reality of rising urban minority unemployment under transforming (and possibly even growing) city economies, together with the improbability of government programs (or the private sector) stimulating sufficient entry-level job generation in the cities, call for a shift in policy emphasis from subsidized job targeting to resident skill upgrading. It also calls for greater appreciation of the instrumental role 'migration plays in alleviating localized unemployment problems and resulting social overhead.

Regarding the latter, revised policies should be considered that would partially underwrite more distant job searches and relocation expenses of the structurally unemployed. Additional policies must be aimed at further reducing housing and job discrimination and other institutional impediments to the relocation of disadvantaged persons who wish to leave distressed urban areas. Finally, existing policies should be reviewed to insure that they are not inadvertently attracting or bonding large numbers of disadvantaged minorities to inner-city areas that offer limited opportunities for employment.

All of the above, of course, must be complemented by broader development policies fostering renewed national economic growth and job generation. *Retraining and/or relocation of structurally displaced urban residents will not reduce overall unemployment without an expanding private sector creating millions of new, permanent jobs.* Improved education and technical training programs for urban minorities, stricter enforcement of civil rights legislation, aid in job search and relocation, and policies promoting substantial national employment growth must be vigorously and simultaneously pursued if rising rates of urban minority unemployment and welfare dependency are to be stemmed.

Author's Note: The analysis presented herein was supported by the Office of Policy Development and Research, U.S. Department of Housing and Urban Development and the National Science Foundation. The views expressed are solely those of the author and should not be attributed to either HUD or NSF. Much of this paper is derived from "Entry Level Jobs, Mobility, and Urban Minority Unemployment," *Urban Affairs Quarterly*, September, 1983.

Appendixes

Appendix to Chapter 3

This essay is based on economic data collected for one hundred metropolitan areas in 1967 and 1977. These include the fifty largest SMSAS (table 3A.1) and a stratified, proportional random sample of the remaining smaller metropolitan areas, selected to minimize sampling error along regional and population growth dimensions (table 3A.2). These hundred metropolitan areas represent a substantial share of national economic activity. Just over half of total U.S. nonfarm employment is located in the fifty largest metropolitan areas. The fifty smaller SMSAS contain about 5.6 percent of total national employment. Within the limits of sampling error, this suggests that by 1977 about 23.6 percent of nonfarm employment was located in SMSAS smaller than 750,000 population.

Economic and employment data for manufacturing, retail, services, wholesaling, and the mineral sectors are compiled from the 1967 and 1977 *Economic Censuses*. Data for transportation, communication and public utilities (Trans/Com), for finance, insurance, and real estate (FIRE), and for services omitted from the *Census of Selected Services* are from *County Business Patterns*. Federal and local government employment data are from the *Census of Government*. All data were adjusted for 1977 SMSA boundary definitions.

These data represent an unusually complete enumeration of economic and employment activity in the U.S. metropolitan areas over the 1970s. However, several caveats should be kept in mind. First, self-employed persons and nonpayroll firms are excluded; state government workers also are omitted since no source reports numbers of state employees by city. Second, data suppression to protect confidentiality sometimes causes economic activity to be undercounted for some smaller SMSAS. Finally, data for FIRE, Trans/Com, government, construction, and mining are reported by central county rather than central city. In cases where the central county is substantially larger than the central city, the central city share of employment in these sectors is overstated. Places where the central county is contiguous with the SMSA are excluded from tables computing the central city share of total economic activity.

Information on the distribution of employment across major occupational categories is reported for only a limited number of cities, and no information is available on the distribution of employment by occupation within industrial sectors for years in which the *Economic Censuses* are taken. Data on the distribution of employed persons by occupation within each of the nine one-digit SIC categories are drawn from the 1970 Census of Population, taken between the beginning and ending dates of the data series used in this

Table 3A.1   Fifty largest metropolitan areas by region

Region	Metropolitan Area
Northeast	New York City, NY-NJ; Philadelphia, PA-NJ; Boston, MA; Nassau–Suffolk, NY; Pittsburgh, PA; Newark, NJ; Buffalo, NY; Rochester, NY; Providence–Warwick–Pawtucket, RI-MA; Albany–Schenectady–Troy, NY
North Central	Chicago, IL; Detroit, MI; St. Louis, MO; Minneapolis–St. Paul, MN-WI; Cleveland, OH; Milwaukee, WI; Cincinnati, OH-KY-IN; Kansas City, MO-KS; Indianapolis, IN; Columbus, OH; Dayton, OH; Toledo, OH
South	Washington, DC-MD-VA; Dallas, TX; Houston, TX; Baltimore, MD; Atlanta, GA; Miami, FL; Tampa–St. Petersburg, FL; New Orleans, LA; San Antonio, TX; Memphis, TN-AK-MS; Louisville, KY-IN; Fort Lauderdale–Hollywood, FL; Birmingham, AL; Norfolk–Virginia Beach–Portsmouth, VA-NC; Greensboro–Winston-Salem–High Point, NC; Nashville–Davidson, TN
West	Los Angeles–Long Beach, CA; San Francisco–Oakland, CA; Anaheim–Santa Ana–Garden Grove, CA; San Diego, CA; Denver, CO; Seattle, WA; Riverside–San Bernadino–Ontario, CA; Phoenix, AZ; San Jose, CA; Portland OR-WA; Sacramento, CA; Salt Lake City–Ogden, UT

Source: U.S. Department of Commerce, Bureau of the Census, *Current Population Reports*, P-25 series.

analysis. The summary industry-by-occupation matrix is shown in table 3A.3 This matrix, multiplied by the vector of urban employment by industry category, has been used to estimate the level and distribution of changes in urban employment in each of the nine major occupational groups.

Table 3A.2 Fifty small and mid-sized metropolitan areas by region

Region	Metropolitan Area
Northeast	Jersey City, NJ; Long Branch–Asbury Park, NJ; Harrisburg, PA; Utica–Rome, NY; Binghamton, NY-PA; Stamford, CT; Lewiston–Auburn, ME
North Central	Grand Rapids, MI; Lansing–East Lansing, MI; Davenport–Rock Island–Moline, IA-IL; Evanston, IN; South Bend, IN; Lorain–Elyria, OH; Hamilston–Middleton, OH; Springfield, MO; Champaign–Urbana–Rantoul, IL; Steubenville–Weirton, OH-WV; Bay City, MI; Lafayette–West Lafayette, IN; Kokomo, IN; Bloomington, IN; La Crosse, WI
South	Baton Rouge, LA; El Paso, TX; Shreveport, LA; Huntsville, AL; Lakeland–Winter Haven, FL; Roanoke, VA; Savannah, GA; Lubbock, TX; Asheville, NC; Sarasota, FL; Fort Myers, FL; Amarillo, TX; Lake Charles, LA; Lynchburg, VA; Clarksville–Hopkinsville, TN-KY, Tallahassee, FL; Longview, TX; Bradenton, FL; Panama City, FL; Owensboro, KY; Midland, TX
West	Honolulu, HI; Fresno, CA; Tuscon, AZ; Stockton, CA; Modesto, CA; Reno, NV; Richland–Kennewick, WA

Table 3A.3 Percentage of all workers
in major occupational categories, by industry

| | Industry | | |
Occupational Category	Manufacturing	Retail	Services
Professional, technical and kindred workers	10.06	2.20	36.46
Managers and administrators (except farm)	5.22	14.92	6.16
Sales workers	2.69	25.08	0.92
Clerical and kindred workers	12.46	16.24	16.74
Craftsmen and kindred workers	19.62	8.22	5.47
Operatives (except transportation)	40.07	7.24	3.33
Transportation equipment operatives	3.05	2.76	0.87
Laborers (except farm)	4.57	5.00	1.45
Service (including private household)	2.26	18.34	28.59
Total	100.0	100.0	100.0

Appendix to Chapter 4

Table 4A.1

	Structural change factors			
	Corporate complex changes (I)	Price-productivity changes (II)	Economic distress changes (III)	Market center changes (IV)
Asheville, NC	−0.14	−0.33	−0.08	−0.27
Atlanta, GA	0.30	−0.13	0.40	0.91
Atlantic City, NJ	1.79	−1.33	0.85	−0.08
Augusta, GA-SC	−0.25	1.00	0.00	−0.74
Austin, TX	0.06	1.93	−0.30	−1.08
Bakersfield, CA	−1.42	1.39	−0.11	1.28
Baltimore, MD	−0.14	−0.27	0.28	0.12
Baton Rouge, LA	−1.07	1.80	−0.44	0.77
Battle Creek, MI	0.18	−0.15	−0.48	−0.13
Bay City, MI	2.05	0.91	−0.10	−0.91
Beaumont–Port Arthur–Orange, TX	−1.49	2.84	0.14	0.69
Billings, MT	−1.09	−0.32	−0.60	−0.04

Wholesale	Trans/Com	FIRE	Construction	Mining	Government
4.28	7.64	5.06	4.49	10.87	16.53
15.43	7.28	15.98	9.37	6.25	10.64
20.89	1.30	22.29	0.73	0.77	0.21
22.72	24.34	48.24	6.30	9.36	39.88
9.66	22.14	1.75	56.25	25.07	6.92
8.46	3.25	0.32	4.97	34.85	1.59
10.63	22.75	0.23	3.81	7.22	1.38
6.43	8.09	1.14	13.11	3.98	2.97
1.50	3.22	5.01	0.95	1.63	19.88
100.0	100.0	100.0	100.0	100.0	100.0

Source: Compiled from data in U.S. Bureau of the Census. 1970 Census of Population, Vol. 2. Special Subject Reports: Occupation by Industry, Table 1.

Manufac-turing multiplier changes (V)	Residen-tiary function changes (VI)	Local cyclical behavior					
		$\bar{Y}_t{}^*$	m	ALPHA	BPOS	BNEG	R^2
0.44	0.28	0.0204	0	0.0276	0.64	2.14	0.45
−0.63	0.31	0.0408	0	0.0288	0.78	1.25	0.74
−0.17	−3.44	**	**	**	**	**	**
−0.11	0.20	0.0324	0	0.0312	0.34	0.85	0.43
−0.72	−0.92	**	**	**	**	**	**
1.14	0.18	0.0312	−1	−0.0336	1.57	0.02	0.41
−0.67	0.00	0.0144	0	−0.0204	1.13	0.81	0.79
0.45	−0.05	0.0468	0	0.0228	0.79	0.54	0.21
−0.02	0.00	0.0001	0	−0.0120	0.83	1.42	0.43
−0.60	1.48	0.0108	0	−0.0096	1.28	2.12	0.43
0.60	0.77	0.0276	0	0.0204	0.76	1.49	0.33
0.02	0.42	0.0516	0	0.0120	1.58	1.64	0.51

Table 4A.1   (continued)

| | Structural change factors | | | |
	Corporate complex changes (I)	Price-productivity changes (II)	Economic distress changes (III)	Market center changes (IV)
Binghamton, NY-PA	−1.01	−0.62	0.79	−0.05
Birmingham, AL	−0.45	0.95	−0.82	0.20
Bloomington–Normal, IL	1.67	−1.32	0.32	−1.64
Boise City, ID	−0.60	1.41	−0.55	−1.28
Boston, MA	−0.66	−1.06	0.53	−0.04
Bridgeport, CT	4.96	0.46	0.25	0.04
Brockton, MA	0.05	−0.24	0.09	0.56
Buffalo, NY	−0.08	−0.04	0.31	0.07
Canton, OH	−1.86	−0.12	0.24	1.20
Cedar Rapids, IA	0.10	−0.44	−0.60	0.03
Champaign–Urbana–Rantoul, IL	−0.09	−1.11	0.36	−0.68
Charleston–North Charleston, SC	−0.06	−0.38	−0.43	−0.71
Charlotte–Gastonia, NC	−0.50	−0.89	−0.26	0.91
Chattanooga, TN-GA	−0.33	−0.74	−0.28	0.54
Chicago, IL	−0.48	−0.30	−0.26	−0.11
Cincinnati, OH-KY-IN	−0.51	−0.41	0.00	−0.19
Cleveland, OH	−0.31	−0.22	−0.01	0.01
Columbia, SC	0.23	0.18	−0.14	−0.70
Columbus, GA–AL	−0.21	−0.59	−0.04	−0.69
Columbus, OH	0.40	−0.29	−0.05	0.21
Corpus Christi, TX	0.02	2.55	0.15	1.05
Dallas–Fort Worth, TX	0.80	0.08	−0.15	−0.14
Davenport–Rock Island–Moline, IA-IL	−0.57	0.83	−0.61	0.18
Dayton, OH	1.38	0.00	0.43	0.21
Decatur, IL	0.84	0.17	−0.02	1.36
Denver–Boulder, CO	0.44	−0.29	0.04	−0.48
Des Moines, IA	−0.30	0.28	−0.30	−0.03
Detroit, MI	−0.17	−0.31	−0.21	−0.42
Dubuque, IA	−0.18	0.80	−0.17	−0.16
El Paso, TX	−0.17	0.91	1.07	−0.33
Elmira, NY	0.09	0.23	0.62	0.99
Erie, PA	−0.63	0.18	−0.10	−0.20

Manufac-turing multiplier changes (V)	Residen-tiary function changes (VI)	Local cyclical behavior					
		$\bar{Y}_t{}^*$	m	ALPHA	BPOS	BNEG	R^2
−0.13	0.31	0.0096	0	−0.0324	1.41	1.07	0.85
−0.87	0.03	0.0300	0	0.0036	0.82	0.49	0.47
−0.03	0.18	**	**	**	**	**	**
−0.83	−1.21	0.0672	1	0.0780	0.44	1.85	0.31
−0.16	−0.33	0.0204	0	0.0005	0.83	1.10	0.79
−0.91	−0.37	0.0096	0	−0.0240	1.21	1.06	0.68
−0.37	0.87	0.0324	0	−0.0024	1.30	1.46	0.76
−0.74	0.30	0.0060	0	−0.0276	1.26	1.27	0.77
0.34	0.86	0.0168	0	−0.0204	1.27	0.92	0.60
−0.13	0.74	0.0252	0	0.0240	0.59	1.49	0.49
1.18	1.16	**	**	**	**	**	**
−0.51	0.36	0.0444	0	0.0096	0.96	0.30	0.49
−0.51	−0.56	0.0336	0	0.0228	0.58	0.78	0.43
−0.52	−0.51	0.0276	0	0.0204	0.54	0.99	0.50
−0.23	−0.04	0.0084	0	−0.0024	0.75	1.26	0.70
−0.10	1.13	0.0204	0	−0.0168	1.31	1.06	0.82
−0.46	0.28	0.0096	0	−0.0252	1.15	0.85	0.83
−0.74	−0.10	0.0528	−6	0.0036	1.14	−0.08	0.35
0.98	−0.27	0.0180	0	0.0180	0.41	1.07	0.35
−0.21	−0.09	0.0288	0	−0.0144	1.43	1.08	0.88
1.86	−0.70	**	**	**	**	**	**
−0.32	−0.66	0.0408	0	0.0180	0.83	0.65	0.72
0.02	0.63	0.0144	0	−0.0120	0.86	0.58	0.29
−0.02	0.99	0.0132	0	−0.0180	1.13	0.99	0.62
0.18	−0.13	**	**	**	**	**	**
−0.02	−0.58	0.0516	0	0.0336	0.90	1.18	0.76
−0.74	0.21	0.0336	0	0.0072	0.84	0.57	0.41
−0.48	0.16	0.0120	0	−0.0156	1.10	1.14	0.50
−0.12	−2.88	0.0312	0	0.0012	0.94	0.59	0.16
0.44	−0.59	0.0420	0	0.0528	0.16	1.05	0.35
−0.47	0.54	0.0036	0	−0.0156	0.99	1.83	0.57
−3.58	1.01	0.0192	0	−0.0036	1.02	1.24	0.50

Table 4A.1 (continued)

	Structural change factors			
	Corporate complex changes (I)	Price-productivity changes (II)	Economic distress changes (III)	Market center changes (IV)
Eugene–Springfield, OR	0.13	−0.343	−0.67	0.11
Evansville, IN-KY	0.17	−0.32	−1.14	0.24
Fall River, MA-RI	−0.75	−1.50	−0.18	0.42
Fargo–Moorehead, ND-MN	−0.57	1.41	−0.30	−2.05
Fayettevillle–Springdale, AR	2.34	1.19	−0.80	1.06
Flint, MI	1.46	−0.93	−1.52	−1.92
Fort Lauderdale–Hollywood, FL	0.39	−0.29	1.12	0.39
Fort Smith, AR-OK	0.13	0.47	−0.22	−0.88
Fort Wayne, IN	1.35	0.09	−0.33	0.34
Fresno, CA	−0.22	0.37	−0.99	−1.01
Galveston–Texas City, TX	−0.40	1.94	0.17	1.44
Gary–Hammond–East Chicago, IN-IL	0.27	0.87	−0.05	−0.13
Grand Rapids, MI	0.06	−0.20	0.05	−0.74
Great Falls, MT	1.66	−0.28	−0.66	−0.78
Green Bay, WI	−1.00	0.36	−0.57	0.69
Greensboro–Winston-Salem–High Point, NC	0.27	0.56	0.27	0.18
Greenville–Spartanburg, SC	−0.79	−0.99	−0.14	−0.47
Harrisburg, PA	−0.09	0.06	0.21	0.55
Hartford, CT	0.38	−0.43	0.50	0.66
Honolulu, HI	0.27	1.17	11.84	−1.27
Houston, TX	−0.16	1.27	−0.68	0.10
Huntsville, AL	−2.02	−1.87	0.15	−1.22
Indianapolis, IN	0.21	−0.22	−0.28	−0.01
Jackson, MI	−0.03	−1.07	−0.71	4.90
Jackson, MS	−0.14	2.98	0.63	1.05
Jacksonville, FL	−0.03	−0.84	−0.17	−0.15
Jersey City, NJ	−0.10	−1.32	0.22	1.82
Johnstown PA	0.00	0.27	−0.88	−0.60
Kalamazoo–Portage, MI	0.45	−0.06	−0.34	−0.96
Kansas City, MO-KS	−0.17	−0.37	−0.54	−0.43
Kenosha, WI	−0.05	−2.95	−0.90	−0.57
Knoxville, TN	−0.02	−0.07	−0.64	−0.06
La Crosse, WI	−0.81	−0.26	−0.28	−0.93
Lafayette, LA	0.58	−0.35	−2.05	−0.03

Manufacturing multiplier changes (V)	Residentiary function changes (VI)	Local cyclical behavior					
		$\bar{Y}_t{}^*$	m	ALPHA	BPOS	BNEG	R^2
0.36	1.96	0.0396	0	0.0060	1.48	1.76	0.62
0.38	−0.16	0.0264	0	0.0072	0.89	1.21	0.25
0.21	−0.18	0.0168	0	0.0108	0.80	1.91	0.60
−0.15	0.76	0.0432	0	0.0108	1.41	1.64	0.61
0.61	−0.71	0.0540	1	0.0120	1.51	1.32	0.49
−0.85	0.18	0.0108	0	−0.0660	2.03	0.49	0.10
0.57	−0.70	0.0720	−6	0.0672	0.88	2.00	0.26
1.62	−0.81	0.0360	1	0.0288	0.98	2.04	0.50
−0.54	−0.17	0.0252	0	−0.0012	1.08	1.18	0.45
0.23	−0.67	0.0444	1	0.0792	0.26	2.87	0.46
0.92	−0.36	0.0240	−3	−0.0084	0.15	−1.58	0.29
−0.06	0.16	0.0180	0	−0.0192	1.14	0.65	0.28
0.44	−0.24	0.0300	0	0.0084	1.13	1.66	0.71
−1.30	2.00	0.0192	0	−0.0420	2.04	1.52	0.48
0.24	−0.24	0.0408	0	0.0384	0.83	2.06	0.59
−0.17	0.27	0.0300	0	0.0288	0.46	1.15	0.59
−0.63	−0.84	0.0360	0	0.0372	0.47	1.30	0.39
−0.60	−0.66	0.0240	0	−0.0048	1.00	0.84	0.68
−0.65	0.52	0.0204	0	−0.0288	1.32	0.32	0.55
0.43	1.00	**	**	**	**	**	**
0.13	−0.23	0.0600	0	0.0420	0.58	0.37	0.49
1.27	−0.14	0.0264	0	0.0180	0.56	0.96	0.60
−0.33	0.18	0.0240	0	0.0036	0.95	1.23	0.73
−0.60	−0.27	0.0132	0	0.0288	0.33	1.88	0.52
2.38	−2.41	0.0456	0	0.0312	0.71	0.97	0.55
−0.83	−0.77	0.0336	0	0.0180	0.50	0.33	0.25
−1.25	−0.30	0.0108	0	−0.0168	0.61	1.20	0.46
−1.10	−0.13	0.0144	0	−0.0756	2.12	−0.12	0.37
−0.39	0.89	**	**	**	**	**	**
−0.57	−0.11	0.0216	0	0.0084	0.79	1.22	0.72
1.19	−0.92	0.0360	0	−0.0540	2.79	1.67	0.26
−0.58	0.91	0.0264	0	0.0072	0.80	0.87	0.52
0.68	1.90	0.0348	1	0.0120	0.96	1.07	0.33
0.30	−1.54	0.0732	0	0.0348	1.13	0.54	0.41

Table 4A.1 (continued)

Structural change factors

	Corporate complex changes (I)	Price-productivity changes (II)	Economic distress changes (III)	Market center changes (IV)
Lake Charles, LA	−1.15	3.81	−0.11	0.53
Lancaster, PA	−1.28	−0.85	0.69	0.21
Lansing–East Lansing, MI	0.31	0.08	−0.64	0.25
Las Vegas, NV	−1.22	−0.94	−0.07	0.24
Lawrence–Haverhill, MA-NH	0.45	−0.37	−0.01	0.40
Lewistown–Auburn, ME	−0.27	−0.72	−0.11	0.42
Lexington–Fayette, KY	0.61	0.09	−0.09	−0.92
Lincoln, NE	0.23	−0.87	−0.49	−1.19
Little Rock–North Little Rock, AR	0.16	0.95	0.01	0.43
Long Branch–Asbury Park, NJ	−2.00	−0.36	0.39	5.19
Los Angeles–Long Beach, CA	−0.06	−0.99	0.17	−0.49
Louisville, KY–IN	0.83	0.32	0.12	−0.65
Lowell, MA-NH	0.02	−1.37	−0.53	−0.01
Lubbock, TX	−0.19	1.00	0.00	−0.49
Lynchburg, VA	−0.52	−0.57	0.45	−0.13
Macon, GA	−0.38	0.39	0.37	−0.18
Madison, WI	0.30	−0.29	0.16	−0.25
Memphis, TN-AR-MS	0.30	0.03	−0.34	0.03
Miami, FL	−0.40	−1.73	−0.59	−0.45
Milwaukee, WI	−0.96	−0.24	−0.14	0.19
Minneapolis–St.Paul, MN-WI	−0.16	−0.47	−0.15	−0.13
Mobile, AL	−0.87	1.39	−0.76	−1.19
Modesto, CA	−0.45	0.06	−0.07	0.33
Monroe, LA	1.01	2.89	−0.70	0.61
Montgomery, AL	−1.21	0.49	−0.04	0.30
Muncie, IN	0.09	4.29	−0.22	0.16
Muskegon–Norton Shores– Muskegon Heights, MI	0.78	1.16	0.00	0.82
Nashville–Davidson, TN	−0.64	−0.37	−0.32	0.33
Nassau–Suffolk, NY	−0.06	−1.89	0.91	1.14
New Bedford, MA	−0.73	−1.14	0.16	0.55
New Britain, CT	−0.86	−0.23	0.50	−2.52
New Brunswick–Perth Amboy– Sayreville, NJ	1.53	−0.71	−0.16	7.19
New Haven–West Haven, CT	−0.21	−0.65	0.64	0.20

Manufacturing multiplier changes (V)	Residentiary function changes (VI)	Local cyclical behavior					
		$\bar{Y}_t{}^*$	m	ALPHA	BPOS	BNEG	R^2
0.60	2.32	0.0372	o	0.0180	0.63	0.48	0.11
−0.91	0.38	0.0252	o	−0.0072	1.10	0.89	0.73
−0.43	0.11	0.0312	−5	−0.0732	2.99	1.27	0.47
−0.27	2.10	0.0732	o	0.0600	0.69	1.02	0.32
−0.72	1.81	0.0192	o	−0.0036	0.94	1.19	0.49
−0.92	0.79	0.0180	o	−0.0096	1.13	1.26	0.50
−0.01	−0.55	0.0456	o	0.0408	0.81	1.86	0.48
−0.16	−0.37	0.0360	o	0.0180	0.81	0.99	0.43
0.60	−0.80	* *	* *	* *	* *	* *	* *
0.66	0.35	0.0360	o	0.0132	0.96	1.06	0.58
0.87	−0.33	0.0252	o	0.0132	0.59	0.81	0.63
−0.51	0.99	0.0228	o	−0.0024	1.05	1.14	0.51
−0.60	−0.21	0.0360	o	-0.0005	1.27	1.29	0.77
1.15	−1.79	0.0324	o	0.0180	0.74	1.05	0.63
−1.11	−1.13	* *	* *	* *	* *	* *	* *
0.37	−0.46	0.0180	o	0.0060	0.63	0.91	0.55
0.83	0.16	0.0372	o	0.0192	1.04	1.61	0.53
0.33	−0.79	0.0288	o	0.0252	0.61	1.34	0.66
−0.30	−1.84	* *	* *	* *	* *	* *	* *
0.69	0.59	0.0192	o	0.0048	0.83	1.26	0.79
−0.28	−0.04	0.0336	o	−0.0060	1.37	1.13	0.87
−0.50	0.09	0.0288	o	0.0012	1.01	0.93	0.52
1.32	−0.70	0.0432	2	0.1368	0.61	7.49	0.44
0.63	−0.08	0.0264	1	0.0156	0.59	0.82	0.23
0.53	−1.19	0.0420	o	0.0300	0.59	0.77	0.34
−0.60	2.00	0.0120	−6	−0.0552	1.80	0.43	0.34
−1.09	0.71	0.0096	o	0.0204	0.43	1.78	0.36
0.02	−0.43	0.0384	o	0.0228	0.74	0.95	0.54
−0.04	−0.94	0.0276	o	−0.0276	1.77	1.11	0.80
−0.77	−0.33	0.0168	o	−0.0060	1.00	1.39	0.58
0.76	−1.86	0.0276	o	−0.0144	1.34	0.90	0.20
−0.29	−1.01	0.0348	o	−0.0036	1.25	0.89	0.70
−0.26	0.60	0.0180	o	−0.0156	1.13	0.84	0.44

320

Table 4A.1 (continued)

Structural change factors

	Corporate complex changes (I)	Price-productivity changes (II)	Economic distress changes (III)	Market center changes (IV)
New Orleans, LA	−0.60	1.10	−0.14	0.63
New York, NY-NJ	−0.36	−0.96	0.65	0.02
Newark, NJ	0.60	−0.76	0.49	0.33
Norfolk–Virginia Beach–Portsmouth, VA-NC	−0.53	0.90	0.21	0.59
Oklahoma City, OK	0.60	0.07	0.04	−0.91
Omaha, NE-IA	1.17	0.73	0.67	0.03
Orlando, FL	−2.14	−1.26	−0.53	0.06
Oxnard–Simi Valley–Ventura, CA	−0.23	−1.64	0.20	−0.65
Paterson–Clifton–Passaic, NJ	1.09	−0.20	0.58	0.51
Pensacola, FL	0.58	0.67	−0.06	−0.42
Peoria, IL	1.26	0.46	−0.20	−0.26
Philadelphia, PA-NJ	0.14	−0.40	0.60	0.35
Phoenix, AZ	0.53	−0.15	0.50	−0.08
Pine Bluff, AR	0.58	−0.14	−1.18	−0.67
Pittsburgh, PA	−1.77	0.36	−0.43	0.13
Portland, ME	0.34	−0.21	−0.30	−1.27
Portland, OR-WA	0.07	0.10	−0.21	−0.83
Poughkeepsie, NY	−0.92	0.23	0.76	0.07
Providence–Warwick–Pawtucket, RI-MA	−0.35	−1.08	0.26	−0.66
Racine, WI	0.71	−0.09	−0.64	0.00
Raleigh–Durham, NC	0.54	−0.10	−0.01	−0.74
Reading, PA	0.58	−0.41	0.53	0.36
Reno, NV	−0.15	−0.23	0.22	−0.76
Richmond, VA	−0.68	0.18	0.29	−0.12
Riverside–San Bernadino–Ontario, CA	0.00	0.14	0.16	0.02
Roanoke, VA	0.86	−0.64	0.16	0.41
Rochester, NY	−0.80	−0.78	0.35	−0.25
Rockford, IL	0.37	0.38	0.31	0.12
Sacramento, CA	0.52	−0.76	0.14	−0.13
Saginaw, MI	−0.34	0.45	−0.93	−0.25
St. Joseph, MO	−0.17	−0.52	0.07	0.08
St. Louis, MO-IL	−0.11	0.24	0.08	0.08

Manufacturing multiplier changes (V)	Residentiary function changes (VI)	Local cyclical behavior					
		$\bar{Y}_t{}^\star$	m	ALPHA	BPOS	BNEG	R^2
0.02	0.50	0.0240	0	0.0108	0.60	0.75	0.52
−1.11	−1.07	0.0048	0	−0.0240	0.77	0.76	0.68
−0.81	−1.01	0.0132	0	−0.0108	0.90	0.88	0.42
0.44	−0.53	0.0348	0	0.0060	1.02	0.85	0.46
0.24	−0.80	0.0420	0	0.0012	0.97	−0.04	0.44
0.75	−1.54	0.0276	0	−0.0060	1.23	1.16	0.77
−0.21	5.04	0.0672	−6	0.0468	0.88	1.01	0.26
1.44	0.22	0.0516	0	0.0132	1.08	0.42	0.56
−0.90	0.26	0.0072	0	−0.0144	1.01	1.30	0.79
−1.98	1.31	0.0372	1	0.0132	0.65	0.21	0.24
−0.47	−0.23	**	**	**	**	**	**
−0.80	0.04	0.0108	0	−0.0120	0.86	0.88	0.82
−1.00	0.25	0.0684	−6	0.0036	1.52	−0.06	0.44
−0.21	0.32	0.0240	1	−0.0084	1.08	0.76	0.36
−1.05	0.58	0.0108	0	−0.0348	1.27	0.47	0.61
−1.55	0.73	0.0336	0	0.0156	0.97	1.37	0.32
−0.11	0.45	0.0396	0	0.0240	0.85	1.28	0.72
−0.59	0.24	0.0252	0	0.0012	0.90	0.99	0.64
0.44	−0.85	0.0144	0	0.0060	1.14	2.45	0.88
0.44	1.04	0.0216	0	−0.0252	1.41	0.72	0.57
−0.40	−0.75	0.0504	−6	−0.0012	1.19	−0.21	0.40
−1.56	0.02	0.0156	0	−0.0048	0.86	1.00	0.52
1.27	−0.53	0.0744	0	0.0516	1.42	2.39	0.42
−1.18	−0.83	0.0336	0	0.0192	0.66	0.88	0.68
0.32	−0.09	0.0420	−6	0.0036	1.18	0.70	0.68
−1.06	−0.62	0.0276	0	−0.0036	1.15	1.01	0.63
0.05	−0.45	0.0156	0	−0.0024	1.04	1.62	0.80
−0.08	0.37	0.0120	0	−0.0024	0.97	1.66	0.57
1.15	−0.09	0.0384	1	0.0432	0.42	1.42	0.45
−0.18	0.45	0.0180	0	−0.0276	1.33	0.59	0.12
0.51	−0.82	0.0120	0	−0.0168	0.98	0.73	0.41
0.26	0.39	0.0096	0	−0.0120	1.02	1.34	0.80

Table 4A.1 (continued)

Structural change factors

	Corporate complex changes (I)	Price-productivity changes (II)	Economic distress changes (III)	Market center changes (IV)
Salem, OR	−0.33	−0.49	−0.48	0.00
Salinas–Seaside–Monterey, CA	−0.04	−1.10	0.25	−1.00
Salt Lake City–Ogden, UT	0.43	−0.24	−0.40	−0.97
San Antonio, TX	0.22	−0.28	0.03	−0.03
San Diego, CA	−0.00	−1.32	0.64	−0.05
San Francisco–Oakland, CA	−0.16	0.11	0.24	−0.03
San Jose, CA	−0.26	−0.42	0.11	−0.63
Santa Barbara–Santa Maria–Lompoc, CA	0.18	−0.47	0.20	−1.91
Santa Rosa, CA	−0.28	0.36	0.50	−0.84
Savannah, GA	0.42	0.07	−0.53	−0.30
Scranton, PA	−0.46	0.19	−0.08	−0.61
Seattle–Everett, WA	0.68	−0.30	−1.12	0.04
Shreveport, LA	0.15	−0.48	−0.58	−0.81
Sioux City, IA-NE	0.35	0.61	−0.89	−0.52
Sioux Falls, ND	−0.09	−0.44	−0.67	0.12
South Bend, IN	−0.40	−0.20	−0.32	−0.41
Spokane, WA	−0.86	0.02	−0.34	−0.60
Springfield, IL	0.04	−0.45	0.61	−0.21
Springfield, MO	−0.42	0.17	0.02	0.70
Springfield–Chicopee–Holyoke, MA-CT	−0.22	−1.10	0.30	0.03
Stamford, CT	6.37	−0.02	−0.36	0.50
Stockton, CA	0.14	−0.68	−0.72	−0.41
Syracuse, NY	−0.44	0.38	0.45	0.81
Tacoma, WA	−0.40	0.18	0.04	−0.42
Tallahassee, FL	0.15	−0.01	−0.13	−0.56
Tampa–St.Petersburg, FL	0.59	−0.37	0.24	−0.13
Terre Haute, IN	1.04	0.27	−0.35	−0.06
Toledo,OH-MI	−0.70	−0.31	0.18	0.27
Topeka, KS	−2.23	−0.81	−0.23	0.55
Trenton, NJ	−0.16	−0.90	0.07	0.12
Tucson, AZ	0.32	−0.47	0.78	−0.08
Tulsa, OK	1.16	0.75	−0.33	−1.47
Tuscaloosa, AL	0.49	1.55	−0.25	0.17

Manufac- turing multiplier changes (V)	Residen- tiary function changes (VI)	Local cyclical behavior					
		$\bar{Y}_t{}^*$	m	ALPHA	BPOS	BNEG	R^2
0.41	−0.38	0.0480	2	0.1572	−0.12	6.55	0.49
1.81	0.16	0.0360	0	−0.0036	1.74	2.11	0.53
0.68	0.47	**	**	**	**	**	**
0.14	−0.66	0.0384	0	0.0168	0.65	0.33	0.51
1.70	0.15	0.0576	0	0.0396	0.62	0.53	0.51
0.82	−0.38	0.0228	0	0.0120	0.59	0.89	0.69
1.63	−0.20	0.0564	1	0.0744	0.20	1.72	0.47
1.16	0.29	0.0408	−6	−0.0168	1.46	0.23	0.54
1.40	−0.36	0.0612	0	0.0468	1.12	2.05	0.56
−1.94	1.56	0.0264	0	0.0300	0.44	1.46	0.35
−0.09	1.99	0.0060	0	−0.0072	0.82	1.35	0.68
−0.21	1.14	0.0348	0	0.0024	1.04	0.70	0.48
0.38	−0.38	0.0324	0	0.0144	0.75	0.92	0.50
−0.12	0.48	0.0168	0	−0.0252	1.28	0.77	0.41
0.59	0.33	0.0408	0	0.0024	1.37	1.22	0.69
0.10	0.63	0.0156	0	0.0084	0.76	1.52	0.60
0.26	0.17	0.0360	0	−0.0072	1.65	1.60	0.73
−0.73	−0.18	**	**	**	**	**	**
1.10	−0.48	0.0408	0	0.0360	0.81	1.85	0.53
−0.44	−0.55	0.0192	0	0.0216	0.62	1.93	0.80
−1.45	0.54	0.0312	0	−0.0108	1.31	0.76	0.54
0.82	−1.03	0.0276	2	−0.0960	0.11	4.60	0.49
−0.30	−0.42	0.0156	0	−0.0132	1.24	1.46	0.85
0.05	0.93	0.0288	0	−0.0072	1.08	0.60	0.53
0.22	0.18	**	**	**	**	**	**
−0.46	0.09	0.0552	−6	0.0372	0.86	1.20	0.45
0.97	−1.08	0.0228	0	0.0024	0.97	1.34	0.46
0.02	−0.51	0.0192	0	−0.0276	1.56	1.15	0.82
0.57	−1.81	0.0312	0	−0.0024	0.80	0.00	0.26
−0.73	−0.67	0.0240	0	0.0072	0.66	0.63	0.60
−0.05	−0.55	0.0588	−6	0.0108	1.22	0.22	0.38
1.34	−1.20	**	**	**	**	**	**
−0.17	−0.97	0.0336	0	0.0504	0.19	1.59	0.21

Table 4A.1 (continued)

Structural change factors

	Corporate complex changes (I)	Price- productivity changes (II)	Economic distress changes (III)	Market center changes (IV)
Utica–Rome, NY	0.32	0.22	0.65	0.12
Vallejo–Fairfield–Napa, CA	0.25	−0.18	0.09	−0.69
Vineland–Millville–Bridgeton, NJ	0.33	0.57	0.45	1.11
Waco, TX	−0.30	−0.09	−0.40	−0.12
Waterbury, CT	3.12	−2.12	0.35	1.66
Waterloo–Cedar Falls, IA	−0.48	1.01	−0.99	0.29
West Palm Beach–Boca Raton, FL	0.57	0.25	0.96	0.87
Wheeling, WV-OH	−1.03	1.13	−0.38	0.20
Wichita, KS	1.07	−0.11	−0.85	−0.66
Wichita Falls, TX	−0.18	2.47	−0.73	−1.24
Wilkes-Barre–Hazelton, PA	0.29	0.10	0.18	0.03
Williamsport, PA	−0.35	0.80	0.21	−0.27
Wilmington, DE-NJ-MD	−3.54	−0.69	0.28	0.10
Worcester, MA	−1.04	−0.73	0.27	0.14
York, PA	−0.66	−0.44	0.79	0.18
Youngstown–Warren, OH	0.06	0.25	−0.22	−0.17

Manufac-turing multiplier changes (V)	Residen-tiary function changes (VI)	Local cyclical behavior					
		$\bar{Y}_t{}^*$	m	ALPHA	BPOS	BNEG	R^2
−0.19	0.58	0.0036	0	−0.0324	1.36	1.30	0.62
1.18	0.19	0.0348	0	0.0036	1.08	0.92	0.43
−0.57	0.22	0.0156	1	0.0456	0.03	1.93	0.37
1.38	−1.12	0.0336	0	0.0156	0.69	0.63	0.41
6.73	5.05	0.0108	0	−0.0192	1.16	1.20	0.40
1.30	−0.26	0.0252	1	−0.0036	0.85	0.35	0.09
−0.03	−0.20	0.0624	2	−0.0504	1.05	−4.45	0.28
−0.91	0.80	0.0132	0	−0.0408	1.72	1.06	0.34
0.37	−0.44	0.0264	0	0.0036	0.90	0.93	0.46
0.55	−0.28	0.0360	0	0.0288	0.42	0.63	0.36
−0.10	1.00	0.0084	0	−0.0396	1.52	0.95	0.56
−1.32	0.47	0.0120	0	0.0004	0.71	1.25	0.50
−1.21	0.70	0.0192	0	−0.0156	1.16	0.90	0.57
−0.59	0.16	0.0228	0	−0.0012	0.97	1.26	0.82
−1.08	−0.21	0.0216	0	0.0012	1.02	1.39	0.76
0.27	0.16	0.0120	0	−0.0408	1.60	0.86	0.44

Estimates from cyclical model were considered unstable or ambiguous.
Annualized growth rates.

Appendix to Chapter Eight

Table 8A.1 Employment and Growth for Selected SMSAS:
High Technology and all Industries

Metropolitan area	Employment (1976)		Employment Growth (%) (1976–1980)	
	Total employment	Hi-Tech employment	All industries	High technology
Albuquerque, NM	133,949.	14,016.	41.7	33.4
Anaheim, CA	615,167.	102,150.	46.5	37.5
Atlanta, GA	899,761.	31,362.	6.9	32.9
Austin, TX	135,811.	7,788.	33.5	182.4
Baltimore, MD	710,828.	24,377.	15.6	63.3
Baton Rouge, LA	139,616.	7,094.	41.3	48.9
Boise City, ID	43,203.	679.	33.2	135.3
Boston, MA-NH	1,682,753.	208,388.	10.5	26.9
Buffalo, NY	513,174.	28,815.	2.9	18.5
Chicago, IL	3,439,570.	336,837.	2.9	−5.6
Cincinnati, OH-KY-IN	584,522.	41,371.	9.3	15.6
Denver-Boulder, CO	682,577.	41,522.	34.7	64.4
Detroit, MI	1,499,361.	73,297.	6.9	15.7
Houston, TX	1,358,504.	126,131.	18.9	47.6
Kansas City, KA-MO	545,141.	37,807.	27.2	5.6
Louisville, KY	380,616.	21,664.	39.2	−5.8
Miami, FL	702,456.	15,222.	5.0	38.2
Milwaukee, WI	629,013.	70,446.	8.3	4.3
Minneapolis–St. Paul, MN-WI	871,042.	84,489.	15.5	−5.4
New Haven, CT	280,972.	23,518.	11.1	22.5
Omaha, NE-IA,	253,527.	11,345.	11.8	10.4
Philadelphia, PA-NJ	1,777,036.	215,875.	1.4	−27.6
Phoenix, AZ	380,035.	38,457.	36.5	43.7
Pittsburgh, PA	897,290.	44,983.	4.7	10.7
Portland, ME	95,660.	2,114.	26.5	55.0
Portland, OR-WA	446,097.	19,214.	24.3	18.3
Raleigh–Durham, NC	198,139.	17,613.	19.5	56.1
Rochester, NY	342,548.	73,755.	12.4	47.7
St. Louis, MO-IL	881,855.	69,826.	14.9	22.9
Salt Lake City–Ogden, UT	252,392.	21,233.	44.5	30.4
San Diego, CA	461,782.	62,334.	25.3	8.9

Table 8A.1 (continued)

Metropolitan area	Employment (1976)		Employment Growth (%) (1976–1980)	
	Total employment	Hi-Tech employment	All industries	High technology
San Jose, CA	521,405.	154,909.	23.6	28.7
Seattle, WA	585,397.	48,286.	37.7	92.4
Tampa–St. Petersburg, FL	432,427.	17,729.	27.6	72.9
Wilmington, DE-NJ-MD	183,634.	31,257.	1.4	−1.4

Table 8A.2 Metropolitan characteristics

Type	Variable	Measure
Sector growth		
	Sector formations [1]	1976–80 new establishments in sector for independent firms for branch establishments
	Sector formation rate [1]	1976–80 new estabs in sector/1976 employment for independent firms for branch establishments
	Sector growth rate [1]	1980 sector employment/1976 sector employment
Strength of economy		
	Employment growth [1]	1980 SMSA employment/1976 SMSA employment
	Employment rate[3]	1.00 minus 1976 SMSA unemployment rate
	Median family income[2]	Median family income in 1975
Business costs		
	Electricity costs[2]	Average monthly commercial payments in 1976
	Wage rates[5]	1976 avg. wage for production workers
	Local tax per capita[4]	ACIR capacity index/effort index
City size and attractiveness		
	Population[2]	1975 SMSA population
	Population density[2]	1975 SMSA population per square mile
	Population growth[2]	1975 population/1970 population
Sector Strength		
	Sector size [1]	1976 sector employment
	Sector share [1]	1976 sector employment/ total SMSA employ
	Agglomeration one [1]	sector share-SMSA/sector share-US
	Agglomeration two[1]	sector employ-SMSA/sector employ-US
Labor quality		
	Percentage technical[2]	1975 Scientists, engineers and technicians/total private sector employment

1 USEEM, Business Microdata Project, Brookings Institution, 1983.
2 Bureau of the Census, City and County Data Book, 1977 and 1980.
3 Bureau of the Census, Metropolitan Area Data Book, 1982 and 1983.
4 Advisory Commission on Intergovernmental Relations, "Interstate Tax Computation" (draft),1983.
5 Bureau of Labor Statistics, Employment and Earnings, Fall 1977.

Notes

Policy Realities and Development Potentials in Local Economics

1 Widely accepted in the sense that it is frequently referred to and understood as an important category of local policy and planning. One need only examine the many titles reviewed in government, development, and planning or policy journals over the past few years to see how important local economic development has become. More evidence for the skeptical can be had by glancing at recent newsletters or periodicals distributed by membership organizations of states, state agencies, governors, cities, mayors, counties, development planners, or public managers. When combined with other national membership organizations now devoted exclusively to questions of economic development (for example, National Council for Urban Economic Development or National Association of Development Officials), it seems that economic development has become a term so widely embraced that it may soon need to acquire many different specialized meanings.

2 For the most part these suggestions would have come from a disparate group of scholars or practitioners outside the planning mainstream. Academic geographers and regional scientists analyzed local area economies within their space-economy models of industrial location and production. Industrial developers from chambers of commerce, utilities, banks, and the real estate industry pursued their traditional area growth objectives (Conway 1980). Developing country or regional specialists continued to improve the theoretical apparatus and policy recommendations applied particularly to the underdeveloped U.S. Appalachian region (Friedmann and Weaver 1979). Wilbur Thompson's early work on the Michigan and Detroit urban economy resulted in an influential book on the performance and structure of urban economies (1965), but the field of urban economics tended to investigate other questions that arose in the 1960s' growth era (Perloff 1973).

3 The principal urban policy documents include President's Commission for a National Agenda for the Eighties (1980), *President's National Urban Policy Report* (1980), and *President's National Urban Policy Report* (1982).

4 Urban policy positions taken during the past half-dozen years by the Carter and

Reagan administrations have been closely analyzed (e.g., Clark 1982), by the National Research Council (1982a, 1982b) in the course of preparing its own urban policy report (Hanson 1983), and by the planning profession (Goldsmith and Jacobs 1982; Glickman 1984a, 1984b; Ahlbrandt 1984; Roistacher 1984; Clarke 1984).

5 The literature on this topic is so voluminous, perishable, and esoteric—or fugitive —that a representative sampling of citations is impossible to draw. However, a few key references and collections of apparent seminal quality or particular relevance to local economic development would include Bell and Lande (1982), Bowles, Gordon, and Weisskopf (1983), U.S. Congressional Budget Office (1983, 1984), Glickman and Van Wagner (1985), Magaziner and Reich (1983), Wachter and Wachter (1981).

6 Here again, a representative sampling of this enormous, often redundant literature is difficult to extract. Chapters 2 and 9 of this book review some of the issues surrounding public-private partnerships. Useful references include Brooks, Liebman, and Schelling (1984), Committee for Economic Development (1982), Fosler and Berger (1982).

7 Recent research by Williams (1984) has demonstrated fruitful theoretical grounds for reformulating neoclassical concepts of the firm as a labor-managed enterprise, thereby opening the way for new interpretations of how investor- and worker-managed enterprises respond to policy initiatives.

1 National Contexts for Urban Economic Policy

1 At the outset it is useful to indicate that the OECD nations are heterogeneous on measures of *economic development* and *urbanization*, both dimensions that concern us. With respect to the economy, income levels, industry mixes, growth rates, and other standard economic variables vary greatly. The major groups of countries can be divided between the relatively wealthy (Northern Europe, North America, and Japan) and those middle-income states primarily along the Mediterranean basin (Portugal, Spain, Italy, Greece, Yugoslavia, Turkey, and a few others). Even within these broad categories there are important exceptions. With regard to urbanization, there are at least four categories: (1) the Mediterranean countries with low urbanization rates, except Italy and Spain; this group is also relatively low-income; (2) nations where older and larger cities are losing population, such as the United States, the United Kingdom, and the Federal Republic of Germany; (3) states with low levels of urbanization, but relatively high incomes (e.g., Norway, Austria) or with rapid economic growth rates (e.g., Finland, Ireland); and (4) nations that are still, in one form or another, being settled (for example, Australia, Canada, New Zealand, and parts of the United States) and have lower population densities (OECD, 1983c). OECD countries also differ in the ways in which government is organized. Some are federalist, most are not; relationships among tiers of government and degrees of public intervention also differ sharply. Therefore, speaking about "the OECD" means taking in a large number of disparate settings. We try to delineate subgroups when possible, but this is not always possible.

2 For instance, tax policies aimed at increasing investment (such as tax credits)

may steer capital formation away from declining cities, the objects of much urban aid. We will return to this when discussing responses to economic change.

3   There are many urban policies that are not growth-oriented. For example, some social services or environmental programs do not have economic growth as their main purpose, although development may be affected indirectly. We will not consider these programs in great detail.

4   Between 1960–69 and 1973–80, the annual growth of real GNP in OECD countries fell from 6.1 percent to 2.3 percent (OECD 1982a). Unemployment rates rose from a 1960–66 average of 3.1 percent to 5.4 percent for 1974–80; by 1982, unemployment worsened further, to a post-Depression high of 8.2 percent. Over the same period, inflation (as measured by the GNP deflator) more than tripled to 9.7 percent per year by the late 1970s. Note that there were greatly differing growth rates among OECD countries, typified most strikingly by the ascendancy of Japan and West Germany and the relative decline of the United States and Great Britain. OECD countries also were at different developmental stages. The Southern European nations have a higher proportion of manufacturing and relatively fewer services, for instance.

5   One can see the sectoral shifts in employment within OECD countries by examining data for the 1960–80 period. Employment in agriculture fell by 2.8 percent per year, while manufacturing gained slightly (0.7 percent/annum) and services grew rapidly (2.4 percent/annum). Importantly, as noted in note 1, these OECD averages mask large differences among countries. The Mediterranean nations are still experiencing significant manufacturing employment increases (for instance, Turkey, 2.9 percent per year), while the more mature Northern European nations fit the trends noted above more closely; in France, Great Britain, Sweden, and The Netherlands declines in manufacturing employment were registered (World Bank 1982).

6   On the role of transnational corporations in world economic development, see OECD (1982b), Barnet and Muller (1974), and United Nations (1978).

7   The product cycle refers to a pattern observed during the development of most products. During the first phase newly discovered or engineered products enter into production. The difficulties normally encountered with new production technology and in developing a new market generally result in relatively slow growth in output and low profits. This phase is followed by one of rapid expansion in output as the manufacturing technology improves; given a quasi-monopoly for the original producer, high profits are realized. The high profit rate attracts other competitors and the production technology tends to become standardized; profit rates decline, and, at some point, the market becomes saturated and total industrial output stabilizes. On this subject, see Vernon (1966), Markusen (1983), Thomas (1974), Norton and Rees (1979), Krumme and Hayter (1975), and Lasuen (1973).

8   Other reasons include falling birthrates and the slowing of international migration (especially in Europe) to large cities where manufacturing jobs have been located.

9   For example, Yugoslavia, Portugal, and Turkey had 30-40 percent urban population in the late 1970s, while the United States, Japan, West Germany, and Bel-

gium had between 75-80 percent of their populations living in cities (OECD 1983c).

10 On regional change in OECD countries, see Hall and Hay (1980), Berry (1973), and Glickman (1979), as well as OECD (1983c).

11 For example, industrial cities in the U.S. Midwest, the Midlands and Merseyside in England, the North and Lorraine in France, and Wallonia in Belgium have experienced job loss.

12 Industrial employment declined by large percentages in several metropolitan areas during the 1970s: Hamburg (17.7 percent), Rotterdam (15.0 percent), Helsinki (14.0 percent), and Tokyo (7.8 percent) (OECD 1983c).

13 High-growth areas include those such as the Santa Clara Valley in California and Kyushu in Japan (the locations of many semiconductor firms), a few international financial centers (such as the business districts of New York City), and energy development regions such as the American Mountain states and the Scottish coast.

14 Many of the migrants were drawn to Northern Europe through the *Gastarbeiter* programs of previous decades and now find themselves without jobs. Often, the jobs that were previously held by these workers have been relocated to other regions and countries.

15 It should be noted that national spending must be considered *net* of taxes paid by a locality. If the amount sent to the central government is more than received locally, there are not likely to be positive budgetary effects on growth. There could be consequences for different sectors, however; those gaining from direct governmental expenditures (for instance, construction firms from highway grants) would have a net gain.

16 Muller (1982) shows that net flows of taxes and spending in 1980 differed widely among U.S. regions. The northern tier regions were net "losers," and the southern and western areas were "winners" in the process of national-level budgeting. Glickman (1979) and Mera (1983) indicate similar differential consequences for Japanese regions. It should be mentioned that much of this uneven pattern of spending and taxing is a direct consequence of progressive tax policies that tax poorer people less heavily than the rich. To the extent that the poor are spatially clustered, the regions in which they live will be favored by tax and social spending policies. In addition, some OECD countries also try to equalize local resources by transferring greater amounts of money to poorer regions. For other case studies of the effects of national spending patterns, see Jussil (1983) about Sweden, and Jensen and Thomsen (1983) on Denmark.

17 Reference is to general tax benefits available economywide. In many OECD countries, such as Great Britain, region-specific tax advantages are provided to induce location in depressed areas (Maclennan and Parr 1979; Allen 1978).

18 The favorable treatment given home ownership by the tax laws in many countries also has important implications for urban spatial structure. Such statutes encourage suburbanization of the population and contribute to the fiscal pressures on central cities.

19 As well as transnational corporations and multinational organizations such as the EC, OECD, and LAFTA.

20 Promotional strategies are fairly common in OECD countries (OECD 1983a); for

Great Britain and West Germany, see Johnson and Cochrane (1981); for the United States, see U.S. Conference of Mayors (1980).

21 Another recent example, the enterprise zone, has been adopted in Great Britain and the United States and includes tax abatements and labor subsidies. Discussions of enterprise zones can be found in Sternlieb and Listokin (1981), Hall (1977), Butler (1980), and Jacobs and Wasylenko (1981).

22 Often university representatives are involved in public-private partnerships.

23 In addition, several countries have adopted legislation that requires notification of plant closings and payment to displaced workers and communities.

24 Central-city revitalization projects usually have an important commercial and retail trade component, but these projects probably shift the spatial distribution of such employment within the city rather than significantly increasing total employment.

2 Urban America, Inc.: Corporatist Convergence of Power in American Cities?

1 See Robert Salisbury's early discussion of these dimensions and their effects on policy formulation (1968). Almost fifteen years later Philippe Schmitter used a similar analytic approach, distinguishing between the structure of interest associations and the type of policymaking process involved, to clarify the conceptual confusion surrounding the use of the term "corporatism" (1982).

2 Essentially both pluralism and corporatism are descriptive, ideal-type configurations. They are complementary and contrasting models rather than contradictory, dichotomous, or mutually exclusive paradigms. Both pluralist and corporatist theorists acknowledge the significance of socioeconomic structures in generating demands and interests; in more recent analyses, both approaches emphasize the concomitant importance of historical, organizational and political processes in shaping interest formation. But where the pluralist sees indeterminate process, the corporatist theorist is more likely to see structure. In the pluralist view, this is a patternless process: there is no theoretical argument that suggests predictable patterns of demands, conflicts among interests, or new relations of group and government. The pluralist perspective assumes that, in an unspecified and problematic way, individuals sharing interests will mobilize into groups and demand political responses to their concerns. Local development policy agendas, therefore, are interpreted as reflecting the demands from a broad range of interest groups seeking public solutions to the private costs of economic change. In Schmitter's descriptions (1979) of these ideal-type configurations, pluralist demand patterns are characterized as "organized into an unspecified number of multiple, voluntary, competitive, nonhierarchically ordered, and self-determined as to type or scope of interest categories" with no claim to a monopoly of representational activity within their respective categories. The pluralist model is based on a subjective definition of interest; since political action is a function of felt needs and mobilization of available slack resources, an unpredictable range of group activity is possible. The relations among groups and government are fluid and competitive; policymaking is characterized by bargaining among interests and

between interests, who remain outside the decision-making structures, and public authority.

In contrast, many corporatist theories interpret structural differentiation processes, and the generation of new interests, in light of crises in capitalist economies. Those interests critical to production — capital and labor — are assumed to be predominant; in particular, capital's search for new forms of profitable investment is seen as a major dynamic that influences contemporary policy processes and policy agendas. Economic crises, for example, prompt demands by investor and producer groups that the public sector share the costs and risks of private development activity and engender new factions within and between capital and labor sectors. Although less well defined, the corporatist model of demand patterns emphasizes the controlled emergence, limited number, singular and compulsory nature, and noncompetitive relations of functionally differentiated categories of units, "recognized or licensed (if not created) by the state" and enjoying representational monopolies within their respective categories (Schmitter 1979). Generally, the corporatist model of group and government relations is restricted to analysis of relationships between the state and economic, or functionally differentiated, interests. If the corporatist model is viewed as a political arrangement rather than a specific structure or economic order, this is not a necessary restriction. The key element in this political arrangement is the attribution of policy authority to private interests; interests no longer remain exogenous to the policymaking process: they are integrated, authoritative participants. The implication is that different degrees and types of corporatism can exist in primarily pluralist systems.

Schmitter's approach (1982) distinguishes between corporatist and pluralist demand patterns and policy processes. He argues that the terms "pluralist" and "corporatist" should be reserved to describe features of demand patterns and that policy formulation processes be characterized as "bargaining" or "consultative" processes. Corporatist demand patterns are identified as those characterized by peak associations acting as representational monopolies for their memberships and able to make commitments to collective agreements in their name. "Bargaining" and "consultative" policy formulation processes range from those with relatively unstructured representation of interests and coordination via bargaining processes to those in which interest representation is structured from "the top down" and accommodation of interests is reached through more formal negotiation and joint decision-making among groups *within* a forum policymaking authority. This distinction clarifies some conceptual confusion in earlier corporatist analyses and emphasizes that the relationship between demand pattern and decisional process is an empirical issue. That is, polities may be characterized by pluralist demand patterns and consultative decision processes, or vice versa, and corporatist demand patterns may be associated with more consultative processes, or vice versa. This adds, though, another layer of terminology that has not been widely adopted.

3 Salisbury makes a strong argument against the likelihood of corporatist patterns of representation in American national politics; this is buttressed with theoretical arguments and some empirical evidence by Schmitter (1983), Safran (1983),

and Wilson (1982). There is no consensus on the conditions favoring corporatist arrangements: the case anticipating corporatist patterns in the United States centers on the absence of those characteristics associated with corporatist development in other countries. For example, at different points, Schmitter has variously identified these conditions as weak traditions of individualistic liberalism, premodern forms of associability, concentrated ownership and geographic locus of capital, and strong and persistent reformist social democratic parties (1981). He also singles out experience with a range of institutional innovations for increasing direct citizen involvement in political decision-making, small size, high international vulnerability, well-established state legitimacy, centralized administrative structure, preponderance of class cleavage over other bases of social and cultural conflict, and ideological hegemony of social democratic over bourgeois values (1983). Safran (1983) notes that corporatist-like arrangements are more likely in countries where physical-geographical forces shape cultural traditions and promote "Malthusian" attitudes toward economic growth, where there are commitments to national socioeconomic planning, and where interest group leaders see such cooperative relations as beneficial. Safran goes on to argue that several "myths" dominant in American political culture make it less likely that the institutional transformations necessary for corporatist representation will occur in the United States: the virtue attributed to the lack of institutional change; the myth of countervailing powers and autonomous bargaining among interests; the belief that equal lobbying opportunities exist for interest groups; the myth of the efficiency of various subsystems as means of participation, including the use of federalism as an alternative to functional representation of interests; and the belief that pervasive class conflict does not exist and, therefore, that state intervention to control interest group conflicts is not necessary (342–43).

Graham Wilson argues that interest groups in the United Staes lack "the unity, membership, and authority essential for the system to be classified as corporatist" (1982, 224). Furthermore, he argues that the characteristics of American government—both the institutions and ideology—do not encourage the formation of such groups; indeed, the multiple channels of access, the fragmentation of power, the separation of powers, the federal structure of intergovernmental relations, weak party system, and the lack of commitment to integrated economic policy and incomes policy do not provide incentives either for such groups to form or for government to seek more direct group participation in policy formulation (224–30). In Wilson's view the size and complexity of the American economy and the absence of a strong labor movement make the emergence of corporatism over time in the United States also unlikely.

While it is true that most of these preconditions do not characterize the United States, it is possible that decision-making in certain policy areas or at certain levels of government or at certain points in time can be more adequately described as corporatist than as pluralist. The National Recovery Administration (NRA) in the 1930s, for example, is often described as a corporatist decision-making structure (Salisbury 1979; Wilson 1982), even though the national political system as a whole at the time continued to be characterized by pluralist policymaking procedures. For reasons discussed below, it is plausible to anticipate trends toward corporatist policymaking patterns at the local level even if this is not an appropriate description of national political processes.

4   See Berger's (1981) account of the research carried out by the Committee on Comparative Politics of the Social Science Research Council in the 1950s and 1960s; Gabriel Almond (1983) presents a vigorous rebuttal of Berger's interpretation in "Corporatism, Pluralism, and Professional Memory," *World Politics* 35:245–60.

5   Only brief attention is given here to changes in demand patterns; this dimension is discussed in the chapters by Wiewel and Mier and by Bradford and Temali that describe changes in the structure of neighborhood-based organizations and their political activities, as well as changes in businesses' approaches to community-based development organizations. See note 2 for descriptions of pluralist and corporatist ideal-type demand patterns.

6   Berger (1981) notes this changing interpretation of the impact of pluralist interest representation on political stability in her introduction (21); in the same volume, Schmitter argues that it is not the volume of demands generated by pluralist systems that creates ungovernability but the processes of pluralist policymaking (in contrast to "consultative" processes) themselves (287). Parallel arguments explaining local fiscal crises, particularly in New York City, as a consequence of systemic "overload" are made by Charles Morris (1980) and Ken Auletta (1980).

7   Most analyses have focused on corporatist arrangements in economic policy areas, particularly incomes policy, or other areas directly affecting a nation's productive capacities. This focus derives from the supposed function of corporatist arrangements: to channel demands to policymakers and provide a forum for consensual decision-making among affected interests on issues where rancorous conflict would impede economic productivity or social peace. One implication is that organized interests in these core policy areas will be involved in corporatist policymaking processes while the less-organized, "distributionally disadvantaged and culturally underprivileged" groups will be relegated to "residual pluralism" processes in peripheral, noneconomic, policy areas (see Schmitter's 1983 discussion). This argument—that interest representation patterns are associated with substantive policy concerns—remains to be tested. There are some indications that more structured modes of interest representation are present in local social welfare policy arenas. The "bureaucratic enfranchisement" model described by Norman and Susan Fainstein (Fainstein, Fainstein, et al. 1983), for example, brings agency clients into the policy process but primarily in an advisory capacity rather than as authoritative policymakers. There are also numerous examples of "partnerships" for local service delivery (Kotler 1981; Ahlbrandt and Sumka 1983; Cunningham and Kotler 1983), although the information on the nature of these partnerships is less reliable. To the extent that corporatist arrangements lead to more consensual local policymaking, it is likely that they could be adopted across a range of policy areas where budget constraints, community cleavages, and other factors make it difficult for local officials to satisfy both their functional and territorial constituencies. Thus, analytic focus on economic policy arenas is more a consequence of the inadequate conceptualization of the relationship between local economic development and service or social welfare policies

than a theoretical argument that these modes only occur in certain policy arenas. See Rich (1982) for a promising start in reconceptualizing local service issues. Kirby (1982) points out that local policy concerns are much more extensive than the "social consumption" issues generally seen as the purview of local policy-making.

8 Hernes and Selvik (1979) produced one of the earliest studies of local corporatism. Based on survey research in Norwegian communities, they argue that the trend toward local corporatist structures in Norway is a consequence of the expansion of local public authority and greater discretionary power for economic planning and development. These new laws and regulations prompted changes in institutional arrangements and interest representation as local political decisions on economic matters became more visible. In the interviews described in this chapter, American local officials report a similar impetus.

British scholars have been particularly active in analysis of local development politics. Cockburn's study (1977) of the London Borough of Lambeth underscores the adoption of corporation management strategies by local government officials; her analysis includes a study of the institutional changes accompanying these approaches, but her focus is on the workings of the local state, not the relations between the local state and local interests. The Marxian framework guiding the research emphasizes conflicts over capitalist reproduction at the community level rather than the institutional apparatus mediating these conflicts. Simmie (1981) and Cawson (1982) make greater use of the corporatist concept in their analysis of British local development politics.

9 The evidence of economic transformation in older industrial cities is now well established (See Sternlieb and Hughes 1975; Weinstein and Firestine 1978; James 1981; Fainstein, Fainstein ct al. 1983; Sawyers and Tabb 1984; Perry and Watkins 1977). In brief, there is increasing loss of manufacturing jobs due to absolute job loss, as urban firms close down and are not replaced (see Massey and Meegan 1982) and relative job loss from shifts to financial management and service sector activities in some cities. Both absolute and relative job loss is accompanied by selective outmigration from the central cities and, increasingly, suburban areas of older metropolises. In addition to these job losses, efforts to eliminate excess capacity and cut costs have brought about a restructuring of the labor force through labor force reduction, substitutions of part-time for full-time employees, or replacement with other production technologies. In addition, the few new jobs added to the urban economy are often not well-matched with the existing labor force and thus do not contribute to resolving unemployment. Financial restructuring through mergers and intrasectoral reorganization also may lead to the abandonment of some otherwise viable operations. As both population and industry leave the city, the revenue base available to support infrastructure development and urban services shrinks; this makes cities less attractive as investment sites and leaves behind urban populations in need of more assistance. For most American cities, economic revitalization is attempted through transformation of existing land uses and shifting of public funds to "more productive" uses.

The tendency in most analyses of the political effects of these processes is to start with a pluralist or structuralist framework rather than to test alternative explanations of urban political phenomena. For example, Fainstein, Fainstein, et al. (1983) provide a valuable, comprehensive account of postwar development politics in American cities; each author uses a structuralist framework and focuses on the historical and political factors shaping coalition formation in specific cities, particularly ways in which past policies shape the definitions of development needs and the emergence of groups and coalitions around those needs. In their concluding essay, Susan and Norman Fainstein suggest that a "national reversion to a Democratic regime" might result in more corporatist patterns, which they define as "more state planning, political determination of relative shares, and stabilization of urban programs embodying both accumulationist and collective consumption tendencies" (279). Mollenkopf's work on national urban policies (1983) and development politics in Boston and San Francisco (1981) also emphasizes the formation of development coalitions; the later work considers the conditions for formation of countervailing coalitions to challenge the dominance of progrowth coalitions in American cities but does not emphasize concomitant changes in institutional structures. Friedland (1982) analyzes policy processes in 130 cities on urban renewal and War on Poverty issues; his interest, however, is in illustrating the constraints imposed by the interests of national corporations and labor unions rather than specifying how these interests are involved in local policy processes. Stone begins with a similar argument on structural constraints (1980) but refines it in applying it to local economic development politics (1984). In contrast, Katznelson (1981) recognizes the inability of either pluralist or structuralist approaches to explain the split between work and community in American politics; his case study of Manhattan stresses the need to recognize the effects on community development of the limitation of class distinctions and politics to the workplace. Finally, Peterson's (1981) *City Limits* presents a counterpoint to these structuralist approaches by arguing for a unitary model of the local community. Because of the political and economic features of American settlement patterns, Peterson claims that enhancing the economic standing of the community, relative to that of other communities, is in the interests of all citizens. This view of the "city as a whole" emphasizes private sector investment decisions as the key to local economic well-being; as Smith and Keller point out, this tends to equate private development interests with "the public interest" (Fainstein, Fainstein, et al. 1983, 160).

10 See note 3 for the arguments against anticipating corporatist interest representation patterns in American national politics. Note, however, that some of the features associated with corporatist arrangements in other countries that are less characteristic of the American national political system—such as small size, vulnerability to changes in larger economic and political systems, economic resource scarcity, concentrated ownership, and geographic locus of capital—are often present at the local level. Some of the preconditions of corporatist patterns, therefore, can be found at the local community, even though they are not features of the national political system.

11 Two types of decisional structures are reviewed: project-level public/private partnerships and local institutional arrangements for formulation of citywide development policy. These are distinct phenomena; the relationship between the inci-

dence of project-level public/private partnerships and the characteristics of citywide policy formulation process is an empirical issue yet to be tested.

12   The research literature is bifurcated between a rich literature of case studies of interest group activities (see Fainstein, Fainstein, et al. 1983; Urban Land Institute 1980; Mollenkopf 1981) and a nascent literature on corporatist links, focused primarily on case studies of historical patterns of state/interest group linkages in national politics. (See Schmitter and Lehmbruch 1981; Lehmbruch and Schmitter 1982.) Some empirical analyses of alternative linkage patterns are available at the national level (Wilson 1983), but few studies of alternative linkage patterns have been conducted at the local level (see discussions in Jones and Bachelor 1984; Hernes and Selvik 1979; Simmie 1981; Olson 1982).

Unfortunately, analysis of the relations between local groups and government is hampered by the lack of systematic information on the types of different arrangements, their composition, and the distributional effects of the decisions they produce. Without such information, it is difficult to determine whether new arrangements reflect nonpluralist representation of interests in development policymaking or whether they merely signify a new symbolic politics that fits within the pluralist paradigm.

13   The Urban Development Action Grant (UDAG) program, adopted as part of the Housing and Community Development Act of 1977, is designed to increase jobs and tax revenues in distressed cities through the stimulation of private investment that would not have occurred "but for" the UDAG injection of public capital. This effort to stimulate economic development through private sector initiative and participation is an explicit policy statement that the public sector cannot and should not attempt urban economic development revitalization without significant private sector involvement in project design and implementation.

Urban development action grants are awarded by the U.S. Department of Housing and Urban Development (HUD) on a competitive basis among eligible cities. Cities qualify for participation in the action grant program by evidencing significant community development need as measured by the UDAG distress index, based on age of housing, poverty, unemployment, per capita income, and employment and population lag/decline. As of June 1982 more than 1,321 action grant projects in 429 cities had been approved by HUD, representing more than $2.2 billion in federal assistance. The sample used in this analysis includes 364 UDAG grant agreements approved during the first four years of the program (1978–81) for 100 cities with populations greater than 100,000. This represents 94 percent of the cities funded during this period. Analyses of the UDAG program are available in Rich (1982), Webman (1980), and the Urban Land Institute (1980).

14   In 1981 the Reagan administration removed the "reasonable balance" requirement, thus making neighborhood involvement less advantageous a factor in the funding process. Since these data report on grant agreements through 1981, the impacts of this change are not reflected in these data.

15   Diversification of local financial capital also may be a distinct influence on interest representation variations, although the data are not available to test this relationship. It is possible that the degree of competition among local financial institutions and the level and type of public debt may influence the extent to

which financial institutions seek more structure representation in the policy process. Other studies suggest that, to the extent that the capital market becomes more diversified with the entry of insurance companies, pension funds, and relaxed strictures on the activities of savings and loan companies and commercial banks, financial institutions may perceive gains from shifting from indirect, less-structured relationships to more institutionalized links with the public sector (see Moran 1982).

3 Restructuring and Growth Transitions of Metropolitan Economies

1   Between 1967 and 1972, for example, ninety-two SMSAS had boundary changes, and more than thirty new SMSAS were added. Boundary adjustments were most common for growing metropolitan areas when SMSA boundaries were expanded to incorporate new counties.

2   These data exclude state government employment, which is not reported by city. This rate of increase masks the even more rapid expansion of employment in local government, which nearly doubled over the decade—partly because of the influx of federal funds for public sector jobs under the now-abolished CETA program.

3   Inferences about the relative degree of centralization of various sectors must be made cautiously because data for some sectors are reported for central county rather than central city. As a result, table 3.3 overstates the central-city share of employment in transportation and communication, FIRE, construction, mining, and government. Cities with the most severe overestimation of central-city employment have been excluded from these tabulations, but some upward bias of the central-city share remains.

4   Sensitivity testing suggests that these broad findings concerning the relative dependence of central cities and suburbs on different economic sectors are relatively robust despite the use of central-county (rather than central-city) data in five sectors. Nevertheless, table 3.4 should be interpreted with care.

5   A description of the data used to estimate changes in employment by occupation is included in the appendix.

6   Following the standard Bureau of Labor Statistics reporting conventions for non-agricultural workers, white-collar workers include professional, technical, and kindred workers; nonfarm managers and administrators; sales workers; and clerical and kindred workers. Blue-collar workers include craftsmen and kindred workers, operatives, and nonfarm laborers. Service workers, described below, are reported separately.

7   The service *sector* is a broad industrial grouping that includes such categories as personal services, business services, health services, and repair services. Service *occupations* are job categories rather than industrial categories; examples of service occupations are waitress, hotel clerk, beautician, repairman, and dishwasher. All industrial sectors employ some service workers, but almost half of all persons pursuing service occupations are employed in the service industry, and sizable numbers also are employed in retailing and government.

8 Regions used are those defined by the U.S. Bureau of the Census. A list of SMSAS by region is included in the appendix.

4 Dynamics, Structural Change, and Economic Development Paths

1 Links between national policies for local economic development and development planning for local economies based on themes presented in this chapter can be found in Bergman and Goldstein 1983a.

2 The increase in direct foreign investment in the United States has occurred disproportionately in the southern manufacturing industries (see Glickman 1981; Hansen 1979).

3 The regression model used to estimate the indicators of local cyclical and growth behavior for each area is:

$$Y_t = \alpha + \beta_1 D_1 \, US_{t+m} + \beta_2 D_2 \, US_{t+m} + u$$
$$t = \text{January 1970 to December 1980}$$

where

Y_t is the local employment growth rate between t and t + 1;

US_t is the U.S. employment growth rate between t and t + 1;

$D_1 = 1$ if $US_{t+m} \geq 0$ (and) $D_2 = 1$ if $US_{t+m} > 0$

$\quad 0$ if $US_{t+m} < 0 \qquad\qquad 0$ if $US_{t+m} \geq 0$;

and m is the characteristic lead or lag or the local economy relative to the U.S. economy.

The value of m for each area was determined by first estimating the model for nine alternative values of m $(-6, -3, -2, -1, 0, +1, +2, +3, +6)$ and then selecting that value that produced the model with the largest R^2.

Employment figures are total nonagricultural monthly employment (wage and scale) from the U.S. Bureau of Labor Statistics, *Employment and Earnings*.

Both Y_t and US_t were calculated after transforming each monthly observation into a three-month moving average to help remove the effects of random and nonrecurring fluctuations.

The effects of serial correlation on the estimates of the regression coefficients and the R^2 were checked by recalibrating the models using a Hildreth-Lu transformation for a sample of areas with models having positive serial correlation. The estimates of the regression coefficients of the models with serial correlation removed did not differ significantly from the estimates of the original models nor did the ordinality of the model R^2s yielded by the nine candidate values of m.

An effect of splitting the independent variable into a positive and a negative component is nonnormal distributions of the disturbances (see Kmenta, 1971). While violation of the normality assumption prevents one from creating confidence intervals and testing hypotheses, it does not lead to biased estimates of the parameters.

There are two potential sources of bias of the parameter estimates. The first results from spurious correlation between the independent variable and the dependent variable since the latter is a subset of the former. The direction of this bias is always positive but is likely to be small because of the relative magnitudes of U.S. total employment level and any SMSA total employment levels. The second potential source is from misspecification of the model due to the omission of relevant independent variables. If the omitted variable(s) are correlated with the U.S. employment growth rate, then biased parameter estimates will result. *Local* causes of an area's employment growth rate should be independent of the U.S. employment growth rate if the small feedback is ignored. Other possible omitted explanatory variables that measure macrolevel investment and trade conditions, however, may be correlated with the U.S. employment growth rate (see Bergman and Goldstein forthcoming). Refinements in the specification of the model to remove potential sources of bias are the subject of continuing work by the authors.

4 Recent work by the present authors reveals the utility of carefully selecting a predefined set of economic variables that measure a local economy's performance, its industrial composition, and its relative productivity or production costs. Seven important structural characteristics emerged from the factor analysis that account for about 73 percent of the total variance in twenty-nine variables measured in the late 1970s for 202 metropolitan economies (Goldstein and Bergman 1983.)

5 Absolute values of less than one standard deviation occasionally offer evidence of substantial influence by a single factor if the majority of remaining factor scores group tightly around the mean of zero.

6 Full definitions and sources of these sixteen and another sixty variables are discussed in Goldstein and Bergman 1983a.

7 These and similar points are presented in Bergman and Goldstein 1983a.

8 Systematic methods of inquiry and conjecture about prospective, preferred futures are reviewed by Hirschhorn (1980), while development paths open to metropolitan economies are reviewed by Knight (1982) and Shostak (1982).

9 For example, methods for forecasting industry employment at detailed SIC levels in metropolitan economies can be markedly improved by taking account of such dynamics (Goldstein and Bergman 1983).

10 In fact, the number of factor scores per area that exceed 0.5 standard deviations is *inversely correlated* with the R^2 of an area's cyclical model (-0.24 rank order correlation coefficient at 0.02 probability). This inverse correlation is interpreted to mean that for some metropolitan areas one has either conformant cyclical evidence or structural change evidence, but not both.

11 The type of analysis and findings presented in the appendix to this chapter should be refined further and kept current by some national agency or organization with a mandate to support local economic development planning.

5 Cyclical Startups and Closures in Key Industries of America's Cities and Suburbs

1 Includes all establishments in Standard Industrial Codes 354, 367, and 371.

2 For a detailed discussion of the creation of this data set, see Howland 1982. For a discussion of the birth adjustment see Howland 1983.

3 Suburban migration figures include all moves in and out of suburbs from central cities and nonmetropolitan areas. Central-city migration figures include all moves in and out of central cities from suburbs and nonmetropolitan areas.

6 High-Technology Sectors and Local Economic Development

1 Definitions of high-technology sectors can be either more or less restrictive and can be based on as many as eighteen screening variables (Battelle–Columbus Laboratories 1982). The U.S. Bureau of Labor Statistics, which identifies thirty-six of 977 industries as high-tech, based on R&D and technical employment twice the U.S. average, is standardizing the definition to some degree. An additional fifty-six industries are "high-tech intensive" because both their R&D spending and technical employment are above the national average (*Business Week* 1983; see also Riche, Hecker, and Burgan 1983).

2 Hanson (1982) vividly points out that the semiconductor industry, one of the most clearly high-technology sectors and one on which other such sectors rely, paradoxically depends on the very manual routine production activity of assembling circuit boards. That work is done either in labor-intensive plants, attracted to low-wage locations, or in highly automated factories that employ few people (Ferguson 1983).

3 The difference between growth and development has rarely been of interest to industrial developers, whose concern has been with growth. The often qualitative side effects of growth are increasingly emphasized in recent research on development (Stöhr 1982).

4 These are (in order): Maryland, Alaska, the District of Columbia, Massachusetts, Utah, Hawaii, Rhode Island, Connecticut, New Mexico, Washington, Vermont, California, Colorado, New York, Wisconsin, North Carolina, and Wyoming (Malecki 1983b).

5 The temptation to use this fund to subsidize restaurants, retail shops, and branch manufacturing plants would have to be resisted to have the full effect.

7 Advanced Services in the System of Cities

1 This classification has its own shortcomings. They are discussed in Noyelle and Stanback (1983). In good part they stem from limitations on the kind of aggregations that can be performed with conventional government data.

2 Findings in the following paragraphs come from Noyelle and Stanback (1983) unless otherwise noted.

3 The 1,150 largest corporations include Fortune's thousand largest industrial firms, fifty largest utilities, fifty largest retailing organizations, and fifty largest transportation companies (Noyelle and Stanback 1983).

4 Based on a count of the location of the head offices of the 11,000 or so industrial divisions of the Fortune's 500 largest industrial firms, fifty largest utilities, fifty largest retailing organizations, and fifty largest transportation companies (Noyelle and Stanback 1983).

5 Based on a sample of Fortune firms (Noyelle and Stanback 1983).

6 The functional nodal centers are host to about twenty percent of the national headquarters of the 1,150 largest corporations (as defined in note 3) and a slightly lesser share of divisional head offices of the largest firms (as defined in note 4).

7 The U.S. Bureau of Labor Statistics' most recent data (March 1983) indicate some of the nation's highest unemployment rates in many of the mining industrial centers.

8 Findings in the following paragraphs are from Noyelle and Stanback (1983) unless otherwise indicated.

9 Brevity being in order, I do not deal here explicitly with the small group of consumer-oriented centers. For many of them, however, problems of transition are not unlike those of the production centers (Noyelle and Stanback 1983).

8 Establishing High-Technology Enterprises in Metropolitan Areas

1 The data base used for this analysis is described in Odle and Armington 1983.

2 Industries were classified as high technology if they met *either* of two criteria: (1) more than 8 percent of jobs in scientific, engineering, and technical occupations *and* at least 5 percent in the scientific and engineering class (Greene, Harrington, and Vinson 1983); or (2) a high ratio of direct and indirect expenditures on research and development to total product sales (Davis 1982).

3 This estimate was taken from Riche et al. (1983, 54), which considered several alternative definitions of "high technology." The references here and elsewhere in this chapter are to "Definition 3," which most closely approximates our definition.

4 These formations of affiliates of existing high-technology firms include acquisitions of previously independent firms and of branches of other multiestablishment firms. The available data did not permit distinguishing these changes in ownership.

5 Factors identified in the JEC study were subjectively selected by hi-tech managers. The results of the survey do not always coincide with empirical evidence of factors associated with new business activity.

6 Although the number of SMSAS was used as the sample size for statistical purposes, the number of formations is a more accurate indicator of the number of observations. For the thirty-five SMSAS there were 13,035 high-technology establishment formations, slightly more than one-third of the U.S. total.

7 Both net changes in the number of establishments and the rate of gross formations were highly correlated with changes in the number of employees and the employment growth rate in all industrial categories.

8 In fact, in most versions of the equations tested the agglomeration measure was stronger and more significant in the standard linear form of the equation, while the labor quality indicator was stronger and more significant in the multiplicative form of the equation. Other results using the multiplicative form were generally similar but somewhat weaker than the additive equations.

9 Using a similar conceptual and methodological framework, Dennis Carlton of the University of Chicago conducted an analysis of independent and branch formations for a limited set of industries (only three four-digit SICS) and a differ-

ent set of independent measures (Carlton 1983).

10   Using ordinary least-squares regression, a simple linear relationship was used rather than a multiplicative form. Although we are measuring change, there is only a single measure compared over a cross section of metropolitan areas.

11   These findings are almost identical to their counterparts in Carlton's study (Carlton 1983) of new firm and branch locations, except the wage factor was significant for both types of formations in his study.

12   Data disaggregated for branches and independents were not available for the non-high-technology sector, so "all formations" were used for this comparison.

13   It is difficult to differentiate the sequence of events, i.e., does industry locate near concentrations of skilled workers or do such workers migrate to concentrations of these industries. Clearly, both types of movement occur.

14   Those very concentrations may result from the presence of other characteristics to which businesses respond but which analysts do not understand.

9   City Venture Corporation: Initiatives in U.S. Cities

1   Unless people gave permission, or the statement has already been published elsewhere with a personal reference, the names of people interviewed are not disclosed. Throughout this chapter, quotes from the study interviews are not referenced, nor are data from field notes and observations. Quotes from other sources are referenced.

2   The original partners are the American Lutheran Church, Benton Corporation, Bertrand Goldberg Associates, Control Data Corporation, Dayton Hudson Corporation, First Bank System, Inc., Honeywell, Inc., Kraus-Anderson, Inc., Minneapolis Star and Tribune Company, Medtronics, Inc., Northwest Bancorporation, Piper Jaffray Hopwood, Inc., Reynolds Metal Corporation, The St. Paul Companies, and the United Church of Christ. The Benton Corporation, Honeywell, and The St. Paul Companies have withdrawn.

3   Herbert Trader (vice president of Control Data Corporation), presentation at the workshop, "City Venture: Creating Partnerships in a Holistic Approach to Job Creation," at the National Training and Information Center conference "Jobs in the '80s—Problems—Priorities—Possibilities" (Chicago, 29 April 1982).

4   City Venture Corporation, "City Venture Corporation," (Minneapolis, 3 May 1979).

5   Herbert Trader, "City Venture Corporation," *Congressional Record*, (26 March 1981).

6   City Venture Corporation, brochure "City Venture Corporation," (November 1981), p. 9.

7   Ibid.

8   City Venture Corporation, "City Venture Corporation," mimeo (3 May 1979), p. 3; see also, Control Data Corporation, "Control Data Business and Technology Center—A New Concept on Space Support Services for Small Businesses," (November 1981).

9   Detailed descriptions of PLATO and Fair Break are contained in Control Data's proposals for Fair Break (e.g., "Proposal for a Fair Break Program," submitted to the South Florida Employment and Training Consortium, 14 August 1980).

10 "Minnesota Cooperation Office—Fostering Job Creation by Helping to Create Innovative Businesses in Minnesota" (undated brochure).

11 "Minnesota Seed Capital Funds, Inc.—Investment Guidelines and Procedures" (undated brochure).

12 For an analysis of the St. Paul Bindery, see Bendick and Egan (1982).

13 City Venture and Control Data officials opposed this study. Thus, interviews with some of the executives in the central offices were not possible.

14 "A Statement by the Urban East Area Coalition to the City Council," mimeo, sent to the City Council of Minneapolis (6 June 1980); Concerned Citizens for Liberty City Revitalization, "Position Statement—An Assessment and Appraisal of City Venture Proposal for Revitalization of the Liberty City Community, Miami, Florida," mimeo, presented to the Private Industry Council of Dade County (28 March 1981); and Concerned Citizens for Revitalization, "An Alternative Planning Process for the Development of a Revitalization Plan for the Liberty City Area," mimeo (2 May 1981).

15 Letter from Walter H. Bruning, Control Data Corporation, to Marvin Gilmore, Jr., Community Development Corporation of Boston (9 March 1981).

16 This change was clear in the sets of interviews conducted in Baltimore over an eighteen-month period.

17 All figures are from city development agencies.

18 "Proposed Project Budget," attached to a memorandum from David Garcia, office of the city manager, to the city council of San Antonio (15 April 1982), and "Exhibit B," attached to "Contract for Professional Services by and between City of Philadelphia and City Venture Corporation" (1 July 1981).

19 The binderies in Benton Harbor and Toledo were started by Control Data but are independently owned.

20 See University City Science Center, *The Science Center* (Philadelphia, no date), and Rensselaer Polytechnic Institute, *Incubator Program Giving Life to New Ideas* (Troy, NY, no date). The three industrial incubators supplied no brochures, but the Industrial Council of Northwest Chicago, which developed the Fulton-Carroll Center, publishes the *Chicago Industrial Bulletin* bimonthly.

21 The Rensselaer project and the Science Center had specific job creation estimates but only general estimates of the skill levels for these jobs.

22 City Venture Corporation, *Jobs for Park Heights—A Program for Economic Revitalization* (March 1981), p. 72.

23 Minnesota Cooperation Office interviews and note 9, above.

24 The Fulton-Carroll incubator had detailed job creation records, but the other incubators had only general estimates. All estimates of job skill levels were general.

25 "Contract for Professional Services by and between the City of Philadelphia and City Venture Corporation" (15 October 1979), attachment 1, p. 30.

26 The City Venture UDAG application was tabled at the 22 September 1980 meeting of the Community Development Committee of the Minneapolis City Council. Research staff attended the later UDAG planning meetings that resulted in City Venture deciding to withdraw.

27 The City Venture contract ended on 30 September 1982. City Venture withdrew

in January 1983.

28 Interviews, contracts, and internal memoranda from the South Florida Employment and Training Program and the Private Industry Council of Dade County, Inc.

29 Contract, note 25, above, and contract, "The City of Philadelphia and City Venture Corporation," (1 August 1980); contract note 18, above, and "Control Amendment–City Venture Corporation," (1 July 1982).

30 City Venture Corporation, *Urban East, Minneapolis, Project Management Plan* (1 March 1980), p. 246.

31 "Community Development Block Grant Professional Services Agreement between the City of San Antonio and City Venture Corporation" (May 1982); and "Memorandum of Understanding," between the City of San Antonio, Vanir Properties, and Control Data Corporation (1 November 1979).

32 See City Venture Corporation, "A Proposal for Preparation and Initial Implementation of a Job Creation and Community Revitalization Strategy for Liberty City" (January 1981), p. 36.

10 Enterprise Activities of Not-for-Profit Organizations

1 For examples other than those presented here, as well as general discussions, see Williams (1982); Skloot (1983, 1985); Neighborhood Development Collective (1982); Cagnon (1982); Wilson (1982); Crimmins and Keil (1983).

2 A corresponding expression of planned community self-sufficiency is the seminal work on Harlem by Thomas Vietorisz and Bennett Harrison (1970).

3 Saul Alinsky, the prototypical neighborhood activist, was a vocal proponent for the preservation of traditional institutions such as the church, schools, and family.

4 For example, see the series of studies on the roles of mediating institutions sponsored by the American Enterprise Institute, beginning with Berger and Neuhaus (1977). For a clear expression of the symbiotic antiplanning sentiment, see The White House (1982). For similar observations on an international scale, see Ward (1982).

5 See, for instance, Savas (1982) and Mier (1982b).

6 The Center, a unit of the School of Urban Planning and Policy, provides technical assistance to neighborhood organizations engaged in economic development efforts. Information on the efforts and experiences of UICUED is available on request.

7 See Molotch (1972), for an analysis of the racial transition in South Shore. Giloth (1981) presents data regarding the disinvestment strategies used in South Shore.

8 These seventeen include the Chicago cases; the others were excluded from this analysis partly because they were known to be reasonably successful. The reader must remember that these cases were not chosen to constitute a statistically representative sample.

9 These issues are discussed in detail in Wiewel et al. (1982).

10 The choice of the expression "nurturing period" is an attempt to distinguish the community organization business start-up process. It is well known that it takes most small businesses three or more years to become profitable. The nurturing

period is perceived as preceding and only partially overlapping with the business growth period.

11 Local Economic Development and Job Targeting

1. For an introduction to these issues, see Beauregard and Holcomb (1983), Bingham and Blair (1984), Harrison and Kanter (1978), Schwartz (1979), and Vaughn and Bearse (1981).

2. See, for example, U.S. Department of Housing and Urban Development (1976) and U.S. Department of Housing and Urban Development (1980).

3. Rutgers University was awarded an evaluation contract to assess TJDP's progress and to disseminate useful information after the demonstration period. The assessment was designed to measure and explain comparative performance on the demonstration's central goals: (1) obtaining jobs for economically disadvantaged people from economic development projects; (2) capturing spin-off business opportunities for small, women's, and minority businesses; and, (3) improving the coordination of employment and training programs with economic development programs to achieve the first two objectives.

   The Rutgers evaluation team prepared two major reports: *An Evaluation of the Targeted Jobs Demonstration Program*, which discusses the demonstration in detail and *Economic Development Projects and Jobs*, which is a technical assistance guide for local practitioners. Case studies also were prepared on all fourteen communities. All of these reports are available from the authors at the Eagleton Institute of Politics, Rutgers University, New Brunswick, NJ 08901.

   The description, explanation, and assessment of TJDP are based on a sizable data base assembled through three waves of field research visits, information submitted by the demonstration sites, and data on comparable projects in other communities. The primary source of information on TJDP consists of a large number of structured interviews conducted by Rutgers staff with people involved in and knowledgeable about TJDP, previous related efforts, and employment and training and economic development projects in general. Overall, 457 people were interviewed—some of them several times. Those interviewed included TJDP staff, elected officials, staff from Private Industry Councils and CETA organizations, small and minority business development groups, economic and community development groups, and planning agencies. Interviews also were held with fifty-five employers, and a structured survey was conducted with eighty-one private employers.

4. TJDP was funded and overseen by six federal agencies—the U.S. Departments of Housing and Urban Development (as the lead agency), Labor, Transportation, Commerce (Economic Development Administration), Small Business Administration, and the now-defunct Community Services Administration. The TJDP sites were Buffalo (NY), Genesee County (MI), Lynn (MA), Metcalfe (MS), Milwaukee (WI), Montanawide, New York City, Paterson (NJ), Philadelphia (PA), Portland (ME), Portland (OR), San Antonio (TX), Seattle (WA), and Wilmington (DE).

5. See The President's Interagency Coordinating Council, Employment Initiatives, processed April 1979.

6 The data for our assessment of job targeting comes from four sources: interviews with TJDP staff and local professionals in employment and training and economic development agencies; Quarterly Jobs Reports submitted by the grantees; interviews and structured surveys with 136 employers who had either hired or agreed to hire through the TJDP agency or who had received economic development aid; and data from the Urban Development Action Grant program. Unfortunately, there was no systematic evidence on the characteristics of people hired under federally assisted economic development projects in the fourteen communities prior to or during TJDP. To judge whether TJDP made a difference in the hiring of economically disadvantaged people, we shall rely on the reports of the TJDP staff and the responses of the employers we interviewed.

7 This "ideal" job targeting strategy was developed toward the end of the evaluation project after the major analysis of the strengths and weaknesses of the fourteen different approaches had been completed.

8 The legal status of job targeting policies was supported by the U.S. Supreme Court in *White* vs. *Massachusetts Council* (No. 81–1003). The Court ruled by a vote of 7–2 that Mayor Kevin White's executive order requiring construction companies conducting public works projects to fill at least half the jobs with Boston residents was not an unconstitutional burden on interstate commerce. However, this clarification of Court policy did not occur until after the demonstration was over. A Supreme Court decision in February 1984, however, ruled that resident quota plans may run afoul of the Constitution. At issue was the Privileges and Immunities clause and an ordinance developed by the government of Camden, New Jersey, to require private contractors to hire city residents for at least 40 percent of their jobs on projects costing more than $50,000.

9 In evaluating the quality of job placements, one also must be sensitive to the growth sectors of urban economies. For an overview, see Robyn Swaim Philips and Avis C. Vidal (1983).

12 Urban Growth, Subemployment, and Mobility

1 See bibliography on segmented labor market framework in Salinas and Rossi (1981). See also a more recent literature review in Cooke (1983, 207–28).

2 See, for example, the report of the President's Commission for a National Agenda for the Eighties.

3 Such a threshold was proposed for the EDA reauthorization legisiation in 1979.

4 See Locke Anderson, "Trickling Down: The Relationship between Economic Growth and the Extent of Poverty among American Families," *Quarterly Journal of Economics* 78, no. 4 (1964): 511–24.

5 For example, in their two-sector model of migration and urban employment, Harris and Todaro (1970) posit that urban industrial employment growth attracts somewhat more migrants than there are jobs to fill, thus increasing the absolute level of urban unemployment.

6 There is a growing literature that analyzes the industrial restructuring accompanying the new international division of labor. See, for example, Hopkins and Wallerstein 1982; Frobel, Heinrichs, and Kreye 1980; and Makler, Martinelli, and

Smelser 1982. Some of the literature has examined the implications for urbanization in the United States (e.g., Noyelle 1983; Cohen 1982).

7 While first quarter earnings were available, yearly earnings were used in order to capture seasonal and other part-year workers.

8 One of the limitations of the CWHS data is occasional faulty reporting of employee location by multiestablishment firms, which produces spurious migration flows.

9 Current Population Surveys have estimated the proportion of involuntary part-time workers to be small: 12 to 15 percent of all part-time workers for 1968 through 1972 (Klein 1975, 5) and just under 20 percent in 1974. Nevertheless, even a direct question to the informant may not result in a correct answer. A housewife may not want to work more than twenty hours a week at a fast food restaurant but would gladly work full-time at a better-paying job with some prospect of upward mobility. Yet it would be logical for her to answer that she is voluntarily working part-time at her present job.

10 Current Population Surveys show that only 13.4 percent of all workers who earned less than $3,000 in 1963 were supporting a family (Cummins 1965, 829). Similarly only a fraction of the subemployed as defined here would actually be family heads, and even a smaller proportion would be heads of four-member households.

11 An important limitation to using a nationwide earnings cutoff for defining the subemployed is that regional cost-of-living differences are ignored. However, adequate data are not available to construct an accurate regional cost-of-living index with the fifty-three metropolitan areas used in this study. The Bureau of Labor Statistics publishes yearly average "lower budgets" for families of four for forty metropolitan areas in the United States; only seventeen of them are among the fifty-three metropolitan areas in the study sample—seven in the Sunbelt and ten in the Frostbelt. Nevertheless, a weighted average of these seventeen cities was used to estimate the relative cost-of-living in each of the two regions. When compared with a U.S. metropolitan price level of 100.0, the aggregate price index was 92.2 for the Sunbelt and 100.9 for the Frostbelt. The impact of this cost-of-living difference on the percentage of subemployed in Sunbelt cities was found to be small: about 3 percent (see detailed analysis in Salinas 1980, 90–93).

12 In fact, however, Harrison and Hill (1978, 9) found a high correlation by industry between wage level and hours worked that was stable over a broad range of cities and regions in the United States. Thus, there is support for using an hourly wage cutoff alone.

13 Subemployment for each year was defined in terms of 1.25 times the official poverty level for the year in question (thus accounting for inflation). Workers with zero earnings for one year but positive earnings below 1.25 times the poverty level in both the previous and following years were considered continuously subemployed for all three years. (This phenomenon was particularly widespread in the years 1970–72 when a high proportion of the subemployed reported zero earnings during the recession peak of 1971.) A person need be subemployed only in 1974 to be in the total sample. However, to be considered long-term subemployed, it is a necessary condition to have had some earnings in 1970 as well. Those subemployed in 1974 who were in the military in any previous year

were considered not in the labor force for that year and therefore could not be counted as continuously subemployed for that year.

14   $.52 - .16(46.4) = 7.4$ for four years, or 1.7 for one year (using compound interest tables).

15   The variance, s^2, for the subemployment rate is 40.0.

16   $.39 \times 1.0 = .39$ over four years.

17   Curiously, of those who moved within the same region, only those in the South/Southwest improved their probability of upward mobility. This fact may reflect continuing southern rural-urban migration rather than intermetropolitan migration. This interpretation would be consistent with the relatively high proportion of blacks making intraregional moves in the South and Southwest, as reported in figure 10 of Salinas (1980).

18   The author thanks Bennett Harrison for his editorial assistance in this section.

19   It could be argued that the earnings mobility of subemployed migrants is understated by concentrating on first-year earnings in the growing SMSA. There may be a lag effect in which the earnings mobility potential is not realized for several years after the move. However, it seems likely that the longer the waiting period, the more the migrant subemployed becomes indistinguishable from the resident subemployed until the probability of the migrants' upward mobility becomes equal to that of the residents. Since the probability of mobility is not greater for residents of growing—compared to lagging—places, there would still be no advantage to relocating.

20   The literature on labor force underutilization differentiates between subemployment and underemployment. The underemployed are those working below their skill potential, regardless of income. Many middle- and upper-income people are underemployed. The subemployed are those members of the work force who hold the economy's marginal jobs or no job at all, regardless of their skill level. The subemployed are all low-income people. While legislative phraseology often refers alliteratively to "unemployment and underemployment," it is assumed here that the priority concern is with low-income workers, and therefore subemployment.

21   The following two arguments sometimes used to support nonintervention will not be addressed here. (1) Subemployment simply reflects an individual's productivity. Since there will always be some workers with low productivity and correspondingly low wages, public sector intervention is useless. Numerous empirical studies, however, have shown an imperfect correlation between marginal productivity and wages, indicating the presence of labor market barriers— e.g., race and gender discrimination—that prevent some people from earning what their potential marginal productivity would allow. Other studies show that the rate of return on human capital—e.g., education and training—also varies by gender and race, thus indicating imperfections in the labor market. (2) Subemployment is primarily voluntary—it permits additional options to the traditional forty-hour work week—and therefore should not be interfered with by the public sector. I would argue, however, that while subemployment is voluntarily chosen over unemployment by many, it is opted for in place of full employment by a minority. Nevertheless, as I point out in the text, not all urban subemployment is a public policy problem—principally just that of the inner-city underclass.

22 For example, Chiswick (1974), although an advocate of the human capital school, shows empirically that the return on investment in education and experience is less for black males than for white males. Chiswick also alludes to a segmented labor market model when hypothesizing regional differences in income inequality: "Income inequality is greater in the Southern states than in the non-South, due partly to (a) greater inequality of schooling, but mainly to (b) a higher rate of return from schooling stemming from the existence of a national labor market for highly educated workers in contrast to the preponderance of local labor markets for those with little schooling (p. 8)."

23 Kasarda (1983) agrees with the structural analysts that the current growth sectors —mainly white-collar services—do not provide sufficient employment opportunities for disadvantaged center-city workers. He cites the case of New York City, where net employment growth has left greater minority employment rates (p. 23). However, for Kasarda the problem appears to be one of *quantity* of employment growth (not the structure of employment growth) and the quality of the *workers* (not the quality or accessibility of the jobs). He advocates a combination of macroeconomic stimulus to create more jobs and retraining to provide disadvantaged workers the skills necessary to get the new jobs. Kasarda also advocates migration assistance to match center-city workers with appropriate job opportunities in growing suburban and nonmetropolitan areas. "Subsidized anchoring" in center cities—i.e., place-specific programs such as community development and welfare that create disincentives to migrate—should also be reduced, he argues. Kasarda does not treat the issues of the disadvantaged migrant's access to jobs once in the destination community, the type of jobs available there, nor whether place-specific government subsidies outweigh other motives for anchoring (e.g., territorial-based networks of mutual assistance).

24 Attempts to link labor supply with labor demand approaches—e.g., first sourcing —have been isolated and often frustrated by lack of monitoring and enforcement mechanisms. It is easy for an incoming employer to agree to hire 10 percent of his workers from local CETA eligible lists, but it is another thing to make sure he does it once he has moved in. Public sector employment (PSE) also links employer with employees, but besides the fact that the political climate makes such a strategy infeasible on a large scale, it is unclear how prepared PSE jobholders are for getting productive private sector jobs after leaving the program.

13 Labor Mobility in National Policy and Local Economies

1 Analysis of the urban impacts of the Reagan administration's budget and tax policies is provided in Kaplan, James, and Phillips (1981); Joint Economic Committee (1984); and in Palmer and Sawhill (1984).

2 Urban policy is implemented in the United States by a political system structured around places. The representatives or governments of places can seldom be expected to foster population decline in their states or communities because such declines would threaten their political power. Mobility programs aimed at poor people or minorities have the additional political handicap of opposition from potential destination places. These political realities have extra power in

the United States because national urban programs have generally been implemented by lower-level governments in a partnership created by intergovernmental aid.

3   Some European countries, notably Sweden, have implemented mobility programs (see Sundquist 1975). However, these programs have yet to be evaluated with enough care to determine their implications for U.S. policy.

4   The Current Population Survey places severe constraints on research on these issues. In particular, geographic details on the residence places of people in the survey are very limited. In most cases, for instance, Levy was forced to use descriptors of the strength of state economies in his analysis rather than the characteristics of metropolitan areas. Metropolitan areas are more relevant for labor market analyses.

5   Working-age persons are persons eighteen- to sixty-five years old, excluding students, retired persons, and farmers.

6   In the simulations, estimates of the expected economic achievements of migrants in their place of origin use statistical relationships between achievement and community economic conditions estimated by Levy for all working-age persons in the Current Population Survey. Simulations of expected achievement in the destination place are based on statistical analyses of the achievement of interregional migrants. Measures of the strength of state economies were selected on the basis of research by Goldberg (1981).

7   To repeat, Levy was forced to relate state economic conditions to the achievements of residents of particular metropolitan areas. This constraint biases Levy's estimates of the returns to migration downward and increases the standard errors of his estimates.

8   Specifically, Levy (1977) related the probability of impoverishment in 1968 to the levels of earnings and nonlabor income received by the person in 1967, to the earnings to be expected by the person in 1968 based upon a variety of characteristics of the person, and to the level of unemployment in the county in which the person lived.

9   This study examined the performance of seventeen CETA prime sponsors in Ohio and an additional fifteen prime sponsors elsewhere in the nation.

10   The study concluded that CETA staff do not live in a universe tightly determined by the unemployment rate. Poor program performance cannot be explained by simply referring to a high unemployment rate. Even in the face of high unemployment, there is much that can be done by a staff that can result in good performance (Ripley 1978, 84).

11   Mitchell (1980) examined the determinants of job retention rates for WIN registrants, job entry wage rates, and job entry or placement rates achieved per WIN staff member. Stepwise regression techniques were used to relate a wide range of explanatory variables of these measures of program success, so the results are difficult to interpret. However, higher local unemployment rates were found to depress job retention rates. Higher rates of employment growth were found to boost job entry wage rates of enrollees.

12   Eligibility for AFDC payments is a major determinant of eligibility for Medicaid, and the scope of Medicaid benefits varies significantly among states. The discus-

sion of the impacts of AFDC on mobility also provides useful insight into the mobility disincentives of Medicaid.

13   There is mixed evidence that differences in benefit levels encouraged relocation during the 1950s and 1960s for the purpose of qualifying for welfare benefits. For an analysis of the effects of welfare programs on mobility in the 1960s, see Glantz (1973).

14   The unit must, however, rent at or below "fair market rent" set by HUD and meet certain minimal quality standards. Mobility among jurisdictions within a metropolitan area is allowed in the Section 8 Existing Program only if interjurisdictional agreements are in effect (but even in this case movement outside a metropolitan area will result in a loss of benefits).

15   Technically, moving costs associated with a job change are an adjustment to gross income and can be claimed without itemizing deductions. The Internal Revenue Service (IRS) determines that a move is related to a job change when the job change would have increased the commuting distance of the job holder by at least thirty-five miles in the absence of a change in residence. IRS rules have the effect of limiting the deduction to persons moving relatively long distances.

16   As outlined by the administration, the voucher program would not necessarily make benefit levels portable, however. The administration has called for the voucher program to be run by the same local housing authorities that run the Section 8 existing program (The Report 1982).

References

Abernathy, W. J., and Utterback, J. M. 1978. "Patterns of Industrial Innovation." *Technology Review* 80, 7: 40–47.

Abramovitz, Moses. 1972. "Manpower, Capital and Technology." In *Human Resources and Economic Welfare, Essays in Honor of Eli Ginzberg.* Edited by Ivar Berg. New York: Columbia University Press.

Abt Associates. 1973. *An Evaluation of the Special Impact Program: Phase II Report.* Cambridge, MA: Abt Associates.

Advisory Commission on Intergovernmental Relations. 1978. *Countercyclical Aid and Economic Stabilization.* Washington, DC: USGPO, December.

———. 1979. *Citizen Participation in the American Federal System.* Washington, DC: USGPO.

Ahlbrandt, Jr., Roger S. 1984. "Ideology and the Reagan Administration's First National Urban Policy Report." *Journal of the American Planning Association* 50, 4: 479–84.

———, and Sumka, Howard. 1983. "Neighborhood Organizations and the Coproduction of Public Services." *Journal of Urban Affairs* 5: 211–20.

Allen, Kevin. 1978. *Balanced National Growth.* Lexington, MA: D. C. Heath.

Alford, Robert R. 1972. "Critical Evaluation of the Principles of City Classification." In *City Classification Handbook: Methods and Applications.* Edited by Brian J. L. Berry. New York: Wiley-Interscience.

Almond, Gabriel. 1983. "Corporatism, Pluralism, and Professional Memory." *World Politics* 35, 1: 245–60.

Anderson, Charles W. 1979. "Political Design and the Representation of Interests." In *Trends Toward Corporatist Intermediation.* Edited by Phillipe C. Schmitter and Gerhard Lehmbruch. Beverly Hills: Sage Publications.

Andrisani, Paul James. 1973. "An Empirical Analysis of the Dual Labor Market Theory." Unpublished Ph.D. dissertation, Ohio State University, Center for Human Resource Research.

Armington, Catherine, and Odle, Marjorie. 1982. "Small Business—How Many Jobs?" *The Brookings Review* 1, 2 (Winter): 14–17.

———, Harris, Candee S., and Odle, Marjorie. 1983. *Formation and Growth of High Technology Establishments: A Regional Assessment.* Final Report to National Science Foundation, Grant No. ISI 82-12970.

Armstrong, R., et al. 1972. *The Office Industry: Patterns of Growth and Location.* Cambridge, MA: MIT Press.

Aronson, Leanne, and Shapiro, Carol. 1981. *State's Role in Urban Economic Development: An Urban Government Perspective.* Washington, DC: U.S. Department of Commerce.

Auletta, Ken. 1980. *The Streets Were Paved with Gold.* New York: Random House.

Bahl, Roy. 1980. *The Impact of Local Tax Policy on Urban Economic Development.* Urban Consortium Information Bulletin. Washington, DC: U.S. Department of Commerce.

Banschick, K. 1982. "High Tech Fever Grabs States, Cities." *High Technology* 2, 2: 18–20.

Barnet, Richard J. 1980. *The Lean Years: Politics in the Age of Austerity.* New York: Simon and Schuster.

———, and Muller, Ronald. 1974. *Global Reach: The Power of the Multinational Corporations.* New York: Simon and Schuster.

Bart, Polly. 1979. *Labor Mobility.* Washington, DC: U.S. Department of Housing and Urban Development.

Bartel, Ann P. 1979. "The Migration Decision: What Role Does Job Mobility Play?" *American Economic Review,* 69, 5: 775–86.

Bates, Thomas, and Osborne, A. E., Jr. 1979. "The Perverse Effects of SBA Loans to Minority Wholesalers." *Urban Affairs Quarterly* 15: 87–98.

Battelle-Columbus Laboratories. 1982. *Development of High Technology Industries in New York State.* Final summary report prepared for the New York State Science and Technology Foundation. Albany: New York State Science and Technology Foundation.

Baumer, Donald, and Van Horn, Carl E. 1985. *The Politics of Unemployment.* Washington, DC: Congressional Quarterly Press.

Beauregard, Robert A., and Holcomb, Briavel. 1983. "Enterprise Zones: The Non-Manipulation of Economic Space." *Urban Geography* 4, 3: 223–43.

Bell, Daniel. 1976. *The Coming of Post-Industrial Society.* New York: Basic Books.

Bell, Michael E., and Lande, Paul S. 1982. *Regional Dimensions of Industrial Policy.* Lexington, MA: D. C. Heath.

Bendick, Marc, Jr., and Egan, Mary Lou. 1982. "Providing Industrial Jobs in the Inner City." *Business* (Atlanta) 32, 1: 2–9.

Berg, Ivar, ed. 1981. *Sociological Perspectives on Labor Markets.* New York: Academic Press.

Berger, Peter L., and Neuhaus, Richard John. 1977. *To Empower People.* Washington, DC: The American Enterprise Institute for Public Policy Research.

Berger, Renee, Moy, Kirsten S., Peirce, Neal R., and Steinbach, Carol. 1982. *Investing in America.* Washington, D.C.: The President's Task Force on Private Sector Initiatives.

Berger, Suzanne, ed. 1981. *Organizing Interests in Western Europe.* Cambridge: Cambridge University Press.

Bergman, Edward M. 1980. "Local Economic Development Planning in an Age of Capital Mobility." *Carolina Planning* 7, 2: 29–37.

Bergman, Edward M. Forthcoming. *Economic Development Planning: Practices, Exper-*

tise and Influence. Lexington, MA: Lexington Books.

Bergman, Edward, and Goldstein, Harvey. 1983a. "Dynamics and Structural Change in Metropolitan Economies." *Journal of the American Planning Association* 49, 3: 263–79. Reprinted and edited in this volume as chapter 4.

———. 1983b. "Local Planning and the National Development Investment Act." In U.S. House of Representatives, Subcommittee on Economic Stabilization of the Committee on Banking, Finance, and Urban Affairs. *Hearings* on HR 10, 98th Congress, April 11.

———. Forthcoming. "Cycles and Shares in U.S. Subnational Economics: Portents for Industrial Policy." In *Economic Restructuring and the Territorial Community*. Edited by Walter B. Stohr et al. Vienna: UNIDO.

Bergsman, Joel. 1971. "Alternatives to the Nongilded Ghetto." *Public Policy* 19, 2: 275–87.

Berndt, Harry Edward. 1977. *New Rulers in the Ghetto: The CDC and Urban Poverty*. Westport, CT: Greenwood Press.

Berry, Brian J. L., ed. 1972. *City Classification Handbook: Methods and Applications*. New York: Wiley-Interscience.

———. 1973. *Growth Centers in the American Urban System*. 2 vols. Cambridge, MA: Ballinger.

Bingham, Richard D., and Blair, John P. 1984. *Urban Economic Development*. Beverly Hills: Sage Publications.

Birch, David. 1979. *The Job Creation Process*. Report to the U.S. Department of Commerce. Washington, DC: USGPO.

———. 1981. "Who Creates Jobs?" *Public Interest* 15, 4 (Fall): 3–14.

Birnbaum, Pierre. 1982. "The State Versus Corporatism." *Politics and Society* 11: 477–501.

Black, Cyril E., and Burke, John P. 1983. "Organizational Participation and Public Policy." *World Politics* 35: 393–425.

Black, J. Thomas. 1980. "The Changing Economic Role of Central Cities and Suburbs." In *The Prospective City*. Edited by Arthur P. Solomon. Cambridge, MA: MIT Press.

Block, Fred L. 1977. *The Origins of International Economic Disorder*. Berkeley: University of California Press.

Bluestone, Barry, and Harrison, Bennett. 1982. *The Deindustrialization of America*. New York: Basic Books.

Bluestone, Barry, Murphy, W., and Stevenson, M. 1973. *Low Wages and the Working Poor*. Policy Papers in Human Resources and Industrial Relocations 22. Ann Arbor, MI: The Institute of Labor and Industrial Relations, University of Michigan and Wayne State University.

Blumberg, Phillip I. 1975. *The Megacorporation in American Society*. Englewood Cliffs, NJ: Prentice-Hall.

Bodner, John, Simon, Roger, and Weber, Michael P. 1982. *Lives of Their Own: Blacks, Italians, and Poles in Pittsburgh, 1900–1960*. Chicago: University of Illinois Press.

Bollinger, L., Hope, K., and Utterback, J. M. 1983. "A Review of Literature and Hypotheses on New Technology Based Firms." *Research Policy* 12, 1: 1–14.

Booth, Alan. 1982. "Corporatism, Capitalism and Depression in Twentieth-Century Britain." *British Journal of Sociology* 33: 200–223.

Borts, George. 1960. "Regional Cycles of Manufacturing Employment in the United States, 1914–1953." *Journal of the American Statistical Association* 55: 151–211.

Botkin, J., Dimancescu, D., and Stata, R. 1982. *Global Stakes: The Future of High Technology in America.* Cambridge, MA: Ballinger.

Bowles, Samuel. 1970. "Migration as Investment: Empirical Tests of the Human Investment Approach to Geographical Mobility." *Review of Economics and Statistics* (November): 356–62.

Bowles, Samuel, Gordon, David M., and Weisskopf, Thomas E. 1983. *Beyond the Wasteland.* Garden City, NY: Anchor Press.

Boyte, Harry. 1980. *The Backyard Revolution.* Philadelphia: Temple University Press.

Bradbury, Katharine, Downs, Anthony, and Small, Kenneth. 1982. *Urban Decline and the Future of American Cities.* Washington, DC: The Brookings Institution.

Bradford, Calvin, with Temali, Mihailo, and Branan, Karen. 1982. "The Politics of Private Sector Initiatives: The Case of City Venture Corporation." Paper presented at the Association of Collegiate Schools of Planning annual meeting, Chicago, October 23.

Brooks, Harvey, Liebman, Lance, and Schelling, Corinne S., eds. 1984. *Public-Private Partnership: New Opportunities for Meeting Social Needs.* Cambridge, MA: Ballinger.

Browne, L. E. 1983. "High Technology and Business Services." *New England Economic Review* (July/August): 5–17.

Browne, Lynne. 1978. "Regional Industry Mix and the Business Cycle." *New England Economic Review* (November/December): 35–53.

Browning, J. E. 1980. *How to Select a Business Site.* New York: McGraw-Hill.

Brueckner, J. K. 1983. "Metropolitan Airline Traffic: Determinants and Effects on Local Employment Growth." Paper presented at North American meetings of the Regional Science Association, Chicago.

Business Week. 1983. "America Rushes to High Tech for Growth." March 28: 84–98.

Butler, Stuart M. 1980. *Enterprise Zones: Pioneering in the Inner City.* Washington DC: The Heritage Foundation.

———. 1981. *Enterprise Zones: Green Lining the Inner Cities.* New York: Universe Books.

Burns, Leland S. 1982. "Metropolitan Growth in Transition." *Journal of Urban Economics* 11: 112–29.

———, and Van Ness, Kathy. 1981. "The Decline of the Metropolitan Economy." *Urban Studies* 18: 169–80.

Bylinsky, Gene. 1981. "A New Industrial Revolution Is on the Way." *Fortune* (October 5).

Cagnon, Charles. 1982. *Business Ventures of Citizen Groups.* Helena, MT: Northern Rockies Action Group.

Cameron, Gordon C. 1983. "Policy Implications of a Changing Urban Settlement Pattern." In OECD, *Urban Growth Policies in the 1980s.* Paris: OECD.

Campbell, Toby, and Bendick, Marc, Jr. 1977. *A Public Assistance Data Book.* Washington, DC: The Urban Institute.

Carlton, Dennis W. 1983. "The Location and Employment Choices of New Firms: An Econometric Model with Discrete and Continuous Endogenous Variables." *Review of Economics and Statistics* 65, 4: 440–49.

Carnoy, Martin, and Shearer, Derek. 1980. *Economic Democracy*. New York: M. E. Sharpe.

Carruthers, N. E., and Pinder, C. C. 1983. "Urban Geographic Factors and Location Satisfaction Following a Personnel Transfer." *Academy of Management Journal* 26, 3: 520–26.

Cartwright, David W., with Renshaw, Vernon, and Levine, Bruce. 1976. *Regional Work Force Characteristics and Migration Data: A Handbook on the Social Security Continuous Work History Sample and its Application*. Washington, DC: U.S. Department of Commerce, Bureau of Economic Analysis.

Cawson, Alan. 1982. *Corporatism and Welfare*. London: Heinemann.

Chandler, Alfred. 1977. *The Visible Hand: The Managerial Revolution in American Business*. Cambridge, MA: Harvard University Press.

Chen, Gavin M. 1984. "Business Formation and Investment in the Minority Community." In *Urban Economic Development*. Edited by Richard D. Bingham and John P. Blair. Beverly Hills: Sage Publications.

Cherniack, Howard D. 1980. "Clusters of Economic Activity: Sub-Metropolitan Structures and Intra-Metropolitan Movement." Unpublished Ph.D. dissertation. Chapel Hill: University of North Carolina.

Chiswick, Barry R. 1974. *Income Inequality: Regional Analysis Within a Human Capital Framework*. New York: National Bureau of Economic Research.

Choate, Pat, and Walter, Susan. 1981. *America in Ruins: Beyond the Public Works Pork Barrel*. Washington, DC: The Council of State Planning Agencies.

Clark, Gordon L. 1983. *Interregional Migration, National Policy and Social Justice*. Totowa, NJ: Rowman and Allanheld.

———, and Gertler, M. 1983. "Local Labor Markets: Theories and Policies in the U.S." *Professional Geographer* 35: 274–85.

Clark, N. G. 1972. "Science, Technology and Regional Economic Development." *Research Policy* 1: 296–319.

Clarke, Susan E. 1984. "Neighborhood Policy Options: The Reagan Agenda." *Journal of the American Planning Association* 50, 4: 493–501.

Clarke, Susan, and Rich, Michael. 1982a. "Partnerships for Economic Development: The UDAG Experience." *Journal of Community Action* 1, 4: 52–56.

———. 1982b. "Financial Federalism: Trends Toward Intergovernmental Management of the Local Economy." Unpublished paper presented at the annual meeting of the American Political Science Association, Denver, September.

Cobb, J. C. 1982. *The Selling of the South: The Southern Crusade for Industrial Development 1936–1980*. Baton Rouge: Louisiana State University Press.

Cockburn, Cynthia. 1977. *The Local State: Management of Cities and People*. London: Pluto Press.

Cohen, Robert. 1979a. *The Impact of Foreign Investment on U.S. Cities and Regions*. Research commissioned by the U.S. Department of Housing and Urban Development. Washington, DC: USGPO.

———. 1979b. "The Internationalization of Capital and U.S. Cities." Unpublished

Ph.D. dissertation. New York: New School for Social Research.

———. 1982. "The New Spatial Organization of the European and American Automotive Industries." In *Regional Analysis and the New International Division of Labor*. Edited by Frank Moulaert and Patricia Salinas. Boston: Kluwer-Nijhoff.

Collins, Lyndhurst, and Walker, David F. 1975. *Locational Dynamics of Manufacturing Activity*. London: John Wiley & Sons.

Committee for Economic Development. 1982. *Public-Private Partnership: An Opportunity for Urban Communities*. New York: Committee for Economic Development.

Committee on Small Business. 1980. *Conglomerate Mergers: Their Effect on Small Business and Local Communities*. U.S. House of Representatives, 96th Congress. Washington, DC: USGPO.

Conroy, Michael E. 1975. *The Challenge of Urban Economic Development*. Lexington, MA: D. C. Heath.

CONTACT. 1982. "Toledo City Venture: Revitalizing a Community." (March/April): 11–13.

Conway, H. McKinley. 1980. *Marketing Industrial Buildings and Sites*. Atlanta: Conway Publications.

Cooke, Philip. 1983. *Theories of Planning and Spatial Development*. London: Hutchinson.

Cox, Andrew. 1981. "Corporatism as Reductionism: The Analytic Limits of the Corporatist Thesis." *Government and Opposition* 16: 78–95.

Crimmins, James C., and Keil, Mark. 1983. *Enterprise in the Nonprofit Sector*. New York: Rockefeller Brothers Fund.

Cromwell, Jerry, and Merrill, Peter. 1973. "Minority Business Performance and the Community Development Corporation." *Review of Black Political Economy* 3, 3: 65–81.

Crouch, Colin. 1984. "Corporatism." *Political Studies* 32: 113–16.

———. 1983. "New Thinking on Pluralism." *The Political Quarterly* 54: 363–74.

Cummins, Laurie D. 1965. "The Employed Poor: Their Characteristics and Occupations." *Monthly Labor Review* 88, 7: 828–35.

Cunningham, James V., and Kotler, Milton. 1983. *Building Neighborhood Organizations*. Notre Dame, IN: University of Notre Dame Press.

Czamanski, Stan, and de Q. Ablas, Luiz Augusto. 1978. "Identification of Industrial Clusters and Complexes: A Comparison of Methods and Findings." *Urban Studies* 16: 61–80.

Daniels, Beldon, Barbe, N., and Seigel, B. 1981. "The Experience and Potential of Community-Based Development." In *Expanding the Opportunity to Produce: Revitalizing the American Economy Through New Enterprise Development*. Edited by Robert Friedmann and W. Schweke. Washington, DC: Corporation for Enterprise Development.

Davis, Lester. 1982. "New Definition of 'High-Tech' Reveals That U.S. Competitiveness in This Area Is Declining." *Business America* (October 18, 1982).

da Vanzo, Julie. 1978. *U.S. Internal Migration: Who Moves and Why*. Santa Monica: Rand Corporation.

Denny, B. C. 1982. "The High-Technology Fix." *Science* 217 (August 27): 791.

Diamant, Alfred. 1982. "Review Article: Bureaucracy and Public Policy in Neocorporatist Settings." *Comparative Politics* 14: 101–24.

Dorfman, Nancy. 1983. "Route 128: The Development of a Regional High Technology Economy." *Research Policy* 12, 299–316.

Dunn, R. 1982. "Parameter Instability in Models of Local Unemployment Responses." *Environment and Planning* 14: 75–94.

Engerman, Stanley. 1965. "Regional Aspects of Stabilization Policy." In *Essays in Fiscal Federalism.* Edited by Richard Musgrave. Washington, DC: The Brookings Institution.

Fainstein, Susan S., Fainstein, Norman I., et al. 1983. *Restructuring the City: The Political Economy of Urban Redevelopment.* New York: Longman.

Farrell, K. 1983. "High-Tech Highways." *Venture* 5, 9: 38–50.

Feagin, Joe R. 1983. *The Urban Real Estate Game.* Englewood Cliffs, NJ: Prentice-Hall.

Feldstein, Martin. 1973. "The Economics of the New Unemployment." *The Public Interest* 33: 3–42.

Ferguson, C. H. 1983. "The Microelectronics Industry in Distress." *Technology Review* 86, 6: 24–37.

Fleigstein, Neil. 1981. *Going North: Migration of Blacks and Whites from the South, 1900–1950.* New York: Academic Press.

Forbes. 1983. "What Drives the U.S. Economy? Services or Goods?" (April 11): 142–49.

Fosler, R. Scott, and Berger, Renee A., eds. 1982. *Public-Private Partnerships in American Cities.* Lexington, MA: Lexington Books.

Freeman, C. 1982. *The Economics of Industrial Innovation.* Cambridge, MA: MIT Press.

———, et al. 1982. *Unemployment and Technological Innovation.* Westport, CT: Greenwood Press.

Friedenberg, H., and Bretzfelder, R. 1980. "Sensitivity of Regional and State Nonfarm Wages and Salaries to National Business Cycles, 1948–79." *Survey of Current Business* 60, 5: 15–27.

Friedland, Roger. 1980. "Corporate Power and Urban Growth: The Case of Urban Renewal." *Politics and Society* 10: 203–23.

———. 1982. *Power and Crisis in the City: Corporations, Unions, and Urban Policy.* London: Macmillan.

———, Alford, Robert, and Piven, Frances Fox. 1978. "Political Conflict, Urban Structure, and the Fiscal Crisis." In *Comparing Public Policies.* Edited by Douglas Ashford. Beverly Hills: Sage Publications.

Friedman, Robert, and Schweke, William, eds. 1981. *Expanding the Opportunity to Produce: Revitalizing the American Economy Through New Enterprise Development.* Washington, DC: Corporation for Enterprise Development.

Friedmann, John. 1982. "Urban Communes, Self-Management, and the Reconstruction of the Local State." *Journal of Planning Education and Research* 2, 1: 37–53.

Friedmann, John, and Weaver, Clyde. 1979. *Territory and Function: The Evolution of Regional Planning.* Berkeley: University of California Press.

Friedmann, John, and Wolff, G. 1982. "World City Formation: An Agenda for Research and Action." *International Journal of Urban and Regional Research* 6: 307–43.

Frobel, Folker, Heinrichs, J., and Kreye, O. 1980. *The New International Division of*

Labor. Cambridge: Cambridge University Press.

Fuchs, Victor. 1968. *The Services Economy*. New York: Columbia University Press.

——. 1977. *The Service Industries and U.S. Economic Growth Since World War II*. National Bureau of Economic Research, Working Paper #211. Palo Alto: Stanford University.

Fuguitt, Glenn V., and Voss, Paul R. 1979. *Growth and Change in Rural America*. Washington, D.C.: Urban Land Institute.

Galaskiewicz, Joseph. 1979. *Exchange Networks and Community Politics*. Beverly Hills: Sage Publications.

Ganz, Alexander, and O'Brien, Thomas. 1973. "The City: Sandbox, Reservation, or Dynamo?" *Public Policy* 21 (Winter): 107–23.

Garn, Harvey A., and Ledebur, Larry Clinton. 1980. "The Economic Performance and Prospects of Cities." In *The Prospective City*. Edited by Arthur P. Solomon. Cambridge, MA: MIT Press.

Gatons, Paul, and Brintnall, Michael. 1985. "The Competitive Approach: Urban Development Action Grants." Sage Urban Affairs Annual 26 (Forthcoming).

Gelfand, Mark I. 1975. *A Nation of Cities: The Federal Government and Urban America. 1933–1965*. New York: Oxford University Press.

Gilchrist, Bruce, and Shenkin, Arlaana. 1980. "The Impact of Computers on Employment: A Look Behind the Statistics." *Futurist* 15, 1 (February).

Giloth, Robert. 1981. *Disinvestment in South Shore's Large Rental Properties*. Chicago: Center for Urban Economic Development.

Glantz, F. B. 1973. *The Determinants of the Intermetropolitan Migration of the Disadvantaged*. Boston: Federal Reserve Bank of Boston.

Glasmeier, Amy, Hall, Peter, and Markusen, Ann. 1983. *Recent Evidence on High Technology Industries' Spatial Tendencies: A Preliminary Investigation*. Berkeley: Institute of Urban and Regional Development.

Glickman, Norman J. 1979. *The Growth and Management of the Japanese Urban System*. New York: Academic Press.

——, ed. 1980. *The Urban Impacts of Federal Policies*. Baltimore: Johns Hopkins University Press.

——. 1981. "Emerging Urban Policies in a Slow-Growth Economy: Conservative Initiatives and Progressive Responses." *International Journal of Urban and Regional Research* 5, 4: 492–528.

——. 1984a. "The Reagan Administration's Urban Policies: Introduction." *Journal of the American Planning Association* 50, 4: 470.

——. 1984b. "Economic Policy and the Cities: In Search of Reagans' Real Urban Policy." *Journal of the American Planning Association* 50, 4: 471–78.

Glickman, Norman J., and Alford, Robert R. 1982. "The State in an Internationalized Economy." Mimeographed.

Glickman, Norman J., et al. 1982. *Policy in Conflict: Economic and Urban Policies*. Report to the U.S. Economic Development Administration. Washington, DC: U.S. Department of Commerce.

Glickman, Norman J., and Van Wagner, Marcia. Forthcoming. "Two Cheers for Industrial Policy: A Critical Look at Some Urban and Distributional Issues." In *Industrial Policy Debate: Regional, State and Local Issues*. Edited by H. A. Goldstein.

Goering, John M. 1979. "The National Neighborhoods Movement: A Preliminary Analysis and Critique." *Journal of the American Planning Association* 45, 4: 506–14.

Goldberg, Robert. 1981. *Geographic Targeting of Economic Development Aid.* Washington, DC: U.S. Department of Housing and Urban Development.

Goldfield, David R. 1982. "National Urban Policy in Sweden," *Journal of the American Planning Association* 48: 24–38.

Goldsmith, William W. 1974. "The Ghetto as a Resource for Black America." *Journal of the American Institute of Planners* 40, 1: 17–30.

———. 1982. "The Biggest Banana Republic." *Working Papers for a New Society* 9, 2 (March): 24–30.

———, and Jacobs, Harvey. 1982. "The Improbability of Urban Policy: The Case of the United States." *Journal of the American Planning Association* 48, 1: 53–66.

Goldstein, Harvey A., and Bergman, Edward M. 1983. *Methods and Models for Projecting Industry Employment for States and Substate Areas* (Washington, DC: U.S. Department of Labor.

Goodman, R. 1979. *The Last Entrepreneurs: America's Regional Wars for Jobs and Dollars.* New York: Simon and Schuster.

Gordon, David. 1972. *Theories of Poverty and Underemployment.* Lexington, MA: D. C. Heath.

Gordon, David M. 1976. "Capitalism and the Roots of Urban Crisis." In *The Fiscal Crisis of American Cities.* Edited by Roger E. Alcaly and David Mermelstein. New York: Vintage.

Gordon, David. 1979. *The Working Poor: Towards a State Agenda.* Washington, DC: Council of State Planning Agencies.

Gramlich, Edward. 1979. "State and Local Budget Surpluses and the Effect of Macroeconomic Policies." Study for Joint Economic Committee of U.S. Congress. Washington, DC: USGPO, January 12.

Gravelle, Jane G. 1982. "Effects of the 1981 Depreciation Revisions on the Taxation of Income from Business Income." *National Tax Journal* 35: 1–20.

Gray, Thomas, and Phillips, Bruce, 1983. *The Role of Small Firms in Understanding the Magnitude of Fluctuations in the Economy.* Washington, DC: Office of Advocacy, U.S. Small Business Administration.

Green, Larry. 1983. "Rust Bowl: Steel Mills Waste Away." *Los Angeles Times* (April 25).

Greene, R., Harrington, P., and Vinson, R. 1983. "High Technology Industry: Identifying and Tracking an Emerging Source of Employment Strength." *New England Journal of Employment Training* (Fall 1983).

Greenstone, David, and Peterson, Paul. 1973. *Race and Authority in Urban Politics.* New York: Russell Sage.

Greenwood, Michael G. 1975. "Research in Internal Migration in the United States: A Survey." *Survey of Economic Literature* 13: 397–433.

Gregory, William H. 1968a. "Several Firms Planning Urban Programs, But Sales Prospects Vague." *Aviation Week and Space Technology* (July 11): 38–51.

———. 1968b. "Industry Probes Socio-Economic Markets." *Aviation Week and Space Technology* (June 10): 41–57.

Grzywinski, Ron, and Marino, Dennis. 1981. "Public Policy, Private Banks and Economic Development." In *Expanding the Opportunity to Produce*. Edited by Robert Friedman and William Schweke. Washington, DC: Corporation for Enterprise Development.

Gurwitz, A. M. 1982. "The New Faith in High Tech." *Wall Street Journal* (October 27): 24.

Gurwitz, Aaron S., and Kingsley, G. Thomas. 1982. *The Cleveland Metropolitan Economy: An Initial Assessment*. Executive summary. Santa Monica: Rand Corporation.

Hall, Peter. 1977. "Green Fields and Gray Areas." Speech to the Royal Towne Planning Institute. Mimeographed.

Hall, Peter, and Hay, Dennis. 1980. *Growth Centres in the European Urban System*. London: Heinemann Education.

Hall, P., Markusen, A. R., Osborn, R., and Wachsman, B. 1983. "The American Computer Software Industry. Economic Development Prospects." *Built Environment* 9, 1.

Hampden-Turner, Charles. 1975. *From Poverty to Human Dignity*. Garden City, NY: Anchor Press/Doubleday.

Hamer, Andrew. 1973. *Industrial Exodus from Central City*. Lexington, MA: D. C. Heath.

Hamilton, F. E. Ian. 1974. *Spatial Perspectives on Industrial Organization and Decision-Making*. London: John Wiley & Sons.

Hansen, Niles. 1979. "The New International Division of Labor and Manufacturing Decentralization in the United States." *Review of Regional Studies* 9: 1–11.

Hanson, D. 1982. *The New Alchemists: Silicon Valley and the Microelectronics Revolution*. Boston: Little, Brown.

Hanson, Royce. 1983. *Rethinking Urban Policy: Urban Development in an Advanced Economy*. Washington, DC: National Research Council, Committee on National Urban Policy.

Harris, Candee S. 1983a. "High Tech Jobs: A Statistical Profile, 1976–1980." *Entrepreneurial Economy* 13: 2.

———. 1983b. *Icebergs and Business Statistics: A Comparison of Business Failures and Dissolutions*. Working Paper No. 19. Washington, DC: The Brookings Institution.

———. 1984. "Plant Closings and Job Loss: The Magnitude of the Problem." *The Annals* 475: 15–27.

Harris, John R., and Michael P. Todaro. 1970. "Migration, Unemployment and Development: A Two-Sector Analysis." *American Economic Review* 60, 1 (March): 126–42.

Harrison, Bennett. 1974. *Urban Economic Development*. Washington, DC: Urban Institute.

———. 1978. *Labor Market Structure and the Relationship Between Work and Welfare*. Cambridge, MA: MIT–Harvard Joint Center for Urban Studies.

———. 1982. "The Tendency Toward Instability and Inequality Underlying the 'Revival' of New England." *Papers of the Regional Science Association* 50: 41–65.

Harrison, Bennett, and Hill, E. 1978. "The Changing Structure of Jobs in Older and

Younger Cities." Cambridge, MA: Joint Center for Urban Studies, New England Political Economy Project Working Paper No. 2.

Harrison, Bennett, and Kanter, Sandra. 1978. "The Political Economy of State 'Job Creation' Business Incentives." *Journal of the American Institute of Planners* 44: 424–35.

Harrison, Bennett, and Sum, A. 1979. "The Theory of 'Dual' or Segmented Labor Markets." *Journal of Economic Issues* 13, 3: 678–706.

Hauser, Phillip M. 1960. *Population Perspectives.* New Brunswick, NJ: Rutgers University Press.

Hawley, Amos H. 1971, 1981. *Urban Society,* 2d ed. New York: John Wiley & Sons.

Hekman, J. S. 1980a. "The Future of High Technology Industry in New England: A Case Study of Computers." *New England Economic Review* (January/February): 5–17.

———. 1980b. "Can New England Hold Onto Its High Technology Industry?" *New England Economic Review* (March/April): 35–44.

———. 1983. "Branch Plant Location and the Product Cycle in Computer Manufacturing." Chapel Hill: University of North Carolina School of Business. Mimeographed.

Hernes, Gudmund, and Selvik, Arne. 1979. "Local Corporatism." In *Nonmetropolitan Industrial Growth and Community Change.* Edited by Gene F. Summers and Arne Selvik. Lexington, MA: Lexington Books.

Hicks, Donald, ed. 1982. *Urban America in the Eighties: Prospectives and Prospects.* New Brunswick, NJ: Transaction Books.

Hirschhorn, Larry. 1980. "Scenario Writing: A Developmental Approach." *Journal of the American Planning Association* 14, 2: 172–83.

Hopkins, Terence K., and Wallerstein, Immanual. 1982. *World Systems Analysis: Theory and Methodology.* Explorations in the World Economy, vol. 1. Beverly Hills: Sage Publications.

Howland, Marie. 1982. *Using the Dun and Bradstreet Data for the Analysis of Business Cycles,* Washington, DC: Urban Institute.

———. 1983. *Cyclical Effects at the Local Level. A Microeconomic View,* Washington, DC: Urban Institute.

———. 1984. "Regional Variations in Cyclical Employment." *Environment and Planning A* 16: 863–77.

Ingrassia, L. 1983. "Four Cities Vie for High-Tech Joint Ventures." *Wall Street Journal* (May 12): 27, 32.

Jackson, Gregory, and Masnick, George. 1981. *Regional Diversity: Growth in the U.S. 1960–1990.* Boston: Auburn Publishing House.

Jacobs, Jane. 1984. *Cities and the Wealth of Nations.* New York: Random House.

Jacobs, Susan S., and Wasylenko, Michael. 1981. "Government Policy to Stimulate Economic Development: Enterprise Zones." Austin: Lyndon Baines Johnson School of Public Affairs, University of Texas. Mimeographed.

James, Franklin J., Jr. 1974. "The City: Sandbox, Reservation or Dynamo: A Reply." *Public Policy* 22 (Winter): 39–51.

———. 1976. *Recession and Recovery in Urban Economies: A Summary of Recent Experience.* American Collegiate Schools of Planning paper no. 13.

————. 1981. "Economic Distress in Central Cities." In *Cities Under Stress: The Fiscal Crisis of Urban America*. Edited by Robert Burchell and David Listokin. New Brunswick, NJ: Center for Urban Policy Research, Rutgers University.

————, and Blair, John P. 1983. "The Role of Labor Mobility in a National Urban Policy." *Journal of the American Planning Association* 49, 2: 307–15. Reprinted and edited in this volume as chapter 13.

Jensen, Ib, and Thomsen, Niels Peter. 1983. "The Danish Block Grant System." In OECD, *The Urban Impacts of National Policies*. Paris: OECD. Pp. 28–32.

Johnson, Nevil, and Cochrane, Allan. 1981. *Economic Policy-Making by Local Authorities in Britain and Western Germany*. London: George Allen and Unwin.

Joint Economic Committee of the Congress. 1982. "Location of High Technology Firms and Regional Economic Development." Washington, DC: Joint Economic Committee.

————. 1984. *Urban America 1984: A Report Card*. Washington, DC: Joint Economic Committee.

Jones, Bryan D., Bachelor, Lynn W., and Wang, Richard. 1981. "Rebuilding the Urban Tax Base: Local Policy Discretion and the Corporate Surplus." Paper presented at the Midwest Political Science Association meeting, Cincinnati.

Jussil, Sune. 1983. "The Swedish Tax System." In OECD, *The Urban Impacts of National Policies*. Paris: OECD. Pp. 23–27.

Kain, John F. 1975. "The Distribution and Movement of Jobs and Industry." In *Essays in Urban Spatial Structure*. Edited by John F. Kain. Cambridge, MA: Ballinger.

Kaplan, Marshall, James, Franklin, and Phillips, Robin. 1981. *The Regional and Urban Impacts of the Administration's Budget and Tax Proposals*. Washington, DC: Joint Economic Committee of Congress.

Kasarda, John D. 1980. "The Implications of Contemporary Redistribution Trends for National Urban Policy." *Social Science Quarterly* 61, 3/4: 373–400.

————. 1982. *Urban Structural Transformation and Minority Opportunity*. Report prepared for the Office of Policy Development and Research, U.S. Department of Housing and Urban Development, Washington, DC.

————. 1983. "Entry Level Jobs, Mobility and Urban Minority Employment." *Urban Affairs Quarterly* 19 (September): 21–40. Reprinted in part and edited in this volume as chapter 4.

————. 1984. "Hispanics and City Change." *American Demographics* 6, 11 (November): 25–29.

Katznelson, Ira. 1981. *City Trenches*. New York: Pantheon.

Keeler, Emmitt, and Rogers, William. 1973. *A Classification of Large American Urban Areas*. R-1246-NSF. Santa Monica: Rand Corporation.

Kelly, Rita Mae. 1977. *Community Control of Economic Development*. New York: Praeger.

King, Leslie J., Casetti, E., Jeffrey, D., and Odland, J. 1972. "Spatial-Temporal Patterns in Employment Growth." *Growth and Change* 3, 1: 37–42.

Kirby, Andrew. 1982. "The External Relations of the Local State in Britain: Some Empirical Examples." In *Conflict, Politics, and the Urban Scene*. Edited by K. R. Cox and R. J. Johnston. London: Longman.

Klein, Deborah P. 1975. "Exploring the Adequacy of Employment." *Monthly Labor*

Review 98, 10: 3–9.

Kmenta, Jan. 1971. *Elements of Econometrics.* New York: Macmillan.

Knight, Richard V. 1982. "City Development in Advanced Industrial Societies." In *Cities in the 21st Century.* Edited by Gary Gappert and Richard V. Knight. Beverly Hills: Sage Publications.

Koch, D. L., Cox, W. N., Steinhauser, D. W., and Whigham, P. V. 1983. "High Technology: The Southeast Reaches Out for Growth Industry." *Economic Review.* (Reserve Bank of Atlanta) 68, 9 (September): 4–19.

Kotler, Milton. 1981. "Partnerships in Community Service." *Journal of Community Action* 1: 45–51.

Kovaleff, Theodore P. 1974. "Industrialization and the American City." In *Cities in Transition.* Edited by Frank J. Coppa and Philip C. Dolce. Chicago: Nelson Hall.

Krumme, Gunter, and Hayter, Roger. 1975. "Implications of Corporate Strategies and Product Cycle Adjustments for Regional Employment Changes." In *Locational Dynamics of Manufacturing Activity.* Edited by Collins Lyndhurst and David Walker. London: John Wiley & Sons.

Kuznets, Simon. 1955. "Economic Growth and Income Inequality." *American Economic Review* 45, 1: 1–28.

Lasuen, Jose R. 1973. "Urbanization and Development—The Temporal Interaction Between Geographic and Sectoral Clusters." *Urban Studies* 10: 163–88.

Lawrence, Robert. 1983. "Is Trade Deindustrializing America?" In *Brookings Papers on Economic Activity.* Edited by G. Perry and G. Burtless. Washington, DC: The Brookings Institution.

Lehmbruch, Gerhard. 1982. "Introduction: Neo-Corporatism in Comparative Perspective." In *Patterns of Corporatist Policy-Making.* Edited by Gerhard Lehmbruch and Philippe C. Schmitter. Beverly Hills: Sage Publications.

Lehmbruch, Gerhard and Schmitter, Philippe C. 1982. *Patterns of Corporatist Policy-Making.* Beverly Hills: Sage Publications.

Leon, Carol Boyd. 1982. "Occupational Winners and Losers: Who Were They During 1972–1980?" *Monthly Labor Review* (June).

Levy, Frank. 1977. *How Big is the American Underclass?* Washington, DC: Urban Institute.

———. 1981. *Migration's Impact on the Economic Situation of Minorities and the Disadvantaged.* Working Paper 1480-02. Washington, DC: Urban Institute.

Levy, J. M. 1981. *Economic Development Programs for Cities, Counties, and Towns.* New York: Praeger.

Levy, Paul. 1979. "Unloading the Neighborhood Bandwagon." *Social Policy* 10, 2: 28–32.

Lewis, H., and Allison, D. 1982. *The Real World War.* New York: Coward, McCann, and Geoghegan.

Liebert, Roland. 1974. "Municipal Functions, Structures, and Expenditures: A Reanalysis of Recent Research." *Social Science Quarterly* 54: 765–83.

Lineberry, Robert, and Fowler, Edmund. 1967. "Reformism and Public Policies in American Cities." *American Political Science Review* 61: 701–16.

Lipsky, Michael. 1968. "Protest as a Political Resource." *American Political Science Review* 62: 1144–58.

Litvak, Lawrence, and Daniels, Belden. 1979. *Innovations in Development Finance.* Washington, DC: Council of State Planning Agencies.

Lowry, Ira S. 1980. "The Dismal Future of Central Cities." In *The Prospective City.* Edited by Arthur P. Solomon. Cambridge, MA: MIT Press.

Lund, L. 1979. *Factors in Corporate Locational Decisions.* Information Bulletin No. 66. New York: The Conference Board.

McCarthy, Kevin, and Morrison, Peter. 1979. *Demographic and Economic Development Trends in Non-Metropolitan Areas.* Santa Monica: Rand Corporation.

McElyea, J. R. 1974. "Setting Your Sights on R&D Sites." *Industrial Research* 16, 5: 46–48.

McGraw-Hill Book Company. 1980. *Plant Site Selection: A Survey of Business Week's Executive Subscribers in Industry.* New York: McGraw-Hill.

Maclennan, Duncan, and Parr, John B. 1979. *Regional Policy: Past Experience and New Directions.* London: Martin Robinson.

Magaziner, Ira, and Reich, Robert B. 1983. *Minding America's Business.* New York: Vintage.

Makler, Harry M., Martinelli, A., and Smelser, N. 1982. *The New International Economy.* Sage Studies in International Sociology 26. Beverly Hills: Sage Publications.

Malecki, E. J. 1980. "Dimensions of R&D Location in the United States." *Research Policy* 9, 1: 2–22.

———. 1981. "Product Cycles, Innovation Cycles, and Regional Economic Change." *Technological Forecasting and Social Change* 19: 291–306.

———. 1983a. "Technology and Regional Development: A Survey." *International Regional Science Review* 8, 2: 89–125.

———. 1983b. "Federal and Industrial R&D: Locational Structures, Economic Effects and Interrelationships." Final Report to the National Science Foundation. Norman: University of Oklahoma, Department of Geography.

Mandleker, Daniel R., Feder, Gary, and Collins, Margaret P. 1980. *Reviving Cities with Tax Abatement.* New Brunswick, NJ: Center for Urban Policy Research.

Manpower Report to the President. 1983. Washington, DC: USGPO.

Manson, Donald. 1983. *Economic Analysis of Effects of Business Cycles on the Economy of Cities,* Washington, DC: Urban Institute.

Markusen, Ann R. 1985. "The Sectoral Differentiation of Regional Economies." In *Profit Cycles, Oligopoly and Regional Development.* Edited by Ann R. Markusen. Cambridge, MA: MIT Press.

———. 1983. "High-Tech Jobs, Markets and Economic Development Prospects: Evidence from California." *Built Environment* 9, 1: 18–28.

Martin, Andrew. 1973. *The Politics of Economic Policy.* Beverly Hills: Sage Publications.

Massey, Doreen, and Meegan, Richard. 1982. *The Anatomy of Job Loss.* London: Methuen.

Mera, Koichi. 1983. "Population Stabilization and National Spatial Policy of Public Investment: Lessons from the Japanese Experience." Mimeographed.

Meyer, John, Schmenner, Roger, and Meyer, Leslie. 1980. "Business Location Decisions, Capital Market Imperfections, and Development of Central City Employment." Cambridge, MA: MIT–Harvard Joint Center for Urban Studies.

Michelson, Stephen. 1979. "Community-Based Economic Development in Urban

Areas." In *Central City Economic Development*. Edited by Benjamin Chinitz. Cambridge, MA: Abt Books.

Mier, Robert. 1982a. "Enterprise Zones: A Long Shot." *Planning* (April): 10–14.

———. 1982b. "Jobs Generation as a Road to Recovery." Paper presented at Cities Congress on Roads to Recovery, Cleveland State University, Cleveland, September.

———. 1983. "High Technology Based Development: A Review of Recent Literature." *Journal of the American Planning Association* 49, 3: 363–65.

Mitchell, John S. 1980. *Implementing Welfare-Employment Programs: An Institutional Analysis of the Work Incentive (WIN) Program*. R&D Monograph 78. Washington, DC: U.S. Department of Labor.

Mohl, R. A. 1976. "The Industrial City." *Environment* 18, 5: 28–38.

Mollenkopf, John. 1983. *The Contested City*. Princeton, NJ: Princeton University Press.

———. 1981. "Neighborhood Political Development and the Politics of Urban Growth: Boston and San Francisco, 1958–78." *International Journal of Urban and Regional Research* 5: 15–39.

Molotch, Harvey. 1972. *Managed Integration: Dilemmas of Doing Good in the City*. Berkeley: University of California Press.

Moore, Frederick T. 1984. Review of *Innovation and Growth* by F. M. Scherer. *Finance and Development* 20 (December): 48.

Moran, Michael. 1982. "Finance Capital and Pressure Group Politics in Britain." *British Journal of Political Science* 11: 381–404.

Morris, Charles. 1980. *The Costs of Good Intentions*. New York: Basic Books.

Moser, C. A., and Wolf, Scott. 1961. *British Towns: A Statistical Study of Their Social and Economic Differences*. Center for Urban Studies, Report No. 2. Edinburgh: Oliver and Boyd.

Moulaert, Frank, and Salinas, Patricia, eds. 1982. *Regional Analysis and the New International Division of Labor*. Boston: Kluwer-Nijhoff.

Muller, Ronald E. 1980. *Revitalizing America: Politics for Prosperity*. New York: Simon and Schuster.

Muller, Thomas L. 1982. "Regional Impacts." In *The Reagan Experiment*. Edited by John L. Palmer and Isabel V. Sawhill. Washington, DC: Urban Institute Press.

National Commission on Neighborhoods. 1979. *People, Building Neighborhoods*. Washington, DC: USGPO.

National Council for Urban Economic Development. 1978. *Coordinated Urban Economic Development: A Case Study Analysis*. Washington, DC: NCUED.

National Economic Development Law Project. 1974. *A Lawyer's Manual on Community-Based Economic Development*. Berkeley: NEDLP.

———. 1983. *Community Economic Development Strategies: Creating Successful Businesses*. Berkeley: NEDLP.

National League of Cities. 1983. *Report of the Community and Economic Development Policy Committee to the Resolutions Committee*. Sixtieth annual Congress of Cities and Exposition. New Orleans, November 26–30.

National Research Council. 1982a. *National Policy and the Post Industrial City*. Washington, DC: National Academy Press.

———. 1982b. *Critical Issues for National Urban Policy*. Washington, DC: National

Academy Press.

Nedelmann, Birgitta, and Meir, Kurt G. 1979. "Theories of Contemporary Corporatism: Static or Dynamic?" In *Trends Toward Corporatist Intermediation*. Edited by Philippe C. Schmitter and Gerhard Lehmbruch. Beverly Hills: Sage Publications.

Needham, Barrie. 1982. *Choosing the Right Policy Instruments*. Aldershot, Eng.: Gower.

Neff, P., and Weifenbach, A. 1949. *Business Cycles in Selected Industrial Areas*. Berkeley: University of California Press.

Neighborhood Development Collective. 1982. *Entrepreneurship in the Nonprofit Sector*. Washington, DC: NDC.

Neighborhood Housing Services. 1980. *Creating Local Partnerships*. Washington, DC: USGPO.

Noble, David F. 1984. *Forces of Production*. New York: Knopf.

Nordlinger, Eric. 1981. *On the Autonomy of the Democratic State*. Cambridge, MA: Harvard University Press.

Norman, C. 1983. "Texas Uses Oil to Fuel Research." *Science* 220 (April 22): 390–93.

Norris, William C., 1979. *Technology and Corporate Governance*. Bloomington, MN: Control Data Corporation.

———. 1982. "A New Role for Corporations." Presentation at Control Data Corporation and American Academy of Arts and Sciences conference, Social Needs and Business Opportunities, Minneapolis, September 25.

Norton, R. D. 1979. *City Life-Cycles and American Urban Policy*. New York: Academic Press.

———, and Rees, J. 1979. "The Product Cycle and the Spatial Decentralization of American Manufacturing." *Regional Studies* 13: 141–51.

Noyelle, Thierry J. 1983a. "The Rise of Advanced Services: Some Implications for Economic Development in U.S. Cities." *Journal of the American Planning Association* 49, 3: 280–90. Reprinted and edited in this volume as chapter 7.

———. 1983b. "The Implications of Industry Restructuring for Spatial Organizations in the United States." In *Regional Analysis and the New International Division of Labor*. Edited by Frank Moulaert and Patricia Salinas. Boston: Kluwer-Nijhoff.

———. 1983c. *The Coming of Age of Management Consulting and Its Implications for New York City*. Report to New York City's Office of Economic Development. New York: Conservation of Human Resources.

———. 1984a. *Technological Change and Employment: Preliminary Findings from the Case Study of Financial Industries*. New York: Conservation of Human Resources.

———. 1984b. "Rethinking Public Policy for the Service Era." In *Economic Development Commentary*. Washington, DC: CUED, Summer.

———, and Stanback, Thomas M. 1983. *The Economic Transformation of American Cities*. Landmark Studies. Totowa, NJ: Rowman and Allanheld.

Oakey, R. P. 1983. "New Technology, Government Policy and Regional Manufacturing Employment." *Area* 15, 1: 61–65.

O'Connor, James. 1973. *The Fiscal Crisis of the State*. New York: St. Martin's Press.

Odle, Marjorie, and Armington, Catherine. 1983. "Weighing the USEEM Files for

Dynamic Longitudinal Employment Analysis." Working Paper No. 10, Business Microdata Project. Washington, DC: The Brookings Institution.

Offe, Claus. 1981. "The Attribution of Public Status to Interest Groups: Observations on the West German Case." In *Organizing Interests in Western Europe*. Edited by Suzanne Berger. Cambridge: Cambridge University Press.

Olson, Mancur. 1982. *The Rise and Decline of Nations*. New Haven: Yale University Press.

OECD. 1979. *Interfutures: Facing the Future*. Paris: OECD.

——. 1981. *Recent International Direct Investment Trends*. Paris: OECD.

——. 1982a. *Historical Statistics, 1960–1980*. Paris: OECD.

——. 1982b. *Positive Adjustment Policies: Managing Structural Change*. Paris: OECD.

——. 1983a. *Managing Urban Change*. Volume 1: *Policies and Finance*. Paris: OECD.

——. 1983b. *The Urban Impacts of National Policies: Proceedings of an OECD Experts' Meeting*. Paris: OECD.

——. 1983c. *Urban Statistics in OECD Countries*. Paris: OECD.

Palmer, John L., and Sawhill, Isabel V. 1984. *The Reagan Record*. Cambridge, MA: Ballinger.

Park, David. 1982. "Woodlawn Struggle Today." *News and Letters* (Detroit, August–September).

Park, S. O., and Wheeler, J. O. 1983. "The Filtering Down Process in Georgia: The Third Stage in the Product Life Cycle." *Professional Geographer* 35, 1: 18–31.

Pennings, J. M. 1982. "The Urban Quality of Life and Entrepreneurship." *Academy of Management Journal* 25, 1: 63–79.

Perlman, Janice. 1976. "Grassrooting the System." *Social Policy* (September/October): 4–20.

Perloff, Harvey. 1960. *Regions, Resources and Economic Growth*. Baltimore: Johns Hopkins University Press.

——. 1973. "The Development of Urban Economics in the United States." *Urban Studies* 10, 289–301.

——. 1978. "The Central City in the Post Industrial Age." In *The Mature Metropolis*. Edited by Charles L. Leven. Lexington, MA: Lexington Books.

Perry, David, and Watkins, Alfred, eds. 1977. *The Rise of the Sunbelt Cities*. Beverly Hills: Sage Publications.

Peters, James. 1983. "Job Targeting: What Planners Can Do." *Planning* 26: 26–29.

Peterson, Paul. 1981. *City Limits*. Chicago: University of Chicago Press.

Philips, Robyn Swaim, and Vidal, Avis C. 1983. "The Growth and Restructuring of Metropolitan Economies: The Context for Economic Development Policy." *Journal of the American Planning Association* 49, 3: 291–306. Reprinted and edited in this volume as chapter 3.

Philpot, Thomas. 1978. *The Slum and the Ghetto*. New York: Oxford University Press.

Pierce, Neal R. 1981. "Local Private-Public Enterprise—Context and Trends." In *Expanding the Opportunity to Produce: Revitalizing the American Economy Through New Enterprise Development*. Edited by Robert Friedman and W. Schweke. Washington, DC: Corporation for Enterprise Development.

Piore, Michael J. 1971. "The Dual Labor Market: Theory and Implications." In *Problems in Political Economy*. Edited by David Gordon. Lexington, MA: D. C. Heath.

Porter, M. E. 1980. *Competitive Strategy*. New York: Free Press.

Porter, Paul R. 1976. *The Recovery of American Cities*. New York: Two Continents.

Pred, Allan. 1977. *City Systems in Advanced Economies*. New York: Halsted Press.

President's Commission for a National Agenda for the Eighties. 1980. *Urban America in the Eighties*. Washington, DC: USGPO.

President's National Urban Policy Report. 1978, 1980, 1982, 1984. Washington, DC: U.S. Department of Housing and Urban Development.

Rawls, John. 1971. *A Theory of Justice*. Cambridge, MA: Harvard University Press.

Ray, D. Michael, and Murdie, Robert A. 1972. "Canadian and American Dimensions." In *City Classification Handbook: Methods and Applications*. Edited by Brian J. L. Berry. New York: Wiley-Interscience.

Rees, John, and Stafford, Howard. 1983. A review of *Regional Growth and Industrial Location Theory: Towards Understanding the Development of High-Technology Complexes in the U.S.*. Washington, DC: Office of Technology Assessment.

Reich, Michael, Gordon, David, and Edwards, Richard C. 1973. "A Theory of Labor Market Segmentation." *American Economic Association Papers and Proceedings* 63, 2: 359–65.

Reich, Robert. 1983. *The Next American Frontier*. New York: Times Books.

Renaud, Bertrand. 1982. "Structural Change in OECD Economies and Their Impact on Cities in the 1980s." Paris: OECD. Mimeographed.

Report of the President's Housing Commission. 1982. Washington, DC: USGPO.

Rich, Michael J. 1982. "Hitting the Target: The Distributional Impacts of the Urban Development Action Grant Program." *Urban Affairs Quarterly* 17: 285–301.

Rich, Richard C. 1982. "The Political Economy of Urban Service Distribution." In *The Politics of Urban Public Services*. Edited by Richard C. Rich. Lexington, MA: Lexington Books.

Riche, R. W., Hecker, D. E., and Burgan, J. V. 1983. "High Technology Today and Tomorrow: A Small Slice of the Employment Pie." *Monthly Labor Review* 106, 11: 50–58.

Ripley, Randall B. 1978. *CETA Prime Sponsor Management Decisions and Program Goal Achievement*. Washington, DC: USGPO.

Robert Morris Associates. 1981. *Annual Statements Studies*. Philadelphia: Robert Morris Associates.

Rohatyn, Felix. 1979. "Public-Private Partnerships to Stave Off Disaster." *Harvard Business Review* 57, 6 (November–December): 6–9.

———. 1981. "The Older America: Can It Survive?" *New York Review of Books* 27, 21: 13–16.

Roistacher, Elizabeth A. 1984. "A Tale of Two Conservatives: Housing Policy Under Reagan and Thatcher." *Journal of the American Planning Association* 50, 4: 485–92.

Rothschild, Emma. 1981. "Reagan and the Real America." *New York Review of Books* 28, 1: 12–15.

Ruin, Olaf. 1974. "Participatory Democracy and Corporatism: The Case of Sweden." *Scandinavian Political Studies* 9: 171–84.

Safran, William. 1983. "Interest Groups in Three Industrial Democracies: France, West Germany, and the United States." In *Constitutional Democracy*. Edited by Fred Eidlin. Boulder: Westview Press.

Salinas, Patricia Wilson. 1980. *Subemployment and the Urban Underclass*. PB 81-132219. Washington, DC: N.T.I.S.

———. 1981. "Targeting the Subemployment." *Man, Environment, Space, and Time* 1, 2.

———. 1982. "Longevity of Individual Low Income Employment in Growing and Declining Metropolitan Areas." *Journal of Regional Science* 22, 3: 367–72.

———, and Rossi, C. 1981. "Economic Development and Urban Subemployment: An Annotated Bibliography on Theory, Data, and Policy." *CPL Bibliography No. 55*. Chicago: Council of Planning Librarians.

Salisbury, Robert H. 1964. "The New Convergence of Power in Urban Politics." *Journal of Politics* 26: 775–97.

———. 1968. "The Analysis of Public Policy: A Search for Theories and Roles." In *Political Science and Public Policy*. Edited by Austin Ranney. Chicago: Markham.

———. 1979. "Why No Corporatism in America?" In *Trends Toward Corporatist Intermediation*. Edited by Philippe C. Schmitter and Gerhard Lehmbruch. Beverly Hills: Sage Publications.

Sarbib, Jean-Louis. 1979. "The Future of American Cities and Regions in an International Economy: Two Scenarios." Unpublished paper. Chapel Hill: University of North Carolina, Department of City and Regional Planning.

Savas, E. E. 1982. "Strategy for Cities." Speech at the Cities Congress on Roads to Recovery, Cleveland, June 11.

Sawyers, Larry, and Tabb, William K., eds. 1984. *Sunbelt/Snowbelt: Urban Development and Regional Restructuring*. New York: Oxford University Press.

Scherer, Frederick M. 1984. *Innovation and Growth: Schempterian Perspectives*. Cambridge, MA: MIT Press.

Schmenner, Roger W. 1982. *Making Business Location Decisions*. Englewood Cliffs, NJ: Prentice-Hall.

Schmitter, Philippe C. 1979. "Modes of Interest Intermediation and Models of Societal Change in Western Europe." In *Trends Toward Corporatist Intermediation*. Edited by Philippe C. Schmitter and Gerhard Lehmbruch. Beverly Hills: Sage Publications.

———. 1981. "Interest Intermediation and Regime Governability in Contemporary Western Europe and North America." In *Organizing Interests in Western Europe*. Edited by Suzanne Berger. Cambridge: Cambridge University Press.

———. 1982. "Reflections on Where the Theory of Neo-Corporatism Has Gone and Where the Praxis of Neo-Corporatism May Be Going." In *Patterns of Corporatist Policy-Making*. Edited by Gerhard Lehmbruch and Philippe C. Schmitter. Beverly Hills: Sage Publications.

———. 1983. "Democratic Theory and Neocorporatist Practice." *Social Research* 50: 885–928.

———, and Lehmbruch, Gerhard. 1979. *Trends Toward Corporatist Intermediation*. Beverly Hills: Sage Publications.

Schurmann, Franz, and Close, S. 1979. "The Emergence of Global City U.S.A." *The*

Progressive, p. 485.

Schwartz, Edward. 1979. "Neighborhoodism, a Conflict in Values." *Social Policy* 9, 5: 8–14.

Schwartz, Gail. 1979. "The Scope for Local Government Action." In *Central City Economic Development*. Edited by Benjamin Chinitz. Cambridge, MA: Abt Associates.

———. 1981. "American Planning Association's Policy Statement on Economic Development." Washington, DC: American Planning Association.

Sears, Carl, and Hawkins, Robert G. 1979. *Foreign Firms in New York City: A Survey Study*. Occasional Paper in Metropolitan Business and Finance #1. New York: New York University, Salomon Brothers Center.

Sekera, June. 1982. *Corporate Initiatives in New Business Development: Five Case Studies*. Washington, DC: Corporation for Enterprise Development.

Shearer, Dick, and Carnoy, Martin. 1981. *Economic Democracy.* New York: M. E. Sharpe.

Short, John R. 1982. "Urban Policy and British Cities." *Journal of the American Planning Association* 48, 1: 39–52.

Shostak, Arthur. 1982. "Seven Scenarios of Urban Change." In *Cities in the 21st Century*. Edited by Gary Gappert and Richard V. Knight. Beverly Hills: Sage Publications.

Simmie, J. M. 1981. *Power, Property, and Corporatism*. London: Macmillan.

Singlemann, Joachim. 1979. *From Agriculture to Services*. Beverly Hills: Sage Publications.

Skloot, Edward. 1983. "Should Not-For-Profits Go Into Business?" *Harvard Business Review* 61: 3–7.

———. 1985. "Enterprise and Commerce in Nonprofit Organizations." In *Handbook of Nonprofit Organization*. Edited by Walter Powell and Paul DiMaggio. New Haven: Yale University Press.

Solomon, Arthur P. 1980. "The Emerging Metropolis." In *The Prospective City*. Edited by Arthur P. Solomon. Cambridge, MA: MIT Press.

Stanback, Thomas M., Jr. 1980. *Understanding the Service Economy*. Baltimore: Johns Hopkins University Press.

Stanback, Thomas M., Jr., Bearse, Peter J., Noyelle, Thierry J., and Karasek, Robert A. 1981. *Services/The New Economy.* Totowa, NJ: Allanheld, Osmun.

Stanback, Thomas M., Jr., and Noyelle, Thierry J. 1982. *Cities in Transition*. Totowa, NJ: Allanheld, Osmun.

Stein, Barry. 1973. "How Successful are CDCs; An Interim Response?" *Review of Black Political Economy* 3, 3: 82–89.

Sternlieb, George, and Hughes, James W., eds. 1975. *Post-Industrial America: Metropolitan Decline and Inter-Regional Job Shifts*. New Brunswick, NJ: Center for Urban Policy Research.

———. 1977. "New Regional and Metropolitan Realities of America." *Journal of the American Institute of Planners* 43, 3: 227–40.

Sternlieb, George, and Listokin, David, eds. 1981. *New Tools for Economic Development: The Enterprise Zone, Development Bank, and RFC*. Piscataway, NJ: Rutgers University, Center for Urban Policy Research.

Stohr, W. 1982. "Structural Characteristics of Peripheral Areas: The Relevance of the Stock-in-Trade Variables of Regional Science." *Papers of the Regional Science Association.* 49: 71–84.

Stone, Clarence. 1976. *Economic Growth and Neighborhood Discontent.* Chapel Hill: University of North Carolina Press.

———. 1980. "Systemic Power in Community Decision-Making." *American Political Science Review* 74: 978–90.

———. 1984. "City Politics and Economic Development: Political Economy Perspectives." *Journal of Politics* 46: 286–99.

Storper, Michael, and Walker, Richard. 1983. "The Theory of Labor and the Theory of Location." *International Journal for Urban and Regional Research* 7, 1: 1–43.

Struyk, Raymond J., and James, Franklin. 1975. *Intrametropolitan Industrial Location.* Lexington, MA: Lexington Press.

Sundquist, James L. 1975. *Dispersing Populations: What America Can Learn From Europe.* Washington, DC: The Brookings Institution.

Suttles, Gerald. 1978. "Changing Priorities for the Urban Heartland." In *Handbook of Contemporary Urban Life.* Edited by David Street and Associates. San Francisco: Jossey-Bass.

Syron, Richard F. 1978. "Regional Experience During Business Cycles—Are We Becoming More or Less Alike?" *New England Economic Review* (November/December): 25–34.

Tabb, William K. 1979. "What Happened to Black Economic Development?" *Review of Black Political Economy* (Fall): 392–415.

Teitz, Michael B. 1981. *Small Business and Employment Growth in California.* Berkeley: University of California, Institute of Urban and Regional Development.

Thomas, Lillian, and Forrester, Eugene. 1982. "T.W.O.: A One-Man Show." *The Chicago Journal* (August 11).

Thomas, Morgan. 1974. "Structural Change and Regional Industrial Development." In *Spatial Aspects of the Development Process.* Edited by Frederick Helleiner and Walter Stohr. Proceedings of the Commission on Regional Aspects of Development of the International Geographical Union, vol. 2, London, Ontario.

Thompson, Wilbur R. 1965. *A Preface to Urban Economics.* Baltimore: Johns Hopkins University Press.

———. 1980. "The Durable Past of the Urban Future." In *Explorations in Public Policy.* Edited by M. M. Harding and M. E. Osman. Memphis: Southwestern at Memphis Press.

———, and Mattila, John M. 1959. *An Econometric Model of Postwar State Industrial Development.* Detroit: Wayne State University Press.

Toffler, Alvin. 1970. *Future Shock.* New York: Bantam Books.

Treadwell, D. 1976. "The Second War Between the States." *Business Week* (May 17).

Treadwell, David, and Redburn, Tom. 1983. "Workplace: Site of Latest Revolution." *Los Angeles Times* (April 24).

Truman, David. 1951. *The Governmental Process.* New York: Knopf.

United Nations. 1978. *Transnational Corporations in World Development: A Reexamination.* New York: United Nations.

Urban Land Institute. 1980. *UDAG Partnerships: Nine Case Studies.* Washington,

DC: ULI.

Urguhart, Michael. 1981. "The Services Industry: Is It Recession-Proof?" *Monthly Labor Review*, pp. 12–17.

U.S. Bureau of the Census. 1970. *Census of Population*. Volume 2. *Special Subject Reports: Occupation by Industry*, table 1. Washington, DC: USGPO.

———. 1973, 1975, 1979. *County Business Patterns*. Washington, DC: U.S. Department of Commerce.

———. 1981. *Statistical Abstract of the United States*. Washington, DC: USGPO.

U.S. Bureau of Labor Statistics. 1983. *Employment and Earnings*. Washington, DC: U.S. Department of Labor.

U.S. Conference of Mayors. 1980. *Local Economic Development Tools and Techniques: A Guidebook for Local Government*. Washington, DC: U.S. Departments of Housing and Urban Development and Commerce.

U.S. Congressional Budget Office. 1979. "The Effects of the Tokyo Round of Multilateral Trade Negotiations on the U.S. Economy: An Updated View." Washington, DC: USGPO.

———. 1980. *The Long Term Costs of Lower Income Housing Assistance Programs*. Washington, DC: USGPO.

———. 1982. *The Federal Role in State Industrial Development Programs*. Washington, DC: USGPO.

———. 1983. *The Industrial Policy Debate*. Washington, DC: USGPO.

U.S. Department of Commerce. 1982. *Minority Business Enterprise Today: Problems and Their Causes*. Washington, DC: USGPO.

U.S. Department of Housing and Urban Development. 1976. *Community, Economic, and Manpower Development Linkages*. Section I. Washington, DC: USGPO.

———. 1979. *The Impacts of Foreign Direct Investment on U.S. Cities and Regions*. Washington, DC: U.S. Department of Housing and Urban Development.

———. 1980. *Evaluation of the Community Economic Development Program: Long-Term Evaluation and Final Report*. Washington, DC: USGPO.

———. 1982. *An Impact Evaluation of the Urban Development Action Grant Program*. Washington, DC: USGPO.

U.S. House of Representatives. 1983. *A Bill to Amend the Public Works and Economic Development Act of 1965 and the Appalachian Regional Development Act of 1965*. HR10. 98th Congress, 1st session.

U.S. International Trade Administration. 1983. *An Assessment of U.S. Competitiveness in High Technology Industries*. Washington, DC: USGPO.

U.S. Office of Technology Assessment. 1983. *Encouraging High-Technology Development*. Background Paper No. 2. Washington, DC: Office of Technology Assessment.

U.S. Small Business Administration. 1983. *The State of Small Business: A Report of the President*. Washington, DC: USGPO.

Van Horn, Carl, et al. 1984. "Leveraging Development Dollars with Business and Jobs Targeting." *Resources* 2, 1: 1–5.

Vaughan, Roger. 1977. *The Urban Impact of Federal Policies*. Volume 2, *Economic Development*. Santa Monica: Rand Corporation.

———, and Bearse, Peter. 1981. "Federal Economic Development Programs." In *Expanding the Opportunity to Produce*. Edited by Robert Friedman and William

Schweke. Washington, DC: Corporation for Enterprise Development.

Vernez, G., Vaughan, R., Burright, B., and Coleman, S. 1977. *Regional Cycles and Employment Effects of Public Works Investments.* Santa Monica: Rand Corporation.

Vernon, Raymond. 1966. "International Investment and International Trade in the Product Cycle." *Quarterly Journal of Economics* 80, 190–207.

Victor, Richard B., and Vernez, Georges. 1981. *Employment Cycles in Local Labor Markets.* R-2647-EDA/RC. Santa Monica: Rand Corporation.

Vidal, A., Phillips, R. S., and Brown, H. James. 1982. "The Growth and Restructuring of Metropolitan Economics During the 1970s." Working paper. Cambridge, MA: MIT-Harvard Joint Center for Urban Studies.

Vietorisz, Thomas, and Harrison, Bennett. 1970. *The Economic Development of Harlem.* New York: Praeger.

Vietorisz, Thomas, Meir, R., and Giblin, J. 1975. "Subemployment: Exclusion and Inadequacy Indexes." *Monthly Labor Review* 98, 5: 3–12.

Vining, R. 1946. "Location of Industry and Regional Patterns of Business Cycle Behavior." *Econometrica* 14, 1: 37–68.

Vinyard, JoEllen. 1976. *The Irish on the Urban Frontier: Nineteenth Century Detroit, 1850–1880.* New York: Arno Press.

von Einem, Eberhard. 1982. "National Urban Policy—The Case of West Germany." *Journal of the American Planning Association* 48, 1: 9–23.

Wachter, Michael, and Wachter, Susan M., eds. 1982. *Toward A New Industrial Policy?* Philadelphia: University of Pennsylvania Press.

Walton, John. 1982. "Cities and Jobs and Politics." *Urban Affairs Quarterly* 18: 5–18.

Ward, Peter M., ed. 1982. *Self-Help Housing: A Critique.* London: Mansell.

Warren, Charles R. 1980. *The States and Urban Strategies: A Comparative Analysis.* Washington, DC: U.S. Department of Housing and Urban Development.

The Washington Papers. 1983. Chicago: Washington for Mayor Campaign.

Watts, H. D. 1981. *The Branch Plant Economy.* London: Longman.

Webman, Jerry A. 1980. "UDAG, a Targeted Urban Economic Development Program: Initial Directions and Prospect." In *The Urban Development Action Grant Program.* Edited by Richard P. Nathan and Jerry A. Webman. Princeton, NJ: Princeton University, Urban and Regional Research Center.

Weinstein, Bernard L., and Firestine, Robert E. 1978. *Regional Growth and Decline in the United States.* New York: Praeger.

Weiss, M. A. 1983. "High-Technology Industries and the Future of Employment." *Built Environment* 9, 1: 51–60.

Whichard, Obie G. 1981. "Trends in the U.S. Direct Investment Position Abroad, 1950–1979." *Survey of Current Business* 61, 2: 39–56.

Whipple, Daniel. 1975. "Unemployment Among the Poor of Six Central Cities." *Monthly Labor Review* 98, 10: 52–53.

White House. 1982. *The Administration's Enterprise Zone Proposal.* Washington, DC: Office of the Press Secretary, March 23.

Wiewel, Wim, Ridker, Jim, Mier, Robert, and Giloth, Robert. 1982. *Spin-off Businesses: Planning the Organizational Structure of Business Activities: A Manual for Not-for-Profit Organizations.* Chicago: Center for Urban Economic Development.

Williams, Robert. 1982. "Why Don't We Start a Profit-Making Subsidiary?" *The Grants-*

378

manship Center News 10, 2.

Williams, Robert B. 1984. *Inside the Labor-Managed Firm: An Economic Analysis.* Unpublished Ph.D. dissertation, Department of Economics, University of North Carolina at Chapel Hill.

Williamson, Jeffrey G. 1965. "Regional Inequality and the Process of National Development: A Description of the Patterns." *Economic Development and Cultural Change* 13, 4 (part 2): 3–45.

Wilson, Cicero. 1982. "Service Enterprises: An Opportunity for Neighborhood Organizations." *The Entrepreneurial Economy* 1: 11.

Wilson, Frank. 1983. "French Interest Group Politics: Pluralist or Neocorporatist?" *American Political Science Review* 77: 895–910.

Wilson, Graham. 1982. "Why is There No Corporatism in the United States?" In *Patterns of Corporatist Policy-Making.* Edited by Gerhard Lehmbruch and Philippe C. Schmitter. Beverly Hills: Sage Publications.

Wilson, James Q. 1973. *Political Organizations.* New York: Basic Books.

Wilson, William J. 1983. "Inner-City Dislocations." *Society* 21, 1: 80–86.

Wolff, M. F. 1982. "Reluctant to Relocate." *Research Management* 24, 6: 5.

Wood, P. A. 1969. "Industrial Location and Linkage." *Area* 2 (1969): 32–39.

World Bank. 1982. *World Development Report, 1982.* Washington, DC: World Bank.

Zimmer, Basil. 1975. "The Urban Centrifugal Drift." In *Metropolitan America in Contemporary Perspectives.* Edited by Amos H. Hawley and Vincent P. Rock. New York: John Wiley & Sons.

Zunz, Oliver. 1982. *The Changing Face of Inequality: Urbanization, Industrial Development and Immigrants in Detroit, 1880–1920.* Chicago: University of Chicago Press.

Index

Contributors

Edward M. Bergman is Professor of Planning, Department of City and Regional Planning, University of North Carolina at Chapel Hill.

Robert A. Beauregard is Associate Professor of Planning, Department of Urban Planning and Policy Development, Rutgers University.

John P. Blair is Professor and Chair, Department of Economics, Wright State University.

Calvin Bradford is Director, Cooperative Community Development Program, Hubert H. Humphrey Institute of Public Affairs, University of Minnesota.

Susan E. Clarke is Associate Professor, Department of Political Science, University of Colorado at Boulder.

David S. Ford is Associate Director, Center for Human Resources, Institute of Management and Labor Relations, Rutgers University.

Norman J. Glickman is Hogg Professor of Urban Policy, LBJ School of Public Affairs, University of Texas at Austin.

Harvey A. Goldstein is Associate Professor of Planning, Department of City and Regional Planning, University of North Carolina at Chapel Hill.

Candee Harris is a research consultant in Washington, D.C.

Marie Howland is Assistant Professor of Urban Affairs, Institute for Urban Studies, University of Maryland at College Park.

Franklin J. James is Associate Professor and Research Director, Institute for Urban and Public Policy Research, University of Colorado at Denver.

John D. Kasarda is Professor and Chair, Department of Sociology, University of North Carolina at Chapel Hill.

Edward J. Malecki is Associate Professor of Geography, Department of Geography, University of Florida at Gainesville.

Robert Mier is Executive Director, Chicago Economic Development Commission.

Thierry J. Noyelle is Research Scholar, Conservation of Human Resources Project, Columbia University.

Robyn S. Phillips is Assistant Professor of Economics, University of California at San Diego.

Patricia Wilson Salinas is Associate Professor, Graduate Program in Community and Regional Planning, University of Texas at Austin.

Mihailo Temali is Executive Director of North End Area Revitalization, Inc., St. Paul, Minnesota.

Carl E. Van Horn is Associate Director, Eagleton Institute of Politics, Rutgers University.

Avis C. Vidal is Assistant Professor of Planning, JFK School of Government, Harvard University.

Wim Wiewel is Acting Director, Center for Urban Economic Development, University of Illinois at Chicago.

Robert H. Wilson is Associate Professor of Public Affairs, LBJ School of Public Affairs, University of Texas at Austin.